Claus Volkenandt / Christian Kaufmann (Eds.)

Between Indigenous Australia and Europe: John Mawurndjul

Art Histories in Context

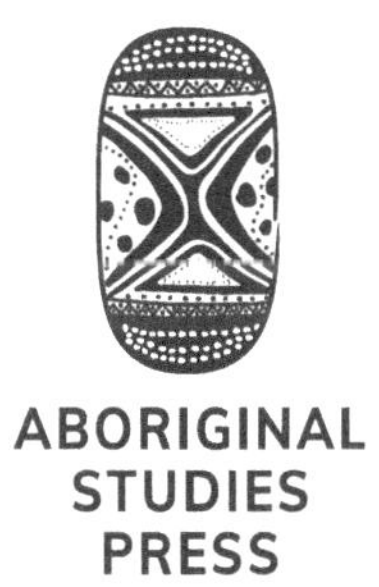

ABORIGINAL STUDIES PRESS

Reimer

This book has been realized with the financial support of the Swiss National Science Foundation

First published in 2009 by Dietrich Reimer Verlag GmbH, Berlin
www.reimer-verlag.de
ISBN 978-3-496-02809-3

Bibliographic information published by the Deutsche Nationalbibliothek
The Deutsche Nationalbibliothek lists this publication in the Deutsche Nationalbibliografi e; detailed bibliographic data are available in the internet at http://dnb.d-nb.de.

First published in Australia and New Zealand in 2009 by Aboriginal Studies Press
www.aiatsis.gov.au
ISBN 978-0-85575-666-6
Reprinted in 2021, 2026

Aboriginal Studies Press
is the publishing arm of the
Australian Institute of Aboriginal and Torres Strait Islander Studies
GPO Box 553, Canberra ACT 2601
Phone: (61 2) 6246 1183
Fax: (61 2) 6261 4288
Email: asp@aiatsis.gov.au
Web: www.aiatsis.gov.au/asp

A cataloguing-in-publication data entry is available from the National Library of Australia, www.trove.nla.gov.au

Aboriginal and Torres Strait Islander people are respectfully advised that this publication may contain names and images of deceased persons, and culturally sensitive material. AIATSIS apologises for any distress this may cause.

Cover design: Nicola Willam, Berlin
Cover: John Mawurndjul painting at Milmilngkan, 2004 (Photo Erika Koch)
Layout: Alexander Burgold, Berlin

Between Indigenous Australia and Europe: John Mawurndjul

List of contents

Guido Magnaguagno
Foreword 7

Claus Volkenandt & Christian Kaufmann
Introduction 9

Jon Altman
A brief social history of Kuninjku art and the market 19

PART 1: The local contexts of bark painting

Luke Taylor
Painted energy: John Mawurndjul and the negotiation of aesthetics in Kuninjku bark painting 31

Apolline Kohen
An arts adviser perspective on producing art for Balanda 47

Jon Altman
Brokering Kuninjku art: a critical perspective on the complex processes of mediating with the market 53

Judith Ryan
Rarrk on bark: John Mawurndjul's medium of power and beauty 61

PART 2: Identifying contexts of art

Howard Morphy
Art theory and art discourse across cultures: the Yolngu and Kunwinjku compared 75

Claus Volkenandt
Why we need an intercultural art history 103

Kitty Zijlmans
Intercultural perspective as context: beyond othering and appropriation? The case of John Mawurndjul 113

Anne-Marie Bonnet
Dilemmata of otherness 123

PART 3: Between Europe and Australia: from local to global

Christian Kaufmann and Richard McMillan (†)
From bark to art: Karel Kupka between Arnhem Land and Basel 137

Sally Butler
Translating the spectacle: John Mawurndjul's intercultural aesthetic 161

Jean-Hubert Martin
Art of the Aborigines between new-age mysticism and politics 175

Till Förster
What is local about local art? Contemporary African artists between international art world and local life-world 183

PART 4: Tomorrow's museums for today's art

John Onians
30,000 years of Australian art – a neuropsychological approach 199

Paul S. C. Taçon
The Creativity Centre: where science meets art 211

Marianne Eigenheer
Rendering visible – new practices for old institutions 217

Bernhard Lüthi
Recognising Indigenous Australians: a new context for art 223

Colour Plates I–XXVI ..... after 112

List of authors 229

Index 233

Map of Arnhem Land 240

Guido Magnaguagno

Foreword

Classic, Eurocentric or at least Western-trimmed, art history – in earlier days actually the only accepted form of art history – has run its course. Today we speak, think and act on a global scale and pursue "art histories in context", in other words, art histories that are embedded in their specific socio-cultural environments. For traditional art-market art, cocooned in its regular support institutions, this extension generates an immense richness of novel questions as regards content, essential renewal and analytic rejuvenation. An encounter with 'anthropological museum art' in its new and contemporary form confers on the encrusted, treadmill 'art world', which has become increasingly geared to consumer culture spectacle, a highly creative impulse.

This at least is how I saw and experienced the international, multi-disciplinary and highly productive symposium that was held at the Museum Tinguely in Basel from 22 to 24 September 2005 on the occasion of the exhibition *«Rarrk» – John Mawurndjul. A Journey Through Time in Northern Australia*. Only rarely have I had the chance to enjoy such an intensive exchange of thoughts, ideas and experiences between Australian and European anthropologists and the art scholars as during these three stimulating days. For once 'crossing over' was not a mere catchphrase – on the contrary, mutual recognition of each other's approaches and methods yielded stimulating insights for both disciplines. And the fact that with the artist John Mawurndjul and the political activist Gary Foley, who has been battling for Aboriginal rights for years, two personalities were not only present, but actively took part in the discussion lent the meeting genuine authenticity. At the end of the event many participants left the venue with the impression of having been part of a truly historical and exemplary occasion.

Therefore I believe it is logical and compelling that the symposium lectures, given by some of the most renowned Australian anthropologists and sociologists with their focussed and long-standing knowledge on Aboriginal cultures, and the important interventions and comments from the European perspective are held in record in the form of the present reader; I see it as a testimony to the state of affairs, in other words, I believe it shows what potential is inherent in a meeting and exchange between firmly established viewpoints and the 'Other' . Often, even the remotest form of 'otherness' is actually closer than you would expect, and could, even should, be reflected and incorporated into one's own scholarly work and future projects, thus raising the old-fashioned notion of 'international understanding' to a new level of understanding. In this sense, the memorable event and the present volume have a mission.

Like the symposium, the present publication was excellently designed, organised and edited by Claus Volkenandt and Christian Kaufmann. In an exemplary manner and in a noteworthy process of interlacing, an anthropologist from the Museum der Kulturen Basel and an art historian from the University of Basel have succeeded in extending and crossing the boundaries of scholarly disciplines and our intellectual horizons. I should heartily like to thank them and the sponsors, The Swiss National Science Foundation (SNSF), for presenting us with a publication, that lends the notion of 'world art' a very real and tangible shape.

Guido Magnaguagno

Claus Volkenandt & Christian Kaufmann

Introduction

The present volume grew out of an international symposium that was held at the Museum Tinguely in Basel from 22 to 24 September 2005 on the occasion of the exhibition *«Rarrk» – John Mawurndjul. Journey Through Time in Northern Australia* which was initiated by Bernhard Luethi and generously supported by F. Hoffmann-La Roche AG.[1] Both exhibition and symposium were on John Mawurndjul and his oeuvre (see fig. 1), in other words on an Indigenous Australian contemporary artist. The brief reference already contains the clues to the central motives and themes that generated this volume: special emphasis is placed on the anthropological index of the Indigenous and how it seems to merge quite naturally with the internationally defined concept of contemporary art. Indigenous and international, anthropology and art history, contemporary artist and Aboriginal origin are categories that one – and by this we primarily mean self-referencing European notions – usually does not perceive as belonging together; on the contrary, more often one tends to register their contradicting qualities.

Nevertheless, it is becoming increasingly evident that the two categories do form parts of a single whole and reference each other, and this is what makes the current volume so topical. It addresses issues and discourses within the framework of globalisation as an economic, social and cultural emergence. Contemporary art, i.e. contemporary artists and their works, figure in, and are shaped by, all three of these tightly interwoven and interdependent dimensions of the global process. Within this overall framework, the volume's special focus is on the question as to how art is encountered and dealt with in, and between, cultures.

John Mawurndjul and his work provide the field for bringing together the general framework and the thematic focus. One of the volume's main aims is to relate some of the basic issues ensuing from the globalisation perspective to the specificity of John Mawurndjul's art, in order to ascertain where they share common ground and what dissociates them. This does not mean that the general is to be tested on the specific, nor is the

1 See also Kaufmann C. and Museum Tinguely (eds.) «*Rarrk*» – *John Mawurndjul. Journey Through Time in Northern Australia,* Schwabe AG, Basel, 2005.

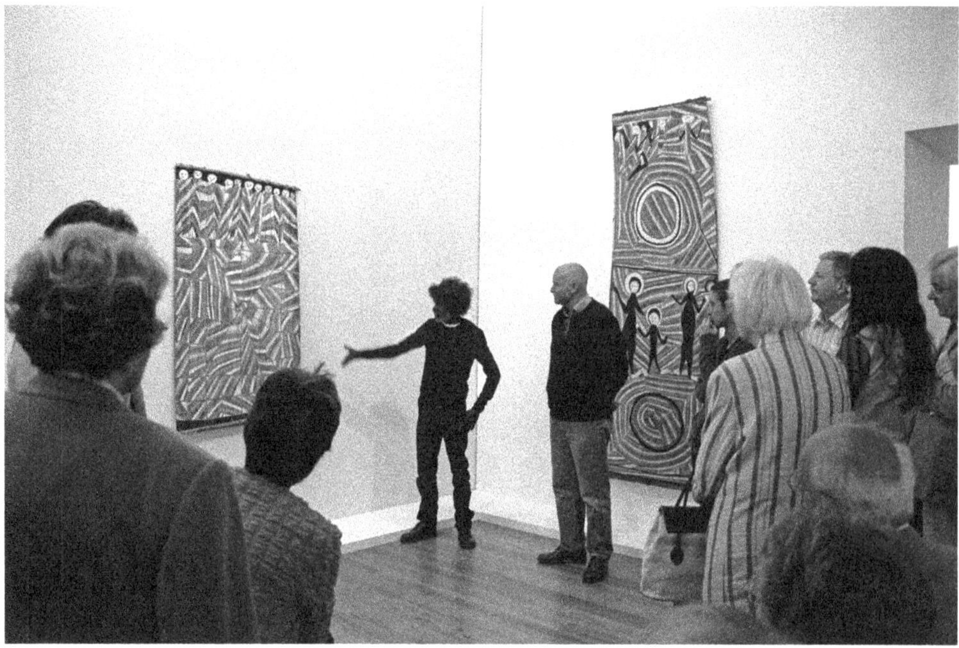

Fig. 1: John Mawurndjul in the Basel exhibition at the opening of the symposium, with Ian Munro translating, 2005. Photo Erika Koch.

singular to be raised to general validity; rather, the aim is to mediate between categorical reflection and actual or concrete situation. In the process, the attempt is made not only to do justice to the singularity of the artist and his works but also to make visible and trace the contours between cultural globalisation and its ramifications on the artist, his works and the way viewers encounter and perceive the works.

In other words, the aim is to thematise some basic issues concerning contemporary world art with a specific view on John Mawurndjul and his works, the conditions of their creation and the mode of their presentation in art museums such as in Sydney, Basel or Hanover where they were shown lately. In this sense, the present volume is different from earlier approaches to intercultural issues in the field of visual arts. When broaching issues of cultural relationships of power in art and art history these usually tend to be in the vein of postcolonial criticism, or else they address the question of the locus of the image and the global passage of images, where migration becomes the key to a trans-national cartography of contemporary art.

In our case, the road to new perspectives of contemporary world art begins in the introduction with the conditions under which John Mawurndjul's works are created and then sketches their journey through the various institutions of the art world. The approach presupposes that the works of John Mawurndjul have already been encountered and definitely been allocated the status of art. Also, the neat order of first describing work creation followed by the works' passage into the art world is somewhat ideal-typical. We leave it to the single contributions to provide a more differentiated and concretised view.[2] But in the sense of an introduction we shall first follow the path as indicated above.

I.

John Mawurndjul normally lives at his outstation Milmilngkan in western Arnhem Land in the northern part of Australia. It is here that he produces the majority of his paintings. They are paintings on bark. For producing them he needs a variety of materials: bark as a base, colour pigments, a brush and fixatives. In the initial steps of his artistic practice John Mawurndjul procures the materials he needs for his paintings. In practical terms this means he first has to go out and collect a bark from a Eucalyptus tree (stringy bark), strip it, dry it over the fire, then flatten it and finally smooth the surface by rubbing it down. All these steps John Mawurndjul attends to himself. For procuring the pigments John Mawurndjul proceeds in a similar manner: he collects the minerals from which he produces his colours from special sites on land surrounding his home. This is not a mere mechanical process. Whilst collecting ochres and white clay he communicates intensely with his clan ancestors, this means the work-step forms part of a ritual performance. This is necessary because the minerals are not regarded as crude materials that one simply extracts from the ground, but as a substance that is symbolically charged through its association with the Dreaming and ancestral mythology. Before using it he has to communicate with his ancestors and the creator beings to receive their permission and reassurance, a step which is itself contingent on his status as a clan elder. This shows that the materials are not freely accessible, and certainly not purchasable in the next do-it-yourself store. On the contrary: access and usage are subject to his initiation status and the terms of traditional lore; the pigments are spiritually charged, by virtue of their origin.

Mawurndjul paints his pictures at his Milmilngkan outstation. Usually you see John Mawurndjul sitting cross-legged in the shade of the porch of his house, quietly and meticulously applying to the bark lying in front of him line by line of crosshatching (*rarrk*). Technique and method – starting from the procurement of the bark and the pigments, the brushes which he makes himself, to the position he sits in whilst painting – are in accordance with the traditional mode of bark painting, with the exception of the fixatives he uses. These are synthetic and he purchases them from a store. However, Mawurndjul has no qualms about this; it neither affects his self-image as an Indigenous artist nor does he regard it as a breach of tradition as some Western viewers might see it, who often tend to an 'either-or-view' of things, to a clear dividing line between tradition and present. This is not the case here; on the contrary, Mawurndjul sees himself and his bark painting absolutely in line with the age-old tradition of rock art, a tradition that, as we know, goes back in the

2 In order to avoid unnecessary duplication we almost completely do without bibliographic references in the introduction, and refer to the single contributions.

history of humanity anywhere between 9,000 and 60,000 years. This knowledge grants him a high degree of self-confidence, a quality that is absent in European Modernism that severed its ties with historic tradition. Moreover, in his reference to early rock art Mawurndjul sees the duty both to continue and to renew this age-old tradition.

It shows that when we are talking about John Mawurndjul and his image of self as an artist we are not only confronted with a different form of relationship to the concept of tradition and an alternative understanding of historicity, but also to a different presence of tradition which compels us to consider alternative ways of viewing and handling the concept. Actually, it is even questionable whether 'tradition' is the appropriate term for what we are trying to express in words since the term carries far-reaching (here only implicated) connotations of a European understanding of history.

When Mawurndjul has finished a work he takes it to Maningrida, about 80 kilometres away from Milmilngkan, and delivers it to Maningrida Arts and Culture (MAC), the local support organisation for artists from Arnhem Land that takes over the task of marketing and selling their works. To be exact, he does not merely hand over his paintings, he sells his works to MAC which from then on is responsible for mediating his paintings and getting them to the market – in Mawurndjul's case the global market. Before they are actually put up for sale the works are measured, documented and evaluated. Through this process the works cross the threshold and enter into the world of art, in both a material as well as a media sense. One could say that this step marks the publication of the works, for an audience that is radically different from the one that his art addressed in ritual and clan contexts before. Put even more succinctly: it is actually the first time that the art works have to face an audience. This shift in function and target group raises a number of questions that the act of transfer itself engenders: what happens to the works' earlier secret meanings – do they persist or do they disappear? What about the ban on, or at least the danger of, viewing that non-initiates were formerly subject to – is it upheld or has it become ineffective, lost its threatening dimension? Does this form of publication not lead to a profanation of ritual properties – with potentially serious consequences for the clan and ritual system? But on the other hand, do such questions not simply reflect the European experience of secularisation, the depletion of the significance of religion that the old continent has gone through? Is it not equally justified to say that by altering the traditional iconic idiom and by making his works public – irrespective of the context within which this occurs – John Mawurndjul is consciously recharging and updating tradition and thereby ensuring its continued existence?[3]

On the premises of MAC in Maningrida there is a small, affiliated ethnographic museum, called the Djómi Museum.[4] This means that one encounters on the same plot –

3 Our text tries to describe what Ivo Kummer's dual video installation mediated to the audience at the exhibition.

4 See also the museum's self-description at www.maningrida.com/mac/museum.php (viewed on 20 February 2007): "The Djómi Museum functions as an integrated element in the community's cultural and regional development. It promotes the richness of the region's artistic expression, it is the custodian of a wealth of historical and cultural material and an active source and repository of valuable reference and research data. Djómi is an official regional museum of the Museum and Art Gallery of the Northern Territory."

depending on which entrance you take – two completely different worlds: on the one hand a world of art, on the other an ethnographic collection. Thus, in a very confined space history and present of the fundamental debate on how to approach and deal with non-Western art, or, to be more precise, art that is often labelled Indigenous or regional, meet head-on. Between the two entrances, and separating them into two worlds – although here the two look very similar – stands the fundamental question "what is art?" and, in conjunction with it, the issue of the presentation of art. To paraphrase, and expand on, a statement made by Guido Magnaguagno on an informal occasion, the difference we are talking about here is the distinction between 'market art' and 'ethnographic museum art'. It is a distinction between two genres of art: the former must be able to prevail in a space without additional contextualisation (apart from a white wall), while the latter cannot function without (usually cultural) contextualisation. At the latest by the time they arrive in Maningrida, John Mawurndjul's works are joined by a series of questions that will accompany them on their journey through the various art institutions until they reach their final destination – in our case Basel. In the present case (and significant in view of the preparations for the exhibition and symposium in Basel), their first stop on the journey through the world of art was the Art Gallery of New South Wales in Sydney, Australia, that is to say: an art museum. It was there that in 2004 the exhibition *Crossing Country: the Alchemy of Western Arnhem Land Art* was shown and which featured John Mawurndjul as an important representative. Above all, it featured him in the 'white cube'. The event naturally attracted the attention of the media and the art world, and John Mawurndjul found himself having to explain his works, and having to speak in public and answer questions. He spoke in his own language, Kuninjku, so it needed an interpreter for the people in Sydney to be able to understand what he was saying. The language barrier and having to rely via an interpreter inevitably broached the issue of the social and cultural status of Aborigines in (white) Australian society today. This meant that John Mawurndjul's public appearance and his words also carried a highly political message, although he does not directly or openly address politics as such in his art works. Rather, the politically provocative potential of his work is lodged in the self-conscious mode with which John Mawurndjul asserts motives and themes from his own culture and encodes them in a specific iconic language. This display of self-confidence allows Aboriginal politics to acquire a new and distinct profile, although, it must be added, today Indigenous Australians are compelled to set their priorities differently: they are fighting for sheer survival, which leaves little to no room for refining profile.

During the *Crossing Country* exhibition in Sydney a symposium was organised under the motto "A day of artist talks, lectures and discussion providing a comprehensive insight into the historical and contemporary contexts of western Arnhem Land art."[5] Here too, John Mawurndjul was asked to give a talk, but it was in a different context, far from the bustle of the exhibition and the attention it drew from the media. The occasion provided

5 http://www.artgallery.nsw.gov.au/sub/crossingcountry/3_EVENTS/events_symposium.html (viewed on 19 February 2007).

an opportunity – as did the exhibition catalogue – to turn to the work of John Mawurndjul and take a closer, one could even say critical look at it from an art historical perspective. This means that the works were subjected to the process of 'art historicisation', in the course of which art history, anthropology and economics, in their guise as academic disciplines, were given the floor to present their by no means compatible perspectives on the work and artist personality of John Mawurndjul. Other topics discussed included the maturing and differentiation of Mawurndjul's art in the course of his career, its place in the tradition of bark painting in western Arnhem Land, the question of continuance and innovation in his work, iconographic and reference issues, but also questions dealing with style and whether his bark painting commands an aesthetics of its own. Other issues focused on the art market and John Mawurndjul's self-conception as an artist. Also of significance were the interviews John Mawurndjul gave and the statements he made in the context of the exhibition; they provide important clues for art historical and anthropological research.

Integrating John Mawurndjul and his works into an art historical, that is, a scholarly discourse provides the chance for applying not only distinct, but differing modes of contextualising his works – that is why above we spoke of by no means compatible (scholarly) perspectives – in other words, we can distinguish between different reference frames. One such reference pertains to the context of the creation of the works, that is, the living and working conditions at Milmilngkan outstation and/or the traditional function and spiritual background of bark painting. The other reference frame relates to the museum context, or, to apply a more ambitious vision, to a globally oriented imaginary museum where the works are, above all, viewed and judged from the perspective of their formal qualities. What stands to debate in these differing contextualisations is defining the apposite reference point for a suitable practice of dealing with the works. This is not merely a matter of difference between academic disciplines and their approaches, for example between art history and anthropology. It goes beyond that and addresses the fundamental question of the nature of scholarship and understanding, and what role the museum should play in this field. Put in more general terms, what stands to debate is the difference between applying a universalistic and a contextualistic approach to art.

The present volume contains contributions on John Mawurndjul and his works from both perspectives. However, they do not stand as alternatives that exclude each other, rather they attempt to explore the opportunities and probe the boundaries of each approach. Some of the authors also reflect on the circumstances and terms under which the works are received and dealt with in practice.

The journey of John Mawurndjul's works from Australia to Basel, and in Basel the transfer to an art museum once more accentuates the question of contextualisation and therein the issue of the appropriate practice of dealing with the works. On the one hand, this ensues from the increased cultural distance that the journey created, calling for more cultural contextualisation at the works' final destination; at the same time, distance also provides the chance for a more decidedly aesthetic appreciation of the works. On the other hand, the pertinence of the issue developed from the special circumstances in Basel, since the options and the venue of presentation constituted central issues of the exhibition concept. The Basel exhibition was the result of an intellectual collaboration and an institutional cooperation, namely between an ethnographic museum and an art museum. Such a form of cooperation immediately evokes Europe's entangled history of exhibition practices and its institutions: the traditional place for displaying non-European cultures, including their art, is, at least in the tradition of German-speaking countries, the ethnographic museum or collection respectively. The ethnographic museum lumps together and displays cultural products, which European institutions keep strictly apart and exhibit separately when their own cultural achievements are at issue. In terms of museum types this means that a clear line is drawn between historical museums and art museums, between historical collections and art galleries.

On the old continent, art museums reacted to the growing output of European and, later, Western art in general, by establishing new institutional bodies to accommodate the increased artistic produce. These included art associations and societies, exhibition halls, museums of arts and crafts and, last but not least, museums of contemporary art. The ethnographic museums, for their part, did not change, at least not until very recently and then only in very few cases, and kept on amassing both traditional cultural products and new (transformed) artistic achievements from non-European cultures. Thus the question concerning the appropriate venue for displaying contemporary, non-European art triggers a controversial debate. Where should it be shown: in the above-mentioned, comparatively new museums of contemporary art, which, as their name implies, focus on modern, present-day art but do not incorporate non-European art? Or should it be shown in ethnographic museums that admittedly collect and also exhibit modern creative products from non-European cultures but at the same time appear not to be able to come to terms with the label 'autonomous art' and, to that effect, with the European concept of art – a concept that from the start seems to be inclined to assign everything non-European subordinate significance?

At the same time one must question how the European-Western white-cube mode of presentation as practised in art museums could be reconciled with cultural contextualisation, which forms one of the tenets in the presentation strategies of ethnographic museums. Is it possible to implant a white cube into an ethnographic museum, or vice versa, feasible to integrate cultural contextualisation in an art museum? Does this not merely lead to an aesthetizisation of the ethnographic museum or ethnographisation of the art museum respectively? On the other hand, the question must be allowed whether a contraposition of this nature is actually relevant in a museum world that is constantly challenging its own set of norms. In fact, would it not make more sense to apply both approaches when displaying contemporary non-European art, irrespective of the type of venue? The fact that many artists would opt for the art museum does not really satisfactorily solve the problem of finding the mediation mode that truly does the works justice.

What goes for the institutional level also applies to the actual encounter with the works of John Mawurndjul in an art museum. Based on the European tradition of presenting works of art, the art museum's white cube is geared to the sensuous perception of the works shown therein. The intention is an eidetic encounter with the works within the framework of aesthetic experience. However, from a European perspective of viewing, the works of John Mawurndjul display a high index of cultural otherness in terms of iconic encoding, materiality and their uneven and corrugated formats. The encounter takes place in a tension field between sensuous challenge and unfamiliar presentation, between aesthetic proximity and uncertainty about the works' original contexts of creation and intended meaning. Going a step further, one could ask whether, in the environment of a European (art) museum, the viewer experiences the cultural otherness that the works of John Mawurndjul emanate as a challenge or as alienation.

In methodological terms, the question is how to accommodate otherness between reflexive approximation and exclusive reconstruction. In other words – pointedly articulated here as alternatives – do we approach the cultural otherness in John Mawurndjul's works in full awareness of its presence but also of its unreachability, or do we try to find orientation in the contexts of their creation and original significance? Put differently, do we enter into a direct visual dialogue in order to fathom the layers and explore the boundaries of the works we encounter, or do we – and herein lies its exclusiveness – absolutely disregard the place of the encounter – a European art museum – and its significance for understanding the works? The two approaches mark opposite ends of the field of intercultural reflection through which we are seeking to probe the conditions, but also the limits, of an encounter with Mawurndjul's works. It is exactly these questions that the present volume wishes to address in order to explore ways of reaching an understanding of his works, what options of understanding there are but also whether and where the boundaries to understanding lie, as seen from the perspective of contemporary world art. If we apply the approach to include visitors to museums in general it soon becomes apparent that the issues raised here do not relate to art works of non-European provenance only. For non-specialists the works of mediaeval artists, even of artists of the 17th and 18th century, are just about as unfamiliar as are the works of John Mawurndjul; in the former case because we are no longer familiar with the living conditions and world views of that era, in the latter because we have not yet become familiarised with cultural alterity. To further explore the difference between historically motivated and culturally informed otherness would certainly be a worthwhile task for the future.

II.

The list of contents and the thematic emphases of the book follow the journey of John Mawurndjul's works as outlined above, from their origins in western Arnhem Land through the various art institutions and into the world of academic investigation. The focus is on the interrelatedness of the contexts within which we go in search of the works and encounter them, and from which the differing art histories grow in their quality as historiographies of art. In the process, basic questions bearing on the encounter and the mode of coming to terms with art within, and between, cultures take centre stage. The questions are explored along the path that John Mawurndjul's works took in four main parts: (1) deals with the local contexts within which the works of John Mawurndjul are created and stand, (2) reflects on the interrelatedness of art, context and art histories, (3) raises the issue of the globalisation of contexts and the shifts it engenders in the receptive attention, and, to conclude, (4) throws a light on the institutional consequences that the questions raised here could have.

Specific issues are woven like threads into the volume and are discussed from shifting perspectives within two levels of order. Next to the vertical order given by the four main parts, the threads crosscut and interlink the single contributions horizontally, thus tying in further the individual texts into the overall plot. In summary, the threads address the following topics: an art historical appraisal of bark painting as an art form in its own right (contributions by Ryan, Morphy, Volkenandt); an inquiry into, and reflection on, the modalities of a contemporary artist's biography, in this case John Mawurndjul's, examining the unfolding of a life story in a field of tension between the expectations on the part of his family and kin, his own goals and artistic aspirations, and his international renown and responsibilities in the world of exhibitions and collectors (Taylor, Kohen, Altman, Butler); an expansion of art history's traditional 'outside' view by exploring how local communities perceive changes to their own art traditions and what effect this has on the artists' strategies and framework of action (Morphy, Taylor, Altman, Bonnet); the significance of trans-cultural reflection on art and the necessity it engenders to explore, describe and practise novel modes of intercultural perception, discourse, criticism and valuation (Zijlmans, Bonnet, Martin, Butler, Onians); and finally, the urgency to develop and critically explore significant groups of works and collections and incorporate them in intercultural projects – exhibitions and other visual modes of mediating artistic expression – in order to include them in the debate on what art has to say (Taçon, MacMillan/Kaufmann, Ryan, Eigenheer, Lüthi).

III.

Symposium and exhibition together formed an entity. This is worth mentioning especially in view of the different and contradictory ways in which in Australia and Europe the achievements of Indigenous Australians are appreciated and valuated as markers of cultural autonomy. While in Australia Aboriginal artists remain disadvantaged in terms of access to the market and face a political atmosphere in which the bygone spectre of forced assimilation is again knocking at the door, and in which they have to fight for their rights, Jean Nouvel, the architect of the new Musée du quai Branly in Paris, went novel ways when he invited several Aboriginal partner artists – prominently among them John Mawurndjul – to leave imprints of their art work on this new cultural centre with all its service facilities such as museum shops, study centres and media library. The work was carried out between September 2005 and the opening of the museum on 20 June 2006. As against the new museum building on the quai Branly, the Mawurndjul exhibition in Basel chose to create both a historical and a cultural bridge to John Mawurndjul's art in order to provide a space for reflecting on the mode of presentation. The historical bridge was in the form of a display of bark paintings from the Kupka collection, that were shown in rooms adjacent to the actual *«Rarrk»* exhibition. In a special sense it provided a double arch: for one, because on his journeys to Arnhem Land from the 1950s onwards Karel Kupka collected bark paintings not as ethnographic objects but from the aspect of their aesthetic quality, that is as art works in their own right; for the other, because the works he collected in western Arnhem Land represented a specific period and tradition of bark painting that preceded John Mawurndjul, which again meant that the viewers received as a complementary context an impression of the artistic and cultural background to his works. The cultural bridge consisted of a video installation that was located in a separate room, showing John Mawurndjul in his living and working environment. The installation, in fact, consisted of two film projections: the first was a large-scale projection using the entire back wall as a screen, the second film, shown parallel, was screened on a TV set standing in the middle of the room. Two rows of benches were placed so that the viewers could watch both films simultaneously. The film which was made by Ivo Kummer and his crew from Switzerland together with John Mawurndjul and his wife Kay Lindjuwanga on-site in Australia evokes in its dual projection mode an impressive portrait of the artist as a person. Without any form of off-commentary, Mawurdjul presents himself in the original contexts of his work, from Milmilngkan to Sydney. While the film on the TV screen portrayed Mawurndjul in action, that is, working, explaining and showing, the projection on the wall captured the environments – both country and urban – through which he moves and which constitute his reference frames. John Mawurndjul and Kay Lindjuwanga also took part in the symposium where their presence left an indelible imprint.

To end we should like to express our gratitude to a number of institutions and people for their contribution to the success of the symposium project. The Basel Symposium was held at the Museum Tinguely. Independent of the museum budget, the event was made possible through generous contributions by the Freiwillige Akademische Gesellschaft, Basel, the Max Geldner-Stiftung, Basel, as well as the Schweizerische Akademie der Geistes- und Sozialwissenschaften and the Swiss National Science Foundation. In the name of all participants we should like to thank all of them for making this event possible. Through their hospitality the director and the staff members of the Museum Tinguely created an atmosphere that made us all feel comfortable and that markedly contributed to the success of the event. In his opening speech and greeting, Prof. Meier-Abt, vice-chancellor for research at the University of Basel and member of the Research Council of the Swiss National Science Foundation, expressed the authorities' commitment to support intellectual enterprises of this kind. We also thank all the authors who contributed to this volume, not only for the texts as such but also for their willingness to adapt and revise their contributions so that new insights gained in discussions and conversations in and around the symposium have been allowed to flow into the volume and contribute to our knowledge and understanding. Alas, one person who from the start was a keen supporter of both the exhibition and the symposium was not granted the grace to witness the publication of this volume. Unfortunately Richard McMillan, who came across the tracks of Karel Kupka in Australia whilst working on the artistic legacy of the Australian painter Tony Tuckson (1921–1973), died on 12 July 2006. One text is a completely new contribution. We have included it because in it Sally Butler describes a visit to the exhibition and discusses the exhibition strategy from the viewpoint of an Australian art historian. Finally we should also like to thank Nigel Stephenson who not only translated the original German texts into English but also provided the text editing for the publication. Without his commitment this book would probably never have seen the light of day.

Jon Altman

A brief social history of Kuninjku art and the market

Introduction

In this contribution I want to focus on the development of Kuninjku art for the market over the past 50 years, but I do this via a wider focus on Kuninjku social history, which is itself part of a bigger story of white Australian colonisation of Arnhem Land, and the intended and unintended impacts of the state and its policies. I will argue that this history can be understood as a series of phases starting with a period of Kuninjku subjugation (in the early 1960s), survival (1960s), then revival (1970s and 1980s), followed by consolidation (1990s) and finally, 2005 in Basel, celebration – of cultural, political and economic success. It is paradoxical, perhaps, that my narrative runs very counter to an Australian government and popular media discourse of 30 years of policy failure since the early 1970s, during the periods that I describe as revival, success and now celebration from a Kuninjku perspective.

In making my presentation, like all social scientists, I use a particular set of lenses, in my case the disciplines of social anthropology and economics as well as empirical data from over 25 years research, in collaboration with Kuninjku; this is just one of many lenses that can be used to look at some of the social history I want to relate in this contribution.

So let me emphasise at the outset that this is but one partial perspective and one that is still emerging, even after all these years. In their own contributions my colleagues provide their perspectives, from different disciplines, on Kuninjku art generally and that of John Mawurndjul in particular.[1]

Art of course is nothing without people, it is something that emanates from particular social and cultural and historic contexts, reflecting traditions, economies, polities: and political and social change.

1 Altman, Jon, 'From Mumeka to Basel: John Mawurndjul's Artistic Odyssey' in Kaufmann C. and Museum Tinguely (eds.), «*Rarrk*» – *John Mawurndjul. Journey Through Time in Northern Australia,* Schwabe AG, Basel, 2005, pp. 30–41.

While the exhibition «*Rarrk*» – *John Mawurndjul. Journey Through Time in Northern Australia* was clearly about the celebration of the achievements of one exceptional artist, this artist like all others obviously lives within and draws his inspiration from a wider community. While this is an obvious point, it is perhaps worth emphasising at the outset that a feature of Kuninjku sociality is the requirement to meet the demands of social relatedness, something that can be at odds with securing one's personal autonomy, inventiveness, creativity – and at odds with the notion of the individual creator as we celebrate it.

Social history of the Kuninjku community

While here we are focussing on «*Rarrk*», I want to look just a little more broadly at the art of the Kuninjku community of which John Mawurndjul is a member. This can be contextualised a little via another exhibition *Crossing Country: the Alchemy of Western Arnhem Land Art* held in Australia in 2004. That retrospective covering nearly 100 years was not just about Kuninjku artists, but included artists from the larger Kunwinjku-ian culture bloc that is described today by the linguistic term Bininj Kun-wok, literally "the language of Aboriginal people" (see figs. 2 and 48).

Most of the contemporary work in that exhibition and obviously shown in «*Rarrk*» (as distinct to the art Karel Kupka collected from further west mainly painted by Kunwinjku dialect speakers) has been produced in the last 25 years.[2] It emanates from the small Kuninjku community whose lands lie southwest of the township of Maningrida established in 1957 and who number just over 300 people today (out of a regional population of about 2,500). This community is demarcated by a distinct language dialect and distinct practices. Its members live in an area of 2,000–3,000 square kilometres of tropical savannah when they are not in the township of Maningrida. Kuninjku are but one of about 10 often intermarrying, often co-residing language communities, or societies, in the larger Maningrida region that was established by colonial fiat and is now an administrative region.

My topic here is the social history and art of this Kuninjku community, defined in this bounded manner probably more in the minds of visiting linguists and academics like myself than by Kuninjku people themselves.[3] That aside, I want to tease out how members of this community have become so prodigiously involved in contemporary world fine art. Not very long ago, certainly in terms of European art traditions that are often measured in centuries, this was not so. Indeed it was only in the early 1960s that a party blazing a road from Oenpelli to Maningrida contacted the remnants of this community. They found a small group living at Marrkolidjban, some suffering from the introduced disease leprosy, some from yaws. Other parts of this community were already in the township of

2 Kunwinjku dialect speakers live in western Arnhem Land with most at the township of Oenpelli (Kunbalanja), Kuninjku dialect speakers live in and around the Mann and Tonkinson Rivers (and in Maningrida).

3 See Borsboom, Ad, 'Thomson at Gaartji', in Rigsby, B. and N. Peterson (eds.), *Donald Thomson, the Man and Scholar,* Academy of the Social Sciences in Australia, Canberra, 2005, pp. 159–169.

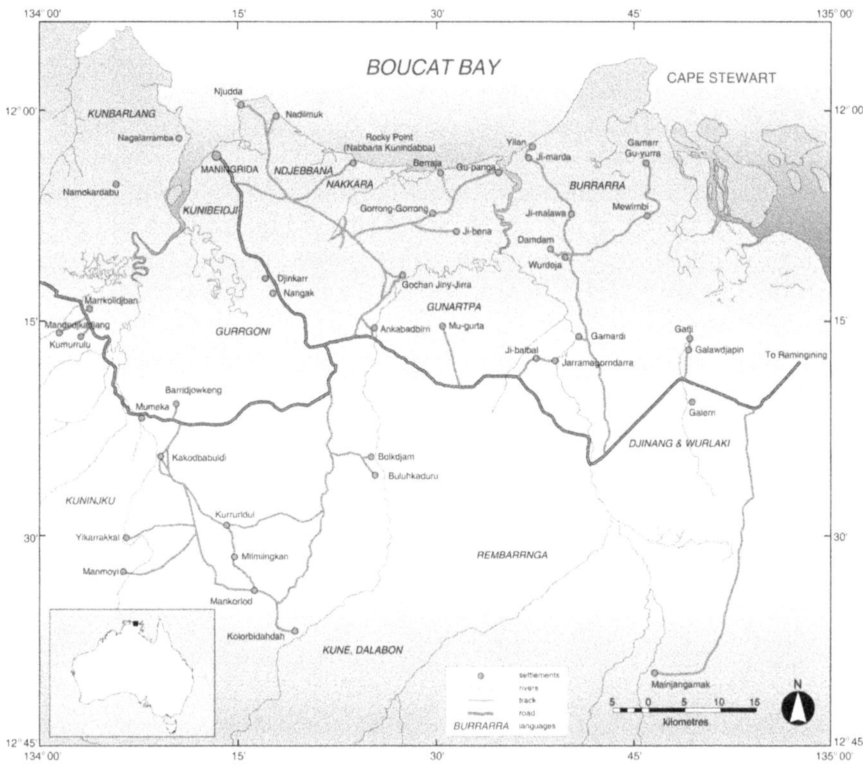

Fig. 2: Outstations, roads and languages in the Maningrida region, Arnhem Land, 2006. Courtesy Bawinanga Aboriginal Corporation.

Maningrida and some were at nearby Oenpelli (150 kms west). It was this stoic remnant, led by men like Peter Marralwanga and Anchor Kulunba that stayed behind garrisoning their country and their Dreamings (see pl. I).

The following events changed all that. A township had been established by state authorities at Maningrida during the assimilation era in 1957, after a Native Affairs trading post had been there briefly in 1949 and 1950. Kuninjku people were persuaded to come into Maningrida for treatment of their children at the newly-established local leprosarium. Dr John Hargreaves insightfully realised the futility of forcibly removing sufferers to Darwin, a practice that had been undertaken with poor outcomes, both for the sufferers and their families.

While in the bush in the Arnhem Land reserve, Kuninjku had been nominal wards of the state. When they moved to Maningrida they became effectively so, under the authority of white Welfare Branch staff. This marked the nadir of Kuninjku experience of white contact, at least in living memory (there are some Buluwana myths about severe drought and deaths that also sound pretty catastrophic), marginalised on the land of others, not so much by the Dekurridji traditional owners of Maningrida, themselves disempowered, as by the complex mix of Aboriginal and white politics that occurred in such artificial social settings. To put it bluntly, Kuninjku were maladapted to township living, in part because they were the last people in these parts to experience contact with colonisation and the wider Australian society; and conversely, because they remained the best adapted to, and most comfortable with, bush living.

In the 1960s, Kuninjku survived in Maningrida, but this survival was partly predicated on maintaining contact with their country, for sustenance and spiritual succour. In those days, maintaining such links was close to miraculous, frowned upon and discouraged by the white authorities and difficult to undertake in the absence of the private ownership of vehicles owing to the remoteness of country, 50–100 kilometres southwest of Maningrida.

In early 1970s, a 'revolutionary' social movement often referred to as the outstation movement, saw Kuninjku migrate back onto their country. They could now do this for several reasons. First, there was a radical change of Aboriginal affairs policy, from the conservative assimilation to the progressive self-determination in 1972. Simultaneously, there was a greater acceptance of cultural diversity within Australia as part of broader global decolonisation. There was growing recognition that assimilation had been a costly failure (which coincidentally we now seem to be revisiting). Pursuing mainstream goals in very remote, very non-mainstream contexts was extremely difficult. Second, there was greater recognition of the rights of Indigenous people, as colonised Australian citizens, to exercise choice about how and where they lived and formal legal recognition of their land rights from 1976.

Fortunately for Kuninjku, during the 1960s they had flaunted the authorities and had retained bush skills. In 1972, they gained access to some rudimentary transport, a tractor and land rover, in large part from cash earned from the early sale of art. And they returned to outstations on their country.[4] It was the return to live on country that saw a rejuvenation of the Kuninjku community and a ramping up of their engagement with the market via the arts. When living in Maningrida in the 1960s, Kuninjku were not prolific artists, although a few like Mick Kubarkku and Crusoe Kuningbal, and closely associated artist Wally Mandarrk, certainly produced art for sale. It was the returning to live on country in the early 1970s that provided the impetus and inspiration for the Kuninjku fine art that we celebrate today.

Why did the rejuvenation of these artistic practices, that have their origins in rock art and ceremonial designs, occur? Again there are at least three complex, and inter-linked, reasons. First, there were economic imperatives. Art was an important source of cash to buy the basic market goods to which the Kuninjku domestic economy had become accustomed in the 1960s. Second, return to country was associated with a rapid revival of the harvesting (or customary) economy and of ceremonial life; people were inspired to paint. Third, art provided a means of reinforcing distinct Kuninjku values and beliefs both within Kuninjku society, but also to wider audiences. As noted earlier, Kuninjku art has

4 See Altman, J. and M. Hinkson, 'Mobility and Modernity in Arnhem Land: The Social Universe of Kuninjku Trucks', *Journal of Material Culture* 12 (2), 2007, pp. 181–203.

to be recognised as a complex economic, cultural and political product without privileging any one explanatory factor over the other. It is important to note that Kuninjku living at outstations were not just living in 'artist colonies'. The art is just one element of the diverse Kuninjku community economy. In 1979–80, when I lived at Mumeka it was the harvesting of wildlife that was by far the most important element of this economy. Over the last 25 years the form of this economy has altered, it is now a hybrid made up of the customary (hunting), the market (the arts) and the state (income support and welfare). The precise composition of this economy is flexible, sectors overlap, and there are changes both seasonally and from year to year and from place to place in the region.

The social history of Maningrida Art and Culture (MAC)

The social history of Kuninjku art correlated very closely with the social history of Maningrida Art and Culture (MAC). This institution has been instrumental in the development of Kuninjku art. In describing MAC I use the term 'social history' because MAC is a very live, organic and dynamic institution with managers or arts advisers, staff and a membership of artists (see also this volume Kohen pp. 47–52 and Altman pp. 53–59).

MAC has an unusually long history for an Aboriginal arts organisation, initially set up in 1963, coincidentally, the same year that the bush-remnants of the Kuninjku community, including John Mawurndjul, were migrating to Maningrida. It was established by a missionary in a secular government settlement, partly to formalise some fairly informal, sometimes-unsavoury, art dealings between blacks and whites occurring in the new township, and partly as a service to the community and to potential parishioners. For a decade from 1963 to 1973, MAC was pretty rudimentary and its services focussed on the relatively more urbane regional artists from the Djinang, the Burada and the Ganalpingu language communities who were better able to explain the meanings of their art and whose art was more palatable to Western tastes. Unintentionally again, even in the 1960s, Kuninjku were relatively neglected owing to regional arts politics and broader judgments about aesthetics and value being made by the fine arts market.

The early 1970s were, as already mentioned, the first years of self-determination, the outstation movement and land rights. But this was also the time of the birth of the modern Australian cultural policy signified by the establishment of the Australia Council. This new national arts patronage institution supported the establishment of a separate Aboriginal Arts Board (AAB) and this in turn resulted in more formalised funding and a role for community-based, community-controlled arts centres.[5] Given its existence and relative longevity even then, Maningrida Arts and Crafts (as it was then called) was among the first supported by the state from late 1972.

5 For a more detailed discussion of this period see Altman, J.,'Brokering Aboriginal Art: A Critical Perspective on Marketing, Institutions and the State', Kenneth Myer Lecture, Centre for Leisure Management Research, Deakin University, Melbourne, April 2005, pp. 1–24 (available at www.anu.edu.au/caepr/).

This made a difference because the first salaried 'arts advisers' (as they were then called, although they had no training in the arts) Dan Gillespie, and then Peter Cooke, were committed to assist artists mainly via the collection and marketing of art, irrespective of where they resided, including at outstations. And there are some wonderful stories from the early days of collection trips by boat up the Liverpool River and by truck over bone-crunching tracks, always providing a means to get the art to market. Quickly from the mid-1970s, MAC was primarily servicing the majority of bush-based, rather than town-based, artists many of whom were Kuninjku.

MAC, in collaboration with artists, was involved from the early 1970s in mediating with the wider fine arts world about what this art was, educating the buyers and collectors, cajoling the public and public institutions to see that art from the region was not just exotic ethnographica, or artefacts. It was in fact 'real' fine art, embodying and encoding meanings and political statements from extant, not extinct cultures. Many of these meanings were not clear and so needed to be translated for wider audiences. The 20-year period from 1973 could be termed the 'great transformation'.[6]

This great transformation was based on a very active partnership between Kuninjku artists and, almost invariably, non-Aboriginal arts advisers. This complex partnership evolved with one party producing the art and modifying it incrementally and expertly for the market; and the other party operating as inter-cultural mediator, providing market messages (often via price, but also other exhibitions feedback) to Kuninjku artists, and also translating and communicating the meanings embedded in the art to Western art audiences.

The challenge both parties faced in selling Kuninjku art as fine art was immense because much of the heritage and style of Kuninjku art was bold and raw and powerful, and fundamentally different. It also appeared handicapped by a lesser appeal to the Western aesthetic than more decorative regional styles, like those of eastern Arnhem Land (see Morphy pp. 75–102). And it was certainly less popular than other regional styles from central Australia that has more readily adopted Western media, acrylic paint and canvas, like the Papunya Tula western desert art that was internationally accepted from the late 1980s. A perennial issue was that of permanence: would ochres and pigments fixed on bark in the Kuninjku way (using PVA wood glue as a fixative) survive in the long term? This was certainly an issue for the fine art markets with an eye on longer-term investment.

There is no doubt in my mind that part of the Kuninjku agency in this great transformation involved the active recruitment of anthropologists and arts advisers (and the Bawinanga Aboriginal Corporation or BAC outstation resource agency) to an understanding of Kuninjku art, its links to Dreamings, country and customary ways. Kuninjku somehow managed to capture the imagination of arts advisers, in large measure through their self-representation and actual practice as people living on country and maintaining Kuninjku land, language and cultural practices.

---

6 Altman, J., 'Brokering Kuninjku Art: Artists, Institutions and the Market' in Perkins, H. (ed.), *Crossing Country: The Alchemy of Western Arhem Land Art*, Art Gallery of NSW, Sydney, 2004, pp. 173–187.

Artistic transformations

And yet all the while, as evidenced in the «*Rarrk*» exhibition, leading Kuninjku artists were subtly and innovatively modifying their art in many ways. Indeed some Kuninjku art forms have declined or disappeared, while others like wood carving, the *mimih* (spirit beings), *yawkyawk* (mermaids), *namorrorddo* (malevolent spirits), Buluwana (spirit figure), *lorrkkon* (hollow log) and bark paintings have proliferated; and others have been transformed. At the same time different sections of Kuninjku society, most notably women, have become significant bark painters in their own right, something that was not evident 25 years ago and that has escalated rapidly since the early 1990s.

Maningrida Art and Culture (MAC) and its advisers have also changed, especially since the early 1990s, as art from the region generally has engaged more actively with cosmopolitanism. In terms of physical infrastructure, the MAC premises are illustrative of such change in both scale and sophistication over time. MAC began in 1963 as a downstairs room in the missionary's manse, moved to a purpose-built, but very small, tin shed in 1968, and then to a series of buildings. Even the current MAC space with offices, galleries, packing rooms, freezer rooms, a library, a cultural research office, storage spaces and the nearby Djómi community museum and repository of art is proving inadequate for contemporary needs and the current level of engagement with the international and national arts community.

And the arts advisers too have become increasingly sophisticated. Initially they aimed to just collect art and document it and try to sell it – Dan Gillespie (pers. comm. 7 March 2004) tells a tale from the early days of how, while working for Gowan Armstrong in 1971, he took some small barks, like a travelling salesman, to Sydney when on holidays from his job as a school teacher and tried to find an outlet via a tribal art dealer in Oxford Street. The dealer agreed to buy some of this art, but when the consignment of barks larger than the suitcase sized 'samples' arrived he complained bitterly to Armstrong that the young assistant was sending him 'rubbish' that was unsaleable.

Over time, the arts advisers have come with more and more knowledge of the arts world and more and more university degrees. And they have started to make collections, broker exhibitions and commissions in public arts institutions and key commercial galleries in Australia and in major arts institutions in Europe. They have participated in major arts projects, mentoring and advising artists and travelling with them both in Australia and overseas, even promoting the art of emerging artists via internet, and so on. More recently, arts advisers have increasingly become agents for the top artists who need sound, lifelong career development plans like any top artist. Sometimes this is a problem because art advisers always come and go (to paraphrase Peter Carroll "*Balanda* (whites) come, *balanda* go: *bininj* (local blacks) are here forever"),[7] although MAC has been successful in retaining the

7 The precise reference is a chapter title by Carroll, P., 'Balanda Come, Balanda Go: Bininj Are Here Forever', in Loveday, P. and A. Webb (eds.) *Small Towns in Northern Australia* (North Australia Research Unit of the Australian National University, Darwin, 1989, pp. 177–188.

good ones longer than most. Being an artist's agent is also difficult because arts advisers at places like Maningrida need to look after the interests of literally hundreds of artists, not just the few very best.

To date, Kuninjku appear to have coped reasonably well with these institutional challenges: they have subtly adapted the art for the market; a new generation of artists is emerging, new and distinct 'family group' schools of art are emerging and there have been gender shifts that now allow and celebrate the achievements of women artists.

But, as the «*Rarrk*» exhibition tours through Europe there are some emerging issues for the Kuninjku arts movement, a movement that is now based on the art produced by more than half of the Kuninjku adult population from a prodigiously talented community. First, given that the inspiration for the art comes from the land, people's relations to country through ceremonial and customary practices, is there a danger that excessive professionalisation of top artists will undermine these crucial activities, e.g. will there be no time to hunt or to participate fully in regional ceremonies that can go on for weeks on end? Second, can MAC institutionally cope with having hundreds of artists in its catchment, with only some in the top echelon? What is the viability of this crucial arts infrastructure and does it have the capacity to sustainably cope with success? Third, is the arts practice sustainable, is there intergenerational transfer of the artistic inspiration and successful practice? In particular, today Kuninjku live comfortably, in a psychological if not physical sense, in Maningrida township, rather than at outstations: is there a danger that township living will sever the inspirational links to country that animates much Kuninjku art? And finally, will the notoriously fickle fine arts market maintain its very recently discovered fascination with Kuninjku art, or will it quickly move elsewhere?

These are obviously hard questions that need to be considered and that need to be raised to provide some balance to what is my very positive and optimistic interpretation of the development and growth of the modern Kuninjku art movement in the last 30 years.

And if there is some cause for future concern, one can draw some solace from reflecting back on the last 40 years and the resilience and adaptability of Kuninjku people and their art: since 1963 we have seen a journey from the 'Gunwinggu problem' (as these people were referred to in official dispatches from settlement authorities right up to early 1970s) into the current Kuninjku artistic *cause celebre* being acknowledged and recognised at the Museum Tinguely in Basel, a cosmopolitan locus for celebrating the best in world art.

Ultimately we end with a lovely paradox. Those apparently least well adapted to the market 40 years ago, now dominate MAC and the goods, almost exclusively art, exported from the Maningrida region: 15% of the regional population are responsible for more than 50% of MAC sales. And the most celebrated artists are now Kuninjku – so those who were 'bushiest', most marginalised and apparently least well adapted to market engagement are now producing the art that the market values most highly – how times change!

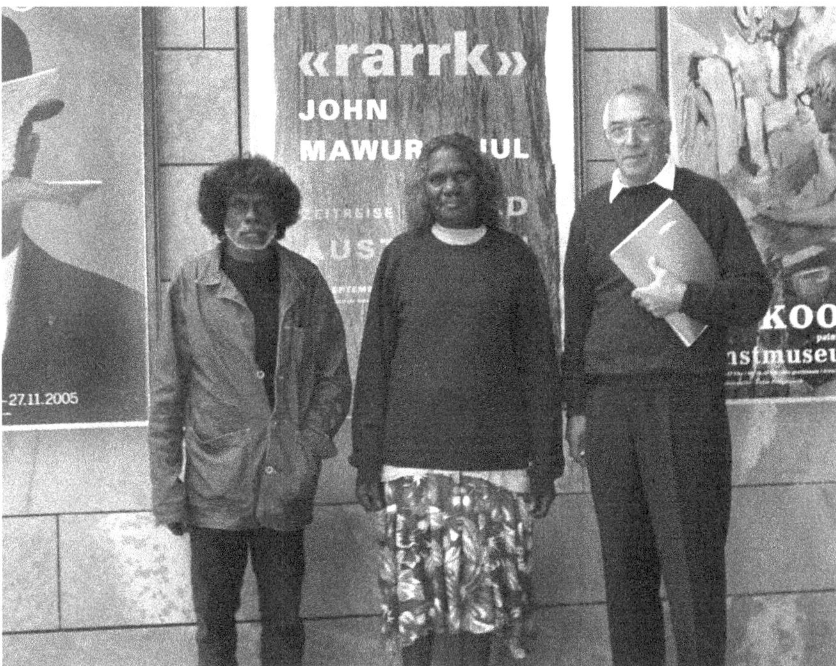

Fig. 3: John Mawurndjul with Kay Lindjuwanga and Bernhard Lüthi in Basel, 2005 (Detail). Photo Erika Koch.

Conclusion

To briefly conclude and summarise: forty years ago, the colonising state embarked on a project to sedentarise (to stop what was then regarded as problematic nomadism), to centralise, and to then 'civilise' Kuninjku in accord to assimilationist thinking of the time.

This historic epoch was bad for Kuninjku, but not all bad – modern medicine was instrumental in eradicating the introduced scourge of leprosy and Kuninjku survived, although their survival was jeopardized by unintended marginalisation at Maningrida township – and the ill effects of that time are still experienced by some adults today who, as children and infants, experienced malnourishment in the communal settlement kitchen and associated illness and morbidity.

While Kuninjku have steadfastly resisted assimilation and refused to join the mainstream on the state's terms, in the last 40 years they have incrementally increased their engagement with the market, with the wider Australian society and with globalisation, but on their own terms. Kuninjku people have managed this engagement skilfully by enlisting white and black allies and institutions, arts advisers, curators, public arts institutions, commercial galleries and, nearer to home, key personnel within BAC and MAC.

In recent times, especially in 2004 and 2005, there have been renewed pressures by the Australian state to revisit the state project of assimilation and to incorporate Indigenous

Australians, like the Kuninjku, into the mainstream. Again this is being promulgated under the apparently benevolent rhetoric of 'practical' reconciliation, the aspiration for social and economic equality between Indigenous and non-Indigenous Australians. These are simplistic motherhood goals that, while undisputable in terms of human rights, are fraught with dangers. At such a time, distinct Kuninjku ways – their ability to maintain their community, and language, way of life, cultural practices and art forms, even land rights – are all under threat. It makes no sense for the state to revisit a project that failed so abysmally 40 years ago but it seems intent on trying to do so.

There is an alternative. Might it not be more productive to recognise and celebrate this important art movement, based on cultural difference, and focussing on its contributions to Australia's national and international artistic and cultural statuses, as shown in the «*Rarrk*» exhibition (see fig. 3 and Pl. XXVI)?

And at a time when indigenous minorities everywhere are asserting their rights, challenging the homogenizing cultural influences of globalisation in their distinct and at times very desperate political ways, it is appropriate to consider just how effectively Kuninjku people have managed to assert their identity and distinctiveness, quietly and cleverly and with dignity, fighting against the powerful forces of incorporation. Kuninjku people have chosen to produce and reproduce their very special cultural heritage the best way possible for us and for them: fighting with their fabulous art.

PART 1
The local contexts of bark painting

Luke Taylor

Painted energy: John Mawurndjul and the negotiation of aesthetics in Kuninjku bark painting

Introduction

My interest in Kuninjku art started in 1980 as I was concerned to document an important world art system from Arnhem Land that seemed quite distinct from that of neighbouring groups. The artists were keen to emphasise that they painted in a way that was different to those painters who lived further east among Yolngu speaking Aboriginal groups. While I possessed a strong interest in art history, I realised that the only way I could get to understand the Kuninjku sense of their own art history was through anthropological research. The mode of my research was to be ethnographic involving a detailed consideration of how the paintings had meaning for the people who were producing them, how local people understood the interconnections between different artists, and what features of paintings were most admired locally. It was to be a detailed consideration of the activity of painting in its particular social context.[1]

At the outset it must be clear that these paintings are made for the commercial market which is now global in scope. However, despite profound intercultural contacts, what became apparent through the fieldwork was the strong integration of painting with processes of local identity formation. Indeed bark painting promoted a strong sense of the connection between people and country in the face of the encapsulation of Kuninjku within the Australian nation state. Bark painting was also involved in processes of group identification at a more local level as particular Kuninjku artists and families emphasised their way of doing things as distinct from other families.

As an example of these processes, and in order to address the recent major retrospective of painting entitled *«Rarrk» John Mawurndjul. Journey Through Time in Northern Australia* at the Museum Tinguely in Basel, Switzerland, I wish to focus this discussion on work by the famed Kuninjku artist John Mawurndjul. Mawurndjul's own development as an artist reveals how he was taught to paint themes of local cultural importance and how his current work comprises innovative reinventions of these themes. Ultimately the analysis also sheds

1 For a more extended discussion see Taylor, L., *Seeing the Inside: Bark Painting in Western Arnhem Land*, Clarendon Press, Oxford, 1996.

light on the particular way that Kuninjku construct metaphors of their place in the world, how artists articulate the content of a unique cultural viewpoint.

A local art history

In a discussion with the author in 2004 Mawurndjul spoke of three phases in his bark-painting career.

The first and early period of his painting from the late 1970s until the mid-1980s is characterised by predominantly small bark paintings of favourite subjects such as *namarrkon* (lightning), *mimih* (trickster spirit), *bambirl* (echidna), *yawkyawk* (young girl), *ngaldadmurrng* (saratoga fish), *birlmu* (large barramundi fish) and Ngalyod (rainbow serpent). In this period of his life Mawurndjul was being taught the iconographies for the correct depiction of particular species. Kuninjku artists must undergo a relatively long period of apprenticeship to learn to reproduce the outline form of species in order to produce a work that can be recognised by other Kuninjku. Paintings of animals are conceived to be iconic in the sense that the outline form of the painting is said to capture the unique body features of the particular species. Iconicity is understood here as the culturally perceived resemblance between signifier and signified components of the sign.[2] From an analytic perspective the young artist should not be considered to be modelling his works from life so much as learning an extensive set of iconically motivated forms that Kuninjku regard as 'correct'.

In the second period from the mid-1980s until late 1990s Mawurndjul was painting much larger works, particularly of Ngalyod the Rainbow Serpent. Ngalyod is conceived as the most important of Kuninjku subjects and Mawurndjul's elaborate paintings of this being emphasise its transformative powers. Ngalyod is conceived to be able to take on many different body shapes and Kuninjku artists take a key role in revealing these different forms. The paintings are not meant to be iconic so much as conceived in a more abstract way as representations that appropriately reveal Ngalyod's fantastic powers. At this time Mawurndjul had developed independence from his teachers, had travelled extensively within Australia and occasionally overseas. He developed a strong knowledge of his broader audiences, relationships with curators in major institutions, and an understanding of the collections held in some of these organisations. He realised that these audiences were interested in paintings of more important ancestral subjects and he considered representations of Ngalyod to be most appropriate to this end.

In the current period, that commenced from the late 1990s, Mawurndjul relates that his work now concentrates on experiments with Mardayin paintings. These are relatively large works that involve elaborations of the designs painted on bodies in the Mardayin ceremony. These paintings are non-iconic and comprise multicoloured patterns of crosshatched, parallel lines or *rarrk* contained within a grid of dotted dividing lines. The paintings are

2 Munn, Nancy, *Walbiri Iconography*, Cornell University Press, Ithaca, 1973, p. 87.

primarily conceived to be representations of ancestrally created landscapes, particular places called *djang* where the ancestral beings are said to still reside under the earth. While Mawurndjul is careful to reproduce the particular framework or grid that is a culturally recognised sign for the specific location, Mawurndjul's creativity lies in the way he varies the patterning of *rarrk* across the surface of the work to suggest the ancestral energy that is said to emanate from the places. These works have found favour with a global art market that is generally more receptive to abstract art due to developments in painting in Western centres and, within Australia, audiences have gradually come to appreciate the ceremonial significance of these more geometric designs.

In examining these different types of painting in Mawurndjul's development as an artist, this essay also provides an analysis of the multiple forms of representation that exist in Kuninjku art. In particular the way that artists make use of both iconic and non-iconic representations and how, in their development as artists, they gradually come to understand and use the potentiality of these different systems of representation to create new forms.

Early bark paintings

Mawurndjul started painting on bark in the same manner as many Kuninjku artists by depicting subjects that are well known to all Kuninjku. These include paintings of animals that are regularly hunted as well as the lesser spirit figures such as *mimih*. *Mimih* are a kind of trickster spirit that live in the rock country and there are a multitude of stories relating to these beings that are broadly known.[3] A common way of learning to paint these subjects involves helping a more senior artist to complete a work. The older artist completes the outline of the figure as a base of white paint called *delek* (calcium magnesium carbonate) for the younger artist to infill with *rarrk*. Until the early 1980s, Mawurndjul's elder brother Njiminjuma was assisting Mawurndjul in this way by providing bark with the *delek* figure outline completed.

Learning to paint a multitude of animal species can take young artists a long time. Often a young artist will look to a close senior relative to acquire these skills. Elsewhere,[4] I have called this learning process an "apprenticeship" although it could be described as a relatively informal teaching process. Young artists may look to their father or elder brother for assistance in the first instance, and later, when they are married, to their father-in-law. Essentially though a young person may approach any senior person with whom he co-resides for tuition. It is common among Kuninjku to see a senior and junior artist working together on a painting. In the 1980s it was very uncommon to see a woman learning in this way although currently a number of Kuninjku women are apprentice artists.

The focus of such learning is upon how to employ an iconic code in the representation of animals. The *delek* outline encodes features of the body shape of animals that are thought to be essential to its representation. Identification may involve the recognition of

3 Taylor, L., 1996, *op. cit.*, pp. 183–189.
4 Taylor, L., 1996, *op. cit.*, pp. 70–101.

peculiar features such as the thick snout of the estuarine crocodile (*Crocodylus porosus*) as opposed to the long thin snout of the freshwater Johnstone's crocodile (*Crocodylus johnstoni*). Alternatively, general features of body proportion such as a heavily muscled body may be used to distinguish the large kangaroo species from the more gracile forms used in the depiction of rock wallabies. Sometimes the outline for a species may be quite distinctive as in the representation of the spatulate beak of the royal spoonbill (*Platalea regia*) or the brush tail of the little rock wallaby (*Peradorcas concinna*). Similarly, very attenuated human body forms are instantly recognised as *mimih* spirits which are said to be so thin that a gentle breeze may break their necks.

Young artists regularly make mistakes in these depictions, which may draw laughter and derision from onlookers. Senior artists can correct mistakes by simply overpainting the white outline with the red background colour and repainting the *delek*. Since individuals in Kuninjku society possess specific ceremonial rights in respect to the depiction of particular species, it is important that young artists learn to paint the correct species and not infringe the rights of others.

The importance of this apprenticeship for young Kuninjku artists reveals a societal concern to protect the meaningful system of iconic representation. Learning to paint is often reinforced by the telling of stories that relate to the way that the species gained the particular form that they have. Indeed, in Kuninjku society there are also stories that relate to the depiction of important internal organs of the species or cuts of meat that may be taken from the animal after it has been killed. These organs may be shown using x-ray techniques.[5] The sharing of particular cuts of meat among the kin of the hunter is a vitally important practice among Kuninjku.

The importance of correct figure depictions is dramatised in public on ceremonial occasions when artists must paint the designs for particular species on the bodies of participants who will perform the dance for that species. In this heightened emotional atmosphere, it is most certainly true that artists must have a mastery of the iconography. While bark paintings are produced in the relative seclusion of the camp and generally sold to a distant audience, paintings produced on the ceremonial ground are exposed to the full glare of the gathered participants. In this context the owning group have the right to wear the design, however those of the opposite moiety, those who call the design 'mother' are considered to be the *djungkay* or managers of the design and must work to produce the design on the owner's body. This responsibility of managers to work for owners on ceremonial occasions necessitates that the design iconography is shared at least between owners and managers. However, when we consider the initiatory aspect of these ceremonies, understanding of the meaning of such paintings is also conveyed by senior people to the much wider social group that convenes for the purpose of the ceremony.

The completion of bark paintings made for sale involves the infill of the *delek* with very fine patterns of multicoloured parallel lines called *rarrk*. The white outline is first divided by lines called *rungkalno* which mark body sections such as the key joints or portions of

5 Taylor, L., 1996, *op. cit.*, pp. 224–241.

flesh. The *rarrk* is created by using a very fine and long-haired brush. A first set of parallel lines is produced in the section and when it is dry a second set of parallel lines is overlain across the first. Variations in the sequence of colours used create vibrant banding effects. Similarly variation of the angle at which the top layer overlays the bottom layer can be used to create different optical effects. A very acute angle creates moiré patterns which seem to move as the viewer moves around them.

While every young Kuninjku man has the responsibility to learn to paint *rarrk* in the context of ceremony, not everyone is considered good at it. Mawurndjul's father was not known as a bark painter although he taught his son his ritual responsibilities and instructed him in the production of *rarrk*.[6] Mawurndjul relates that:

> I saw my father doing the rarrk for the Mardayin ceremony and tried to do it myself with my back all doubled over, I ended up being better than any of them at it. They gave me a job in the Mardayin ceremony to paint some rarrk. When they all saw me doing it they said "wow', he's got the hang of it. You've left us behind my son," they said to me.[7]

Early bark paintings reveal Mawurndjul's exceptional ability at producing fine *rarrk*, *rarrk yahwurd* (little or tight *rarrk*). The lines in Mawurndjul's early works are like fine threads in a loose weave textile and the overall effect of the *rarrk* in such paintings is one of softness. Often the *rarrk* in such paintings is produced in a single colour red or in bands of red and orange that are very similar in tone. If this were continued across the whole work it might produce a work of soft focus that recedes into the red background of the bark. However Mawurndjul injects drama into such works by leaving body features such as the head, hands and feet unpainted. These features glow with the brilliance of the white paint *delek*. The strength of these paintings derives from the counterpoint between the unpainted and infilled sections of the work. The white paint lends a ghostly quality to the image and is reminiscent of some of the last paintings in the caves of this region that are also completed in *delek* often without further elaboration.

---

6 The word *rarrk* is used throughout Arnhem Land to refer to designs that make use of crosshatching components. Crosshatching is a description of the way the designs are painted as a set of parallel lines which are overlain by another set of parallel lines. A very thin brush consisting of a few very long fibers is used to make these lines. Colour changes in the respective sets of lines create a banding effect. The Mardayin ceremony for which these designs are produced was performed throughout the region although it is referred to generally as Ngarra in the east. In western Arnhem Land the term *rarrk* can also be used to refer to the whole design that is worn in the Mardayin ceremony. A full Mardayin ceremony has not been performed in western Arnhem Land for many years although senior men still look after the sacred objects for the ceremony and knowledge about Mardayin can be exchanged and incorporated in other important ceremonies.

7 John Mawurndjul quoted in Garde, Murray, 'Ngalyod in my Head: The Art of John Mawurndjul', in *John Mawurndjul: John Bulunbulun*, Annandale Galleries, Sydney, 1997, n. p.

"Ngalyod gets in my head"

Mawurndjul says that there was a middle period in his art that focussed upon larger paintings, particularly multiple interpretations of Ngalyod. Ngalyod is a major figure in Kuninjku religious life and a subject to which many artists return. Given that Ngalyod features in so many aspects of Kuninjku life there is enormous potential for individuals to investigate their own visual interpretations of this figure.

Mawurndjul's painting *Ngalyod, rainbow serpent, devouring the yawkyawk girls*, 1984, (see fig. 4 and pl. II) reveals a serpent looping around the painting, twisting backwards across its body a number of times and the young girl figures and parts of their bodies are depicted enmeshed in Ngalyod's crushing embrace. The moiré effects of the *rarrk* give a sizzling energy to the snake figure much like the rainbow effects that can be seen in snake-skin. Ngalyod is depicted as a snake figure with a crocodile head.

Kuninjku language speakers say that Ngalyod was the first being that made the world and that every other ancestral being came out of its body. People imagine this being as the 'mother' of all other species, of all the humans, of all of the ceremonies, of all the sacred objects and clan lands. Ngalyod is particularly associated with water and dwells in deep billabongs in the dry season. People say that waterlilies on the surface of the water at these places are attached to Ngalyod's back. If people damage such places, called *djang*, Ngalyod will come up out of the earth and devour them. It is both creator and protector of *djang* sites. Many creation myths told by Kuninjku involve Ngalyod. Typically other ancestral beings, also called collectively *djang*, are said to walk the earth in the creation period moulding the unformed land into features of landscape. These stories end when the ancestral being encounters Ngalyod who rises up out of the water, encircles the other being, swallows it, and takes it down into the water again. The powers of the ancestral beings remain at these places. Depictions of these moments of site creation are a very common subject in paintings. Kuninjku believe that the spirits of unborn humans also reside at these sacred places.

Kuninjku also say that Ngalyod makes the wet season. Ngalyod is said to rise up out of its watery home, arc into the sky and spit out the rain that forms a torrential downpour. The rainbow seen after the rain is another manifestation. When we imagine Ngalyod's power we must imagine the cyclonic weather that can characterise the wet season and the torrents that run across the earth and flood the low lying country. Following the rains the earth is replenished. The otherwise dry savannah is transformed by brilliant green spear grass, animals travel to eat the grass and birds flock to the floodplains. Kuninjku say that Ngalyod regurgitates all of the animals back into the world. Each year Kuninjku perform ceremonies such as Kunabibi to ensure that Ngalyod maintains the cycle of the seasons. Ngalyod also has this much more positive connotation as the bringer of life through the imagery of water.

While artists strive for a correct iconic interpretation of ordinary animals, ancestral beings such as Ngalyod are considered to have extraordinary powers which include the ability to change their body form. In successive paintings artists may reveal different interpretations of body form appropriate to the stories for particular places. These paintings are

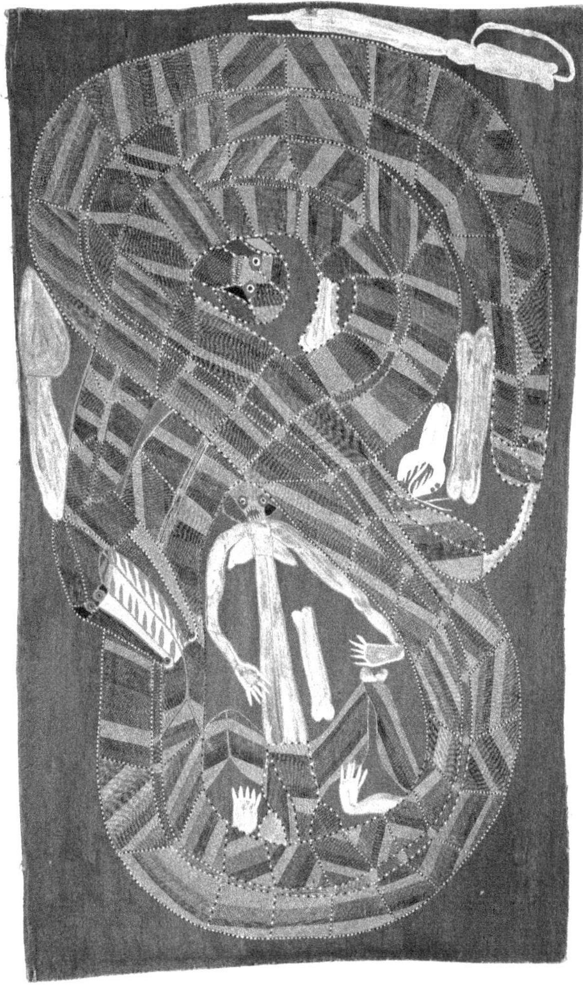

Fig. 4: John Mawurndjul, *Ngalyod, rainbow serpent, devouring the yawkyawk girls*, 1984, earth pigments on bark, 123.5 x 74 cm, National Gallery of Australia, Canberra. 84.1956.
Photo National Gallery of Australia.
© 2008, ProLitteris, Zürich.

created through the amalgamation of the body forms of different species, be it snake and crocodile or snake and water buffalo or a combination of any of the other species that 'came out of' Ngalyod's body. This variety of means of representing the being highlights the relative freedom of senior artists to interpret the complex body of knowledge that relates to Ngalyod. Other components of the body of these Ngalyod representations such as the inclusion of waterlilies growing out of Ngalyod's back or fish tails highlight the association with water.

If we may view the schema for representing particular animals as a syntagmatic chain of iconically motivated signifiers of particular body features, paintings of Ngalyod require artists to construct a new chain by combining the signifiers of different species. The representation of a single body part, such as the distinctive horns of the water buffalo,

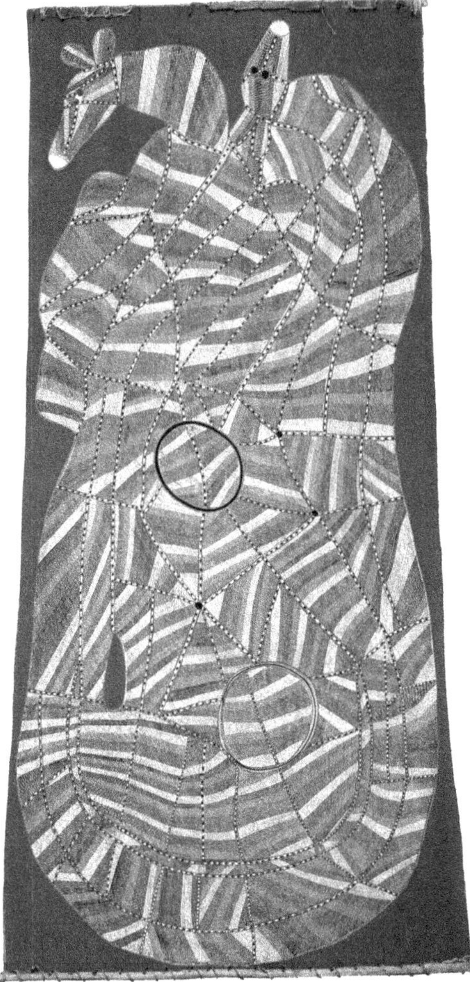

Fig. 5: John Mawurndjul, *Rainbow serpent's antilopine kangaroo*, 1991, earth pigments on bark, 189 x 94 cm, National Gallery of Australia, Canberra. NGA 91.874. Photo National Gallery of Australia. © 2008, ProLitteris, Zürich.

to signify a particular species in the Ngalyod representation is an example of synecdochic substitution. The creativity rests on a *bricolage*[8] technique through the combination of fragments of syntagmatic sets into a new set to create new meanings. The paintings would not be effective were it not for the way that a recognisable part of a familiar representation is used to stand for the whole. The conjunction of body parts, which synecdochically relate to other wholes, establishes a new relationship between the different species. The paintings reveal that the qualities of these other species are combined in Ngalyod. The socialisation of Kuninjku artists involves learning an interpretative framework or template[9] that allows

8 Lévi-Strauss, Claude, *The Savage Mind*, Weidenfeld & Nicolson, London, 1976 [1962], p. 150n.
9 Morphy, Howard, *Ancestral Connections*, University of Chicago Press, Chicago, 1991, p. 243.

them to transpose understanding of the representation of animals into understanding the representation of ancestral beings which are believed to be able to change their shape.

As well as showing Ngalyod as the 'mother' of these other species at the beginning of creation, paintings of Ngalyod also emphasise the strength and dangerous powers connoted by these species. The crocodile and snake are the only indigenous species considered dangerous to humans in this landscape. Water buffalo were released in Arnhem Land by the British in the 1830s and since then they too have been incorporated in Kuninjku mythology as the other major dangerous being in this country. A feature of iconically motivated systems of representation is that the representation of new species requires the invention of new schema for their representation. Kuninjku are now adept at painting buffalo, and representation of the two long horns is also a recognisable reference to this species in paintings of two-horned Ngalyod.

Another example of Mawurndjul's experimentation with this theme *Ngalyod*, 1988, was included in the *Magiciens de la Terre* exhibition in Paris in 1989. In this work the form of Ngalyod fills most of the surface of the bark and waterlily leaves are incorporated in the figure form. However the bulk of the figure allows Mawurndjul to experiment with ways of creating excitement within its interior. The sinuous rhythms of its backbone are the focus for radiating bands of colour and dotted section lines echo these forms and are suggestive of ribs. Circular elements that represent waterholes are also incorporated within Ngalyod's body and these signal the dual aspect of the image that can be read as a figure but also as a landscape. Thus, Mawurndjul highlights Ngalyod's role in land creation and the figure can be interpreted as a kind of map. The work *Rainbow serpent's antilopine kangaroo*, 1991, (see fig. 5) is another beautiful example of this theme. Here Ngalyod is shown as a dual figure with the head of the antilopine kangaroo and the twists and turns of these figures writhing together fills out the body of the figure. However Mawurndjul also incorporates circular motifs to suggest the places created by the being. In essence the figures become a foil for the expression of the creative energies that radiate from the sites in the landscape.

Mardayin paintings

Mawurndjul's experimentation with paintings of Ngalyod that can be conceived as maps reveal a broader concern for paintings of country, of the way that country can be conceived as transformations of the ancestral essence, and of expressions of these powers that exist in landscape. Paintings such as *Mimih at Milmilngkan*, 1989, (see fig. 6) focus attention upon the abstract representation of landscape and refer directly to the style of painting used in the Mardayin ceremony. Mardayin is a ceremony that highlights the powers of ancestral beings in maintaining the human and natural life cycles and performance in the ceremony demonstrates the dancer's spiritual identification with particular ancestral beings and the lands created by them.

Toward the late 1990s Mawurndjul concentrates on these Mardayin-style geometric paintings. As we have seen above Mawurndjul learnt about this ceremony as a young man and currently he has responsibility for sacred objects used in it. Because of the importance

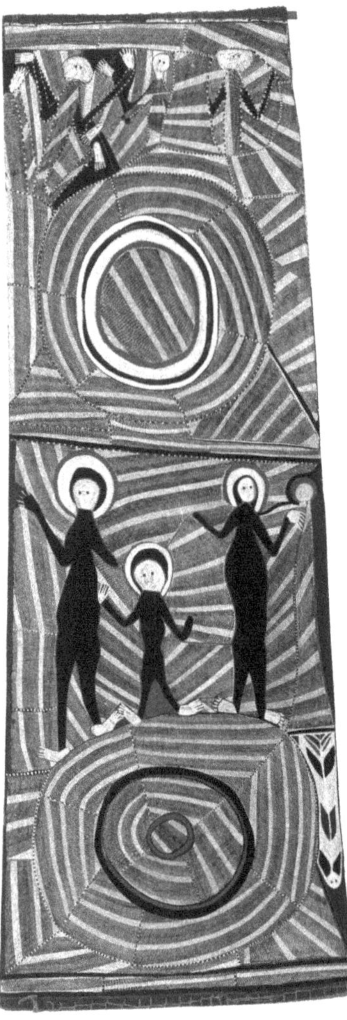

Fig. 6: John Mawurndjul, *Mimih at Milmilngkan*, 1989, natural pigments on eucalyptus bark, 249 x 95 cm. Purchased 2002. Collection: Art Gallery of New South Wales. © John Mawurndjul/2008, ProLitteris, Zürich, Photograph: Brenton McGeachie.

of this ceremony and the powers of the paintings used in it Kuninjku were generally reticent to paint these subjects for the commercial market. However, from his travels Mawurndjul became aware that occasionally older artists such as Yirawala and others had produced Mardayin paintings and this created a precedent both for their production by Kuninjku and for their acceptance in Australian and overseas markets. In addition, the decline in the widespread performance of the ceremony created the conditions where bark painting became an important means of demonstrating an artist's knowledgeable status vis-à-vis other Kuninjku and for passing on this knowledge. Mawurndjul makes the point that he derives inspiration from the 'inside', restricted, designs of ceremony but that his bark paintings are an elaboration and 'outside', or public, version of the themes:

> Yes, I can do them [Mardayin body paintings], but I will not do them the same way on my barks. I will make them different. I will use the 'outside' version of them, or change them so they are not like the 'inside', more restricted or secret, designs. People can look at the designs, but they won't know what they mean....But buried inside are secret meanings which others don't need to know. Other senior Aboriginal men will look at the painting and know what those deeper levels of meaning are and understand them.[10]

Body paintings worn in the Mardayin ceremony are wholly geometric works. They are painted on the chest and thigh of the dancers. They are comprised of a grid of dotted dividing lines which may incorporate circular elements painted black which represent waterholes. Often the grid is a highly symmetric design and different geometric arrangements of the grid distinguish different clan groups. The spaces inside the grid are infilled with *rarrk*. The designs are interpreted to represent the important sites in the clan lands of the wearer. For example the motifs representing the waterholes may be shown by lines that represent a creek or tunnel that links the waterholes while other lines may be interpreted as cliffs or rocky bars across the creek. In addition these designs may be interpreted as a kind of x-ray design with the patterns seen as body parts of the original ancestor and, by extension, the body parts of the person who wears the design. These designs are said to have been owned by the original creator beings and passed on to humans at the end of the creation period. The designs are thus considered to be inherently powerful and communicate their power to the wearer.

As distinct from paintings of animals which are iconic in character, these Mardayin paintings are not meant to be interpreted as representations of the outline form of the ancestor. Rather, it is important that the designs for different clans can be readily distinguished and each design is comprised of a different geometric pattern for dividing the rectangular outline. For example the dividing pattern may be a rectangular grid framework of dotted lines that cross at right angles, a set of squares criss-crossed by diagonal dividing lines, or a set of squares divided by a single diagonal. As Mawurndjul explains above, the paintings cannot be 'read' by the uninitiated. Rather, we may describe such designs as a whole sign identified with a particular ancestral locality. Elsewhere[11] Morphy has characterised such designs as 'identificational' in as much as the code for interpreting the meaning of the design is either known or not known by the viewer and forms part of a knowledge base that is considered restricted to those who have been initiated to the meanings of the ceremony. As Morphy has pointed out, the different characteristics of iconic and non-iconic representational systems are employed by Aboriginal artists in different realms of life, the non-iconic systems being particularly employed in restricted ceremonial contexts.

If one compares Mawurndjul's very large geometric works with representations of the designs used in ceremony, the first major distinction is the difference in scale. Early

---

10 Mawurndjul, J., 'My Head is Full Up with Ideas', in Ducreux, A.-C., Kohen, A. and F. Salmon (eds.), *In the Heart of Arnhem Land, Myth and the Making of Contemporary Aboriginal Art*, Musée de l'Hôtel-Dieu, Mantes-la-Jolie, Paris, 2001, pp. 51–55.

11 Morphy, H., 'What Circles Look Like', *Canberra Anthropology* 3 (1), 1980, pp. 17–36.

Mardayin paintings by Yirawala and others are chest sized and the *rarrk* patterning is very regular. Mawurndjul's new paintings by contrast can be taller than a person. Background grid patterns relate the design to the ceremonial works, but this element generally recedes in comparison to the focus upon the energy fields of crosshatching that swirl across the work.

Works such as *Mardayin ceremony*, 1999, that was included in the 12th Biennale of Sydney 2000 are a tour de force example of the dynamism of this theme. A fine tracery of thin dotted lines forms the background grid for the painting and indeed relates it to the grid used in the body paintings that represent this place.[12] However the energy of the painting is conveyed by the circular motifs that Mawurndjul interprets as lights glowing in the billabong at Kakodbebuldi, a place in his mother's country that he takes ritual responsibility for as *djungkay* or manager. Rays of light and ancestral energy are evoked by the intersections and flows of *rarrk* around the work. These lights are described to be like sources of Mardayin power in the earth at the bottom of the billabong and the *rarrk* itself is conceived as an expression of this power radiating from these sources.[13] *Mardayin ceremony*, 2000, is also a masterful representation of this theme. Here the focus is upon the rayed patterns of *rarrk* that move across the whole work and are only gently corralled by the grid. The fine *rarrk* against a light background conveys a general softness to the painting as a whole.

In some works it is this energy that becomes the focus. The grid which carries the particular locational associations of the design recede into the background. Mawurndjul is experimenting with the visual effects of different forms of crosshatching. Kuninjku say that what they strive for in their paintings is a liveliness and expressiveness, or *kukkmarkk,* literally good body, shape or form. The same term can be used for example to describe the positively valued qualities of a person who smiles a lot and is expressive in their face or, if describing a tree, that is full of vigour and the leaves and bark are smooth. By contrast a painting that does not achieve these effects could be described as 'dead'. In these paintings of swirling *rarrk* Kuninjku look to see if the paint is bright, carefully applied and, in effect, 'jumps out' at the viewer. These visual effects are captured in their description of good painting quality as *kabimbedmeh,* literally shining paint. For Kuninjku the desired aesthetic effect is thus an expression or emanation. Artists are inspired to express the energies that run through the landscape and through their own bodies and in turn to create a work that emanates these powers to those who view the paintings. This desired aesthetic effect is taken to be an expression of ancestral energy in much the same sense as that described by Morphy of *bir'yun* in Yolngu art.[14]

---

12 Taylor, L., 1996, *op. cit.*, pp. 227–234; and Taylor, L., 'Fire in the Water: Inspiration from Country', in Perkins, H. (ed.), *Crossing Country: The Alchemy of Western Arnhem Land Art*, Art Gallery of NSW, Sydney, 2004, (pp. 115–130), pp. 126–127.

13 John Mawurndjul, 2001, in Ducreux, A.-C., Kohen, A. and F. Salmon (eds.), *op. cit.*, p. 58.

14 Morphy, H., 'From Dull to Brilliant: The Aesthetics of Spiritual Power Among the Yolngu', *Man* (N.S.) 24 (1), 1989, pp. 21–40.

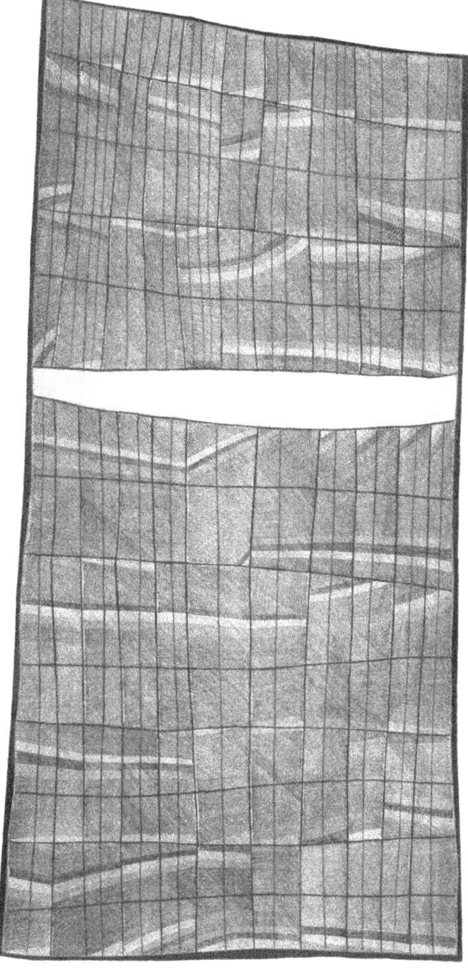

Fig. 7: John Mawurndjul, *Mardayin at Kudjarnngal*, 2003, earth pigments on bark, 152.5 x 76 cm, National Gallery of Victoria, Melbourne. Presented through the NGV Foundation by Judith and Leon Gorr, Ricci Swart, Nellie Castan and Anita Castan, 2003. NGV 2003.663. Photo National Gallery of Victoria. © 2008, ProLitteris, Zürich.

In Mawurndjul's most recent works such as *Mardayin at Kudjarnngal*, 2003, (see fig. 7 and pl. III) which was one of a group of paintings that won Mawurndjul first prize at the Clemenger Contemporary Art Award in 2003, the paintings gain their force by a grid that is not dotted and through waves of *rarrk* that run across the grid. There are very subtle flows of energy in such work as bands of white and red move horizontally in wave forms. Mawurndjul told me that these days he selects the 'strong' red and yellow ochres, often trading with other artists who live further afield to obtain them. The new works gain some of their glow by the pure saturated quality of the red paint in the thicker lines of *rarrk*. A counterpoint is provided by a thick band of pure *delek* which indeed represents the *delek* to be found at the site. Here again the contrast between the filled and unfilled sections of the painting creates an abrupt surprise, a tension in the heart of the work that evokes the connection between landscape and the sacred energies radiating from it. Mawurndjul is the first Indigenous artist to win this award and for him it was taken as testament to the growing equality between Indigenous and non-Indigenous contemporary artists in Australia.[15]

Conclusion

While John Mawurndjul speaks readily of his personal creativity in bark painting, he also acknowledges his debt to those artists who taught him and more broadly to the Kuninjku way of painting. What I have shown in this chapter is that Mawurndjul's individual expression involves an exploitation of potentialities that exist in Kuninjku representational systems. Mawurndjul's paintings of Ngalyod draw upon the iconic representational system for depicting animals and ancestral beings in animal form. Mawurndjul's current experiments lie with the potentialities of the non-iconic Mardayin system of representing landscape and elaborations of the crosshatching in different works to suggest the ancestral energy associated with these sites.

These two different ways of painting are related in that they make use of elaborations of body forms to construct meaning. Paintings of transforming figures elaborate the relationships between different species by connecting different body parts while Mardayin paintings are related to x-ray paintings in the way they elaborate the internal infill of the body outline. Kuninjku artists manipulate these two different axes of the representation of body form to create meaning. Kuninjku artists create metaphors about the body to give meaning to many other areas of their experience. Understanding about the connection of humans to each other, humans to ancestors, humans to animals, humans to landscape, and ancestors to landscape can all be modelled through body imagery. Visceral metaphors abound in Kuninjku cultural life partly as a result of the way that meanings are created through the artistic system. Body imagery is particularly apt because of the way that interior complexity and processes are encapsulated and masked by the skin. This in turn relates to the structuring of many bodies of knowledge among Kuninjku into 'inside', or restricted, and 'outside', or public, realms. Aesthetic categories are also interlinked to this broader system such that 'liveliness' is a positively valued criterion while a bad painting can be described as 'dead'.

An analysis of Mawurndjul's art leads us to an important understanding about the arts that have been characterised as traditional. While Mawurndjul was initially taught to paint by rote, learning culturally appropriate schema for representing animals, ultimately he learned to understand the productivity of the Kuninjku artistic system and how to create innovative works. What he learned was an interpretative intellectual structure or template for creating paintings that are inspired by his knowledge of the transformative powers of the ancestral beings. He maintains a tradition in the abstract sense that the template for creating paintings is shared between the generations while individuals are free to

15 The Clemenger Contemporary Art Award is a triennial exhibition and award held at the National Gallery of Victoria's Ian Potter Centre. It is an invitational award and in 2003 fifteen of Australia's finest artists were invited to exhibit. Mawurndjul was one of four Indigenous artists invited to exhibit.

create works that are lively and new. While individual creativity is encouraged through the new global marketing frameworks for Aboriginal art, Mawurndjul's output also maintains techniques of image production that have enormous time depth. Part of the richness of Mawurndjul's art comes from these obvious links with the art of his mentors, his creativity derives from a wellspring of cultural knowledge and an understanding of his social identity. The expressiveness of his painting is ultimately a religious expression, a celebration of ancestral powers understood to work through individuals.

Apolline Kohen

An arts adviser perspective on producing art for Balanda

The production of art in the Maningrida region (see fig. 8) is vital to artists as both an expression of their identity and as a source of income. Maningrida Arts and Culture (MAC) is the bridge between the artists it represents and the Balanda (non-Aboriginal) audience which the art is produced for.

Like other artists working in the Maningrida region in central Arnhem Land, John Mawurndjul connects with the commercial market through Maningrida Arts & Culture. MAC is what is known as an arts centre and is primarily the point of purchase of works produced in the Maningrida region which are then marketed to the world. MAC is owned by the Aboriginal artists themselves and was established in 1973, although art works have been produced and marketed since the establishment of Maningrida community in 1957.

Artists primarily produce work on their own country and art works are made of traditional materials and natural pigments, the exception being PVA fixative. Even the production of the most basic art work requires considerable skill and customary knowledge. It is important to know that artists represented by MAC have never lost their land, language or culture. This is why to this day John Mawurndjul is so comfortable with his identity.

How does an arts centre work? I will confine my comments to the functions of MAC because other Aboriginal arts centres in Australia have their own unique practices and policies. The relationship between the artists and MAC is essentially a commercial one but these relationships can be, and often are, extremely complex. On a typical day, I buy and sell many different kinds of art work of differing quality and value (see fig. 9). I also provide encouragement to emerging artists, offer hopefully constructive criticism to others, pay someone telephone's bill, negotiate the purchase of a 4WD for an artist, engage in many long-distance calls with galleries and collectors, email images all over the world, entertain clients, supervise the packing and freight, deal with a couple of conservation emergencies, etc. Life in the arts centre is hectic and unpredictable. There are never two days that are the same but the dramas and frustrations are beautifully balanced by the thrill of having exciting and innovative art works arriving through the door.

MAC is housed in a converted soup kitchen built in the 1960s. The building is inadequate and inappropriate for the display, storage and conservation of art. Fourteen of us work in the building, two of us are non-Indigenous. In addition to supporting 700 hundred

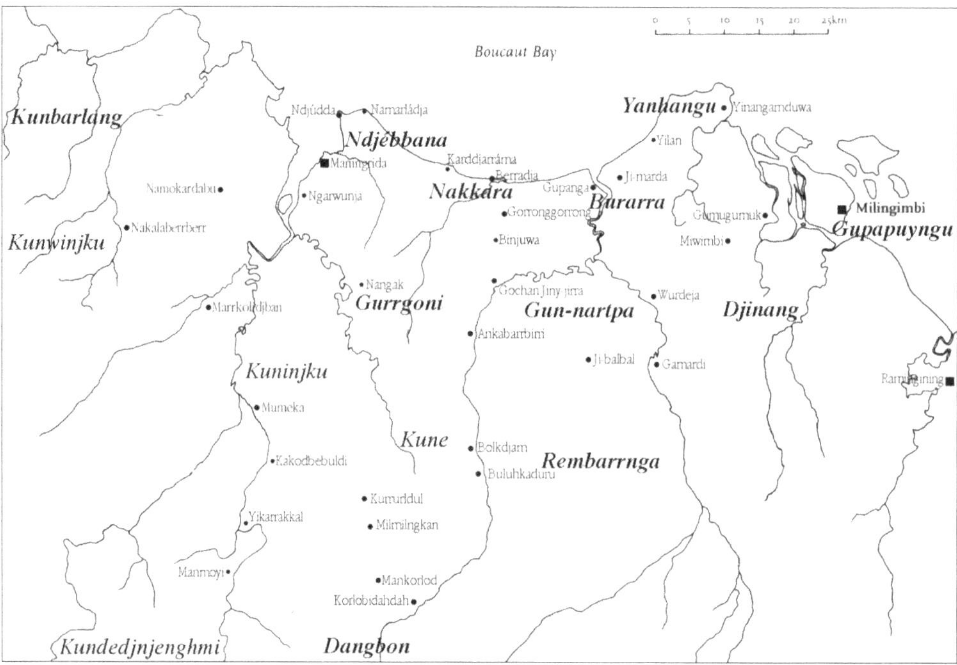

Fig. 8: Map of language groups in the wider Maningrida area, 2006. Courtesy Maningrida Arts and Culture.

artists, MAC is a significant local employer of Aboriginal people in the community. People work in packing and freight areas, photography, conservation, visual display and conduct tours through the community museum. Additionally, the arts centre engages in cultural maintenance activities including the production of dictionaries, music recording, preservation of the archives, supporting researchers and students and responding to the community's request with regard to cultural maintenance.

A significant feature of MAC is its total acquisition policy by which I mean that MAC buys each and every art work that is brought in by an artist. This creates reliability and security for the artists, insures that their work is treated with respect, boosts the career of young and emerging artists and provides an income to ageing artists who have passed producing their best work. The opportunity to have access to an additional income through the production of art works is an important factor in the Maningrida economy. In order to underwrite the total acquisition policy the arts centre is compelled to function as an effective and profitable marketing organisation. MAC achieves this by continuously stimulating the production of quality art works. A wide range of art works is produced in the region: the most well known are bark paintings but increasingly MAC is gaining renown for wooden sculptures, traditional material culture such as dilly bags, innovative fibre art, ceremonial regalia, musical instruments and limited edition prints. Over 10,000 individual

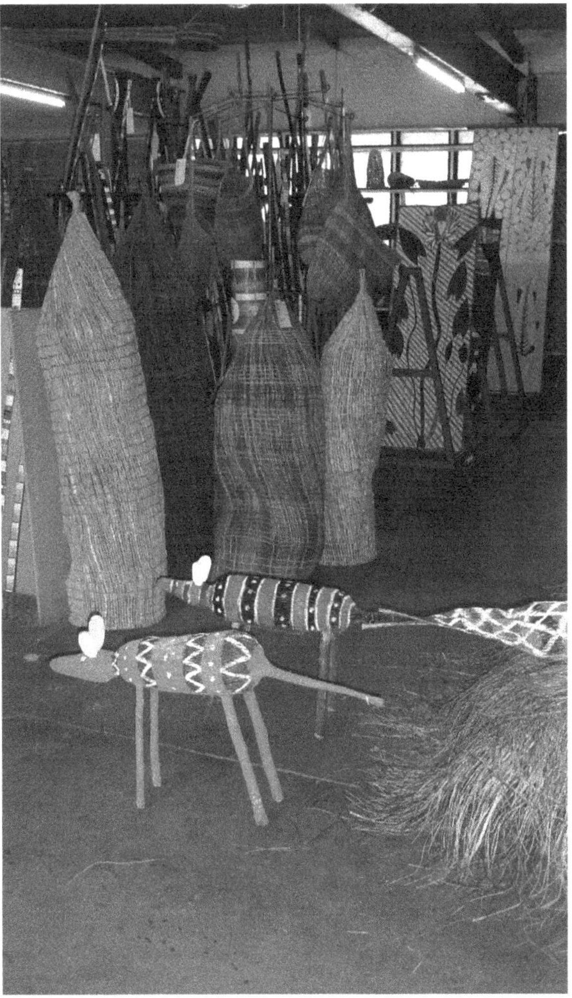

Fig. 9: Inside Maningrida Arts and Culture. Photo Apolline Kohen.

art works are produced every year. The volume and diversity of production obviously creates its own marketing dilemmas. Without question the highest quality works can be categorised as fine art and are marketed mostly through an extensive exhibition programme. There were 26 such commercial exhibitions last year alone. Some of the works, such as Mawurndjul's paintings, are in high demand and 'stars' like him require skilful insertion into the market in order to maximise the returns to MAC and the artists. The bulk of Maningrida art works is bought by galleries and shops in Australia and overseas for routine commercial resale, while a small number of collectors and art enthusiasts visit Maningrida to buy directly; the arts centre has its own website with purchase online facilities, and in 2004 MAC opened a retail outlet in Darwin, the nearest city, approximately 500 kilometres away from Maningrida. There is a growing interest in unique objects such as fish traps and mats for interior design and 3D installations.

I will now explore the unusual way in which artists view the commercial art market. The basic economic determinants of supply and demand can resonate in unconventional ways with Aboriginal people. For many, the transaction at the counter of MAC marks an end to their interest in, and engagement with, the market. For others, the transaction marks both the symbolic recognition of the art work and confirmation of their skills and knowledge. At this point, either the arts adviser or the artists themselves may initiate a dialogue aimed at developing a deeper mutual understanding of both production and market. In its simplest form the dialogue may include information about seasonal factors affecting production such as the difficulties of obtaining bark in the dry season or, at the opposite end, the problem of excessive moisture during the rains which is liable to produce cracks through shrinkage as the bark dries. A critical part of the dialogue involves discussions about the art works' content and meaning. The level of information conveyed is left to the discretion of the artist but such information forms the basis of high-quality documentation which in itself serves as a certificate of authenticity. The technical craftsmanship of the work is a fundamental point of discussion. It is not uncommon for art works to suffer damage while being transported to the arts centre and minor repairs are sometimes required to make the work marketable. The quality and appeal of the work is then discussed with the artist. Clearly the arts adviser has an onerous responsibility as the artist relies heavily on his or her advice and guidance in matters of likely market response, aesthetics and value. This generally leads to an agreement on purchase price, and payment by cheque follows. However, the dialogue is not necessarily concluded herewith. It is quite common to exchange information about upcoming exhibitions, developments in style, to provide feedback on the success or failure in the market, provide encouragement and discuss various other factors affecting the artist's career.

Not so very long ago the market was a complete enigma to Aboriginal artists. They knew that Balanda people wanted to buy their work, but the reasons why were a source of complete mystery. Obviously artists want to produce work of greater appeal and value, and this has stimulated a desire for an understanding of the market. Here the arts adviser assumes the role of educator. A successful relationship between the arts adviser and the artist relies heavily on trust. Sadly, in the history of Aboriginal art in Australia this trust has too often been misplaced.

One successful way for artists to better understand market mechanisms, collectors and the Balandas' love of Aboriginal art is to get involved in an exhibition project or a commission which offer the opportunity of direct interaction. For example, the making of the exhibition *Crossing Country: the Alchemy of Western Arnhem Land Art* in 2004 involved the active participation of many Kuninjku artists through interviews published in the catalogue, the making of a film, their presence at the opening of the exhibition and their participation in floor talks and at the symposium. It triggered an interest in educating Balanda about Kuninjku art and culture, encouraged artists to produce fantastic art and made Kuninjku artists confident about their popularity on the market place. A commission such as the current Musée du quai Branly project which involves eight Aboriginal artists,

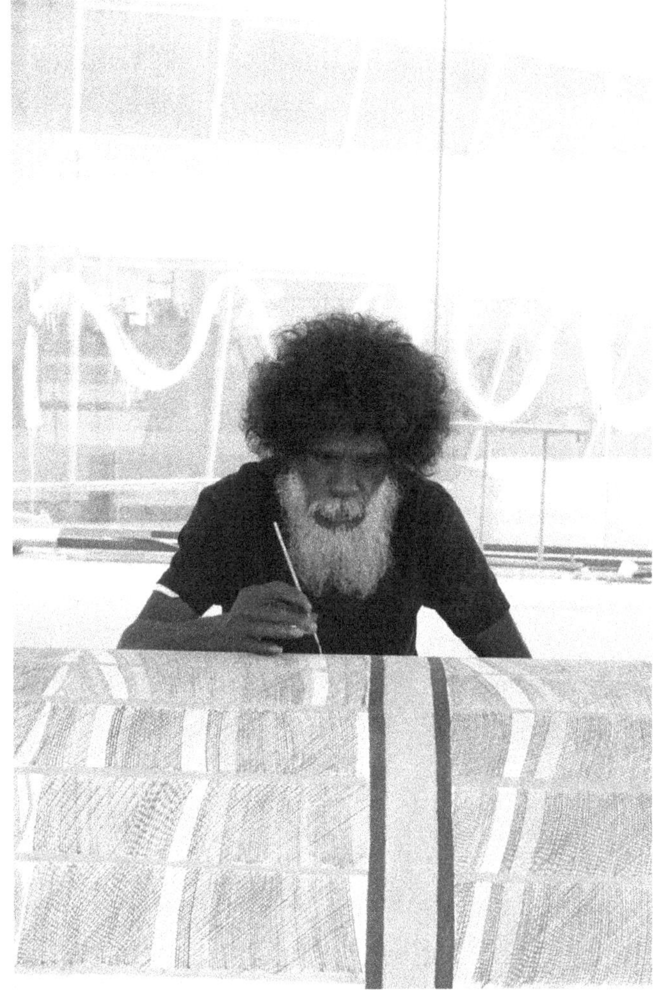

Fig. 10: John Mawurndjul painting the hollow cover for the column in the bookshop of the Musée du quai Branly, Paris, September 2005. © Photo Scala, Firenze – Musée du quai Branly, 2005.

including John Mawurndjul, is seen as a major form of recognition by the community. Prior coming to Basel John Mawurndjul spent three weeks in Paris working on a column in the bookshop of the Musée du quai Branly (see pl. IV). On a daily basis, I sent photos of the work in progress to Maningrida as many artists and community members wanted to know how John Mawurndjul was handling his project (see fig. 10). Many Maningrida people feel that Mawurndjul is representing the community through this project and is acting as an ambassador of central Arnhem Land art and culture. No need to say that Mawurndjul did not let them down. The result is stunning and powerful, reflecting his genius and attachment to country.

The reasons why individual artists produce work vary somewhat. The key components are the desire to preserve and display cultural heritage, the education of both Balanda and younger generations of Aboriginal people, and the obvious income benefits. The most desirable consumer commodity in our region is a 4WD vehicle, enabling convenient access to country for people and their families. The production of art is often the only way people can generate the considerable sums required for the purchase and running costs of these vehicles. Access to trucks, as they are called, dominates daily life for some. Trucks, in turn, contribute significantly to Aboriginal people's ability to produce food and art works, and the loss or failure of a truck causes considerable stress, and often an alarming reduction in art production. Consequently, an effective arts adviser requires knowledge of the condition of community vehicles. The output of individual artists can often be predicted with great accuracy if one is up to date with the state of their truck. The urgency to buy or repair a truck often stimulates an eruption of art production but, more interestingly, this is often accompanied by a discussion on career development targeting a higher income. Common questions asked at these times include "what is it that Balanda want?", "what do I have to do to be in an exhibition?", "why is John Mawurndjul's work in such high demand?" or "how much do I owe the workshop?" I do not want to trivialise the subject of vehicles. They really do play a pivotal role in people's lives, and this does not look like changing in the nearer future.

As in many, if not all, cultures, Kuninjku people aspire to higher incomes. The phenomenon of the professional Aboriginal artist is a recent one. Traditionally, no Aboriginal person could be described as a professional artist, although art may have been a significant component of their life. Professional artists require professional marketing and it falls to the arts centres to provide this. A disturbing development in the Aboriginal arts trade in Australia has been the emergence of the so-called carpetbaggers. These are individuals who directly approach established artists with offers of immediate payment for their work. This payment usually takes the form of cash, but can also be alcohol, vehicles and recently, and most alarmingly, drugs. Carpetbaggers are the enemy of arts centres, artists and good quality art. As opposed to arts centres, carpetbaggers tend to neglect the artist's career development, target only big name artists and pay the bare minimum for a work. In their most evil manifestation they have been known to confine artists to sweatshops. Maningrida Arts and Culture has worked long and hard for the artists and we have managed to keep carpetbaggers largely at bay; however, they remain an ever-present threat. Invariably carpetbaggers are not effective agents for artists. In contrast, MAC is a genuine representative and advocate for the artists. As previously discussed, the establishment and maintenance of key partnerships with institutions, galleries and collectors is fundamental in enabling artists to embark on a career trajectory. The production of art in communities like Maningrida is also often the only non-government money coming to the community and art has an enormous economic impact. The arts centre has a crucial role in the community and needs to represent its artists in the most professional and impeccable manner.

It is important that we do not fail Aboriginal people in this, as art production is seen by Balanda as an activity in which Aboriginal people excel. In Australia, Aboriginal people need all the positive coverage they can get. Art is a major success story for Maningrida, and the self-esteem, wellbeing and growing confidence of the artists cannot be overvalued.

Jon Altman

Brokering Kuninjku art: a critical perspective on the complex processes of mediating with the market

Kuninjku art must travel enormous geographic and cultural distances from its place of origin in remote Arnhem Land, north Australia, to the fine art galleries and public arts institutions of metropolitan Australia and the world.

Sitting here in Basel it is very difficult to imagine the journey taken over time and space, culturally as well as conceptually, by the Kuninjku art we view here, represented by the artistic life work of John Mawurndjul.

In this paper I seek to provide some insights into the complex processes of mediation with the market by giving an historical perspective on the journeys of the art of John Mawurndjul from the late 1970s until today. I shall do this from three vantage points.

I begin with the artist, although the observations that follow are my own. Much biographical material about John Mawurndjul is in the catalogue essay 'From Mumeka to Basel: John Mawurndjul's artistic odyssey',[1] so I will not repeat it here.

I will then move on to consider the institutional frameworks that underpin the complex processes of mediation between John Mawurndjul, an extremely successful Kuninjku artist, and the global fine arts market. Here I will consider the role played by local institutions, especially Bawinanga Aboriginal Corporation (BAC), Maningrida Arts and Culture (MAC) and the arts adviser, as well as wider state policy settings. I will not say much about other important institutions like the commercial galleries sector, the public art institutions (in Australia and overseas) or the secondary art market and the auction houses, although all obviously play crucial roles.

I will conclude with some critical observations about the future: of course a healthy vibrant prognosis is not guaranteed for anything or anyone especially in the arts, but arguably the Aboriginal arts sector is especially vulnerable, dependent as it is on intense mediation and state patronage, located in unimaginably disadvantaged Indigenous communities, and susceptible more than most art to the vagaries of a market that has yet to unambiguously

1 Altman, Jon, 'From Mumeka to Basel: John Mawurndjul's Artistic Odyssey' in Kaufmann C. and Museum Tinguely (eds.) «*Rarrk*» – *John Mawurndjul. Journey Through Time in Northern Australia,* Schwabe AG, Basel, 2005, pp. 30–41.

decide if this art is truly fine art or tribal or ethnographic. The threats to Kuninjku art are multifaceted and very real, especially in contemporary Australia.

I will end though with a degree of optimism drawn in part from the history of the development and resilience of the Kuninjku art movement over the past 40 years and in part from my observations and documentation of its growth and associated embedding in the national arts imaginary since 1979.

The Kuninjku artists

Kuninjku art draws its inspiration and originality from Kuninjku return to country in the early 1970s. Before that institutionalised and sedentarised, some might argue imprisoned in the government settlement of Maningrida in the 1960s, Kuninjku art did not flourish. Indeed it is a wonder that some key Kuninjku men like Mick Kubarkku and Crusoe Kuningbal were able to produce anything for the market given the marginality of their existence in the township, but they did.[2]

That marginality turned into a form of competitive advantage when people returned to live on their land in the early 1970s, supported now in theory, if not fully in realistic practical resourcing, by changed government policy.

Living at outstations was not easy in economic and logistic terms but provided the geographic and cultural distancing and insulation that the Kuninjku community needed to re-establish itself on its lands and to recover from the 1960s trauma of the Maningrida experience. Basically this meant that people were able to reignite some old ways: hunting, ceremonies, and intimate knowledge of country. At the same time art schools developed, focused on particular outstations – as described in fascinating detail by Luke Taylor in his important book *Seeing the Inside.*[3] More and more, people's livelihoods depended on the arts for cash income because when living at outstations there were no mainstream jobs (a situation that continues today). In new ways, art was used to make important political statements about 'on country' living to many people, initially to white authorities, then to other Aboriginal people in the region, and increasingly more recently to other Kuninjku people choosing to live in Maningrida.

One can see all this reflected in the artistic development of John Mawurndjul over three decades 1975 to 2005. While in Luke Taylor's rendering (see above pp. 31–45) the artist reflects on the impact on his art work, I would like to reiterate briefly the social bases in real life: in the early 1970s, John Mawurndjul moved to Mumeka with his father Anchor Kalunba and began to paint in the late 1970s under the tutelage of his elder brother Jimmy Njiminjuma and his father-in-law Peter Marralwanga; this is when I first met him as a young man, already with three children and with no cash income other than what he

2 See Altman, J., 'Brokering Kuninjku Art: Artists, Institutions and the Market' in Perkins, H. (ed.), *Crossing Country: The Alchemy of Western Arnhem Land Art*, Art Gallery of NSW, Sydney, 2004, pp. 173–187.

3 Taylor, Luke, *Seeing the Inside: Bark Paintings in Western Arnhem Land*, Clarendon Press, Oxford, 1996.

earned from art (in those days about $A 3,000 per annum) and with pressures to perform in other arenas in hunting and in ceremony in which he was deeply involved.

In the 1980s, still living at Mumeka, John Mawurndjul also started to travel outside Arnhem Land and see art in public institutions; by now his identity was more firmly established as an artist, but he continued to also participate in other activities. There were some important art breakthroughs in the late 1980s and early 1990s mediated by art adviser Diane Moon and including overseas travel.

By the 1990s, John Mawurndjul was starting to become an artist of renown and this was linked to a move to his own 'outstation' at Milmilngkan near to the most sacred of Kurulk sites at Dilebang, but also opening up opportunity for painting different places like Milmilngkan itself and nearby Kudjarnngal. It was after his father passed away and when new arts advisers facilitated his solo shows in the top Australian commercial galleries like Gabrielle Pizzi and Annandale that he became the foremost living Kuninjku and regional artist.

In the 21st century, this leadership has become even more evident, as winner of Clemenger Prize in 2003 and as scripted leading artist and spokesperson for the Kuninjku arts community at the major retrospective *Crossing Country: the Alchemy of Western Arnhem Land Art* in 2004.[4]

This success of an individual is remarkable in many ways especially in a society where individualism is unusual and politically contested. It can be explained in part by John Mawurndjul's extraordinary energy and artistic creativity: the records of MAC show him producing art year-in and year-out since 1978 (and more specifically in each year since 1985 John Mawurndjul has produced an average of over 30 pieces of art per annum with output in recent years exceeding 50 bark paintings, carvings and hollow logs, not including more recently printed works on paper in collaboration with non-Indigenous artists like Jean Kohen), without respite, without rest and with enormous commitment to excellence.

And through it all, as I have already alluded, John Mawurndjul has chosen to continue living a lifestyle that is geographically and culturally distant from the markets for his art, as have most other key Kuninjku artists.

Paradoxically this has also meant and required a high degree of dependence on BAC to support outstation living and MAC, and its employed arts advisers, to support the marketing of his art, and the Australian state to support both.

The complex processes of mediation

For Kuninjku people today living at outstations, small remote communities on their land, relationships with wider Australia and the rest of the world are to a large extent mediated by the Bawinanga Aboriginal Corporation (BAC), an outstation resource or services agency established originally in the early 1970s and officially in 1979. Similarly, the sale of art is

4 See Perkins, Hetti, 2004, *op. cit.*

mediated for Kuninjku by Maningrida Arts and Culture (MAC), an organisation set up initially with a township focus in 1963 (coincidentally the year John Mawurndjul moved to Maningrida as an unwell child from the bush), but more formally from 1973 with support from the Aboriginal Arts Board of the Australia Council. And finally, while MAC is a community or artist-controlled agency that is now a part of BAC, the pivotal role there is played by the arts adviser or director (see Kohen above pp. 47–52). Kuninjku are fortunate that all these institutions have operated in unison and effectively for a long time, at least in the context of the modern Kuninjku art movement.

Let me illustrate briefly the pivotal role played by each of these institutions and their connectivities that make arts mediation such a relatively complex process.

BAC was established as an outstation service agency located in the township of Maningrida (see Altman above, pp. 19–28). It has historically facilitated Kuninjku return to country, but then moved on to provide the services that enable people to live out there, infrastructure like housing and roads and access to basic services like shopping. Other organisations also assist: for example, the school provides outstation schooling and the medical centre health services. But BAC provides the three things that matter most: access to income support (via the Community Development Employment Projects (CDEP) scheme, a form of work-for-the-dole or workfare); access to vehicles and mechanical repairs; and access to banking and the means to purchase vehicles, the most highly prized commodity (as noted in A Kohen's contribution, above pp. 47–52 and by Altman and Hinkson).[5] From the Kuninjku arts perspective, a crucially important current role is BAC's championing of CDEP as a form of basic income support that allows artists to operate creatively and with the vagaries of the arts. While MAC is at one level just a business arm of BAC it is much more: it is the locus of cultural activity and the links between BAC's servicing role and artists living on, and inspired by, country.

Within MAC, the crucial arts brokering role is played by the arts adviser, usually outsiders or Balanda with an arts background, who invariably come and go. This is both the most pivotal and potentially problematic arts mediation point. Good arts advisers are hard to find and even harder to keep, at least for the sort of time over a career that a top artist generally has an agent relationship (bearing in mind that this analogy has some limitations as the categorisation of an individual, just as being a professional artist, is not so straightforward in the Kuninjku world).

The arts adviser does many things including running a small retail/wholesale arts business in a remote location that services literally hundreds of member artists and artisans. But most importantly in the context of a top artist like John Mawurndjul, the adviser operates as an agent, negotiating the purchase of art from the artist, making important decisions about what to exhibit, where, when and with whom. This is an extremely difficult task because it requires the constant bridging of the cultural gulf between what art means in Kuninjku society and what it means in the global art world. Just very fundamental tasks like ensuring that a quality collection is completed for a planned exhibition in a top gallery

5 Altman, J. and M. Hinkson, 'The Social Universe of Kuninjku Trucks', paper presented at the Cruising Country Symposium, Centre for Cross Cultural Research, the Australian National University, May 2005.

can be extremely challenging when artists have many other competing obligations and considerations in their social worlds.

Both BAC and MAC are supported by the Australian state, which in Australia's federal system means both the federal and the Northern Territory governments. Neither are particularly generous in their support. What these relations of financial dependence mean is that these institutions need to be internally accountable to their members, while also externally accountable to state funding agencies. This, as we shall see shortly, makes them vulnerable to the vagaries of party political and ideologically driven policies and policy change. It is not the case that the success that we might celebrate here in the from of John Mawurndjul's art is either recognised or regarded as sustainable by the Australian state.

It is these diverse levels of mediation between the artist and the arts market, which I have simplified considerably that result in complexity: and while I have alluded to potential contestations in the Kuninjku arts domain, I have only hinted at the contestations that occur in the institutional domains, within BAC and MAC (where Kuninjku have representation) and within state funding agencies (where they need to be represented by BAC and MAC). The mediation process requires artists to interact with these institutions and these institutions to in turn interact with the global arts community and the state.

Structural ambiguities, tensions and threats

Given the complexity in brokering art inter-culturally, it is not surprising that the process is fraught with ambiguities, tensions and threats. This is particularly the case because though we focus here on art, its production is dependent on the maintenance of a particular style of living increasingly between Maningrida and outstations, between town and country. One cannot divorce arts from its broader setting.

Let me very briefly revisit this setting again at the level of the artist, supporting institutions, and the state.

Kuninjku art, like all art, is produced in a social context and consequently one needs to ask what social conditions might be supportive of robust artistic practice? While living between town and country is one issue, a more important one is how to create space for individual success in a society that is very communal and group oriented. This tension requires careful negotiation and some like John Mawurndjul have clearly been able to do this well. Another issue is how to maintain focus on art living within an economy that has constant competition for one's time, in hunting, ceremony and family life. Again some negotiate the real life tensions for the Kuninjku artist, living in, and between, two worlds, aspiring to be a professional artist within the Kuninjku community, living between the country that inspires art and the township with its service conveniences (including access to MAC). Others cope less well with the pressures of arts production and ongoing marginalisation in contemporary Australia. There are major health problems associated with too much tobacco, and on occasions, alcohol, kava and gandja. Some artists die too young, some are cut down in their prime, I have been to too many funerals between 1979 and now and get phoned about too many deaths.

At the institutional level, there are similar pressures. In the regional Indigenous domain there is competition between Kuninjku and other groups for an appropriate and equitable institutional space, something that historically Kuninjku failed to get, but have increasingly managed to secure through the support for their determination to live on outstations as well as their artistic practice. In particular, Kuninjku have managed to attract the appropriate attention of current and recent advisers. Indeed the current financial viability of MAC is largely dependent on Kuninjku production, but will this always be the case?

A critical institutional issue is the role of the adviser, who must constantly cope with the tension of being the manager of a small business employed to look after the interests of all artists, and the demands of being the agent for the very best artists and the demands that such a role entails. This issue to some extent parallels that of individual versus the collectivity in Kuninjku society and again must be carefully negotiated. An associated issue is the nature of the relationship between the adviser and artist: Kuninjku social relations are kin based and intensely social and sometimes it is difficult to establish and maintain boundaries with professional and financial requirements. Ultimately, this tension is encapsulated in the 'for how long' issue: advisers invariably come from another place and another culture and equally invariably, like anthropologists, they leave. This is not always in the best interest of the artist.

The above ambiguities and tensions can, and have, all been resolved, with occasional hiccups, at the regional level. The ambiguities in relations with the state are external and potentially more fraught in part because of dependence and in part because the state, if I can borrow from James Scott, 'thinks like a state'.[6] In the Aboriginal art context, what this means is that the state does not understand the complex processes that I have described that underpin the success of the Kuninjku arts movement. This has never been more true than at the present when the priorities of state policy are at odds with Kuninjku priorities, most particularly to live on their customary lands, a way of life which underpins their artistic expression. But at present the viability of this cultural imperative/aspiration is being questioned and in many cases even attacked by the state, by the allied popular media, and even by some Aboriginal spokespeople with different aspirations. The state's neo-liberal project for Aborigines is focused on economic imperatives in a strictly Western sense, focusing on individualism, mainstream employment, private property and financial independence, terms that have little resonance with Kuninjku imperatives or lived (artistic) reality at either Maningrida or outstations or in between.

And for MAC such policies are threatening because the state response to its success is to continually reduce its small subsidy. Paradoxically, 'thinking like a state' means that rather than the success of artistic practice being recognised and rewarded, it is penalised and jeopardised. Concurrently, the arts adviser must focus more on commercial issues that distract from the core arts support role. BAC too could be under increasing pressure as its core program, the CDEP scheme, is recalibrated to focus on impossible goals of economic independence in situations that will require state subsidy for the foreseeable future.

---

6 Scott, James C., *Seeing Like a State: How Certain Schemes to Improve the Human Condition Have Failed*, Yale University Press, New Haven, 1998.

While uncertainty in fine arts markets cannot be underestimated, there is no doubt in my mind that the greatest source of potential conflict and threat emanates from the state, especially if it tries to blackmail institutions like BAC or MAC to switch their allegiances from what is best for their clients to what is best according to the current policies of mutual obligation and shared responsibility. There is a danger that in the broad Indigenous affairs policy framework, the Kuninjku arts baby, by European standards still in its infancy, will be thrown out with the bath water, something that is rather sad to report to an international audience.

Some reflections on the future

It would be too easy to end this presentation on a negative note, something that I seek to avoid by looking to the future and at the three perspectives that will influence Kuninjku art in reverse to the order in which they were introduced.

The greatest threat to this art movement is posed by the Australian state that has historically provided the requisite patronage to Aboriginal art in the Maningrida region. However, as I hope I have demonstrated, Kuninjku art cannot be differentiated from the every day values and beliefs and actions that constitute being a Kuninjku. The threat from the state will need to be negated, probably through political action, but just how is not clear: suffice to say that at present evidence-based research is not proving sufficient and there is an emerging dominant view that some return to assimilation is needed for Aboriginal advancement. In my view this would be disastrous for Kuninjku.

At the institutional level, Kuninjku artists are fortunate to have robust organisations with histories of success. But even here there is potential vulnerability because experience at Maningrida and elsewhere shows that the institution is only as effective as the next arts adviser and a supportive policy environment.

At the level of the artists there are also challenges. The movement will remain dependent on the maintenance of strong Kuninjku cultural traditions, connections to country, to sacred sites and to the Dreamings. There are emerging indications that the conditions needed to ensure the ongoing vitality and reproduction of this art movement are already in place: not only, as Johnny Mawurndjul says, are today's artists the new generation, but coming up behind them is the next new generation of young artists, many living on country. There is also a very healthy adaptability in the arts movement, evident in the very recent and successful incorporation of women as artists; in the controlled responsiveness of artists to the fine arts market; and in the unquestionable and requisite lifelong commitment to art of the very best.

Given the history of Kuninjku experience with the colonising Australian state and the complex mediating processes required to broker Kuninjku art, it is truly miraculous how quickly this arts movement has developed and flourished. Ultimately, it is this that fills one with optimism about the future. Despite numerous potential hurdles, it is hard to believe that the challenges of the next forty years could possibly match those of the last forty. This is not an argument for complacency, but rather a prognosis that I hope will come to fruition.

Judith Ryan

Rarrk on bark: John Mawurndjul's medium of power and beauty

"In the beginning was the eye, not the word."[1] When we are in the presence of great art, as in viewing the major retrospective *«Rarrk» – John Mawurndjul. Journey Through Time in Northern Australia* and the works collected by Karel Kupka for Basel in 1958 we need to have eyes to see and the mind to sense and conceptualise what the artist is telling us. The ochre marks whether figurative or abstract resist literal translation into words. When engaging with the works in this exhibition, we can look into the beauty of another world in which image and essence reverberate. When we attempt to analyse the aesthetic qualities of the bark medium – that which sets it apart from other forms of painting, Colin McCahon is illuminating:

> Painting to me is like lambs born in spring, rain, wind, sun. Like chopping down trees in the wilderness and living with the slaughtered stumps, of not seeing the beauty I look for, and also seeing the beauty of another world ...[2]

Painting on *Eucalyptus tetrodonta* (Stringybark), a medium unique to Indigenous Australia, has been developed by generations of Aboriginal artists from Arnhem Land into an art form of singular spirituality and aesthetic power. This development is not the fossil tradition of an unchanging society, as is borne out by a study of the stylistic evolution of painting on bark since 1870 when Paul Foelsche made the first substantial collection of barks from western Arnhem Land until the present. It is further exemplified by an analysis of John Mawurndjul's constantly evolving oeuvre which has not occurred in a vacuum and exemplifies the words of Ricoeur: "A tradition is not a sealed package we pass from hand to hand without ever opening, but rather a treasure from which we draw by the handful and which by this very act is replenished."[3]

---

1 Otto Pächt, quoted in Kimball, Roger 'The Rape of the Masters', *The New Criterion* 22 (4), 2003.
2 McCahon, Colin in *Colin McCahon/ A Survey Exhibition,* Auckland City Art Gallery, Auckland, 1972, p. 30.
3 Ricoeur, Paul, *The Conflict of Interpretations,* North-Western University Press, Evanston, 1974, p. 27.

Each piece of Stringybark is organic, textured and retains its indissoluble link with the artist's country. The whole process of painting on bark and the materials of its creation express the artists' reverence for their country, and for ancestral beings and the things that grow and move in the created universe. The artists are the land they paint, as stated by visionary NGV director and my mentor, James Mollison. This deep affinity with country and with *djang* (ancestral beings) is ever present when we behold a bark painting of John Mawurndjul.

The aesthetic uniqueness of a painting on Stringybark lies in its irregularities of surface, shape and design, its matte paint layer and variations of texture. We are dealing with an art work that is raw and not cooked, as seen in examples by Iwaidja, Kunwinjku and Kuninjku artists (see pl. V). The design layer consists of vital, sensitive drawing and living lines that strongly reflect the hand of individual scholar painters, analogous to those of Chinese literati who work with ink in contemplation of the essence of nature absorbed over a lifetime. These qualities flow from the assurance of artists working directly with one line on to a Stringybark surface with the finest of human-hair brushes. Like jazz musicians who improvise, rather than constantly consult the score, there is no need for practice, preparatory sketches, rulers or set squares, digital technology, air brushes or tracing paper. There is no pressure to contrive the subject, the conceptual meaning: that is the artist's birthright, identity, and blood – the indelible cultural law that emanates from each bark painting, as John Mawurndjul states:

> I paint the dreaming stories and places which were instituted by the first ancestors, the sacred sites ... These are the stories my father explained to me and I put them into my head ... I kept thinking and learning about these stories until they were firmly fixed in my mind and they entered my heart. I filled my head to the brim with all of this knowledge and now it is full.[4]

A bark painting calls to mind the words of Colin McCahon, "I hoped to throw people into an involvement with the raw land, and also with raw painting. No mounts, no frames, a bit curly at the edges."[5] It can never be an absolutely flat, framed rectangle contrived for the Western lounge room of the 'Home Beautiful', sitting in a 'tidy town' but is composed of elements of the artist's country. A bark painting – crooked, three-dimensional, vertical, tree-like of shape, ephemeral – has a singular aesthetic which is a product of its materials. The ochre with its gritty particles has a matte and dull, as opposed to a shiny or smooth texture, giving the work an irregularity of surface texture which contributes to a quality of sensibility identified by British art historian Roger Fry. The sheet of fibrous Stringybark also constitutes a raw support, being shaped like an organism, a living thing, rather than a rectangular grid. The bark is sculptural, not flat or parallel with the wall; its edges are crooked, not uniform. It still wants to be a tree, a living thing rather than a geometrical figure, and behaves accordingly. The ochres evade permanence, the bark splits and bends:

---

4 John Mawurndjul, quoted from his statement after winning the prestigious Clemenger Contemporary Art Award, 2003, translated by Murray Garde.

5 McCahon, C., 1972, *op. cit.*

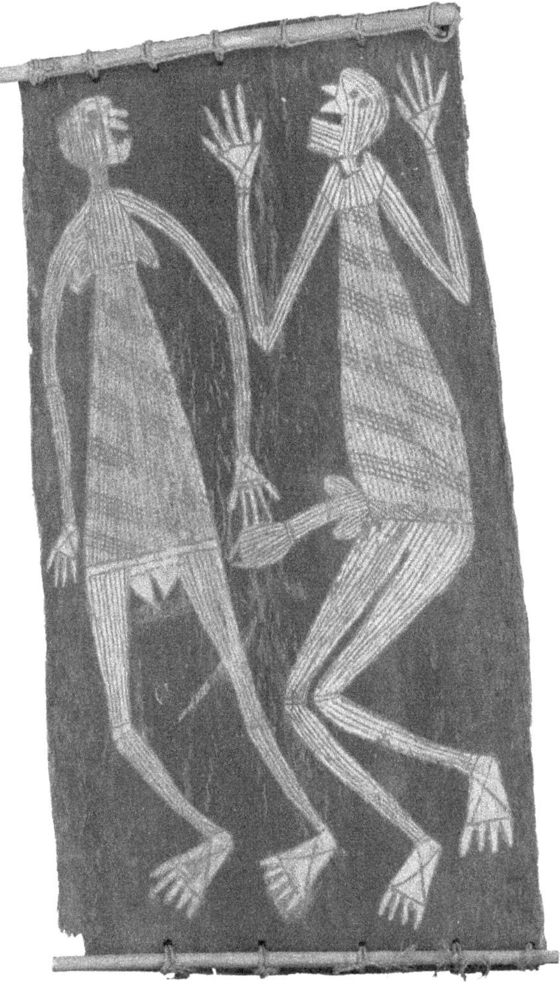

Fig. 11: Paddy Compass Namatbara, *Namarnday spirits*, c. early 1960s, earth pigments on bark, 85.7 x 44.4 cm, National Gallery of Victoria, Melbourne. Gerstl Bequest, 2000. 2000.224. Photo National Gallery of Victoria.

the edges do not confine or circumscribe the image on the organic support, which like life itself is ephemeral.

Dramatic stylistic changes have occurred in bark paintings of western Arnhem Land from the 1870s onwards, when Paul Foelsche, a member of the Northern Territory Police force, made a significant collection of bark paintings from the vicinity of Port Essington, in the Cobourg Peninsula, which together constitute the first works on bark of any great number to enter museum collections. These fluid sketches in white ochre of *mimih* figures with prominent genitalia, fish and other food sources by Garig, Iwaidja and Ilgar male artists are painted in one layer, without subsidiary ornamentation. The uncontrived drawings, collected from bark shelters in exchange for tobacco, prefigure in both style and iconography works of Iwaidja artist, Paddy Compass Namatbara (see fig. 11 and pl. VI)

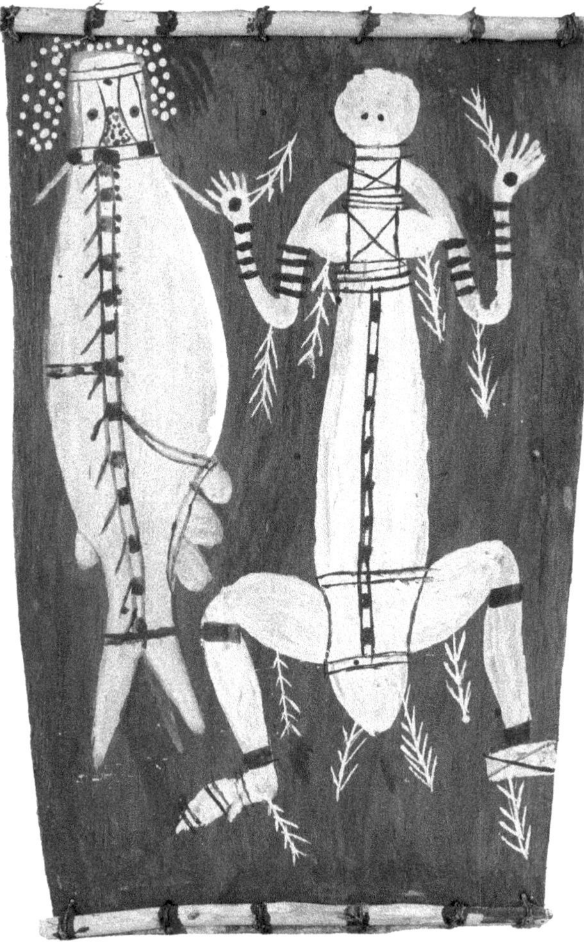

Fig. 12: Jimmy Midjawmidjaw (Kunwinjku c.1897–1985), *Sorcery figure*, 1975, earth pigments on bark, 83.1 x 54.9 cm, National Gallery of Victoria, Melbourne. Purchased through The Art Foundation of Victoria with the assistance of Utah Foundation, Fellow, 1990. O.55-1990. Photo National Gallery of Victoria.

and Kunwinjku artist Jimmy Midjawmidjaw (see fig. 12) collected from Croker Island by Karel Kupka in 1958, where spontaneous drawn elements take centre stage. Here images float against plain grounds as they do on the rock escarpment and artists employ negative space to heighten the power of the icons. These artists worked by drawing in one or two colours only on a plain bark or red-ochre surface, creating spontaneous and brazen sketches, blocked in vigorously. Their pure and dynamic drawings often executed rapidly in one layer are works imbued with the indelible magic of the artist's hand.

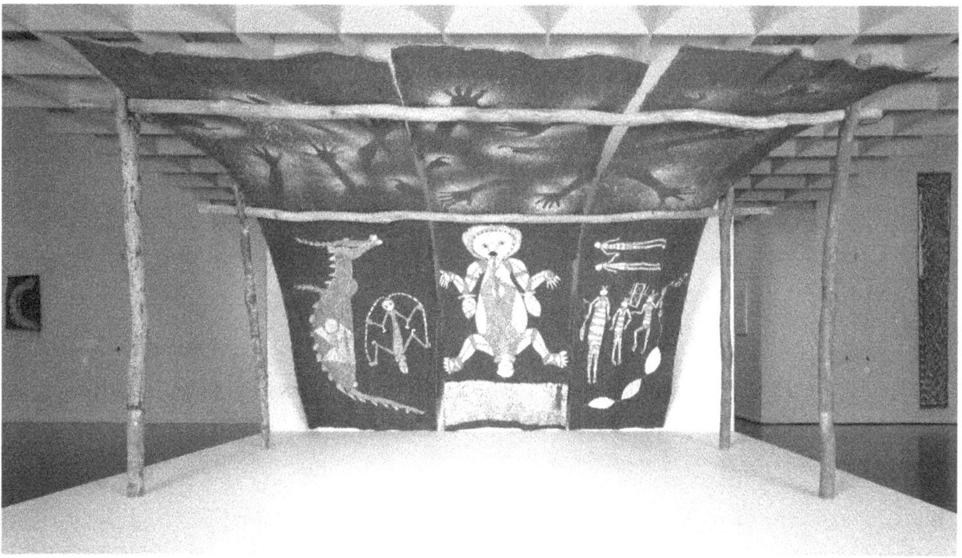

Fig. 13: Bardayal Nadjamerrek and Ngulayngulay Murrumurru (Kunwinjku born 1926 and c.1920–1988), *Bark shelter*, 1987, earth pigments on bark, wood, 153.1 x 300.0 x 265.8 cm (irreg.) (installed), National Gallery of Victoria, Melbourne. Purchased, 1995. 1995.565.a-i. Photo National Gallery of Victoria.

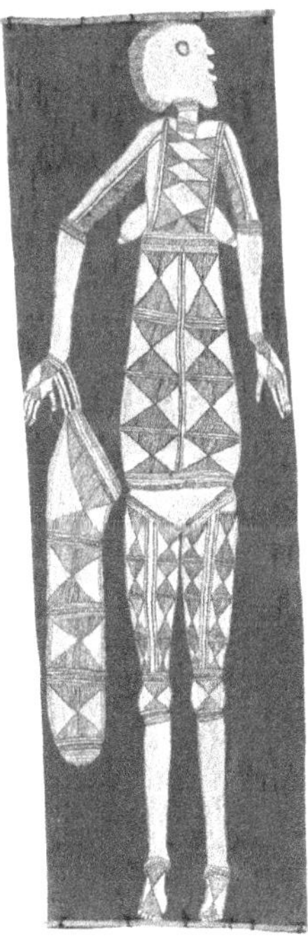

Fig. 14: Lofty Bardayal Nadjamerrek (Kunwinjku born 1926), *Ngalyongddoh djang*, 2005, earth pigments on bark, 157.5 x 47 cm, National Gallery of Victoria, Melbourne. Purchased with funds donated by Supporters and Patrons of Indigenous Art, 2005. 2005.407. © the artist licensed by Aboriginal Artists Agency 2008. Photo National Gallery of Victoria.

Another better-known strategic encounter than that of Foelsche in the 1870s, which eventually led to the evolution of contemporary Aboriginal fine art, occurred in 1912. Baldwin Spencer, 2nd Chief Protector of Aborigines in the Northern Territory, commissioned Gagadju and Kunwinjku artists, from the escarpment country, to paint images similar to those found on rock and bark shelters (see fig. 13), in exchange for sticks of tobacco. With this inspired commission, Spencer set the pattern for later collectors of Aboriginal art, endorsing a form of iconic representation – x-ray images of food sources and spirit beings – which became characteristic of Kunwinjku art from western Arnhem Land for most of the 20th century. The monumental scale of the barks he commissioned is still employed for major works by artists working at art centres throughout Arnhem Land, such as Kunwinjku artist, Lofty Bardayal Nadjamerrek (see fig. 14 and pl. VII).[6]

But the elaborate crosshatched designs produced by Kunwinjku and Kuninjku[7] in secret ritual contexts were not yet incorporated into these secular and public works of art, as Mawurndjul explains: "My father and uncle didn't use crosshatching: that was the old Aboriginal way ... Before Yirawala and Marralwanga, there was no *rarrk* ... it was just like rock art. They took the *rarrk* from the Mardayin ceremony and put it on bark. They started it and we, the new generation, are doing new things. I make my *rarrk* different."[8] Bardayal comments further: "But I can't cut that cross-rarrk, I'm not allowed. That's sacred Mardayin cross-hatching, that's a new kind ... So I keep doing it, that 'old fashioned' kind of rarrk (parallel line work) just like the old people used to do in the rock paintings."[9]

The transfer of sacred body designs, or *miny'tji,* onto sheets of bark and small sculptures was initiated by Yolngu (Aboriginal inhabitants of north-east Arnhem Land) at missions of Milingimbi and Yirrkala from the 1920 and 30s onwards. As in western Arnhem Land, Yolngu art has become increasingly detailed and sophisticated over time and the figurative elements that were prominent until the early 1990s have gradually receded. Crosshatching was relatively sparse in the earliest Yolngu bark paintings of 1920s onwards and consisted more of freely hatched infilling of sections of the composition, with parts of the background left plain. In some cases figurative elements were painted in solid blocks of white pigment against plain red ochre grounds, with little or no crosshatching in marked contrast to the ordered and meticulous patterning of the entire surface characteristic of Yolngu bark

6 Bardayal's *Ngalyongddoh djang*, 2004, is an image close to its original source in rock art, not far removed from those Spencer commissioned.

7 There are two dialects of Kunwinjku language reflecting the regional subdivision of the population into eastern and western communities. The western group or Kunwinjku live mainly around Kunbarlanja (Oenpelli) whereas the eastern group or Kuninjku from the Liverpool/Mann Rivers region have gravitated to outstations serviced mainly through Maningrida. The cultural division between eastern and western Kunwinjku, which is reinforced in ceremonies, is also manifest in art. In this paper, Kuninjku refers to the eastern group, whereas Kunwinjku refers to the western group and to early periods in Kunwinjku art before this distinction came to the fore.

8 John Mawurndjul, from a conversation with Apolline Kohen at Milmilngkan in September 2004, translated by Kay Lindjuwanga, quoted courtesy of Maningrida Arts & Culture.

9 Bardayal Nadjamerrek in an interview with Margie West, November 1994, quoted in West, M., 'Growing up in the Stone Country: The Lives of Bardayal and Kubarkku', in *Rainbow Sugarbag and Moon,* Museum & Art Gallery of the Northern Territory, Darwin, 1995, p. 11.

paintings from 1960 onwards (see fig. 15 and pl. VIII).

By the 1970s and 80s, when Howard Morphy conducted his field research into the work of Narritjin Maymuru, Yolngu artists' facility with the medium was acutely developed, resulting in more elaborated and refined crosshatching. At that time Morphy identified the quality or qualisign of *bir'yun* – brilliance, shining – a visual effect that for the Yolngu signifies a manifestation of *wangarr marr* (ancestral power) as an aesthetic characteristic of Yolngu bark paintings. Since the 1960s, the substantial yellow ochre borders above and beneath the hatched sections gradually diminished in size, until virtually disappearing whilst the proportion of white in the composition increased, serving to accentuate the painting's shimmering visual effects overall – creating a flooding of light (see the progression from 1935–1994 and the origin of Yolngu designs in body paintings, as revealed on *mokuy* sculptures (see figs. 16–17 and pls. IX–X).

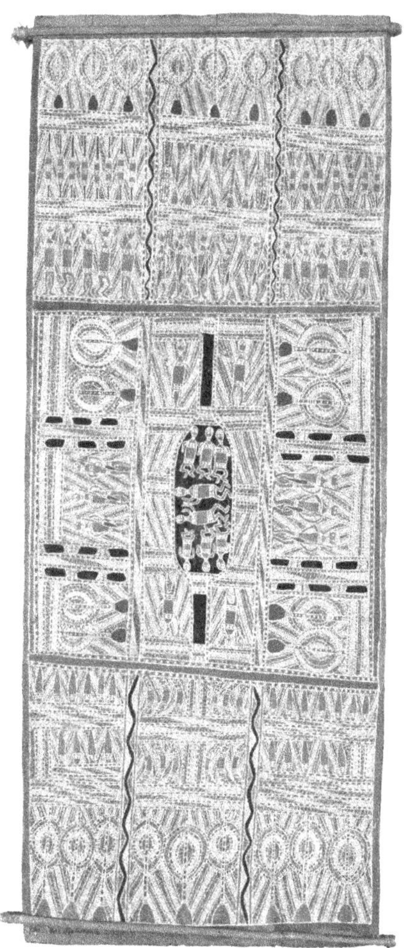

Fig. 15: Mathaman Marika (Rirratjingu c.1916–1970), *Wawilak ceremony*, 1963, earth pigments on bark, 159.1 x 68.2 cm (irreg.), National Gallery of Victoria, Melbourne. Gift of Jim Davidson, 1967. D5 1512. Photo National Gallery of Victoria.

Apart from the Yolngu concept of *bir'yun*, whereby the dense linear striations of hatching create a brilliant shimmer of refinement, the organic materials have a contrary visual impact which is confined to this medium: the ochres in contrast to acrylics are matte rather than shiny. The physical properties also have a metaphorical dimension as suggested by the words of Dhalwangu artist, Gawirrin Gumana from Gangan in north-eastern Arnhem Land, who stated that "I am the people of water, earth and mud."[10] He further explained that his place is "mud, rock, sand, earth, clay and that the painting, like earth and

10 Gawirrin in speech at the opening of *Miny'tji Buku Larrnggay: Bark Paintings from the East* exhibition at the National Gallery of Victoria in March 1995.

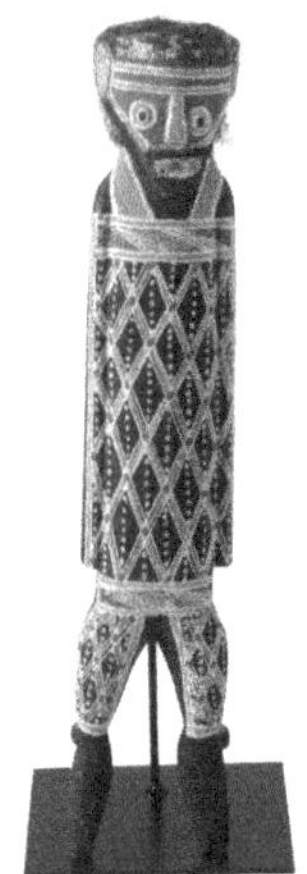

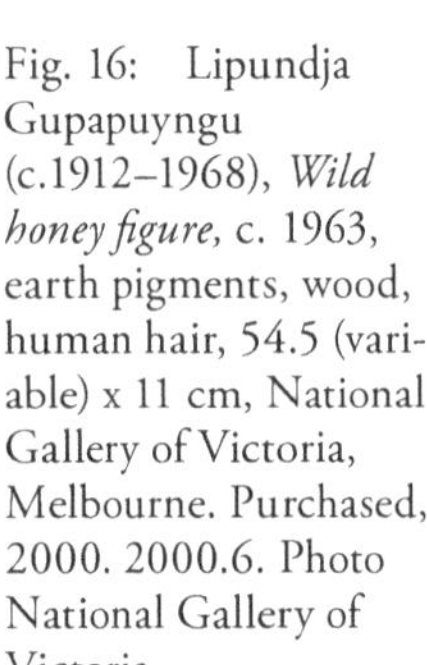

Fig. 16: Lipundja Gupapuyngu (c.1912–1968), *Wild honey figure,* c. 1963, earth pigments, wood, human hair, 54.5 (variable) x 11 cm, National Gallery of Victoria, Melbourne. Purchased, 2000. 2000.6. Photo National Gallery of Victoria.

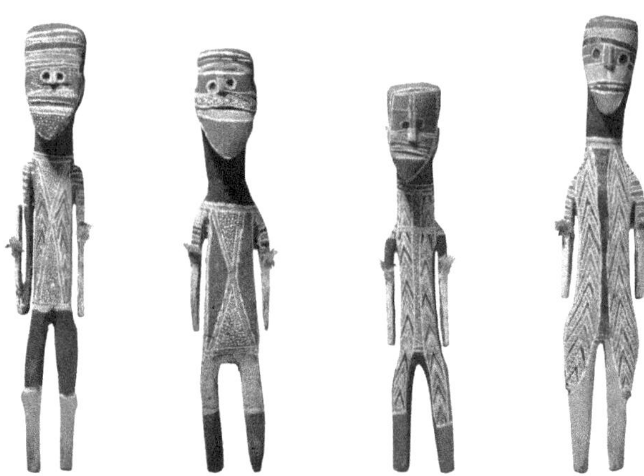

Fig. 17: Luluna Ganalbingu (c.1910–c.1973), *Bumuri/Wayarre – Lunggurrma figures,* 1963, earth pigments, wood, lorikeet feathers, variable dimensions, National Gallery of Victoria, Melbourne. Purchased through The Art Foundation of Victoria with the assistance of Alcoa of Australia Limited, Governor, 1997. 1997.268, 1997.269, 1997.270, 1997.271. Photo National Gallery of Victoria.

rocks, is not for fun but from the heart of the people."[11] Many of the aesthetic properties specific to bark paintings result from the ochres which are from rock, earth, clay, sand, mud – the artist's homeland. This also makes them *ngarra* (sacred) through their use in and association with ceremony, making them dangerous to be touched. The use of ochres on bark is metaphorical of the artist's country. Reticent tone meets subdued tone – tonal colours of earth. Its sound is quiet – from rock, mud, earth, and serious, serious of heart, it tells us something: it is *ngarra.* The bark aesthetic of inwardness is a product of the materials – mud, earth, rock, bark and what they mean to the artist.

Similarly, Mawurndjul uses specific pigments to connote places of spiritual power in his country where ancestors or *djang* went into or became the land. His *Mardayin at Kudjarnngal*, 2003, for example (see fig. 18 and pl. III) refers to a place where Kuninjku people collect *delek* – white pigment, believed to be the metamorphosed excreta of Ngalyod whose sacred power is therefore eternally present at the site. His ancestral potency is manifest in the brilliant shaft of white ochre towards the centre of the bark painting.

---

11 Ibid.

Unlike Kunwinjku artists working on Croker Island during the 1950s and 60s, who made sketches in one layer, the contemporary Kuninjku bark painter builds up a painting in layers, following the procedure established in painting the body for ceremony. A spontaneous underdrawing is now the starting point or cartoon for a composition that is painted in many stages and in exacting detail until the whole surface of the bark is elaborated. First a red ochre, yellow ochre or black ground is applied equivalent to the action of priming a canvas. Upon that ground, Kuninjku artists apply an underlying white silhouette or *rungkalno*, which forms an additional underlayer. On that white silhouette, with a free hand, the artist vigorously paints in the outline or under-drawing in red ochre, setting down the main compositional elements, creating internal lines of division that are filled in with red, white, black and yellow striping at different angles. The under-drawing indicates the artist's hand or drawing style which also informs the subsidiary details. This gives the bark its compositional structure. By painting on larger and larger surfaces, the subdivisions increase in number, the range of ochre tones within the structure stretches, the crosshatching itself optically gyrates and the association with sacred body paintings becomes less literal. Today a Kuninjku painting that is not filled in with crosshatching is considered unfinished because it lacks the full design with all its tonal colours. Yet without the under-drawing, which supplies the bones of the composition, it would lack cohesion, structure.

The greatest bark painting contains a sensibility of design and surface texture, an inner life, a vital rhythm in the drawing that eludes mathematical definition. The art form has a singular aesthetic of spiritual resonance and inwardness. Its power is not the result of technical facility or neatness, but the reverse. It is uncontrived and fluid, rather than calculated, cooked or overworked. Unlike much Western art, prior to Impressionism it is not concerned with mimetic truth, the mirroring of nature, or using the brush as a camera but with elements of life revealed through earth pigments and living lines directly brushed. The land is rendered human and is painted from the inside, with the mind's eye, and is revealed in symbols as if through its bones. The image on the rough and irregular, crooked piece of bark in its vertical, tree-like shape may vary from the minimal to the densely marked, the iconic to the abstract, the plain to the flash, but the organic properties of the bark medium create the dominant aesthetic. The transition from bark to Arches paper or canvas results in a loss of the third dimension, confining the painting to a neat hard-edged rectangle where it lies trapped, unable to extend beyond the frame.

Given the use of terminology such as 'the other' or 'otherness' that has been used during the Symposium, I want to remind you of Gawirrin's dictum "we are all people" and of the words Mawurndjul spoke after he was announced as the winner of the Clemenger Contemporary Art Award:

> Here I am boasting in front of all you European people, but really we are all the same, you and me, Aboriginal and non-Aboriginal, we are the same. But me, I am a painter on bark and exclusively so ... I won't change ... I don't go and paint on paper, paper is not for me, no. I hold on to what my father talked about and taught me and so I keep painting on bark. That's all.

> I'm an Aboriginal man. I'm just like you, like a European person. I have a human heart and I've just won this award ... deep in my heart ... wow, a number one painting.[12]

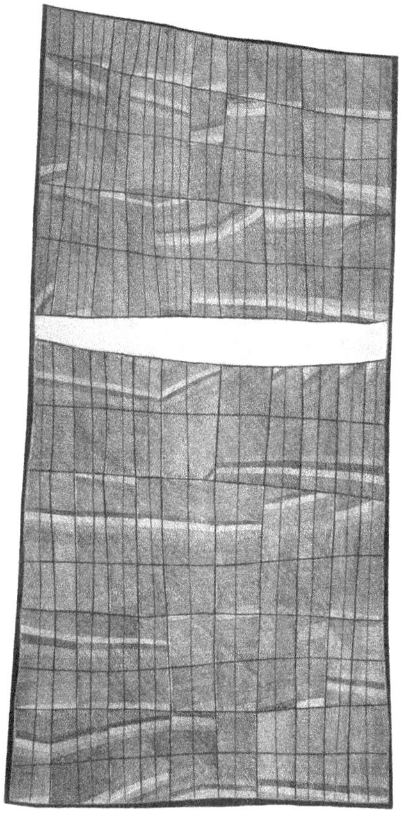

Fig. 18: John Mawurndjul, *Mardayin at Kudjarnngal*, 2003, earth pigments on bark, 152.5 x 76 cm, National Gallery of Victoria, Melbourne. Presented through the NGV Foundation by Judith and Leon Gorr, Ricci Swart, Nellie Castan and Anita Castan, 2003. NGV 2003.663. Photo National Gallery of Victoria. © 2008, ProLitteris, Zürich.

Mawurndjul's statement stresses not that the bark painting medium is the same as other art forms, which I have argued it is not, but that he identifies it as his primary medium. It has associations with what he has been taught and also has singular aesthetic properties. Furthermore he argues that he, like all of us, has a human heart. He has produced a number one painting in a contemporary art award open to all artists: Balanda or Aboriginal. During the artist's walkthrough of his exhibition in Basel we learnt that not only did the Balanda judges regard this as the No 1 painting but so did Mawurndjul. Similarly, when Gawirrin won the 19th Telstra Aboriginal and Torres Strait Islander Art Award he stated: "I did not make this *larrakitj* just for my community, but for the world, so that black and white can walk together."[13]

Mawurndjul's radiant abstractions of sacred geography on Stringybark increasingly demand to be seen in the context of contemporary international art, as evidenced by his winning of the Clemenger Contemporary Art Award in 2003 (see fig. 18–20 and pls. III and XI) and the staging of *«Rarrk» – John Mawurndjul. Journey Through Time in Northern Australia* at the Museum Tinguely, Basel, in 2005. In charting twenty-six years of the artist's practice, the retrospective confirms Mawurndjul's sense of himself as an artist, as revealed in his statement: "I always think of new ways to paint, I always look for something different.

12 John Mawurndjul's speech at the Clemenger Contemporary Art Award, National Gallery of Victoria 17 September 2003, translated by Dr Murray Garde, quoted courtesy of Maningrida Arts & Culture.

13 Gawirrin's speech at the preview of the Telstra Aboriginal & Torres Strait Islander Art Award, Museum & Art Gallery of the Northern Territory, Darwin 2002, as remembered by the author.

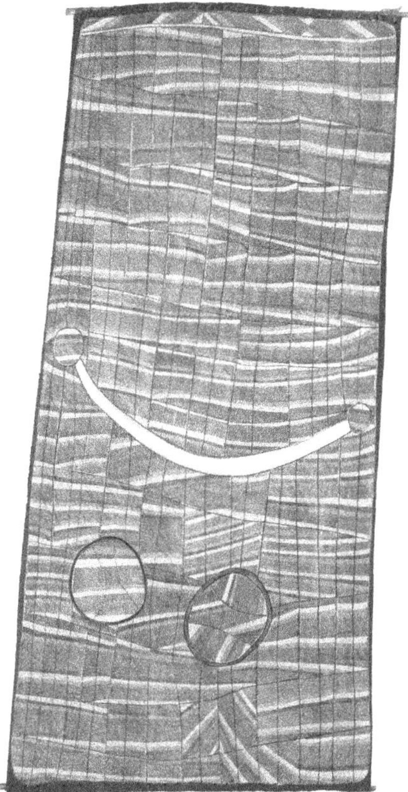

Fig. 19: John Mawurndjul (Kuninjku born 1952), *Mardayin design at Dilebang,* 2003, earth pigments on bark, 212 x 98 cm, National Gallery of Victoria, Melbourne. Presented through the NGV Foundation by Judith and Leon Gorr, Ricci Swart, Nellie Castan and Anita Castan, 2003. 2003.661. Photo National Gallery of Victoria. © 2008, ProLitteris, Zürich.

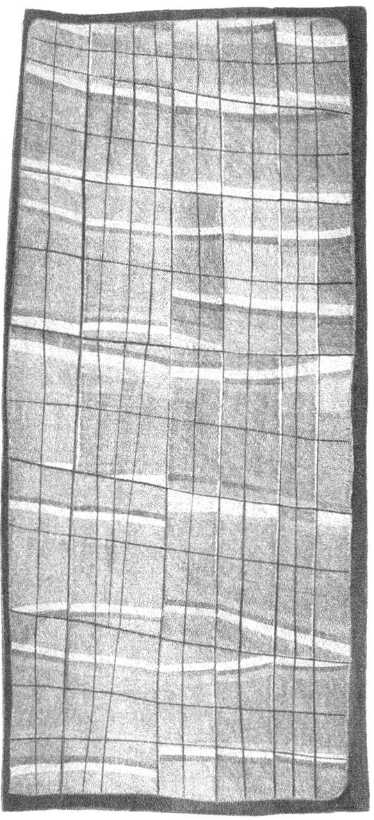

Fig. 20: John Mawurndjul (Kuninjku born 1952), *Mardayin at Dilebang*, 2003, earth pigments on bark, 131.6 x 63 cm, National Gallery of Victoria, Melbourne. Presented through the NGV Foundation by Greg Rosshandler, 2003. 2003.662. Photo National Gallery of Victoria. © 2008, ProLitteris, Zürich.

My work is changing. I have my own style."[14] In Mawurndjul's hands Kuninjku bark painting has been revolutionised into an art of shimmering reflection and shadow, mirroring the incandescent light of ancestral beings whose power is manifest at *djang* (sacred sites). It is no longer concerned to image living things, spirit beings, designs or objects by outlining them against a plain ground and then infilling the form contained by an envelope, but rather to reveal an innermost essence through abstraction: a body of *rarrk* that is stretched over the entire surface. Mawurndjul's *rarrk* on bark is his signature or imprint: it reveals

14 John Mawurndjul from a conversation with Apolline Kohen at Milmilngkan in September 2004, translated by Kay Lindjuwanga, quoted courtesy of Maningrida Arts & Culture.

his identity in the land, his lineage, his understanding of many esoteric layers of ceremony to which only he is privy. But, as with a late Beethoven quartet, the final impression is not about words, the *rarrk* striations in a quartet of natural ochres of varying intensity on an irregular organic surface result in work of "overriding presence and great beauty."[15]

Art exhibitions such as *«Rarrk» – John Mawurndjul. Journey Through Time in Northern Australia* provide opportunities for an exchange of information and knowledge, which constitutes power in Aboriginal society. In this retrospective the restricted and ephemeral designs made for the Mardayin ceremony are transformed into permanent public symbols of the strength of Aboriginal culture in global contexts, and given a Balanda frame of reference.

15 Words of Bill Henson, one of Australia's leading artists and a member of the judging panel for the Clemenger Contemporary Art Award in 2003 who explained that it was the "visual and spiritual dimension of the work" and its "overriding presence and great beauty" that persuaded the judges to make their choice in awarding first prize to John Mawurndjul.

PART 2
Identifying contexts of art

Howard Morphy

Art theory and art discourse across cultures: the Yolngu and Kunwinjku compared

Introduction

I remember having a long conversation with an Australian art-historian as to whether the works in a Canberra exhibition long ago were art works or something else – ethnography or perhaps craft. His argument was that the works were the product of clans, corporate groups, rather than the work of individual creative artists. Moreover they were replicas – copies of designs that had been previously produced by members of the clan, and hence they failed to fulfil some of the main criteria for belonging to the Western category 'art'. Perhaps mistakenly I tried to take up the argument in his terms, by referring to the diversity of styles of painting produced within each clan, pointing out the formal characteristics that differentiated one artist's work from another's, and how it was possible to show the development of formal sequences over time in Yolngu art. "But do they recognise these distinctions?" he enquired. And I had to admit that I did not know, but that more often than not they would deny that there was any difference. To me this was an interesting contradiction to be explored in Yolngu art practice – the contradiction between an ideology of continuity in the production of collective forms and my perception of a rich and innovative practice in which individual artists continually produced new forms. Maybe this innovation was an unrecognised and unconsciously produced epiphenomenon of something else; perhaps change was produced by the process of reproduction in a non-literate tradition, where the record of the past was continually being reproduced through its representations in the present.[1] Changes occurred but they were either unperceived, or not emphasised because they were unimportant. Whatever the explanation, to the art historian the conclusion was obvious: these were not works of art as he understood the category.

The issue is important because it has significance for the ways in which Aboriginal art works are accepted in the Euro-Australian art world, how they are classified, and how

1 Interestingly a point made long ago by Margaret Preston: "This art is never an attempt at rigid realism, they represent but never duplicate; this last feature is hardly possible, as all their designs are from memory or imagination." Preston, M., *Margaret Preston's Monotypes*, Ure Smith Publications, Sydney, 1949, p. 11.

they are catalogued; it has consequences for the recognition of Aboriginal individuals as artists. In this case the issue under debate was whether Aboriginal art should be included in its own right within the Australian National Gallery, or only exhibited in its supposed relationship to European art, side by side with a Fairweather or a Preston. But it could as easily have involved a debate about whether, in cataloguing the works, priority should be given to the clan or group associated with the work or to the individual artist, or whether, in exhibiting works, indigenous categories should be used as the basis for hanging the exhibition.[2] The issues thus range from whether Aboriginal works can be accepted as art, to whether they should be curated as art in a different way from European paintings.

Too often anthropologists and art historians have made assumptions about the differences between Western and non-Western conceptions of 'art' objects. These tend to make the non-Western objects more distant than they prove to be after more rigorous investigation.[3] To understand the significance of the perspectives adopted by an Indigenous as opposed to a European artist, it is necessary first of all to place the objects they produce in their respective cultural contexts and examine those contexts more fully. On the surface, the differences between two cultures' concept of an art object may seem quite profound when measured according to singular criteria. Further investigation into the discourse that surrounds the objects in each case, and an analysis of the ways in which they are conceived and how they are used, may problematise the degree of difference.[4] Differences that at first sight appear categorical may be revealed as differences of emphasis or different interpretations of similar phenomena. In some cases Indigenous Australian artists may appear to prioritise group affiliation over individual agency in attributing works of art to people, but this should not in itself be a criterion for defining works as ethnography

---

2 The National Gallery had been founded in Canberra about the same time as the Aboriginal Arts Board. The founding document was the Lindsay report prepared for the Menzies' government in 1966 and it was finally established by an act of parliament in 1976, under Gough Whitlam's prime-ministership. The Gallery initially had three main foci, World art, Australian art and Primitive art. It would have seemed that Aboriginal art should be able to find a place in one of the latter two categories. However, as a matter of policy, in order not to overlap with other institutional collections, the Gallery had decided at that time not to build up a major holding of Aboriginal art. Whatever the merits of this decision there was a danger that it could be interpreted to imply that Aboriginal art was not primitive fine art and that it was not a significant part of the history of Australian art. For a while it appeared that Aboriginal art was almost the only art in the world excluded from the Australian National Gallery.

3 For a relevant discussion see Van Damme, Wilfried, 'Do non-Western Cultures have Words for Art? An Epistemological Prolegomenon to the Comparative Studies of Philosophies of Art', in Benitez, E. (ed.), *Proceedings of the Pacific Rim Conference in Transcultural Aesthetics*, Sydney University, Sydney, 1997.

4 Margaret Preston was the first Australian artist to emphasise the synergies between Aboriginal art and art in the European tradition (though she did so in the context of rejecting the European tradition as the primary heritage for a truly Australian art). She wrote "Australia has the good fortune to have a native race who paint and draw as they have always done, and with few exceptions look on their [art as] essential[ly] more than merely covering a rock, bark or ground with forms. They feel dimly something they contact in it that they like ourselves vaguely understand." (Preston, M., 1949, *op. cit.*, p. 10–1) While on this occasion somewhat obscurely and inelegantly expressed, we see here Preston's approach to Aboriginal art as more than a model for an Australian modernism, alluding to a sharing of the conception of what art is across cultures.

rather than art. If that were the case then many works of European art should be removed from the gallery since they were produced at a time when individual authorship was a less significant factor in Western art practice and when the concept of art differed markedly from that associated, for example, with modernism.[5]

The works that art historians deal with come from very different cultural contexts and times. It must be presumed that the intention of art history is to understand those works initially in the contexts of their time and of the societies that produced them before relating them to historical processes that link objects across place and time. It is possible to imagine an art history that is only concerned with the history of art objects once they have been included as part of the Western canon or accepted as objects worthy of inclusion in a fine art gallery or museum. However this would be a particularly narrow form of art history and would be of little help in explaining many aspects of the form of the objects being studied. Of course those aspects could be part of a separate study – 'research into the cultural background of objects subsequently included in the Western category of art object'. However, to create this as a separate area of study would be to accept a priori that the place of objects in the original context of their production is irrelevant to understanding how they work as art objects. It would also have the effect of separating the producing cultures from world art history.

Certainly, in many cases, the ways in which non-European art works have been incorporated in the history of European art or influenced the practice of European artists had nothing to do with their original significance in the societies of origin. However it does not follow that in their original context they were not art objects – that is to say objects that can be accommodated by a cross-cultural and cross-temporal definition of art. It is necessary to investigate the sense in which these are the same kind of objects as European art works and the senses in which they differ. Otherwise they have the status of found or adopted objects, or, to use Maquet's apposite phrase, they are art by metamorphosis – objects that are appreciated by the Western art world without reference to their significance to members of the producing cultures.[6] They are part of the history of Western art as objects incorporated within Western art but not part of the history of the objects as art in their own historical and cultural context, a point well made by Susan Vogel.[7]

It is true that some of the objects from other cultures that have metamorphosed into works of art in a European context – that have become examples of primitive fine art – may not be art in the context of the societies that produced them. In that case they are not in

5 Mariët Westermann makes a related point when she writes that "the distinction between 'primitive' art and pre-modern Western art objects in museum collections is not fundamental: no art objects made before the nineteenth century were made to be put into a public museum of the modern kind. Western and non-Western art objects received their differential status in the course of museum history." See Westermann, M., *Anthropologies of Art*, Sterling and Francine Clark Art Institute Williamstown, Mass., 2005, p. xiv.

6 Maquet, Jaques, *The Aesthetic Experience: An Anthropologist Looks at the Visual Arts*, Yale University Press, New Haven, 1986.

7 See Vogel, S., 'Introduction', in Vogel, S. (ed.), *ART/artefact: African Art in Anthropology Collections*, Centre for African Art and Prestel Verlag, New York, 1988. The *locus classicus* of this approach is Robert Goldwater's *Primitivism in Modern Art*, Random House, New York, 1967.

themselves the subject of art history in their indigenous context but of the history of the kinds of objects that they are – a Zande net, for example, may or may not be an art object to the Zande even if it can be considered from certain Western perspectives to be a work of art (see also this volume Förster pp. 183–196 and fig. 35, p. 188).[8] They may of course be relevant to the study of Zande art in that they are part of its contextual background, just as the history of technology is relevant to studying Western art forms and the forms of baskets and spears are relevant to studying Yolngu art – art is a subset of the material culture produced by a society. A similar case might be made for a Dogon ladder or a Tikopean headrest.[9] And that critical approach needs to be applied to all objects encompassed in the Western category of fine art whether they are Mediaeval, Classical, African, Egyptian or Indigenous Australian. There can only be an African or Australian Aboriginal art history if it is acknowledged that some objects are in some sense art objects in the context of the societies that produced them; and that requires the development of a definition or conception of art that is capable of encompassing the diversity of cultures concerned. But the study of non-Western arts will inevitably encompass a different set of objects from those that have been adopted into the Western category of fine art. It will not be restricted to works that have been placed historically in the art gallery as opposed to the ethnographic museum.

Many of the issues that are raised by the curation and marketing of Aboriginal art – the artist as author, the institutional context of art, the role of individual creativity, the autonomy of form – are central to Western art history and art theory, and in turn influence the production of art. The relationship between art theory, art history, and art practice can be seen to be problematic. Art historians not only write about art but also have had a role in defining art and in 'discovering' art. There is of course no simple deterministic relationship between art history and art practice. Art history is not a unitary hegemonic discourse but consists of many discourses, which change over time, and which may reflect quite different views of what art is and artists are. The struggle over the recognition of Aboriginal art

8 Mariët Westermann (2005, *op. cit.*, p. xii) interestingly includes in her definition of art objects "objects made or found by humans, that have the potential to be put into circulation and demand by their visual aspect, not exclusively but at least in part, an aesthetic response to work efficaciously within their culture." While the immediate reference in Western art history may be to Duchamp's found objects as an exemplar of objects that are perceived to have aesthetic properties but were not made as art objects, in many respects primitive art objects fit well into the category of found object, their culture in this context being that of the finder not the maker. It is the disregard of the intention of the maker that makes them into found objects.

9 The reference here is to the debate generated by Susan Vogel's exhibiting of a Zande hunting net in her influential ART/Artefact exhibition (see Vogel, S., *op. cit.*, 1988). I do not intend here to give any opinion as to whether the works concerned are art works in the context of Zande, Dogon or Tikopean cultures. It is also relevant to point out in this context that the works may be appreciated aesthetically in both cultures (the Indigenous and the European) without them being art objects in both. A Tikopean headrest maybe an aesthetically pleasing headrest to a Tikopean and primarily appreciated as an art work by a collector of Pacific art (see Firth, Raymond, 'Tikopean Art and Society', in Forge, A. (ed.), *Primitive Art and Society*, Oxford University Press, Oxford, 1973, pp. 25–48).

has been in part an argument in Western art history and theory about what 'art' is – with questions of ontology.[10]

If Western art history has an important role in Western art practice is there an equivalent area of Aboriginal discourse about their art objects that could play an important role in the exhibition and interpretation of Aboriginal art, even if that art is apparently being exhibited in a non-Aboriginal context? Are Aboriginal views about art and creativity best framed as they conventionally have been, as ethnography, cultural background or cultural context? If this premise is accepted, there is a danger that Aboriginal views will be used to position the works in Western art discourse rather than contributing to the discourse itself. Aboriginal art will be included in a particular way, with essentialised assumptions about its difference from European art – such as "Aboriginal artists are members of groups, the rights in Aboriginal paintings are corporately held, the designs have been handed on unchanged from the Dreamtime." Unless due attention is paid to Indigenous ideas about what kinds of things art works are – ideas which in turn influence artistic practice – all of the changes that occur in Aboriginal art will be perceived as having occurred in the European frame, or as a consequence of the movement of that art into Western contexts, rather than as being influenced by Aboriginal discourses about art. Aboriginal art history will only begin when the works are incorporated within the Western frame. Before that moment all of their life is viewed as an ethnographic artefact, and the existence of an Aboriginal/Indigenous frame for discussing art is denied. In the Yolngu case I argue that, at least from the perspective of the artists themselves, both frames exist, and there is a relatively smooth transition between them.[11]

The ways in which Aboriginal people conceptualise art objects, the ways in which they talk about them and the kind of knowledge that they bring to bear on them has to be the basis of art history's writing about Aboriginal art. And if that information is included within the framework of Aboriginal art history or the approach of Western art historians to Aboriginal art then not only will it open up different possibilities of discourse about the relationships between Aboriginal art and the art of other cultures, including the diverse history of cultures encompassed within the rubric of European art, but it will also reveal synergies that are otherwise obscured by the kind of art history that is overly constrained by a narrow conception of what art is.

My reason for pursuing the idea of an art history/art theory that is synergistic with the Aboriginal discourse about art is partly a pragmatic one. If in European art there is a relationship between art, art criticism and art theory, when introducing Aboriginal art

---

10 As Fred Myers writes "Aboriginal objects are not simply or necessarily excluded by Western art critical categories; they may in fact contribute to or challenge these discourses for the interpretation of cultural activity in productive ways." Myers, F. R., *Pintupi Country, Pintupi Self: Sentiment, Place, and Politics among Western Desert Aborigines*, University of California Press, Berkeley, 1991, p. 30.

11 Fred Myers shows a similar situation in the case of the Pintubi artists where the process of movement of the art from one frame to another is seen to be the product of a dialogic process in which the Pintubi are fully involved rather than a transfer of authority from one group of producers (the painters) to another (the designators). Myers, F. R., *Painting Culture: The Making of Aboriginal High Art*, Duke University Press, Durham N. C., 2002.

to Western contexts one should be attuned to the possibility that an analogous body of discourse exists within Aboriginal society. Aboriginal art discourse is likely to produce a different understanding of the relationships in space and time among art objects than conventional European art history, but both would nonetheless would be encompassed within the rubric of a more cross-cultural art history.

While I do not intend to argue that art history is a cross-cultural concept, there is a greater overlap between Indigenous and Western discourse over art than most theorists allow for. If there is a relationship between the two then it may be possible to see Aboriginal art discourses entering into a dialogue with European art discourses and each being influenced by the other. If there is compatibility between the discourses then this may be shown to have influenced the ways in which Aboriginal art has developed in a post-colonial context. In simple terms it changes the premise of the debate from 'this [piece of information] does not fit, or challenges, the Western definition of art' to 'under an Aboriginal theory of art, or from the perspective of Aboriginal art history, the following is the case'. It presents the European art world with information that it has to come to terms with and accommodate to rather than simply presenting information that can be used to adjust the space the art occupies in European classifications of objects.

Towards a cross-culturally sensitive art history

My aim in this contribution is not so much to produce a cross-cultural definition of art history, as to develop an art history that is sensitive to the different ontologies of art cross-culturally – to different ways in which people talk about and conceive of art works. I am not convinced that art history as an academic discipline is the kind of thing that is likely to prove to be a cross-cultural category, but I believe that, as an institution of Western society, it should become more cross-culturally sensitive; it is important that it articulates with relevant fields of discourse in the societies whose art history is being researched. Art history is in part concerned with dates and sequences, and with relationships between objects in time and space, but it concerns equally the ideas associated with those objects that in part produce them and influence the trajectories of form over time.[12] Art history is part of Western art discourse and as such it has inevitably at times influenced art practice. It is thus all the more important that when it approaches the history of non-Western art it is cognisant of local art discourse and of the ontology of art in the particular case, to ensure that it is not unduly influenced in analysing other art histories in terms of Western presuppositions about the kind of thing art is. In order to understand the trajectory of Indigenous Australian art it is important to consider the kind of thing art is to the producing societies and how that influences the relationships that Indigenous Australians see between art works and the conclusions that they draw from those relationships. By making Indigenous art discourse

12 See Kubler, George, *The Shape of Time: Remarks on the History of Things*, Yale University Press, New Haven, 1962.

part of the data of art history and critically examining the ontological concepts and their relationship to practice we should become aware of conceptual similarities and differences between different traditions. And in the case of different art traditions that occupy the same temporal space we should be able to better understand how they articulate with one another – in the case of Aboriginal art how Indigenous artists embrace contemporary Australian art worlds.

There have recently been signs of a rapprochement between anthropology and art history.[13] The time when anthropologists of art neglected form and avoided concepts such as 'style' and when art historians paid too little attention to social context is over, certainly in individual cases, if not right across the disciplines. The exchange has been an unequal one. The neglect of art by anthropologists has continued to be a negative factor, limiting the opportunities for an art-historical anthropology to emerge. In Africa in particular it has been the art historians who have shown the way, adding the methods of anthropology in the form of long-term fieldwork to the objectives of art history in elucidating the distribution and significance of forms in art.[14] But in Australia and the Pacific the situation has if anything been reversed, with anthropologists playing a leading role in analysing the forms of art and analysing historical relations.[15]

However, this paper is less concerned with the respective contributions of the two disciplines to some joint enterprise, than with the meta-theoretical questions that the combining of art history with anthropology provokes. In other areas of anthropology these kinds of questions have proved productive at the interstices between disciplines: examples are questions about the nature of belief and rationality at the boundaries with philosophy, and about the nature of culture at the boundary with biology, as are the productive debates over ideology, memory and the imagination, among others, at the boundaries with history. Anthropology challenges the assumptions of other disciplines through cross-cultural analysis and is in turn challenged to account for phenomena in other than cultural terms by the general propositions of other disciplines.

In the past anthropology and art history have often been opposed as disciplines. I would argue that they should be complementary. Art history was and is still often cast as a discipline that approaches art in relation to one set of questions and anthropology

---

13 See Volkenandt, Claus, 'Perceptible Boundaries: Aesthetic Experience and Cross-Cultural Understanding with a View to John Mawurndjul', in Kaufmann C. and Museum Tinguely (eds.) *«Rarrk» – John Mawurndjul. Journey Through Time in Norhern Australia*, Schwabe AG, Basel, 2005; and the essays in Westermann, M., 2005, *op. cit.*

14 See for example Boone, Sylvia. A., *The Radiance from the Waters*, Yale University Publications in the History of Art, New Haven, 1986; McNaughton, Patrick, *The Mande Blacksmiths: Knowledge, Power and Art in West Africa*, University of Indiana Press, Bloomington, 1988; and Blier, Suzanne P., *The Anatomy of Architecture*, Cambridge University Press, Cambridge, 1987.

15 See for example Kaeppler, Adrienne, *Artificial Curiosities: Being and Exposition of Native Manufactures on the Three Pacific Voyages of Captain Cook*, Bishop Museum Press, Honolulu, 1978; Thomas, Nicholas, *Entangled Objects: Exchange, Material Culture, and Colonialism in the Pacific*, Harvard University Press, Cambridge Mass., 1991; Thomas, N., *Oceanic Art*, Thames and Hudson, London, 1995; and Morphy, H., *Aboriginal Art*, Phaidon, London, 1998.

as a discipline that approaches art according to another set of questions. There then can occur a series of slippages. The two sets of questions become associated with different kinds of society – art history is an approach to objects as they are exhibited in an art gallery and anthropology or ethnography is associated with works as they are exhibited in an ethnographic museum. In as much as art history maintains these distinctions it is in fact part of the process of reproducing the categorical distinctions between Western fine art and ethnographic artefact since it has defined its field according to the Western category of fine art in its institutional mode – art history deals with art as it is encompassed by Western art worlds.[16] The opposition that is thus created makes art history blind to evidence that contradicts the categorical distinctions between Western and non-Western art.[17] A similar critique can be made from the perspective of anthropology, which in the past tended to over-emphasise the differences between human societies, to create over-defined boundaries around them and to essentialise the Western other.

This association of anthropology with one set of questions and art history with another has set them apart when they attempt to approach the same subject matter. And I will argue that it fundamentally miscast the relationship between the two from the outset. Anthropology is primarily concerned with issues of cross-cultural translation – recording and analysing the world from the perspective of a particular society and reproducing the data in such a way that it can be understood, in its own terms, by members of another. The product of anthropological analysis, the data that anthropologists provide can be subject to the analysis from other disciplinary frameworks – in this case by art historians. Such cross-disciplinary interaction of course requires that the anthropologist records the kind of data that is relevant to the other discipline – data that relates to categories of thought in the case of philosophy, relevant Indigenous knowledge in the case of science, data that is relevant to explaining the form of the object in the case of art history.[18] The net result of a more collaborative approach should be to reveal, where they exist, perspectives from the societies in question that are relevant to the subject of the particular discipline.

It is not so much that Aboriginal Australia will be revealed to have its own discipline of art history, rather that the processes and discourses on which art history is centred will be found to exist more generally cross-culturally. In as much as art history is concerned with

16 See Danto, Arthur, 'The Artworld', *Journal of Philosophy*, 61, 1964, pp. 571–84. The distinguished art historian Hans Belting makes this explicit when he writes "As an art historian, I deal with Western art, where the famous old debate on art and ethnology — that is the debate whether ethnographic art needs an art museum or ethnographic documentation does not apply." Belting, H., 'Towards an Anthropology of the Image', in Westermann, M. (ed.), 2005, *op. cit.*, (pp. 41–58), p. 42.

17 Interestingly Jonathon Hay argues that something synergistic with Western art history has long been a part of the history and practice of Chinese art: "The long history of self-fashioning by Chinese artists led to a further particularity of Chinese painting: the importance from the fourteenth century on of art historical self-inscription, that is, the artist's practice of locating self in history using the painting's own history as a frame of reference." Hay, J., 'The Functions of Chinese Paintings: Towards a Unified Theory', in Westermann, M. (ed.), 2005, op. cit., (pp. 111–123), p. 116.

18 Mariët Westermann (2005, *op. cit.*, p. xvii ff.) provides an excellent discussion on the potential relationship between the two disciplines.

the explanation of form then it must be concerned with theories of art in the societies it encompasses, since their theories about art and the ontology of art, including the theories of the art practitioners, are likely to be relevant to explaining the relationship between objects in space and time. In the case of Western art the relationship between art history, art theory and art practice is subtle since there is an overlap between the discourses – art history and art theory are both concerned with the relationships between objects in time and space and both at different times have influenced Western art practice.

Most academic disciplines are grounded in the common sense knowledge and experience of members of the societies in which they develop. Art history is no exception and has evolved as part of Western systems of knowledge with an inevitable bias towards the common sense understanding of the societies concerned. If we include overlapping fields of discourse and knowledge systems from other cultures then we will enter that process of adjusting the parameters of the discipline to enable it to take part in cross-cultural dialogue in a way that responds to the common sense knowledge and understandings of other cultures.[19] It is possible that the art historians may find themselves extending the boundaries too far. Disciplines are always concerned with maintaining their distinctive boundaries. In the case of art history I would argue that in looking at Aboriginal society from the perspective of providing data relevant to art historians we do find synergies between Aboriginal discourses about art and art history, just as we will find synergies between Aboriginal knowledge about the seasonal cycle in Arnhem Land and Western science. And reflecting back on Western art history it becomes apparent that within its own domain it has always been encompassing of other cultures and times, stretching out for information to make sense of the historical record, from the moment that Winckelmann engaged with the trajectories and contexts of Classical antiquity.[20]

I will begin by outlining the field of discourse in Aboriginal society that overlaps with topics approached by Western art historians when analysing Aboriginal art. The discourse centres on the formal relations between paintings in space and time and the attribution of works to individuals or groups, but will stray into the more specific areas of individual creativity and artistic influence. While these may not be considered as core components of the definition of some contemporary schools of art history they do reflect a concept of art history associated with museum collections and art galleries. I would be interested to know if they were indeed entirely absent from any Western version of art history.

19 Van Damme (1997, *op. cit.*, p. 104) develops a closely related argument when he writes in relation to the development of cross-cultural concepts for art discourse "... it may be possible to commence by local concepts that have a semantic overlap with the Western term. By displaying the overlap – or tertium comparationis or 'family resemblance' – such concepts may then serve as a bridge to another culture's conceptual system and world view. Further exploration of what might be called the artistic and aesthetic vocabulary within a given cultural context may then lead to the delineation of a relevant field of opinion and reflection in this culture's own terms. Moreover in non-Western cultures there may in fact exist concepts that designate such fields – fields that could then be likened to those that in the Western tradition are signified by the terms 'philosophy of art' or 'aesthetics'."

20 Irwin, David, (ed.), *Winckelmann: Writings on Art*, Phaidon. London, 1972.

Aboriginal perspectives on their art

The history of Western art has to contend with different conceptions, even ontologies, of art in space and time; an Aboriginal art history has to accommodate differences between different Aboriginal societies. One benefit of adopting the perspective of Indigenous artists is that it gives us a means to identify regional differences in the way art objects are categorised and related to one another. This may in turn influence the trajectory of art practice and the way in which works are influenced by exposure to other arts. For example some Aboriginal theories about what art is may encourage greater degrees of conservatism to others. My main focus will be on the art of the Yolngu people from the Yirrkala region of north east Arnhem Land. Towards the end I will make a comparison with neighbouring Kunwinjku to the west.

On the surface Yolngu theory about art represents an archetypal Aboriginal view of the world in which the forms of the present are viewed as a reproduction of the forms of the past.[21] Paintings are creations of the *wangarr* Ancestral beings and have been handed on in unchanged form to the present. The designs arose as a result of ancestral action and have been handed on to the social groups who occupied the land. They are the title deeds to the land and rights in them are both shared and closely guarded. Sets of people hold equal rights in the designs and these can only be reproduced with permission from senior members of the owning clan. The contexts of production are closely specified and the form of the designs were set in the past. The only skill involved is that required to replicate the design. The designs are a form of knowledge rather than the product of individual creativity. Over the years I have recorded many statements in which people denied their creativity and emphasised the unchanging nature of their art.

The topic I set off to study in 1974 was art and social change; in particular I wanted to look at the impact of commercialisation on the form of Yolngu bark paintings. Before going into the field I took photographs of most of the bark paintings from the region that were then housed in Australian collections. These photographs included the paintings collected by Donald Thomson in the 1930s and 1940s in eastern Arnhem Land close to the beginning of intensive European contact in the region. On almost my first night in the field I was slowly leafing through my sets of photographs in front of a well-known Yolngu artist, Narritjin Maymuru. After I had shown him several photographs from different points in time he appeared to see right through my project. "I know what you are trying to do, you are trying to show us that our art has changed. We will show you that it hasn't."

On another occasion Narritjin emphasised the dangers of innovation in art when he said: "We can't follow a new way – the new way I cannot do that – I go backwards in order to work. I cannot do any new things because otherwise I might be making up a story –

21 My book *Ancestral Connections* provides a detailed ethnography of Yolngu art and the reader will find many of the points touched on here developed further in the chapters of that book; see Morphy, H., *Ancestral Connections: Art and an Aboriginal System of Knowledge*, University of Chicago Press, Chicago, 1991.

my own thoughts you see – and people over there, wise people, would look at my work and say, Ah! that's only been made up by him."

This view reflects a socio-cosmic perspective on Yolngu art, which is directly reflected in aspects of its form.[22] Paintings are comprised of components which make them readily identifiable as the property of particular clans associated with particular places. This relationship between Ancestral beings, social group and land is often said to be immutable – set in the ancestral past and reproduced in the present. Paintings can be ordered into a number of different sets according to different criteria, the two most common being the set associated with an ancestral track and the set associated with a clan or segment of a clan. There is a multidimensionality to Yolngu paintings which reflects the articulation between the actions of the *wangarr* Ancestral beings and the formation of social groups who inherited the earth from them. Paintings form a complex framework of interlocking genealogies to which people can relate on the basis of kinship and mythical connection.

The Yolngu 'art historian' is able to place paintings on the basis of their form in relation to this grid of connectivity and to state precisely who the painting belongs to, what his or her own relationship to it is, which country it belongs to and which ancestral track. This grid is integral to the interpretation of Yolngu art and one of the consequences is that the body of interpreters, of 'wise people', is regionally quite extensive. Thus most adult Yolngu artists will be able to identify the clan to which a particular painting belongs and provide some account of their mythological significance and topographic reference.[23] There is great interest in paintings, both in ensuring that rights in paintings are not being abused or usurped and in monitoring the extent to which people have maintained knowledge over their paintings. The political significance of this knowledge is considerable since the reality is that land changes hands over time as groups expand and contract, and art is part of the currency of change. In a system where a group's knowledge may be held for them by others until the new generation of leaders are sufficiently mature and authoritative to hold it themselves, groups are kept under control by denying them access to knowledge of the religious law associated with their land. Knowledge of religious law is useful in making a claim of inheritance and succession.[24] The political significance of art means that people will look with interest, though often with the appearance of disinterest, at the paintings

22 The Pintubi perspective well expressed by Fred Myers (2002, *op. cit.*, p. 24) is entirely consistent with Narritjin's reflections on his art "Pintubi representations of their own cultural production are deeply entwined with ideas and practices of personhood, cosmology and the ontological articulation of subjects and objects (Munn [...]). With images said to come from the Dreaming, the emphasis is not on what the painter has done (his or her creativity) but on what is represented, what value that has itself, and the painter's relationship to it. This ontology exotic and intriguing for many Westerners, is not remote from real life and politics."

23 Morphy, H., 'Myth Totemism and the Creation of Clans', *Oceania* 60, 1990, pp. 312–328.

24 Keen, Ian, *Knowledge and Secrecy in an Aboriginal Religion*, Clarendon Press, Oxford, 1994, chapter 5. Keen shows how one Yolngu group attempted to maintain control over another by not releasing knowledge which its members possessed of the other groups songs, denying that group access to its ancestral inheritance.

that are being produced by other clans either in ritual contexts or for sale at the craft store.[25]

The importance of the ancestral grid and of maintaining the formal distinctions upon which it is based have strongly influenced Yolngu interpretation, attribution, and perhaps perception of earlier paintings. It has been common practice for Euro-Australian museum curators to do what I did and take photographs of art in museums back to the field or invite Yolngu into the store rooms to interpret or re-document paintings. While this is certainly a valid exercise it may not produce the anticipated result, if the goal is to identify the individual artist. Although there will often be consistency in the attribution of paintings to particular clans there is likely to be considerable variation as to artist. Indeed the first point of identity is that of the clan, and individual artists' names will only be given if asked for or if that is known in advance to be what is wanted. Usually if the age of the painting is known it will be attributed to one of the senior right-holders of the time who is known to have painted. There is likely to be a bias towards those who have painted more frequently or whose reputation in the European art world is established, or who are close relatives of the person asked. If the age of the painting is unknown, then it is likely to be attributed to a senior right holder who is still alive or who belongs to the recent past. In cases where I had independent information about the artist's hand from contemporary documentation, people would frequently attribute the painting to a different artist. People would even 'misattribute' paintings recently produced by themselves to other artists, especially when the date of production was uncertain.

Even in the case of works that were produced for me during my fieldwork the identity of the individual artist was seldom a topic of interest. The emphasis was on what paintings shared in common rather than what differentiated them. In teaching younger people to paint senior people would emphasise a process of copying, of reproducing things in the correct way, even at the level of detail of precise sequences of crosshatching. Personal style was very rarely referred to and then usually with reference to the figurative component of the paintings and not the choice of colours, detail of the infill, overall structure or form of clan designs. People would sometimes comment on the ant-like nature of Mithinari's human figures and on rare occasions one younger artist claimed to paint animals more 'realistically' than his father. But these cases were exceptions. And yet within a clan different artists produced the same painting in what to me were strikingly different ways. Indeed the same artist often produced very different versions of the same painting each time he produced it. The differences were such that I could readily distinguish between the 'styles' of different individual members of the same clan.

In the 1970s the Manggalili clan was a clan of painters. The four senior artists were Narritjin Maymuru, his sons Mändjilnga and Banapana and his brother Bokarra. It is possible to differentiate between their paintings on a number of different bases.

---

25 On one memorable occasion I was asked by a Yolngu friend if I had seen a design of a particular type at an outstation craft store. It was not certain whether the group concerned retained knowledge of a particular clan design since they generally reproduced designs associated with one segment of their territory only. I feigned ignorance!

There were differences in the frequency of certain figurative representations in different artists versions of the 'same painting'. Narritjin produced far more human figures than any of the others and created detailed action sequences that are absent in the others' paintings. Indeed Narritjin developed, with two other senior artists, a genre of paintings in which myths were represented in episodic form in different segments of the same painting (see fig. 21 and pl. XII). Moreover there were considerable differences in the ways in which figurative representation of particular species were produced by different artists. Narritjin's figures were more rectangular and less flowing than those of his sons. However what I want to focus on here is differences in the technique and colour of infill and the overall effect achieved.

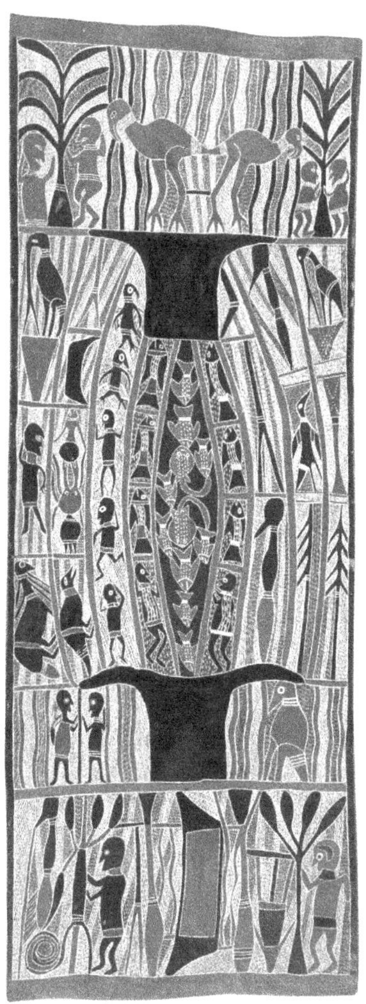

Fig. 21: Narritjin Maymuru, *Djet story*, 1967, earth pigments on bark, ca 150 x 50 cm, National Museum of Australia, Canberra. Copyright the artist's family. Reproduced courtesy Buku-Larrnggay Mulka Art Centre. Photo National Museum of Australia.

Manggalili paintings display forms of infill that are rare in other Yirrkala barks: for example, dotted and dashed infill which occur frequently in Manggalili art are rare in the art of other clans. Narritjin was a past master at this elaborated infill. His art is characterised by the great variety of crosshatching employed in the same painting and by the fact that different parts of the same painting were often elaborated in different ways. The overall colour balance of Narritjin's paintings was very even, with no one colour predominating, and he tended to combine red, black, yellow and white more frequently in the same segment than other artists (see pl. XIII). In contrast Bokarra's paintings were more uniform with a particular pattern of infill predominating in each painting (see pl. XIV). His paintings seemed darker than those of other Manggalili artists, with a greater emphasis on red yellow and black and much less use of white. Banapana's paintings in contrast appear light and bright. He used a predominance of white with yellow and red but very little black (see pl. XV). The composition of his paintings meant that very often large areas of bark were covered with fine long crosshatched lines. Sometimes he used contrasting shades of ochre to create graded contours of colour that had an almost tapestry-like effect.

His older brother Mändjilnga, whose paintings shared many of the same characteristics, used less varied infill but characteristically included more black in his crosshatching.

It would be wrong to over emphasise these individual differences. On many occasions members of the family worked together and in the case of Banapana's paintings the quality of the crosshatching was often a joint product with his wife Maymirrirr. Small barks in particular were the product of two or three people working together, with one marking out the basic design while others worked on the crosshatching. Nonetheless in most cases, adopting a Western art-historical approach, I was readily able to differentiate between paintings produced by the four leading artists, and using micro-stylistic analysis was able to identify the hand of most paintings produced while I was at Yirrkala. Yet I was not taught by Yolngu to do this and from my observation of Narritjin teaching his sons he stressed the importance of copying the order in which he infilled the paintings and emphasised that this was to ensure continuity with the past. It would be wrong to conclude however that he did not recognise the individuality of different people's techniques of infilling and that he did not himself delight in creating particular aesthetic effects. Maymirrirr would sometimes comment on the beautiful effect of the crosshatched lines achieved in one of her and Banapana's paintings. However in public discourse – in official Yolngu art history – such things were not emphasised.

To an extent I think that the issue is a matter of emphasis and of misinterpreting the objectives of a pedagogical technique. As well as being ancestrally set designs, Yolngu paintings are semantically dense and aesthetically powerful objects. The form of the paintings, their meaning and their aesthetic force all derive from the same source, that is the ancestral dimension. What Yolngu see and value as ancestral forms are also forms that they know are reproduced by themselves and they believe that in reproducing them they are moving closer to the ancestral dimension. The ancestral form, however, is an idea that only exists through its replication and the criterion by which the success of a replication is judged is that it is a recognisable token of its type: for example that it has the correct clan designs, that it is an effective encoder of ancestral meanings and that it conveys the power of the ancestral past through the aesthetic effect of its infill.

Infill on Yolngu paintings is thus simultaneously an ancestral form, a semantic component of the painting and the producer of an aesthetic effect. It is possible to produce infill that contradicts the ancestral specifications or fails to evoke the required response, through the use of a wrong colour, or the wrong sign, or an appearance of dullness. However there are considerable areas of flexibility and freedom in the reproduction of ancestral forms and indeed some of those freedoms may make the painting a more successful token of its type than others. Crosshatching is precisely one of those areas in which the individual aesthetic success of the painting is in harmony with ancestral design. The more effective the crosshatching in producing a sensation of shimmering brilliance then the more it evokes a sense of ancestral power.[26]

26 See Morphy, H., 'From Dull to Brilliant: The Aesthetics of Spiritual Power among the Yolngu', in Coote, J. and A. Shelton (eds.), *Anthropology, Art and Aesthetics*, The Clarendon Press, Oxford, 1992, pp. 181–208.

As a pedagogical technique the emphasis on faithfulness to pre-existing form nonetheless allows for the development of variations in individual styles of crosshatching over time. Although people are instructed to produce paintings by following their elders, what they are learning is a technique and the boundaries of what is permissible in a particular painting. Individual variation is thus de-emphasised in the learning process and in the interpretation of paintings but within certain constraints it is allowed and even desirable.

Variation and innovation

On the basis of the information given so far it can be argued as the art historian stated at the exhibition opening, that the emphasis in Yolngu art history is not on the individual autographic aspects of paintings but on the clan sets to which they belong. At the same time it would be wrong to deduce that artistic practice is conservative or that new forms are not consciously being produced. Infill is one example where variation continually occurs. But change also occurs in other aspects of paintings, although there are also remarkable continuities. Most dramatically, certain types of paintings are claimed as inventions by the artists themselves.

There are some categories of Yolngu paintings that are produced specifically for the outside market and which have no set form. In 1973 these were referred to as 'anyhow paintings' as that was what the missionary Chaseling was supposed to have asked people to paint on the first barks that were produced for sale after the founding of the mission station of Yirrkala in 1935. Today they are more commonly referred to as 'hunting stories', or *wakinngu*,[27] making reference to their secular nature. Paintings of this type are today usually produced on small barks, though larger representations of secular scenes can be produced for sale or on commission to illustrate a particular theme.[28]

Another category of invented paintings is associated with a set of public myths that take the form of moral tales for amusing children or instructing them in appropriate behaviour. The Bamabama story, directed against incest, is one and the Djet̲ story, directed against greed and selfishness, is another. Although these stories are associated with songs and particular locations, they are semi-sacred forms and are not represented in the clan's sacra. Nonetheless they are more closely associated with some clans than with others. Djet̲ and Bamabama, for example, are both associated with a limited set of Yirritja moiety clans. According to Narritjin the form of the Djet̲ paintings was invented by him in the 1950s (see fig. 21 above and pl. XII). Djet̲ is a boy who lost his temper when reproached for his

27 *akinngu* refers to the world in its mundane rather than sacred (*madayin*) state and in this context means that the paintings are not part of the sacred property of any clan.

28 My discussion here primarily is centred on bark paintings, which together with soft wood carvings were the main forms of art produced until the 1990s. Subsequently Buku Larrnggay Mulka, the art centre at Yirrkala has established a very successful print workshop. Print making is largely but not exclusively practiced by women artists. Yolngu print making is very diverse and includes images from the sacred art of the clans, but also includes pictorial representations of traditional and contemporary life.

greed. Jumping up and down in a state of hysteria he gradually began to take on the form of a sea eagle, and ended up flying into the sky. The painting is innovative in a number of ways, the most obvious being that it shows the process of transformation from human to animal form.

In this case Narritjin would emphasise with some degree of pride that he had invented the painting. It was a new category of painting, not a *wakinngu* painting, but not a *likanpuy* painting, a sacred clan painting either. Indeed in the case of sacred clan paintings there is a degree of freedom as to how the overall painting is composed and which figurative elements are included as long as it is recognisable as an example of its type. In inventing the new Djet paintings he was involved almost in the reverse process creating a painting that became an example of a type. The Djet paintings include generalised geometric designs that are associated with the Yirritja moiety and often include the outline of a *yingapungapu* sand sculpture, the sculpture for burying fish remains. And the figurative content of the paintings are limited to the creatures mentioned in the myth and the features of the place where the events took place. And the painting once invented became subjected to precisely the same constraints on production and ownership as ancestrally-created forms. The right to produce the painting has spread to a number of closely related Yirritja moiety clans and people can only produce it if they are linked to those clans by descent or marriage.[29]

It is quite possible that we are seeing here a process by which new paintings have always been added to the inventory of ancestral forms, since all memory of their connection with an individual innovator would rapidly have been lost. Indeed Yolngu paintings show considerable evidence of having been influenced by other traditions well before European colonisation and quite independent of any craft industry. Paintings of both moieties include elements from the time when Macassan traders visited the shores of Arnhem Land to trade and gather trepang. Such paintings include representations of Macassan boats, cloth designs, knives, axes; and sacred objects include Macassan anchors, gin bottles, ships masts and many other things. The issue of Macassan influence on Yolngu art has hardly been explored but the evidence exists in song, dance and ritual form of close observation by Yolngu of the Macassan way of life and material culture, which was almost certainly part of a two way process of cultural exchange. Interestingly however Yolngu are as likely to deny that their art has been influenced by the Macassans as to acknowledge their influence. Myth incorporates the Macassans as part of Yolngu ancestral history and distances them from actual historical events.

A sand sculpture in the form of a Macassan proa is sometimes constructed in Yolngu mortuary rituals, which may be evidence of influence from Eastern Indonesian beliefs about the ship of the dead. The sculpture is certainly modelled on the form of Macassan boats. On one occasion sitting beside such a sculpture watching the dancers, I asked Jack

29 In this case the situation is complicated by the fact that the Djet story is primarily associated with a Madarrpa clan place, not a Manggalili one. The fact that Narritjin invented a painting that is primarily associated with another clan's country is unusual and identifies the story as one that exists at a very public level. In fact in the iconography of the Djet paintings Narritjin uses elements that are shared across a number of Yirritja moiety clans.

Marrkarakara, a Marakulu man, if Yolngu had learnt to do such a sand sculpture from the Macassans. "Oh no," he replied. The sand sculpture came from the Dreaming: it represented Dreaming (*wangarr*) Macassans. Yolngu had produced the sculpture long before the actual Macassans began their trading visits. I must have looked a little sceptical for he continued: "Maybe we did not know that the boat was made of wood and the sails were made of cloth until the Macassans came but we always had the design."[30]

A historical view of Yolngu art suggests that it has changed over time in response to influences from outside and to changing internal circumstances. Yolngu are undoubtedly interested in the forms of art; other people's as well as their own.[31] Having developed designs based on Macassan elements, more recently they have invented paintings and sculptures to satisfy new markets for their art. They pay great attention to aspects of the form of paintings and train their children in the skills of its production. Paintings are objects of great value in Yolngu society and following European colonisation Yolngu have actively used art in their attempts to persuade Europeans of the value of their culture. They have seen an analogy between their paintings and carvings and what Europeans produce and classify as art, and have pushed for their paintings to be treated with the same respect and housed in the same institutions as European art.

The form of their art has been influenced by exposure to other arts and to the stimulus of the art market. They have accommodated to European requirements, that artists should be known by name and works should be associated with individual artists. At the same time they have held to a view of the relationships among paintings, which radically contradicts the way in which they are classified, documented and ordered by the European art market. And this internally-focused view has influenced the formal trajectory of Yolngu art much more than the new frames in which it has been included. This Yolngu view of the nature of their art and the principles underlying their art practice can also contradict or challenge the very categories into which Europeans try to place it.

Yolngu 'art history', like all art histories is in part an ideology intimately connected to value creation processes. The ideology underlying Yolngu conceptualisation of agency in paintings prioritises group rights over individual authorship, emphasises the relationship between paintings, social groups and Ancestral beings, and emphasises continuity over change even to the point of denying change. It is moreover a public ideology, an official ideology of the relationship between art and society operating in the context of a system of restricted knowledge in which contradictions disappear with time.[32] At a public level

30 Such ontological positions are of course common to many theories about art and integral to many belief systems. Elizabeth Coleman has pointed out to me the interesting parallels between Yolngu and neoplatonic conceptions of art in which, for example, musical forms pre-exist their composition. They are, in effect, discovered rather than invented or created.

31 Narritjin Maymuru showed great interest in art other than his own and provided Anthony Forge and me with a rich perspective on Abelam art when Anthony asked him and his son Banapana to comment on some of his collection of Abelam paintings, see Morphy, H., 'Style and Meaning: Abelam Art through Yolngu Eyes', *RES: Anthropology and Aesthetics* 47, 2005, pp. 209–230.

32 Over time groups die out and the sacra, including the clan designs, are passed on to the groups that take over the land, and in the process of adjustment new sets of sacra are created and new connections between

of knowledge paintings belong to clans as part of their ancestral inheritance. Thus, when paintings are produced in ritual or made for sale the identity of the artist is much less important than the fact that the production is the instantiation of the use-rights of the group to which the paintings belong. It also means that collaboration between artists in producing a work is considered unremarkable.

Yolngu conceptions of the kind of objects works of art are has had consequences both on the form of art, on the ways in which art is used and the ways in which it has changed over time in response to new circumstances. The continued importance of clan designs in Yolngu art is the most obvious consequence. Clan designs show great continuity and the specifications of difference between one group and the next remain relatively constant over time.[33] However almost as significant is the effect of clanship and kin relations on the themes an artist can use and the direction of influence and inspiration. The introduction of new themes such as Djet̲, Bamabama, and Morning Star occur in the context of clanship. The paintings are innovated within the context of pre-existing clan forms using appropriate clan designs and centring on the myths and practices associated with particular places. Once invented the paintings spread along kinship lines as rights to produce them are extended to mother's and mother's mother's groups, or to groups sharing the same mythology. By no means all changes occur under such constraints – new forms of figurative representations, techniques of crosshatching, and general themes such as mortuary rituals cross-cut clanship even though the particular form they take will be influenced by more localised mythology.

Although a particular view of the historical relations between paintings thus acts as a constraint on production, it would be wrong to conclude that Yolngu art is conservative, or that people do not consciously innovate new forms, or that the skill of individual artists goes unrecognised. From the perspective of European art history these conclusions would seem to be the logical correlates of Yolngu ideology and are precisely the assumptions that were made about Aboriginal art and indeed much non-European art until quite recently. However, as I have shown innovation occurs routinely in Yolngu art and although it is not stressed ideologically as it has been in the recent history of European art it is neither unconscious nor undesired. It is however subject to constraints which shift the emphasis away from the creative individual towards art as the property of groups and integral to the rights that extend throughout networks of kin.

---

places are created. However once the adjustments have been made the new situation is the one that is said to derive from ancestral precedent. The control over knowledge means that disputes over rights in sacra seldom emerge in public even though they may continue to act powerfully beneath the surface. For a more detailed discussion see Morphy, H., 1990, *op. cit.*

33 Clearly clan designs do change over time as they adjust to the demographic exigencies and political process. While in the present Yolngu can control the significance of variations in the form of clan designs by allocating them to particular groups and subgroups in the context of agreement among the participants, the further back in time one goes the harder it becomes to make such determinations. Hence while people can readily identify the moiety of most of the earliest paintings collected by anthropologists they can not always identify the painting at the level of clan. Thus with painted objects collected by Lloyd Warner from Milingimbi in the 1920s present day Yolngu, some eighty years later on, are reluctant to make attributions about the ownership of the designs on some objects.

Yolngu artists produce art in a number of different frames: in Yolngu ceremonial contexts, for the wider Australian art market and for special commissions for museums or international exhibitions. As Yolngu have become increasingly engaged with the art market and increasingly involved in discourse with non-Yolngu artists, some have become more conscious of the innovative processes in their artistic practice and have entered into the kind of dialogue with audiences and potential purchasers of their art that the Western contemporary art market encourages and values. Recent paintings by artists from Yilpara, a remote settlement on Blue Mud Bay, have consciously emphasised components of Yolngu art that resonate with the art market. In a separate study I have introduced the concept of *buwuyak* which I have referred to elsewhere as 'emergent figuration'.[34] The artists employing this technique include Narritjin's daughter Galuma Maymuru and his sister's daughter's child (*gutharra*) Djambawa Marawili.

Yolngu art has always had a strong geometric component, which in the case of sacred forms—both paintings and objects —has often dominated the surface. The paintings made today for sale by the Blue Mud Bay (Djalkiripuyngu) artists emphasise this geometric component. Djambawa, for example, covers much of the surface of the bark canvas with swirling and intersecting patterns of interconnected diamonds. The geometric motifs enable the technique of crosshatching to be applied to maximum effect, creating a dynamic surface of shimmering brilliance which in turn is characteristic of the most sacred Yolngu art.

Buwuyak is a technique or a number of techniques that enable figurative representations to emerge from the background pattern of the clan designs, to become visible when the viewer focuses on a particular area of a painting or sees a motif in a particular way. *Buwuyak* harmonises well with the emphasis in European terms on abstraction.[35] The immanent figurative component allows the representational meaning to be simultaneously both present and absent. The paintings produced can be seen to respond to an external audience whose aesthetic has been influenced by the modernist abstraction of the Western tradition. But though the synergy is exploited, the process of abstraction comes from the relatively autonomous history of Yolngu art. The techniques – the emphasis on the geometric and the play on visibility – come out of the history of Yolngu art and the ability to employ them comes out of the training the artists have received from the previous generation. The effects are ones that Yolngu have always exploited to give insight into the ancestral dimension of existence – to convey the idea of *wangarr*. The particular geometric patterns that are used depend on the clan of the artist and the rights in paintings that he or she has inherited, and the figures that emerge on the surface refer to the mythology of their clan. But today artists will point out that they are doing something that is new, that is the result in part of their own creativity.[36]

---

34 See for example Morphy, H., 2005, *op cit*.

35 The term *buwayak* was first applied to this feature of Yolngu paintings by the artist Wanyubi Marika in discussion with Will Stubbs who runs Buku Larrnggay Mulka art centre. However it is also recorded in Donald Thomson's fieldnotes to describe the masking of body paintings produced in restricted contexts by smearing the surface before they are revealed to people in public places.

36 Keller, C. and Coleman, E. B., 'What is Authentic Aboriginal Art Now? The Creation of Tradition', *International Yearbook of Aesthetics* 10, 2006, pp. 55–80.

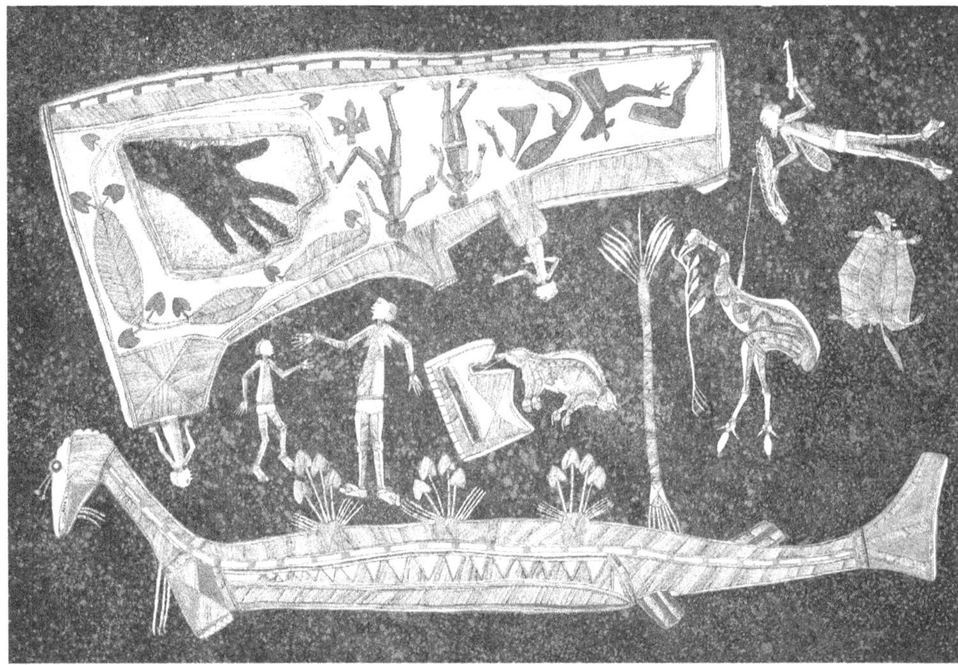

Fig. 22: Lofty Bardayal Nadjamerrek, *The female rainbow serpent beneath waterlilies in her sacred billabong,* 1991, earth pigments on Arches paper, 100 x 150 cm. The Kluge Ruhe Collection of Australian Aboriginal Art, Virginia, 1991.001.006. © the artist licensed by Aboriginal Artists Agency 2008.

Comparing the Kunwinjku

So far I have been looking at an Aboriginal art history from the perspective of the Yolngu people of eastern Arnhem Land (see map, fig. 48, p. 242). It would be quite wrong however to assume that an identical perspective holds sway across Australia. While some features are widely shared, such as the belief in the ancestral origin of certain categories of design, and the dispersed nature of rights in objects and designs, there is also great regional variation. If we compare the Kunwinjku with the Yolngu case very different factors can be seen to influence the perceived relationship between paintings. Among the Kunwinjku variations in infill style have a central role in differentiating between schools of artists, and clanship as such plays a much reduced role in structuring the system, though affiliation through clans remains significant.

Luke Taylor[37] has identified a number of contemporary schools of Kunwinjku art, identifiable in terms of their style and content. These schools centre on co-residential

37 Taylor, L., *Seeing the Inside: Bark Painting in Western Arnhem Land*, The Clarendon Press, Oxford, 1996, see especially chapter 4.

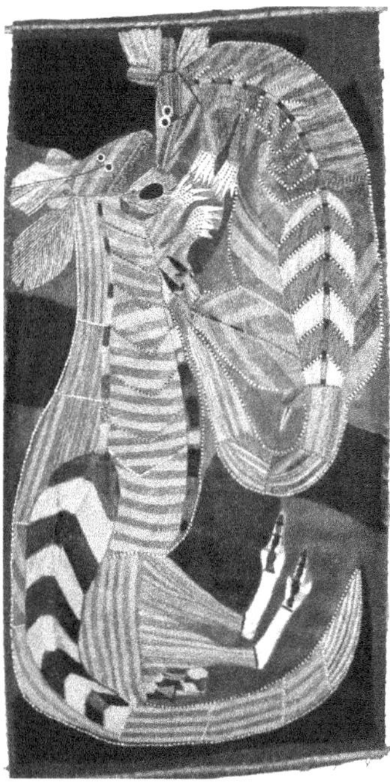

Fig. 23: Peter Marralwanga, *Two rock wallabies,* 1979, earth pigments on bark, 149 x 76 cm. Museums and Art Galleries of the Northern Territory. © the artist's family.

groups of kin oriented towards a particular region. One he labels the Kunwinjku/Dangbon School reflecting the fact that the artists all belong to Kunwinjku clans with strong links to Dangbon country to the south. The artists are all associated with Oenpelli and with the outstation of Manmoyi which is near their own clan lands. The artists in this group included Dick Nguleingulei, Nabarrayal, Kalarriya [Kalareya] and Nabarlambarl. The most striking feature of their work is the use of a crosshatching technique employing very thin parallel lines which on close inspection show a characteristic quiver (see fig. 22 and pl. XVI). It is almost as if they had been painted with a shaky hand and yet the consistency and fine definition of each line contradicts such an interpretation. The artists tend to use a single colour in contrast to many other contemporary painters and claim that the style is the one that used to characterise the rock art. They often work together and share each other's pigments adding to the similarity across their paintings. Although the line work is in some respects austere the outlines of the animal species produces forms of extraordinary elegance and naturalism, the high point of realism in Kunwinjku art.

The second school is that of the Mumeka/Marrkolidjban artists and centred around Marralwanga (see fig. 23 and pl. XVII). Other recent members of the school include his son

Namirrkki [Namirrki], and his sons-in-law Njiminjuma [Njimirnjima] and Mawurndjul. The artists belong to the Kardbam and Kuralk clans and have reciprocal responsibilities for each others' paintings. Marralwanga in turn derived much of his inspiration from Yirawala. Yirawala was originally part of a school of artists based on Croker Island in the 1950s and early 1960s, and many of his early paintings are difficult to distinguish from those of Namatbara, Nangunyari-Namiridali and Midjawmidjaw. The paintings associated with the Croker Island School consist of extraordinarily elaborated and contoured multi-limbed figurative representations of spirit beings as well as finely drawn x-ray figures. Later Yirawala developed a style of complex infill within geometric segments loosely based on the form of Mardayin or Marrayin designs. This resulted in the tapestry style of painting in which the figures occupy a large expanse of the bark canvas allowing room for the development of intricate crosshatched segments that are so characteristic of the later Mumeka/Marrkolidjban works.

Yirawala's paintings tended to be brighter than those of other members of the school, with strong yellow and red ochred lines being emphasised by the white background that he often used. The later Mumeka/Marrkolidjban paintings are dense and deep in their effect and tend to draw the viewer into the bark whereas Yirawala's figures tend to leap out of the surface of the painting. The aesthetic impact of the paintings owes much to the dense, heavy but often flowing nature of the forms lightened by the tapestry of fine crosshatched lines that seem to lightly scratch the surface of the painting. The crosshatching is a constant source of variation, with each segment often differing from the rest and setting off at obverse angles to the others. Yet at the same time the effect can be one of extraordinary unity with the segments blending together as a whole.

Although the composition of the membership of two schools considered so far reflects both place and kinship networks it is partly based on historical contingency and individual relations. Marralwanga deliberately set out to differentiate his paintings from those of Yirawala his original teacher. One of Marralwanga's sons, Birriya Birriya, belongs in turn to a different school from the Mumeka/Marrkolidjban school of his father. The Marrkolidjban II school followed the style of Mandaynjku who, until his death in 1981, was joint leader of the outstation with Marralwanga, and Milaybuma. The paintings of this third school are again based on figurative paintings with infilled geometric segments. However in contrast to Marralwanga these artists produce broad bands of crosshatching in regular colour sequences which create an overall pattern of striped bands across the surface of the figures (see pl. XVIII). Birriya Birriya explicitly says that he follows Milaybuma's style "otherwise people will say I copy my father;" thus presenting an interesting reversal of what is officially considered desirable in north east Arnhem Land.

A final school of Kunwinjku artists is based to the west of the region at Oenpelli centred on members of the Nganjmira family. The paintings show some similarities with the Marrkolidjban artists in that the figures are infilled with alternating bands of single coloured cross-hatching. However whereas Marrkolidjban artists paint mainly single figures, the Nganjmira family, and in particular the youngest member of the family, Robin Nganjmira, paint complex compositions in which *mimih* hunters are combined with animal representations in energetic scenes.

Although the Kunwinjku schools identified by Taylor reflect relations of kinship and clanship, and although the ancestral beings depicted have associations with particular sites, it would be wrong to argue that Kunwinjku bark paintings are clan-based either in their form or content. Certain themes of the art can be produced by people belonging to clans from across the region. Paintings of food animals such as kangaroo and barramundi, for example, are produced by most Kunwinjku artists, and major regional themes such as that of the Rainbow Serpent or Lumaluma can be treated by senior artists of any of the schools.

Taylor shows that it is possible to discern patterns in the adoption of particular themes that reflect both clan membership and authority within the regional ceremonial system.[38] Young artists tend to produce themes associated with their father's clan first, then those connected to their mother or mother's mother, before moving further afield. As people gain in age and status so too the range of themes represented in their art increases. This pattern results in part because rights to paint certain general themes are easily acquired, however it is also the case that learning to paint is a long process in which the skill is gained only slowly. Initial attempts to produce figurative forms are often clumsy and the young artist needs detailed instruction. Younger artists produce a limited number of new forms because of the need to perfect the ones they have already acquired. Not only do they have to learn the way to represent the features that distinguish particular animals or fish but they must learn the elaborate techniques of cross hatching that enhance the aesthetic effect of the painting. Some aspects of form, such as the divisions made in the body of a kangaroo, may be part of ancestral law. Others such as the production of particular effects through cross-hatching is much more subject to individual variation. In both cases however the technique must be learnt.

An old man of ritual authority such as Yirawala or Marralwanga produced paintings on themes drawn from right across the Kunwinjku region. In such cases however there are limits to the set of paintings that an individual produces, but these seem to be set by personal life history and rights gained during the artist's lifetime rather than by clan affiliation. Marralwanga produced paintings of places that he became associated with through residence, kinship, and ceremonial participation, and because such factors vary from individual to individual the set of paintings he produced differed from the sets produced by other artists of his generation.

Contrasts on common ground

Kunwinjku and Yolngu artists thus have very different emphases in their understanding of the relationships between paintings, and between the artist and the work of art. On the surface Kunwinjku art history shares features in common with certain perspectives in European art history. Kunwinjku artists, for example, relate their paintings to earlier

38 Ibid., pp. 95ff.

generations of paintings preserved on rock surfaces. In some cases they are able to identify the individual hand of artists of the previous generation and to assist archaeologists to identify their corpora of works.[39] They emphasise change and originality both within their own corpus and as a basis for differentiating the works produced at one place and time from those of another. They recognise differences between paintings on the basis of micro-stylistic features and adopt different styles from their relatives as a means of asserting personal identity. These characteristics of Kunwinjku art practice and art history may in part explain why an artist such as Yirawala was able to produce a huge corpus, characterised both by its individualistic nature and by its stylistic variability over time.[40]

Just as it is necessary, however, not to over-emphasise the extent to which Yolngu were constrained by their ideology of conformity to clanship, so it is also necessary to emphasise that Kunwinjku artists also operate under some constraints. Although the structure of rights in paintings may appear less clear-cut than in eastern Arnhem Land, it is nonetheless publicly acknowledged and enforced. People who produce paintings without authority or who stray into areas of ambiguity are likely to be reproached, fined, or punished in some other way for their transgression. Kunwinjku artists are incorporated within a master-apprentice structure that simultaneously receives the sanction of ancestral law and is integrated with the system of ritual authority.

The contrast between Kunwinjku art history and Yolngu art history cautions us against positing any essentialised, uniform, and continent-wide Aboriginal art history. Of the two, the Kunwinjku variant could sit more happily within a framework of an art history that emphasises individuality, innovation, formalism and cross-cutting ties of identity. It could be argued that Kunwinjku art practice would have to change less than that of the Yolngu in order to be incorporated in the individualistic autographic framework of a particular kind of Western art world. It might be postulated that the ready acceptance of Yirawala's work had something to do with its pre-adaptation to the requirements of a particular kind of Western art market. However such a conclusion would be highly problematic. In the Kunwinjku and Yolngu cases art is integrated in a similar way within social process and equally subject to a dispersed system of inherited and constructed rights in designs. Moreover Yolngu art practice also allows for the development of innovative artists, such as Narritjin,[41] Mithinari, Malangi[42] and contemporary artists such as Djambawa, Galuma and Wanyubi.

Both Yolngu artists and Kunwinjku artists have in recent years been able to respond to, engage with and influence contemporary Australian art by emphasising features of their art that resonate with a modernist aesthetic. The emphasis on geometric art and the masking of the figurative component that we have seen occurring in the recent paintings of the

39 See for example Haskovec, Ian and Hilary Sullivan, 'Najombolmi: Reflections and Rejections of an Aboriginal Artist', in Morphy, H. (ed.), *Animals into Art*, Allen and Unwin, London, 1989, pp. 57–74.

40 See for example Holmes, Sandra, *Yirawala: Painter of the Dreaming*, Hodder and Stroughton, Sydney, 1992.

41 Morphy, H., Deveson P. and K. Hayne, *The Art of Narritjin Maymuru*, CD Rom, Australian National University, E Press, Canberra, 2005.

42 Jenkins, Susan, *No Ordinary Place: The Art of David Malangi*, National Gallery of Australia, Canberra, 2005.

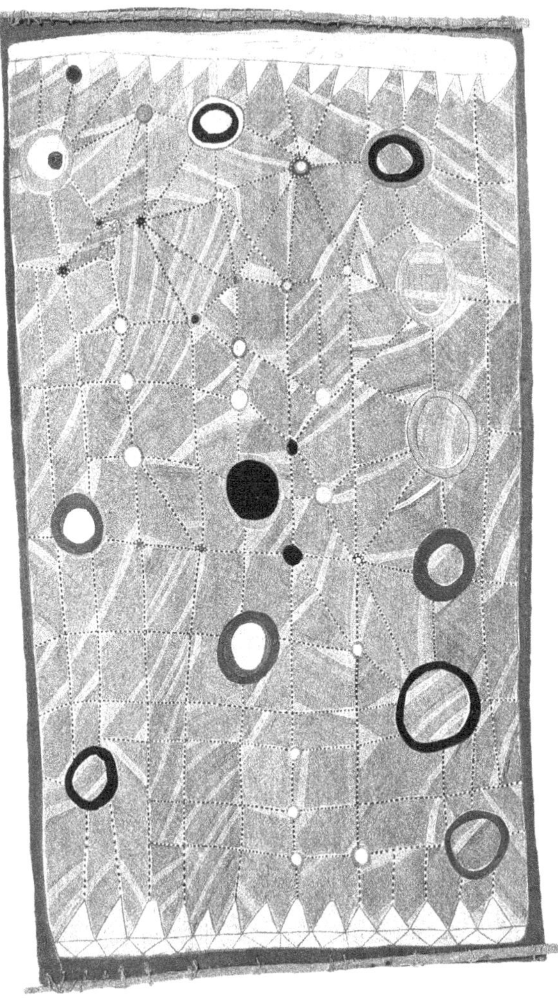

Fig. 24: John Mawurndjul, *Mardayin ceremony*, 1999, earth pigments on bark, 153 x 88 cm, Laverty Collection, Sydney. ID 1170. © 2008, ProLitteris, Zürich.

Yolngu artists from Yilpara is paralleled in the work of the Kunwinjku artist Mawurndjul. However the 'abstraction' in Mawurndjul's case comes out of the trajectory of Kunwinjku art and characterises its particular difference.[43] While Mawurndjul's paintings are similarly located in landscape they are not comprised of clan owned geometric elements (see fig. 24 and pl. XIX). His paintings have evolved out of the deconstruction and reconstruction of the figurative component of Kunwinjku art almost to the point of its disappearance.

---

43 Taylor, L., 'John Mawurndjul – "I've got a different idea"', in Kaufmann C. and Museum Tinguely (eds.) *Rarrk – John Mawurndjul. Journey Through Time in Northern Australia*, Schwabe AG, Basel, 2005, pp. 42–49.

The geometric structure created by this process then becomes the framework for an exquisite layering of crosshatching covering much broader expanses of bark than is the case in contemporary Yolngu art, where the geometry of the clan designs creates the dominant pattern. Coming from their own different but related traditions contemporary Yolngu and Kunwinjku artists respond to the encompassing Australian art market in complementary ways.

However it would be quite wrong to see the artistic production as parallel responses to the market's desire for a particular appearance of abstraction. In both Mawurndjul and Djambawa's case the particular paintings are the outcome of a trajectory of artistic practice that is relatively autonomous from national and global market forces. Mawurndjul's abstraction is patterned by the ancestral landscapes that he represents and the structure of the paintings are motivated by landforms. In Djambawa's case after several years of working through the idea of *buwuyak* and developing techniques that move figurative form beneath the surface for the painting, he invented a new medium which enabled figurative form to rise above the surface of the bark or hollow log. His most recent paintings produced in 2006 for the Asia Pacific Triennale in Brisbane, include moulded figures of mythic subjects – crocodiles on their nest, dugong rising above the surface of the water, overturned canoes. The figures are moulded onto the surface of the bark using his own medium of stringy bark fibre ground into a fine sawdust mixed with wood glue and pigment. An innovation, and yet in the case of all most artistic innovation one that can be placed in a historical context. The figures gain their power because the work as a whole combines different techniques of representation that carry the eye from above to below the surface of the bark, connecting with the Yolngu metaphysics of inside and outside, inner and surface form. Moreover, the previous generation of Yolngu artists used beeswax to mould figures that were subsequently painted. Mountford collected several of them on his 1948 expedition.

Conclusion

This contribution is based on the premise that it might be useful to look at the idea of art history from a cross-cultural perspective that articulates with non-Western discourses about art. I have focused on issues relevant to a particular area of discourse in Western art history, which has influenced the way in which Aboriginal art has been approached both by curators and by the art market. I have been concerned with the process of putting art works into sets on the basis of historical and formal relationships and the attribution of works to individuals. There are many art histories and not all would favour this particular methodological orientation. It has been argued that the particular Western discourse I have outlined is associated with the ideological process that has resulted in the formation of the modern capitalist state, and which is linked to the development of modernism, individualism and beliefs about the value of 'progress'. A form of art history which defines works according to progressive sequences of formal development and emphasises individual creativity and the identity of the individual artist is clearly not going to approach paintings in the same way as Yolngu artists do. What it shares in common with Yolngu art discourse or perhaps art theory is that it provides a framework for relating paintings to one another and in turn relating them to their human producers in a spatiotemporal context. A cross-cultural art history which attempts to take into account different ways of conceiving of the relationships between art works over time is going to be set at this level of generality. It must enable paintings to be placed at least initially in the context of the producer's own art discourse rather than re-inventing them as a component of someone else's art world – neither should works of Aboriginal art be defined as non-art because they do not fit into a particular Western art historical framework. A cross-cultural art history that embraces Kunwinjku art because its art theory shares some features in common with European art theory, but rejects Yolngu art, would clearly be absurd.

Aboriginal 'art histories' are as interconnected with ideological and social processes as European ones. The entry of Aboriginal art into predominantly Western arenas makes it subject to Western art discourse, and this in turn has inevitable consequences for the way in which the art is conceptualised in its Indigenous context. Conforming to the demands of other art discourses can produce values contradictory to those that are central to the place of art in Aboriginal societies. However the relationship between art histories, ideologies and other aspects of social process is a loose one, so art histories themselves are always in the process of change, and change can involve fundamental shifts of perspective. Aboriginal theories about the kind of things art works are can insert themselves in this process of changing Western art discourse and also be subject to change themselves. Art objects can simultaneously be the product of groups and subject to multiple right-holders, and the recognisable product of individuals or a definable set of collaborators. The juxtaposition of art histories brought about by the movement of Aboriginal art into the Western frame, while it simultaneously remains a part of Aboriginal society, brings to the fore new ways of seeing the relationships between objects and people.[44]

Yolngu 'art history' and art theory, the ways in which Yolngu conceptualise the relationships among paintings in terms of their own cultural categories, has affected the response of Yolngu artists to the changed circumstances brought about by European colonisation. It has influenced Yolngu ideas about how their art should be incorporated in the Euro-Australian and global art frames. Yolngu have accepted their identification as individual artists, but they have also argued for a particular kind of individuality. And recently they have begun to influence in significant ways the discourse that surrounds their work in the Euro-Australian arena. The Yolngu conception of the relationships between paintings, and the constraints on individual artists, are having an impact on curatorship and on the Euro-Australian art world, partly because they happen to engage with current debates in European art history/theory. But Aboriginal people have also been influencing more directly the ways in which their paintings are incorporated within the wider Australian frame. Most Australian institutions now consult Aboriginal people before organising exhibitions of their works, and rights in cultural property and indigenous knowledge have entered the legal arena. Exhibition practice now takes account of Aboriginal concerns in

---

44 See for example Thomas, N., *Possessions: Indigenous Art / Colonial Culture*, Thames and Hudson, London, 1999.

matters such as the propriety of exhibiting certain categories of objects to unrestricted audiences, the suppression of dead people's names, consciousness of the extended body of right holders in the case of some works, and Aboriginal categorisations of art works.

Acknowledgements

This chapter has been through many hands which have resulted in major revisions to the argument. I would like to thank Elizabeth Coleman for her insightful reading and Claus Volkenandt and Christian Kaufmann for their critical encouragement. Frances Morphy has always shared her ideas with me as well as jointly undertaking the fieldwork. Pip Deveson and Karen Westmacott undertook considerable editorial work to improve the text.

Claus Volkenandt

Why we need an intercultural art history

When dealing with the works of John Mawurndjul the question of place runs through the debate like a thread. The discussion centres on the relationship between art and context, on the tension between the art gallery as an institution and anthropological fieldwork, and on the difference between encountering the works in a museum and the conditions of their creation. In my contribution to this volume I want to stimulate the debate, especially where the oppositions meet head-on, by looking at art and context, or museum and fieldwork, but not as alternatives that exclude each other. These oppositions rather complement each other as becomes evident when considering the closeness of viewing and the distant origin of the works. In this sense, the following ideas seek answers to ways of understanding otherness from a hermeneutic tradition. To this end I first discuss some of the conditions of understanding otherness as seen from a European perspective, in other words: as either art or context, then I go on to relativise this opposition in an actual encounter with one of John Mawurndjul's works. I end my contribution with a brief summary.[1]

To start, I wish to point out that in the intertwining relationship of self and other and in the wake of globalisation and postcolonial critique the conditions of understanding otherness have changed decisively.[2] Today they are challenged by claims to political, social and cultural alterity that confront Western assertions of supremacy and postulate own

1 The following contribution picks up, and expands on, earlier postulated ideas on the subject; see especially Volkenandt, C., 'Ästhetik der Differenz. Überlegungen zum kunsthistorischen Umgang mit dem Fremden', in Dobbe M. and P. Gendolla (eds.), *Winter-Bilder. Zwischen Motiv und Medium*, Festschrift für Gundolf Winter zum 60. Geburtstag, Siegen, 2003, pp. 304–317; and Volkenandt, C., 'Perceptible Boundaries: Aesthetic Experience and Cross-Cultural Understanding with a View to John Mawurndjul', in Kaufmann, C. and Museum Tinguely (eds.), *«Rarrk» – John Mawurndjul. Journey Through Time in Northern Australia*, Schwabe AG, Basel, 2005, pp. 181–184.

2 See especially Waldenfels, Bernhard, *Topographie des Fremden. Studien zur Phänomenologie des Fremden 1*, Suhrkamp, Frankfurt am Main, 1997; Bronfen, Elisabeth, Marius, Benjamin, and Thomas Steffen (eds.), *Hybride Kulturen. Beiträge zur anglo-amerikanischen Multikulturalismusdebatte*, Stauffenburg Verlag, Tübingen, 1997; Därmann, Iris, *Fremde Monde der Vernunft. Die ethnologische Provokation der Philosophie*, Wilhelm Fink Verlag, Paderborn, 2005; and with a distinct art-historical focus Enwezor, Okwui, 'Die Black Box', in *Documenta11_Plattform5: Ausstellung*, (exhibition catalogue), Hatje Cantz, Ostfildern-Ruit, 2002, pp. 42–55.

identities founded on a different basis.[3] If one is ready to accept this critique of Euro- or Ethnocentrism respectively then one also has to question one's own, in this case European, concepts and terminologies with regard to their origin and scope. This in turn generates the incentive to deal with the European definition of art and the issue of the concept of context. Space allows me to shed light only on some select aspects here.

What follows is not based on a disciplinary distinction, though valid in itself, between art history and anthropology, but rather on a methodological distinction between the alternatives of art and context. By this I do not mean the situational shaping of all understanding – there is no such thing as context-free understanding in this sense, only closer and more distant contextual bonds as captured by the term horizon.[4] As a methodological distinction, art and context relate to options of interacting with works, and the time and location this interaction refers to. To give an example: are we, as scholars, referring to the time and place of the original creation of a work, or are we speaking of time and place in the sense of the aesthetic universe of a museal or medial world of images?[5] In other words, are we talking about contextualistic or universalistic options when dealing with art works on a scholarly basis?[6]

From art or context to contexts of art

If you take a look at the academic discipline of art history with the distinction of contextualistic and universalistic concepts in mind, the European tradition of art history presents you with the model of a universalistic conception: an art history based on the options of an 'ars una' model. In the following, I shall briefly outline this model as it forms the focal mode through which the European tradition has dealt with Western as well as non-Western art.

This aesthetically oriented concept of world art which, for a long time, operated under the label 'ars una', features among its leading representatives two prominent names: André Malraux and Wilhelm Worringer.[7] For Worringer the idea of an 'ars una' is rooted in the fact that "at all times and in all places we find evidence of drawing, painting, writing,

---

3 See Mosquera, Gerardo, 'Das Marco-Polo-Syndrom', in *Havanna. Sao Paulo. Junge Kunst aus Lateinamerika*, Haus der Kulturen der Welt Berlin, Berlin, 1995, pp. 34–39; see also Volkenandt, C., 'Versuch einer Einleitung', in Volkenandt, C. (ed.), *Kunstgeschichte und Weltgegenwartskunst. Konzepte – Methoden – Perspektiven*, Dietrich Reimer Verlag, Berlin, 2004, pp. 11–30, especially pp. 17–22; as well Kitty Zijlmans in this volume.

4 Gadamer, Hans-Georg, *Wahrheit und Methode. Grundzüge einer philosophischen Hermeneutik*, (6th edition), J. C. B. Mohr, Tübingen, 1990, pp. 307–312.

5 Gadamer, H.-G., 1990, *op. cit.*, 'Kritik der Abstraktion des ästhetischen Bewußtseins', (pp. 94–106) and 'Rekonstruktion und Integration als hermeneutische Aufgaben', (pp. 169–174).

6 With the terms contexualistic and universalistic options I am incorporating here art-historically transformed concepts and arguments developed by Waldenfels, see Waldenfels, B., 1997, *op. cit.*, especially pp. 110–117.

7 See Malraux, André, *Das imaginäre Museum*, Campus Verlag, Frankfurt,1987; and Worringer, Wilhelm, *Abstraktion und Einfühlung. Ein Beitrag zur Stilpsychologie*, Piper, München, 1981 [1st ed. 1907].

sculpting etc., so that it is justified to say that in manual-technical terms as well as in terms of the materials processed, a trajectory emerges that leads right up to the art practices and techniques of today."[8]

Thus the idea of an 'ars una' has to do with questions of continuity, creative continuity to be precise, which, because of its persistence throughout the history of mankind, has become an anthropological signum of humanness. This fact is granted special emphasis by 'ars una': the concept does not first and foremost deal with the creative human being as such and the special abilities that distinguish him or her, but rather more with the products of human creativity subsumed under the label 'art'.[9] Whatever the human being in his role as *homo pictor* has crafted through the ages – to be more precise: throughout all the ages – is art.

Thus the concept of 'ars una' is borne by the conviction that, to quote Worringer again, "throughout the history of humanity, from its earliest beginnings to the present day, there is evidence of the existence and the permanence of a distinct, self-determined creative drive that allows us to grant it, under the hallmark 'art', the status of a universe to and in itself among all forms of human activity, such that this world of its own is categorically and unambiguously distinguishable from all other forms of expression of the human activity impulse".[10] In other words: art, forever and at all times.

I need not point out that this concept did not remain undisputed, neither in European discourse nor in the context of postcolonial critique. The critique focuses on the 'ars una' conception's claim to universality: on art as being ubiquitous and omnipresent, not knowing boundaries in space and time. Such a claim to universality was and is unable to withstand the historicisation and geographical differentiation of the concept of art. Especially in the light of postcolonial critique art no longer ranks as a trans-cultural hyper-value but rather, it seems, as an especially successful, and thus tenacious, expression of Eurocentrism with worldwide impact and appeal.[11]

The universality claim of the 'ars una' concept and its representatives, the universalists of art history, have been challenged and contested in the main by the contextualists, by which I mean the proponents of the mainly European, context-bound conceptions in art history and anthropology.[12] One of the hallmarks of this school is the relativisation of universal

---

8 Worringer, W., 'ARS UNA?', in Worringer, W. (ed.), *Fragen und Gegenfragen. Schriften zum Kunstproblem*, München, 1956, pp. 155–163, here notably p. 156.

9 On the resumption of this debate in the context of the 'iconic turn' see Boehm, Gottfried, *Homo Pictor*, Colloquium Rauricum, Vol. 7., K. G. Saur, München/Leipzig, 2001.

10 Worringer, W., 1956, (*op. cit.*, footnote 8), p. 155.

11 See especially Mosquera, G., 1995 (*op. cit.*, footnote 3), pp. 34–39.

12 See Kemp, Wolfgang, 'Kontexte. Für eine Kunstgeschichte der Komplexität', in *Texte zur Kunst 2*, 1991, No. 2, pp. 89–101; Belting, Hans, 'Das Werk im Kontext', in Belting, H. et. al. (eds.), *Kunstgeschichte. Eine Einführung*, (3rd edition), Dietrich Reimer, Berlin, 1988, pp. 222–239; Haustein, Lydia, 'Der Kunst- und Bildbegriff im Spannungsfeld von Kunstgeschichte und Ethnologie', in Kämpf, H., und R. Schott (eds.) *Der Mensch als homo pictor? Die Kunst traditioneller Kulturen aus der Sicht von Philosophie und Ethnologie*, Bouvier Verlag, Bonn, 1995, pp. 86–104; Förster, Till, 'Die Geschichte fremder Künste. Afrikanische Perspektiven und Probleme', in Fößel, A. and Ch. Kampmann (eds.), *Wozu Historie heute?*

claims and the way its representatives occasionally radically challenge the applicability of a European art model to non-European forms of artistic expression.[13]

At its core, this approach could be described as an attempt to counter the de-contextualisation of art works and other creative productions. Put differently, the contextualist approach aims at an understanding (*Verstehen*) that grows from the conjunction of art and context, of creation and the conditions of production. Art, or to put it more generally, anything that has been created and formed, is intrinsically linked to the conditions of its production and its impact. It is located in a specific social and/or cultural space that holds one of the keys and opens a door to understanding. Context renders understanding possible. Herewith the historicity of the concept of art appears to be accounted for and, from the perspective of postcolonial critique, the claim to alterity is upheld by the relativisation of the standards of value.[14]

However, one issue remains to be dealt with: the question of the historical and geographical legitimacy of the context concept. Or, worded more pointedly: is not the concept 'context' simply ideologically less suspect than the concept 'art'? Does not what applies to the historical and geographical differentiation of the concept of 'art' also apply to the 'context' concept? In other words: what or where is the historical and geographical place of the concept of 'context'?

I can only briefly spotlight a few answers to these questions here.[15] The guideline to these answers is the supposition that the idea of context is a specifically European one and that it began to be used in a distinct historical setting, at about the same time that the first museums were established. One could say that it was a compensatory reaction to certain cultural issues provoked by the first wave of bourgeois modernity in Europe. Primarily this includes the de-contextualisation of images around 1800 and their transfer to museums.[16] The philosophical pioneer of the 19th century who dealt with the question of the re-contextualisation of images was Friedrich Schleiermacher; the leading figure to deal with these issues in art history in the 20th century is Erwin Panofsky.

What links the two men is the methodological ideal of reconstruction. To Schleiermacher – as expressed in his aesthetics – a work of art is "also rooted in its ground and soil, in its environment. It loses its significance as soon as it is removed from its environment and is brought into circulation. It is like an object that has been saved from a fire and now carries burn marks."[17] Schleiermacher responds to this by developing a hermeneutics

---

Beiträge zu einer Standortbestimmung im fachübergreifenden Gespräch, Böhlau Verlag, Köln/Weimar, 1996, pp. 123–154.

13 Förster, T., 1996, (*op. cit.*, footnote 12), pp. 146–150.

14 See also Mosquera, G., 1995, (*op. cit.*, footnote 3), pp. 34–39.

15 See also Dilley, Roy, 'Introduction: The Problem of Context', in Dilley, R. (ed.), *The Problem of Context*, Berghahn Books, New York/Oxford, 1999, pp. 1–46; and Danneberg, Lutz, 'Art. "Kontext"', in Fricke H., (ed.), *Reallexikon der deutschen Literaturwissenschaft*, Vol 2, Walter de Gruyter, Berlin, 1997–2003, pp. 333–337.

16 See also Mattick, Paul Jr., 'Context', in Nelson, Robert S. and Richard Shiff (eds.), *Critical Terms for Art History*, University of Chicago Press, Chicago/London, 1992, pp. 70–86, especially 70–76.

17 Quoted from Odebrecht, Rudolf (ed.), *Friedrich Schleiermachers Ästhetik*, de Gruyter, Berlin/Leipzig, 1931, p. 86, (quote translated by N. Stephenson).

that he conceptualises as a study of art. Its task is "the historical and divinatory, objective and subjective reconstruction of rendered speech."[18] Thus it aims to reconstruct the single, concrete work through the mediation of the singularity of its author with the general properties of its linguistic, or in our case more appropriate, iconic potentialities.[19]

Panofsky sees this kind of post-constructive understanding applied by Schleiermacher as a form of historical reconstruction. For Panofsky it ranks as a mode of revitalising the historically defunct by reinstating it in the context of its original meaning under conditions controlled by scholarship.[20] In the present debate between art history and anthropology this methodological ideal still seems to hold good in a transformed sense, insofar as the context provides the basis of understanding.[21]

In any case, seen from this perspective both the 'context' concept and the 'art' concept, or, to be more precise, the concept of autonomous art, are of European origin. Probably they represent two sides of the same European coin, answering to the radical changes by reverting to aesthetic universalism on the one hand, and reconstructive historicisation on the other. For art history, this means that to rely on either art or context as the set of oppositions when dealing with otherness on an academic basis reflects an aporia. It springs from its own, i.e. European, historical development. The question now is: what is the alternative?

The alternative I propose in the following is to position the understanding of non-European art in a field that bridges the global and the local. This allows us to address questions that relate to both art and context.

Through the worldwide dissemination of cultural products and works of art which are then exhibited in the white cube of museums, in the first instance globalisation appears to be responsible for blurring, or grinding down, their distant origin and local fixation. Globalisation, here understood as the global mobility and distribution of goods, de-localises art and culture. At the same time, however, globalised art and culture are re-localised at the venues where they are shown, in line with the traditions, habits and self-conceptions that prevail there.

At this point the necessity of an intercultural art history becomes evident: an art history that puts into perspective authentic understanding drawn from the context of the production of a work with its appropriation as art. The alternative I am speaking of includes bringing into a dialogue the local conditions under which the encounter with art and culture takes place – speaking in European terms: the label 'art' which, in Europe, is given to anything that has been formed and/or created – and the local conditions and

18 Schleiermacher, Friedrich, *Hermeneutik,* re-edited by Kimmerle, H., Winter, Heidelberg 1959, p. 87, (quote translated by N. Stephenson).

19 See also Birus, Hendrik, 'Hermeneutische Wende? Anmerkungen zur Schleiermacher-Interpretation', *Euphorion* 74, 1980, pp. 213–222.

20 According to Erwin Panofsky, 'Einführung. Kunstgeschichte als geisteswissenschaftliche Disziplin', in Panofsky, E., *Sinn und Deutung in der bildenden Kunst,* DuMont, Köln, 1978 [1940], pp. 7–35.

21 For art history see Weddingen, Tristan, 'Art. "Funktion und Kontext"', in Pfisterer, U. (ed.), *Metzler Lexikon Kunstwissenschaft. Ideen, Methoden, Begriffe,* Verlag J. B. Metzler, Stuttgart/Weimar, 2003, pp. 104–107; for anthropology see Dilley, R. (ed.), 1999, (*op. cit.* footnote 15).

cultural setting under which the art work is conceived and produced. We need to seek and attempt a dialogue between the different localities while fully keeping in mind that these are globally bridged.

John Mawurndjul's *Yawkyawk* (2005) in the Museum Tinguely

In the second part of this contribution I want to test these ideas on an encounter with a specific work by John Mawurndjul called *Yawkyawk*, which was created in 2005 (see fig. 25 and pl. XX). In this encounter I attempt to bridge the sensory immediacy of the picture with its distant, but ever-present cultural origin. The starting point of this encounter is the sensory presence of the picture as made possible through its presentation in the Museum Tinguely, in other words in a (European) art museum.[22] The encounter thus takes place within the bounds of an aesthetic experience.[23]

The *Yawkyawk* picture is in portrait format, 1.5 m high and roughly 75 centimetres wide.[24] The first glance reveals a visual event and, at the same time, the invocation of a figure. Figure and structure are interlocked, emerging and receding in unison and opposition simultaneously whilst constantly accentuating each other. These accentuations are brought to the viewer's notice not only through the visual vitality of the image and the contrast between the painting's structure and the figure but also because his eye is locked in the portrait format of the painting.[25] This is effectively underpinned by a thin black line that runs around the bark, thus delineating the theme of the painting from its support. It demarcates a representational field of its own which attracts the viewer's attention and holds it there.

Stepping closer to the painting you clearly recognise the crosshatching that gives the picture its intense visuality. Thin lines consisting of natural earth pigments constitute the base elements and create a design that is regular and irregular at the same time. On the one hand the design is graphically structured by horizontally-running tiers of colour. Out of the crosshatching these flows are compacted, becoming black, white or ochre-coloured bands. On the other hand, black, freehand-drawn lines traversing the bark from top to bottom create a contrasting vertical order. There are also a number of black lines that sort of meander across the picture. Together they form a network of lines. Through the effect of the flow of colours a broad field of topographical and geological allusions is invoked.

22 See O'Doherty, Brian, *In der weißen Zelle / Inside the White Cube*, (ed. Wolfgang Kemp), Merve Verlag, Berlin, 1996.

23 See Boehm, G., 'Bildsinn und Sinnesorgane', *neue hefte für philosophie* 18/19, 1980: Anschauung als ästhetische Kategorie, pp. 118–132 and Boehm, G., 'Sehen. Hermeneutische Reflexionen', in Konersmann, R. (ed.), *Kritik des Sehens*, Reclam, Leipzig, 1997 [1992], pp. 272–298.

24 John Mawurndjul, *Yawkyawk*, 2005. Natural pigments on bark. 148 cm by 72 cm, oblique format, Basel, Museum der Kulturen.

25 See Imdahl, Max, 'Überlegungen zur Identität des Bildes', [1979], in Imdahl, M., *Gesammelte Schriften, Vol. 3: Reflexion, Theorie, Methode*, (ed. Gottfried Boehm), Suhrkamp, Frankfurt/Main 1996, pp. 381–423, especially pp. 394–404.

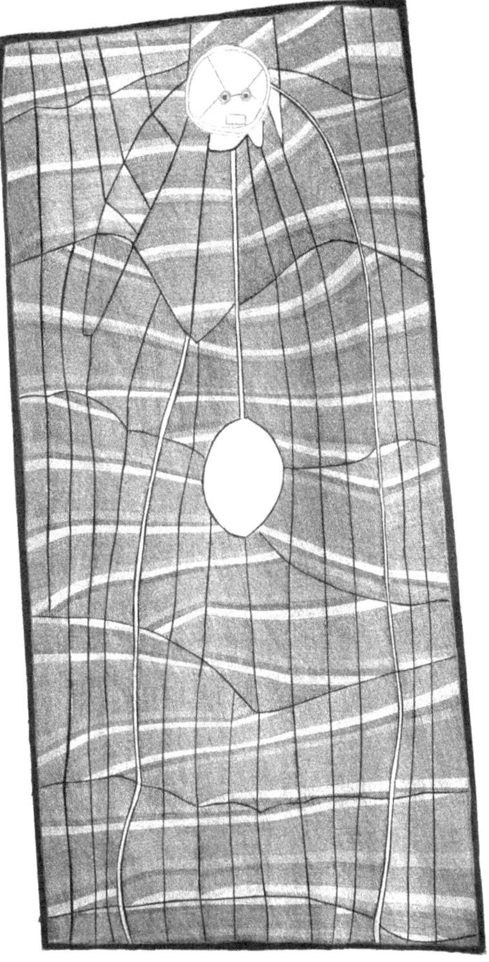

Fig. 25: John Mawurndjul, *Yawkyawk, young girl – waterspirit*, 2005, earth pigments on bark, 154 x 52 cm, Museum der Kulturen Basel. Va 1429. Photo Museum der Kulturen Basel. © 2008 ProLitteris, Zürich.

This set of allusions is sustained by the unevenness of the bark itself. It does not offer a flat painting surface; through the even flow of ups and downs it is given a form of three-dimensionality and acquires the semblance of a landscape relief, it is given bodily form. Probably it is no coincidence that the white almond shape in the picture is located not only near the centre of the image but also in one of the bark's troughs. It creates a visual focal point, forming a highlighted spot in the landscape at the same time. In its formation it corresponds to three similarly configured lines. One passes the almond shape vertically to the left, the other to the right and the third connects it in a straight line with the head-shaped form at the top of the picture. They are reminiscent of features in the landscape while simultaneously strongly invoking a figure.

The invocation is based on rudimentary elements: a strongly stylised head in white that is given a facial expression by a pair of prominent eyes and an adumbrated mouth to which are added two lines, outlining the head's shape. From the perspective of this figure invocation the almond shape looks like an internal organ that is linked to the head in a singular fashion. The intimation of a figure, however, in no way revokes the landscape quality of the image. In fact, the almond shape acts as an important go-between in the picture in the sense that it mediates between the 'outside' and the 'inside' of the figure itself on the one hand and between the figure and the landscape on the other. Put rather succinctly and hypothetically: the landscape stands for the outside of the figure which itself is present in the landscape.

In an attempt to go more deeply into the matter concerning the outside and inside of the figure and its relationship to landscape we must acknowledge that we have reached the limits to our viewing, the boundary of what we can understand through mere contemplation. It becomes apparent that John Mawurndjul works in a different iconic translation mode from the one we are accustomed to in Europe. By translation I mean here the way through which reality (in the widest sense of the term) finds its way into imagery. This qualifies translation as a metaphoric process: the iconification of reality.[26] In order to better understand this translation process in relation to the *Yawkyawk* picture we need to know more about the cultural contexts that inform these works.[27]

In the following I want to suggest at least one or two aspects of these contexts. The *Yawkyawk* picture is based on both iconic and narrative references.[28] The *Yawkyawk* picture's narrative iconography is based on oral tradition, in the broadest sense of the term, on the recounting of creation myths: the Yawkyawk story tells of two sisters who are travelling through the country and decide to set up camp near a waterhole. They prepare the food they have collected nearby, actually so close to the waterhole that it angers the Rainbow Serpent – one of the key figures in the creation mythology – who rises from the billabong and tries to kill the sisters. They flee to the next waterhole into which they dive and hide. Still, the Rainbow Serpent catches and devours them, but spits them out again later. Through this act they metamorphose to become spirit beings who henceforth inhabit the rocky country, especially the freshwater-holes.

Returning to the picture equipped with these contextual rudiments we need to enter into an exchange between this other form of knowledge and our own mode of perception. I want to emphasise this exchange explicitly: the aesthetic presence of John Mawurndjul's

26 See Boehm, G., *Paul Cézanne. Montagne Sainte-Victoire*, Insel Verlag, Frankfurt/Main, 1988, pp. 54–66; and from an intercultural perspective Mersmann, Birgit, 'Bildkulturwissenschaft als Kulturbildwissenschaft? Von der Notwendigkeit eines inter- und transkulturellen Iconic Turn', *Zeitschrift für Ästhetik und Allgemeine Kunstwissenschaft* 49 (1), 2004, pp. 91–109, especially 107–109.

27 This is where anthropology comes in as the academic discipline that traditionally deals with cultural otherness.

28 See Taylor, Luke, *Seeing the Inside. Bark Painting in Western Arnhem Land*, Clarendon Press, Oxford, 1996, pp. 201–208; and Taylor, L., 'Fire in the Water. Inspiration from Country', in Perkins, H. (ed.), *Crossing Country: the Alchemy of Western Arnhem Land Art*, Art Gallery of New South Wales, Sydney, 2004, pp. 115–130, especially p. 122.

paintings and the anthropological and art-historical knowledge we have on them are two sides of the same presence. It is not a matter of contrasting aesthetic presence and cultural knowledge, but of bringing them into a meaningful relationship instead: works are created in a specific setting and undergo reception in a broad variety of contexts. They can either transgress these contexts or resist being absorbed, and may attain new actuality in the same or different contexts.[29] In this sense the knowledge gained from art history and anthropology represents only one building block to the understanding of John Mawurndjul's works. This knowledge must be realised in an eidetic form.

Once again, I can only briefly outline what is meant by eidetic realisation. With both picture and story in mind the ghost-like figure shows one of the Yawkyawk sisters after transformation. She is depicted in her second form of existence and, seen from this perspective, the white almond shape emerges as the waterhole that she now inspirits. At the same time, however, the shape reflects her own story: it figures as the organ into which she was swallowed and thus evokes the events that led to her transformation. But the intertwining of figure and landscape also makes evident not only the fact that, but also how, she indwells and inspirits country.

Turning to the issue of translation, i.e. the iconic translation of reality, we can clearly speak of the iconification of reality: by granting her incorporeal existence a body in the shape of the bark, John Mawurndjul converts the imagined presence of the Yawkyawk girl to an image. Bark painting manifests itself as a process of embodiment that mediates the translation of reality into visible form, in other words, into a picture.

Conclusion

This briefly outlined translation that the *Yawkyawk* picture accomplishes, develops profile when the relationship between art and context is activated or energised. Its potential becomes evident when one neither takes the art aspect of presentation in a museum nor the context dimension of anthropological fieldwork as the exclusive benchmark of understanding. Preferably both aspects should be put into perspective and their mutual relationship stressed. On account of, and as a consequence of, the flexibility in relation to each other I take the specific setting in which I face the picture as the immediate context of the work encounter and define it as the constituting condition of the encounter.

In the case of the *Yawyawk* picture this encounter took place in the white cube of an art museum where it presented itself to me in a visually perceptible form on the wall. For my experience with the painting this had two implications:
a) my sensory access to the image was defined by a European tradition of aesthetic experience, in other words, my background shaped the specific form of visual perception; and
b) by reference to the context of its presentation in a museum it appealed to me as art.

---

29 On the relationship between art and history in European art history see Volkenandt, C., *Rembrandt: Anatomie eines Bildes*, Wilhelm Fink Verlag, München, 2004.

At the same time, however, the sensory examination of the work also revealed my own boundaries to viewing insofar as beyond the museum setting of its presentation other dimensions of the picture came to the fore, namely the question of the *Yawkyawk* picture's reference to reality. Taking into consideration this dimension of the picture, i.e. the painting's ability to translate reality, shifted my perspective and relativised the issue of the universality of art. Thus, from the painting ranked previously as an autonomous work questions arose as to how reality was actually represented by the work.

This in turn raised questions that deal with the local conditions under which the work originated. Evoking the context of creation did not provide the ultimately valid gauge for understanding the work but it contributed important information on the cultural context that proved enriching for both the work and the mode of viewing, without levelling or lowering the aesthetic experience. Both aspects, knowledge of the cultural context and aesthetic experience, were brought to bear on each other in terms of the *Yawkyawk* picture's ability to translate reality on a universal, trans-cultural scale. In European terms, this translation was described as embodiment, a description which in itself is to be taken as an opportunity for dialogue that needs to be continued, on an intercultural basis.

An art history that deals with intercultural issues in this sense draws on the tension that exists between the works' otherness and one's own cultural stamp that makes them look 'other' in the first place. An art history of this kind does not merely bypass this cultural stamp; instead it attempts to bring it to bear as a productive preconception while, at the same time, neither levelling the works' otherness nor declaring this otherness to be their ultimate characteristic. Both moments, otherness and preconception, are present and figure as a tension between proximity and distance, between familiarity and unaccustomedness in the works of John Mawurndjul and the way they are exhibited. Our (European-coined) encounter with the works of John Mawurndjul are marked by aesthetic as well as anthropological moments. Both aspects shape the experience of viewing. They create the tension field within which, and through which, the works of John Mawurndjul are exhibited.

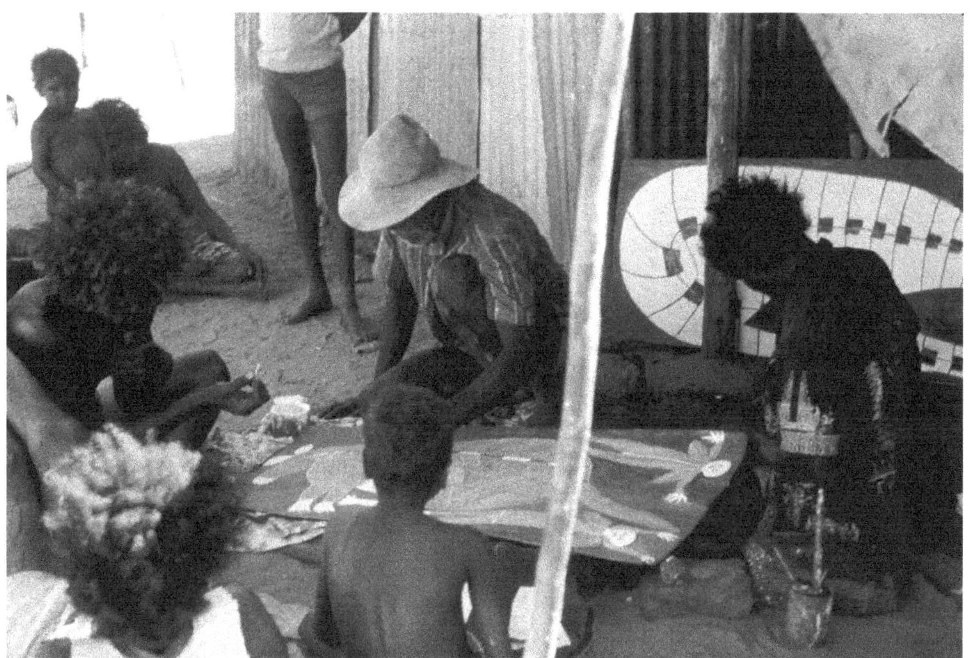

Pl. I: Peter Marralwanga, Ivan Namirrki and Clark Bubbuwanga Namunjdja painting together at Marrkolidjban, 1983. Photo Luke Taylor.

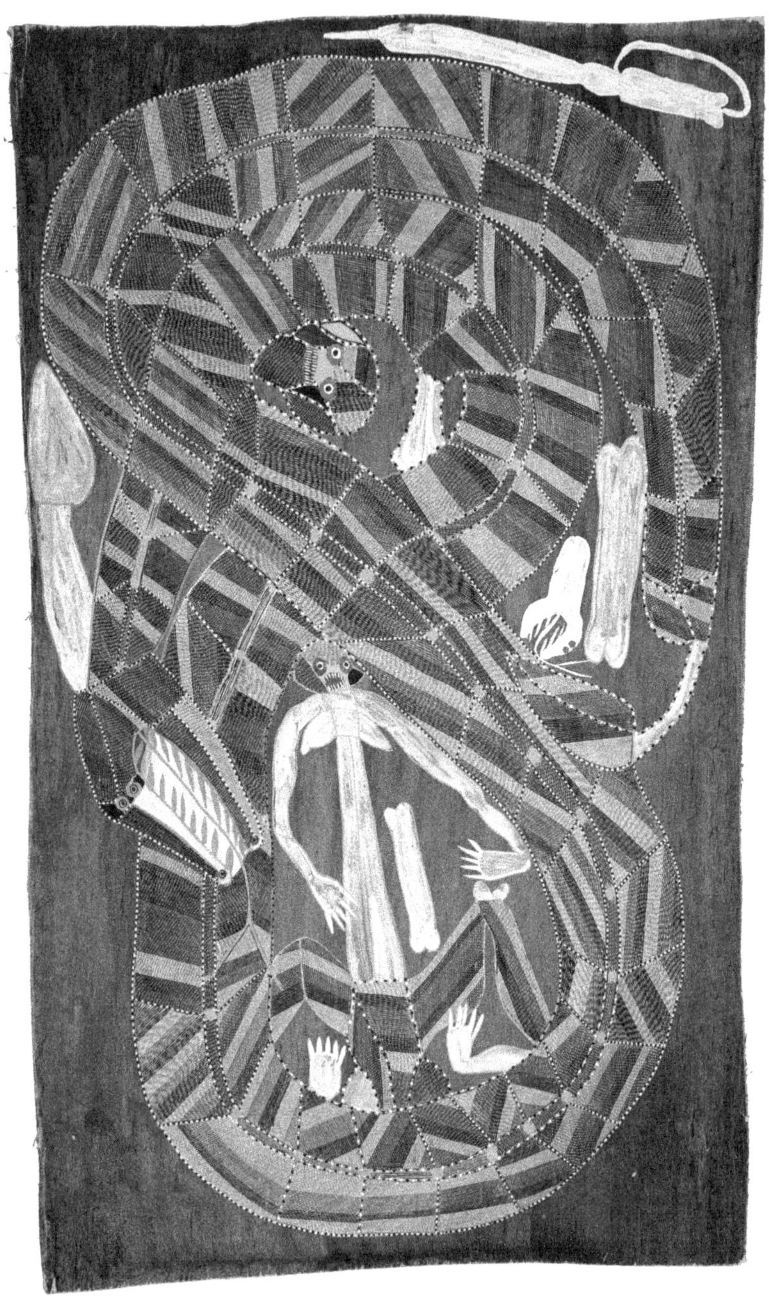

Pl. II: John Mawurndjul, *Ngalyod, rainbow serpent, devouring the yawkyawk girls*, 1984, earth pigments on bark, 123.5 x 74 cm, National Gallery of Australia, Canberra. 84.1956. Photo National Gallery of Australia. © 2008, ProLitteris, Zürich.

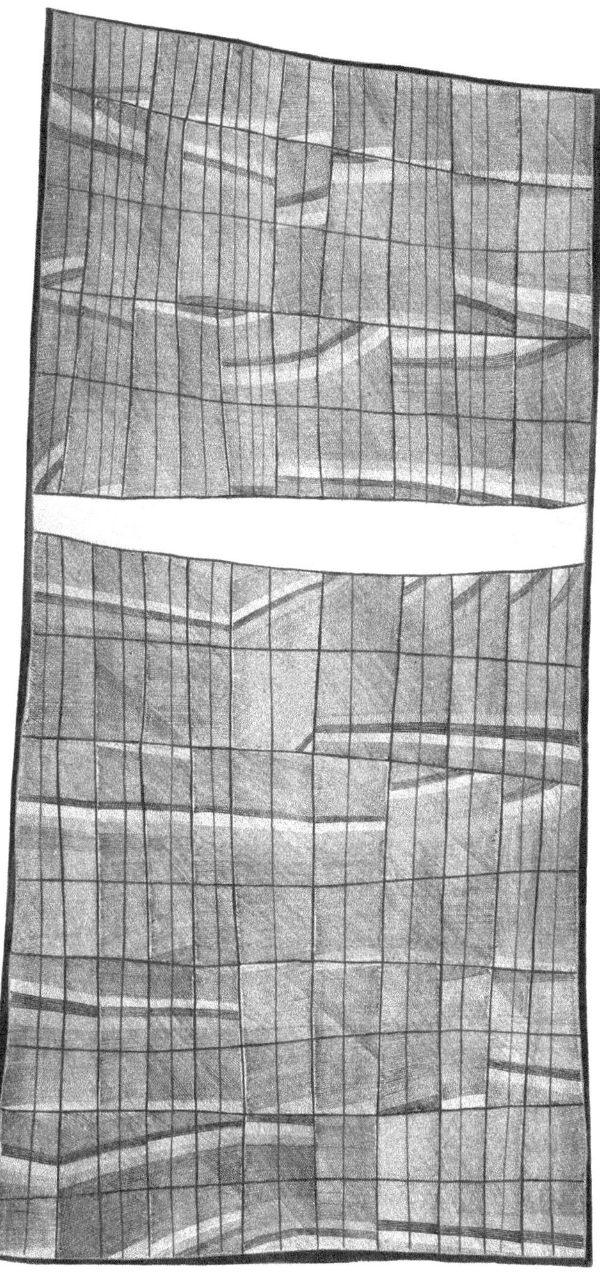

Pl. III: John Mawurndjul, *Mardayin at Kudjarnngal*, 2003, earth pigments on bark, 152.5 x 76 cm, National Gallery of Victoria, Melbourne. Presented through the NGV Foundation by Judith and Leon Gorr, Ricci Swart, Nellie Castan and Anita Castan, 2003. NGV 2003.663. Photo National Gallery of Victoria.

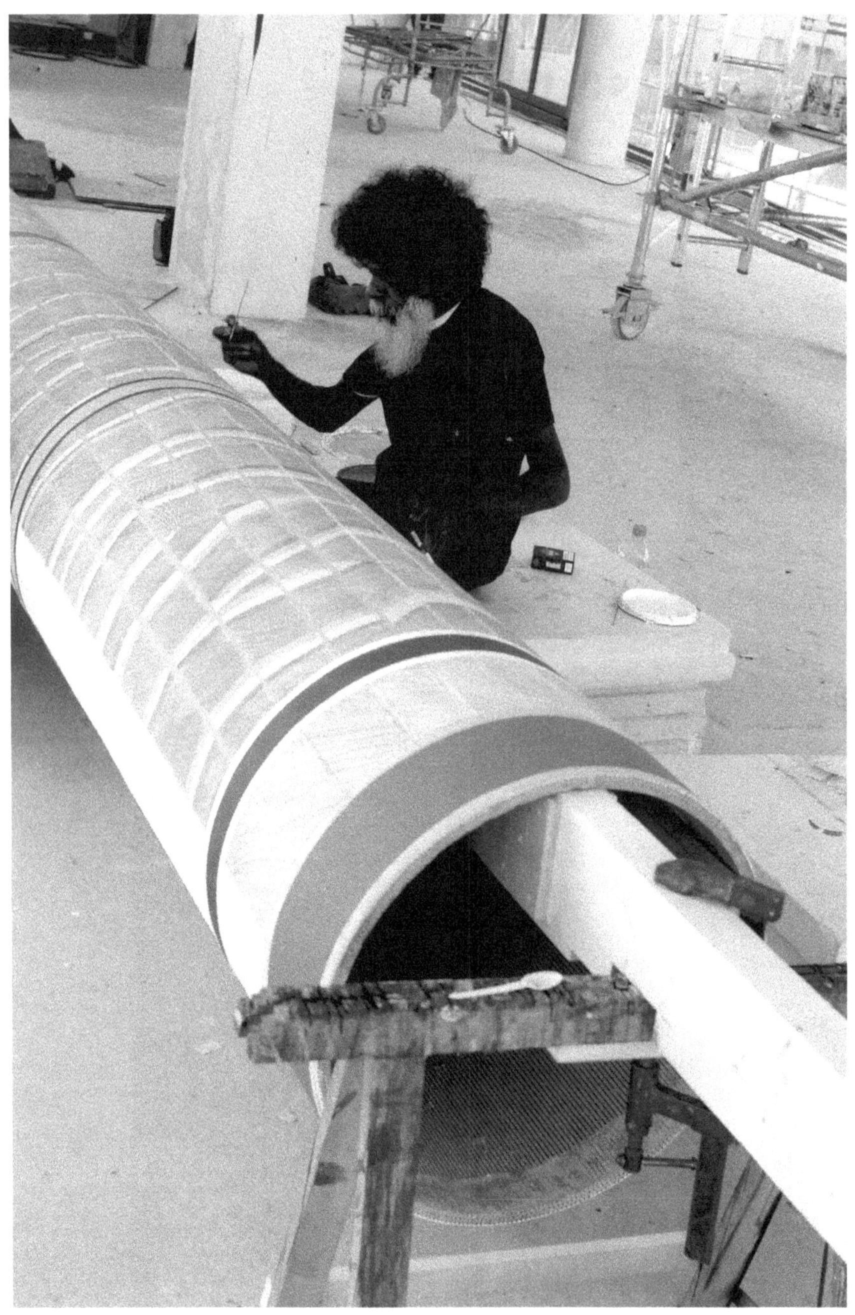

Pl. IV: John Mawurndjul painting in the Musée du quai Branly, Paris, September 2005. ©Photo Scala, Firenze – Musée du quai Branly, 2005.

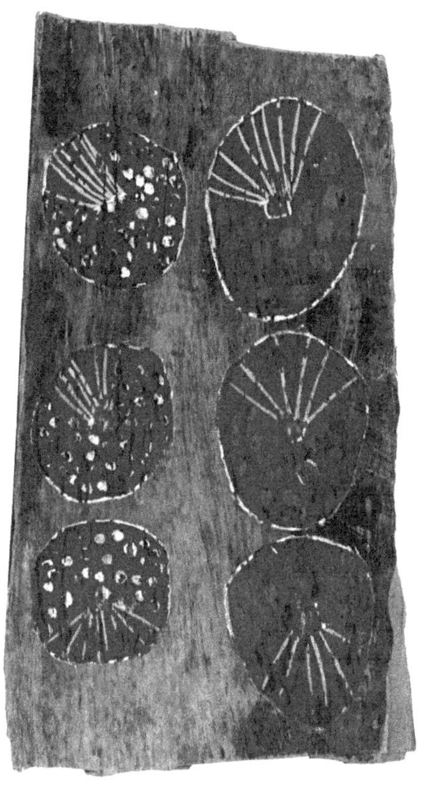

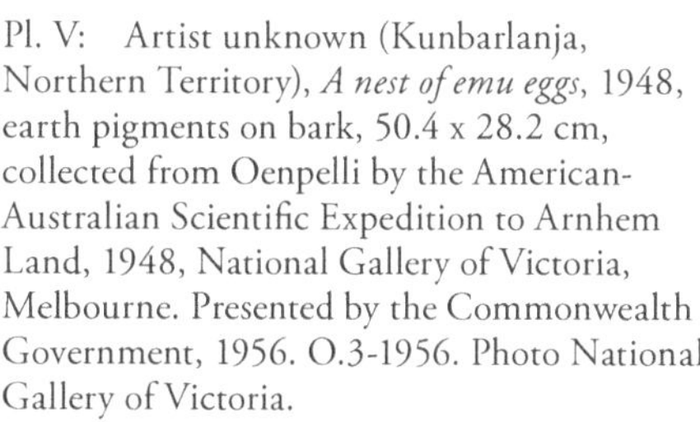

Pl. V: Artist unknown (Kunbarlanja, Northern Territory), *A nest of emu eggs*, 1948, earth pigments on bark, 50.4 x 28.2 cm, collected from Oenpelli by the American-Australian Scientific Expedition to Arnhem Land, 1948, National Gallery of Victoria, Melbourne. Presented by the Commonwealth Government, 1956. O.3-1956. Photo National Gallery of Victoria.

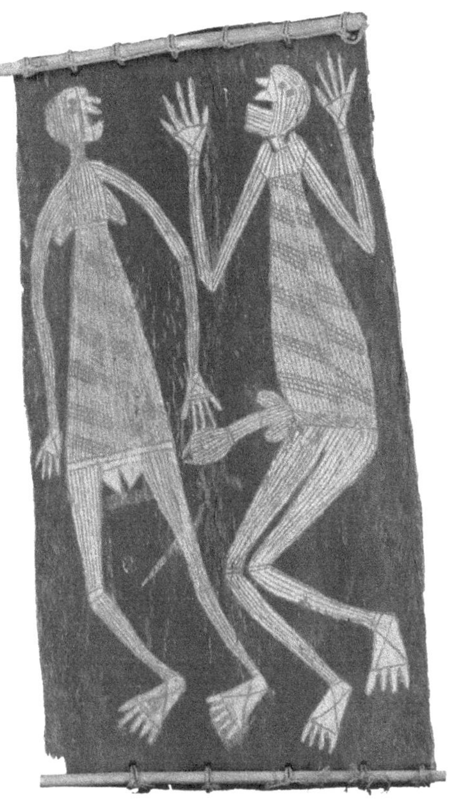

Pl. VI: Paddy Compass Namatbara, *Namarnday spirits*, c. early 1960s, earth pigments on bark, 85.7 x 44.4 cm, National Gallery of Victoria, Melbourne. Gerstl Bequest, 2000. 2000.224. Photo National Gallery of Victoria.

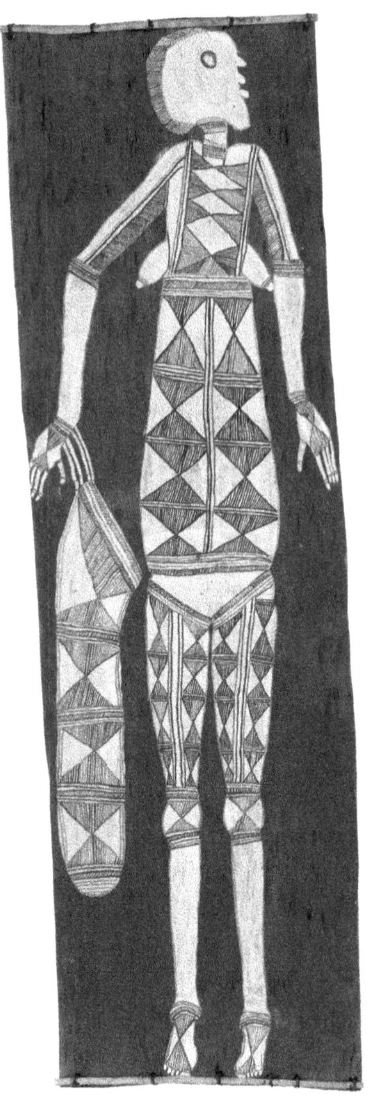

Pl. VII: Lofty Bardayal Nadjamerrek (Kunwinjku born 1926), *Ngalyongddoh djang*, 2005, earth pigments on bark, 157.5 x 47 cm, National Gallery of Victoria, Melbourne. Purchased with funds donated by Supporters and Patrons of Indigenous Art, 2005. 2005.407. © the artist licensed by Aboriginal Artists Agency 2008. Photo National Gallery of Victoria.

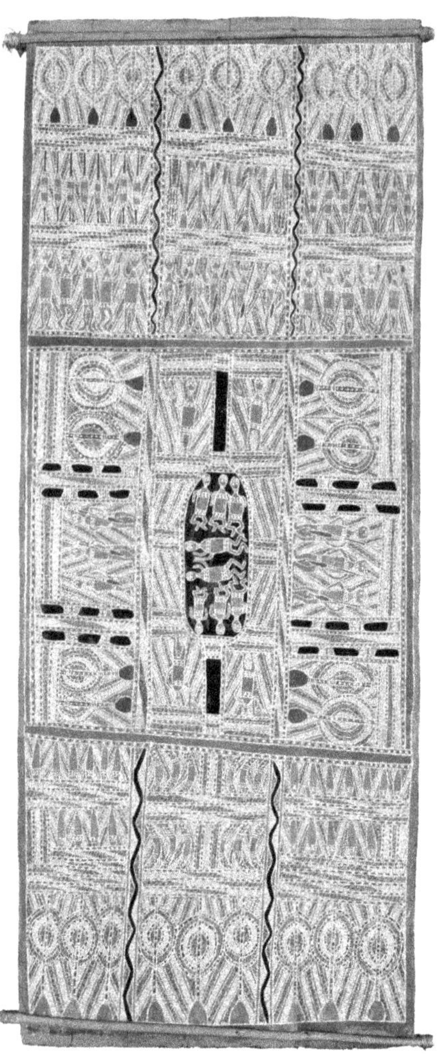

Pl. VIII: Mathaman Marika (Rirratjingu c.1916–1970), *Wawilak ceremony*, 1963, earth pigments on bark, 159.1 x 68.2 cm (irreg.), National Gallery of Victoria, Melbourne. Gift of Jim Davidson, 1967. D5-1512. Photo National Gallery of Victoria.

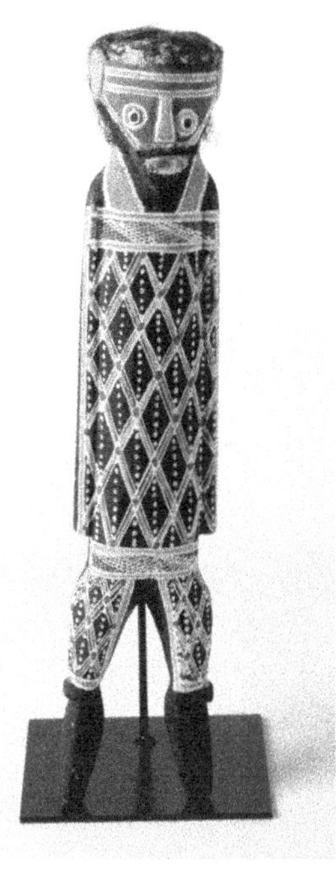

Pl. IX: Lipundja Gupapuyngu (c.1912–1968), *Wild honey figure,* c. 1963, earth pigments, wood, human hair, 54.5 (variable) x 11 cm, National Gallery of Victoria, Melbourne. Purchased, 2000. 2000.6. Photo National Gallery of Victoria.

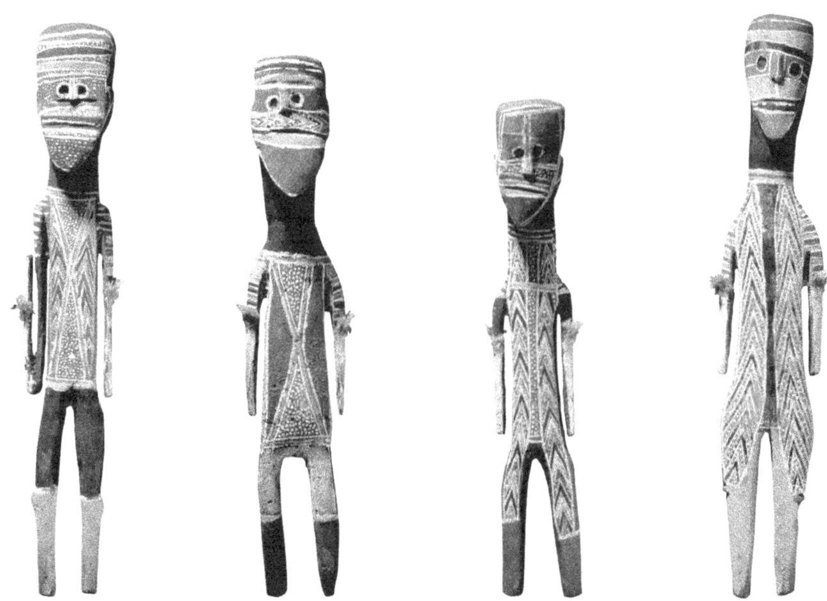

Pl. X: Luluna Ganalbingu (c.1910–c.1973), *Bumuri/Wayarre – Lunggurrma figures,* 1963, earth pigments, wood, lorikeet feathers, variable dimensions, National Gallery of Victoria, Melbourne. Purchased through The Art Foundation of Victoria with the assistance of Alcoa of Australia Limited, Governor, 1997. 1997.268, 1997.269, 1997.270, 1997.271. Photo National Gallery of Victoria.

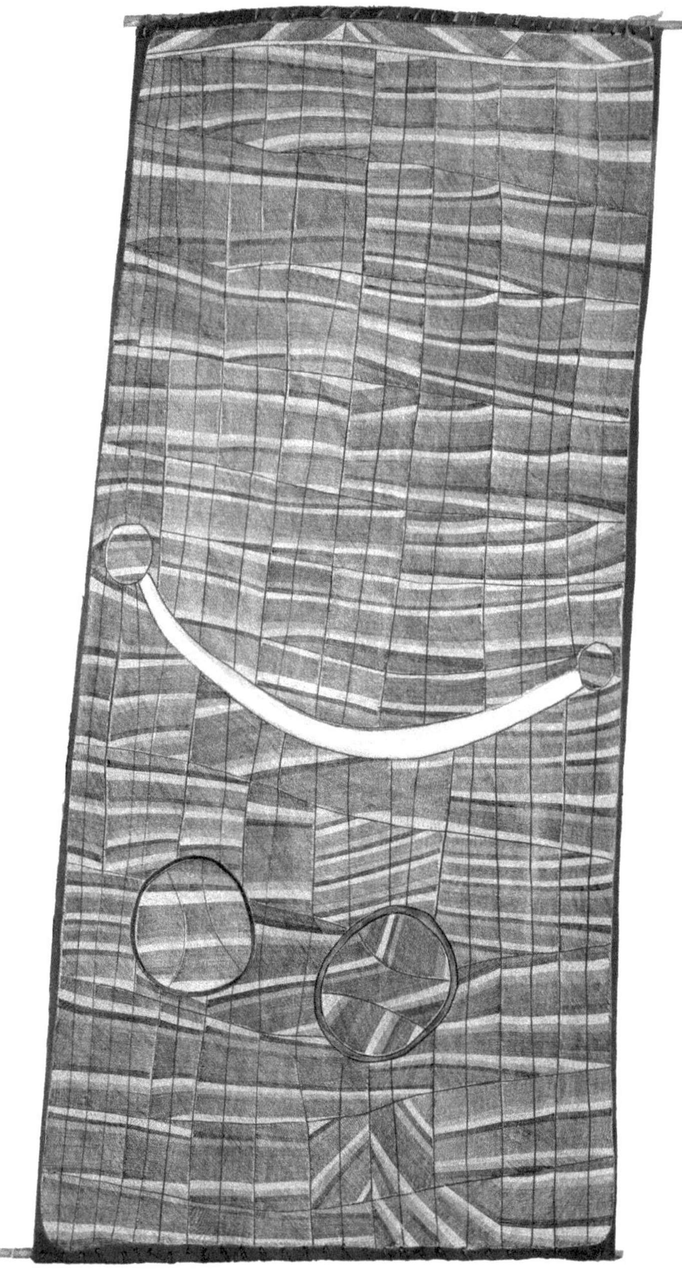

Pl. XI: John Mawurndjul (Kuninjku born 1952), *Mardayin design at Dilebang*, 2003, earth pigments on bark, 212 x 98 cm, National Gallery of Victoria, Melbourne. Presented through the NGV Foundation by Judith and Leon Gorr, Ricci Swart, Nellie Castan and Anita Castan, 2003. 2003.661. Photo National Gallery of Victoria. © 2008, ProLitteris, Zürich.

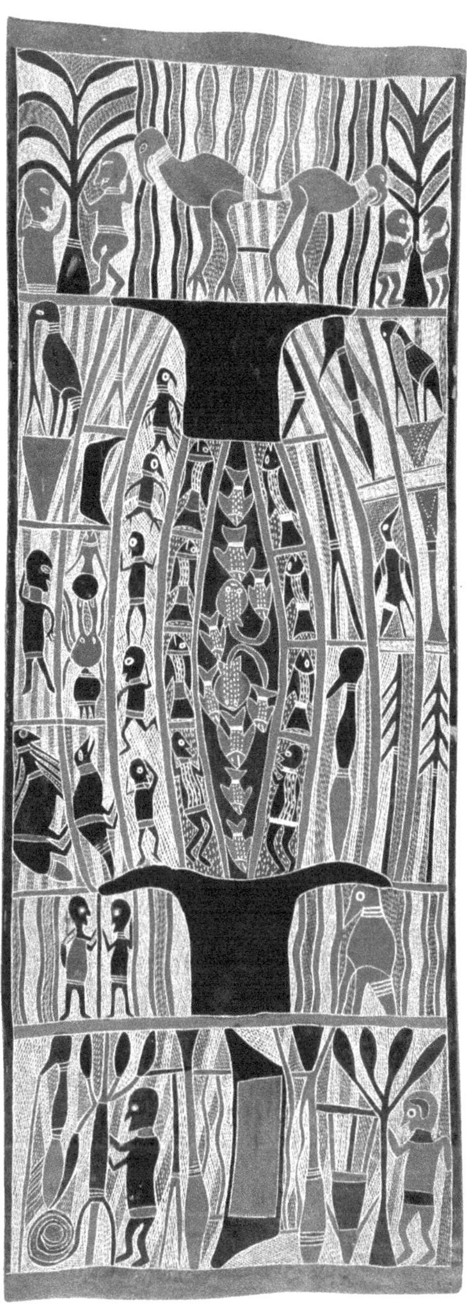

Pl. XII: Narritjin Maymuru, *Djet̲ story*, 1967, earth pigments on bark, c. 150 x 50 cm. The painting illustrates in rich detail the story of Djet̲, and his transformation into a sea eagle. National Museum of Australia, Canberra. © the artist's family. Reproduced courtesy Buku-Larrnggay Mulka Art Centre. Photo National Museum of Australia.

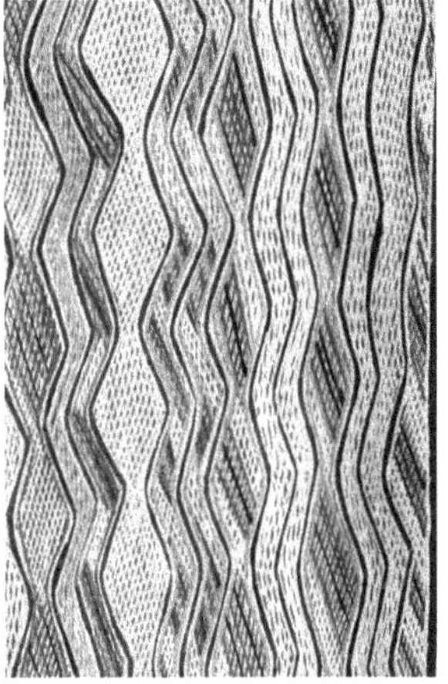

Pl. XIII: Narritjin Maymuru's crosshatching. Detail of a painting: *The Marawili tree at Djarrakpi*, 1976. Photo Howard Morphy.

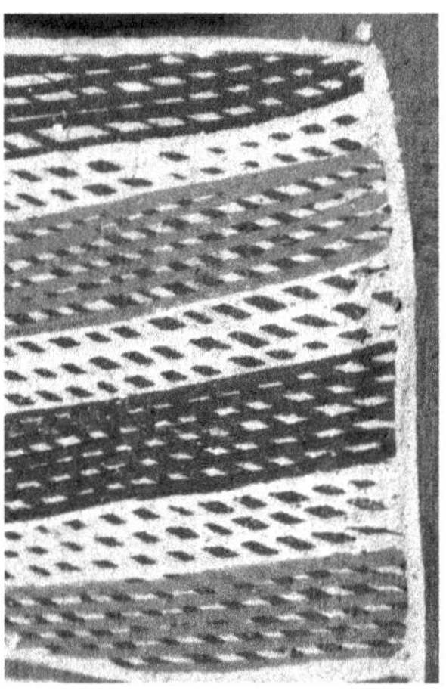

Pl. XIV: Bokarra Maymuru's crosshatching. Photo Howard Morphy.

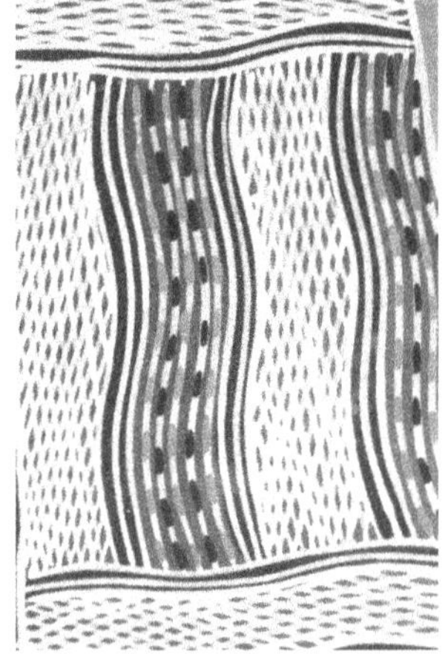

Pl. XV: Banapana Maymuru's crosshatching. Photo Howard Morphy.

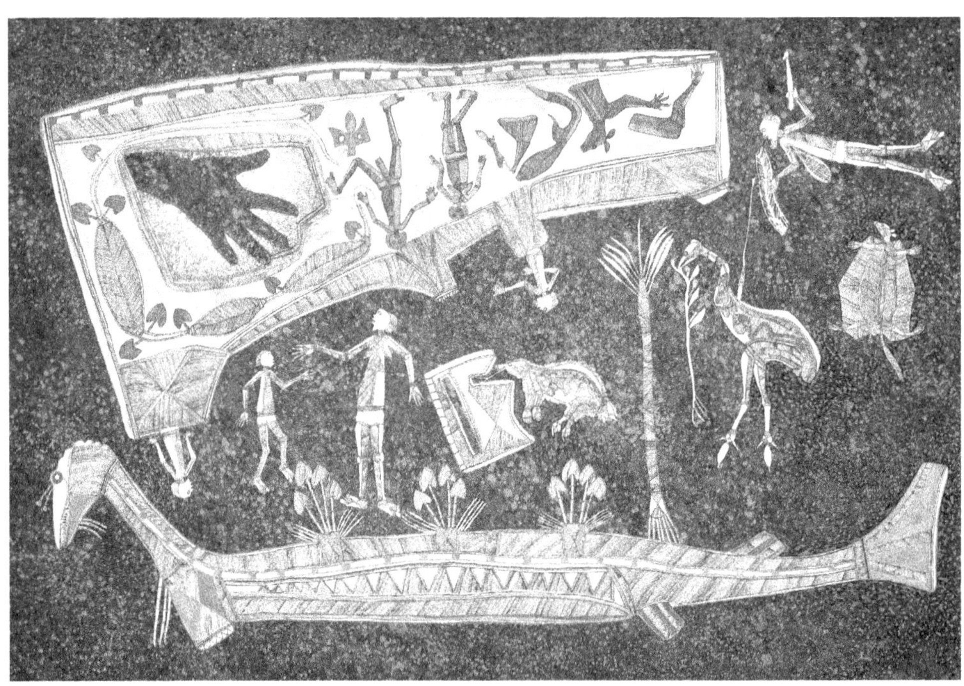

Pl. XVI: Lofty Bardayal Nadjamerrek, *The female rainbow serpent beneath waterlilies in her sacred billabong,* 1991, earth pigments on Arches paper, 100 x 150 cm. The Kluge Ruhe Collection of Australian Aboriginal Art, Virginia, 1991.001.006. © the artist licensed by Aboriginal Artists Agency 2008.

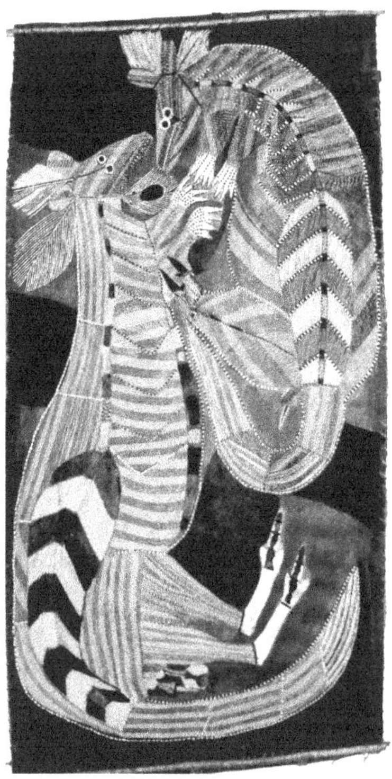

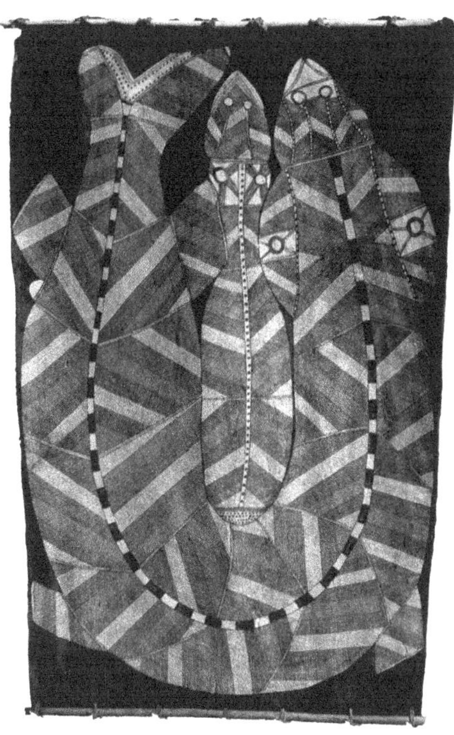

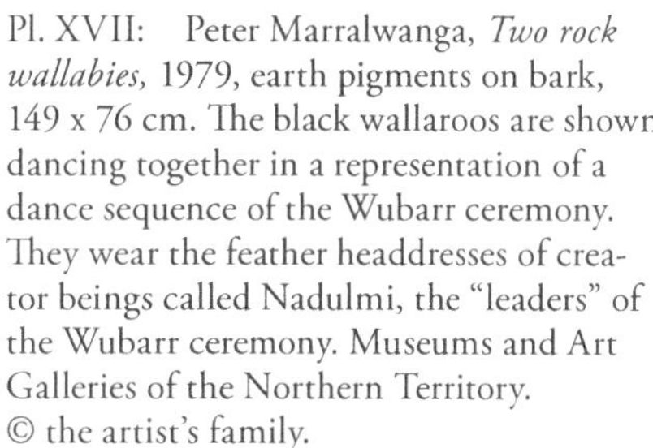

Pl. XVII: Peter Marralwanga, *Two rock wallabies,* 1979, earth pigments on bark, 149 x 76 cm. The black wallaroos are shown dancing together in a representation of a dance sequence of the Wubarr ceremony. They wear the feather headdresses of creator beings called Nadulmi, the "leaders" of the Wubarr ceremony. Museums and Art Galleries of the Northern Territory. © the artist's family.

Pl. XVIII: David Milaybuma, *Yingarna,* 1983, earth pigments on bark [no dim. available]. Yingarna giving birth to the ancestral frog at Kudjidme in his Nadangkorlo clan lands. The frogs are present as large boulders at this site. Yingarna is said to give birth through a hole cut in her side. © the artist's family. Reproduced with permission of Maningrida Arts and Culture.

Captions to Pl. XIII to XV continued from previous page:

Pl. XIII: This segment of the cross hatching represents the body of the lake and Djarrakpi and is particularly intricate even for Narritjin. The lake at Djarrakpi is the source of Manggalili conceptions spirits. At the time, the artist was troubled by the behaviour of some of his sons and by the disruption caused by the mining town of Nhulunbuy. Reflecting on spirit conception he remarked with a sense of irony, 'you never know how the spirits will turn out'.
Pl. XIV: The crosshatching surrounding the figure of a possum illustrates the characteristic density and uniformity of Bokarra's work.
Pl. XV: Banapana's crosshatching is characterised both by the sureness of the line and by the overall brightness of the effect covering large areas with a higher proportion of yellow and white than the other two artists.

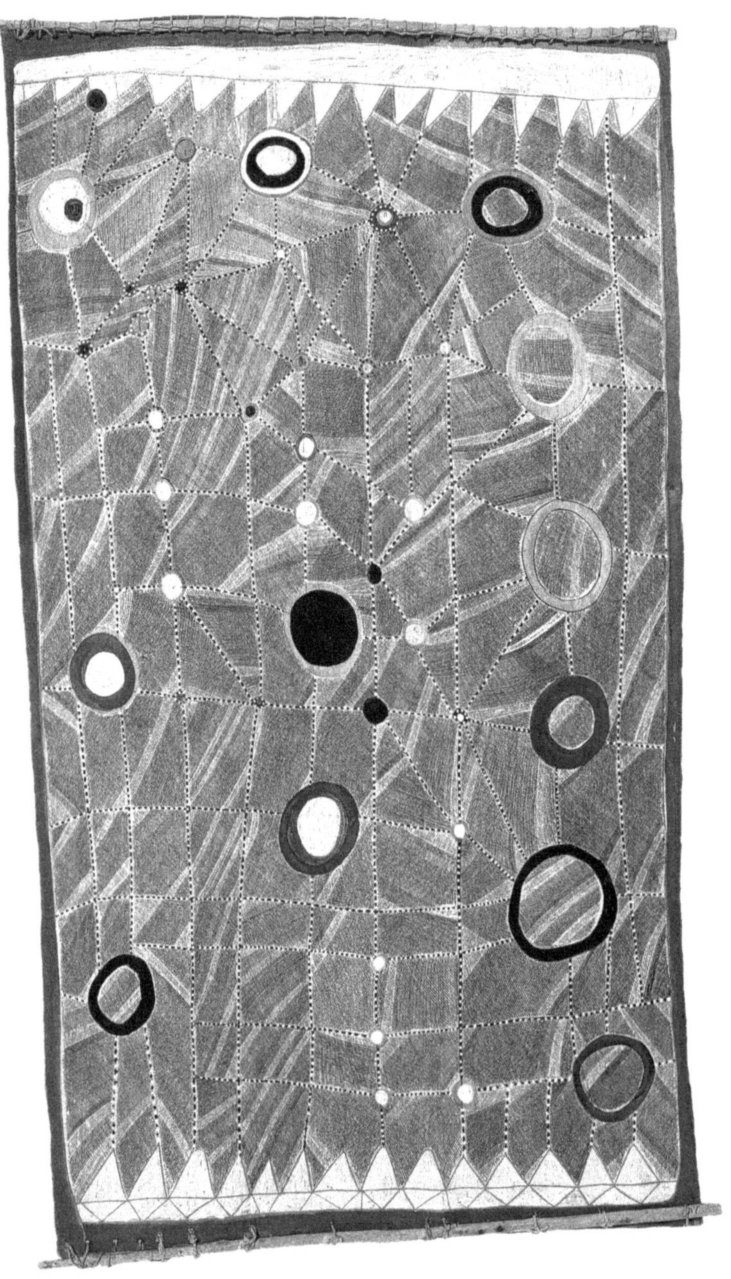

Pl. XIX: John Mawurndjul, *Mardayin ceremony*, 1999, earth pigments on bark, 153 x 88 cm, Laverty Collection, Sydney. ID 1170.

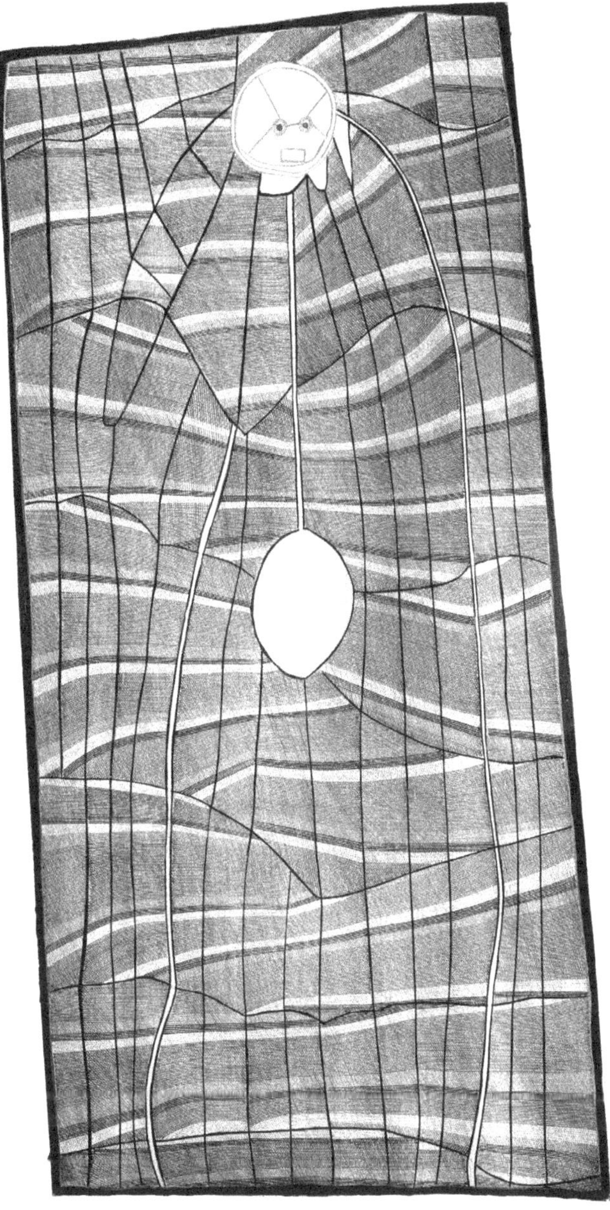

Pl. XX: John Mawurndjul, *Yawkyawk, young girl – waterspirit*, 2005, earth pigments on bark, 154 x 52 cm, Museum der Kulturen Basel. Va 1429. Photo Museum der Kulturen Basel.

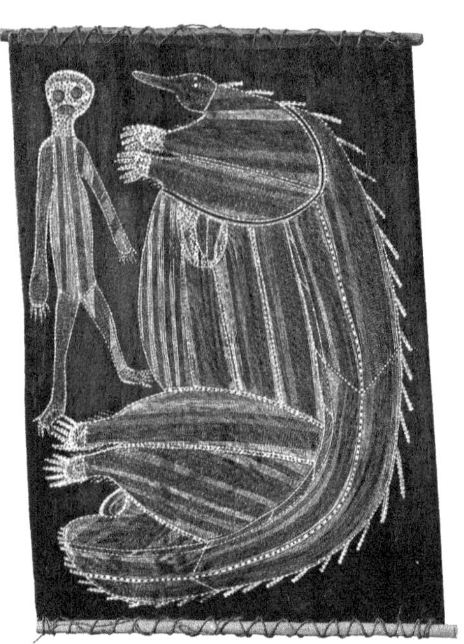

Pl. XXI: John Mawurndjul, *Bambil, echidna and mimih*, 1979, earth pigments on bark, 68 x 46 cm, Jon Altman. Photo Archives of the owner. © 2008, ProLitteris, Zürich.

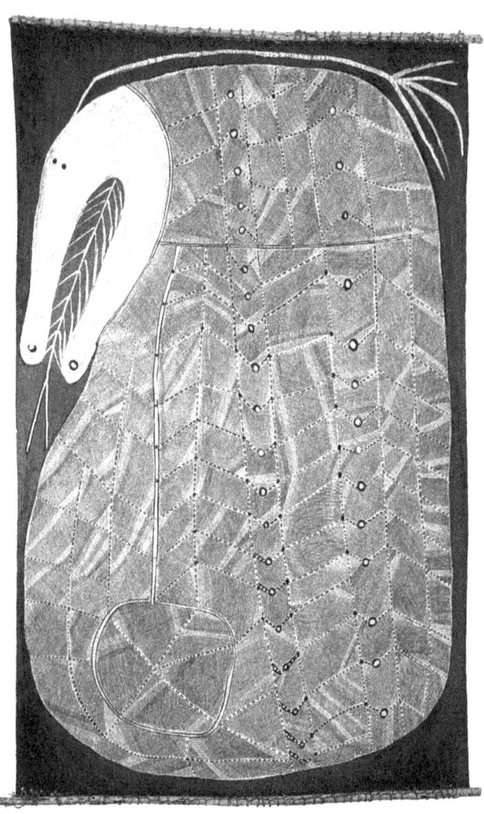

Pl. XXII: John Mawurndjul, *Ngalyod, rainbow serpent*, 1999, earth pigments on bark, 153 x 90 cm, L.A. Moran Collection. Photo Carl Warner. © 2008, ProLitteris, Zürich.

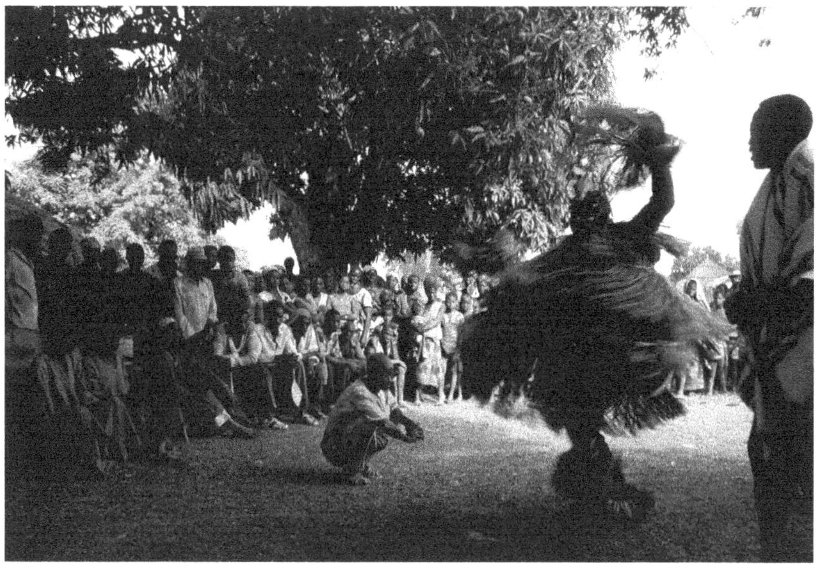

Pl. XXIII: A *korogo* mask performing. This is the work of recent initiates to the ropemakers' secret society. Senufo, Northern Côte d'Ivoire, 1991. Photo Till Förster.

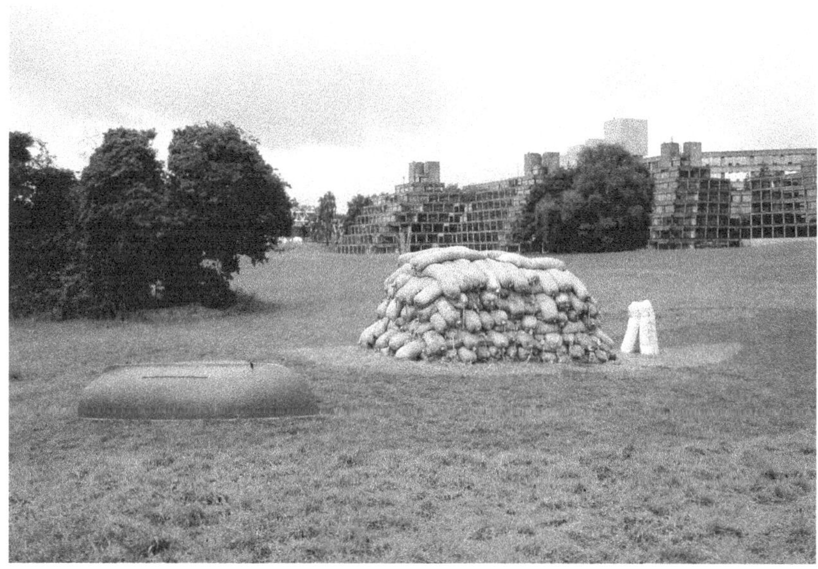

Pl. XXIV: Fiona Foley, *Dandi March, 2005*, rowing boat, 241 khadi bags, salt. Contribution to *Out There,* installation series, summer 2005, University of East Anglia, Norwich. Image courtesy of the artist. Photo Sainsbury Centre for Visual Arts, University of East Anglia, Norwich.

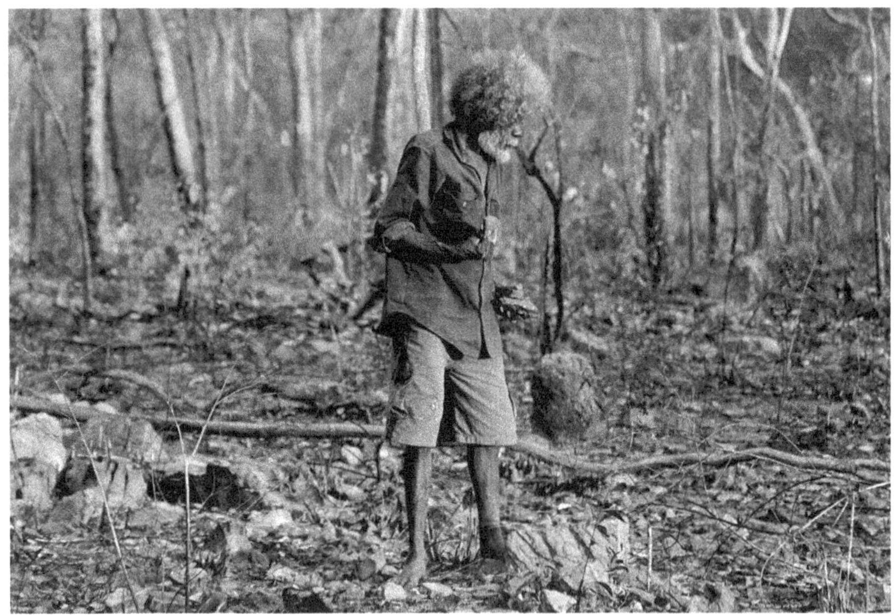

Pl. XXV: John Mawurndjul collecting ochre material for painting at home, 2004 (Detail). Photo Erika Koch.

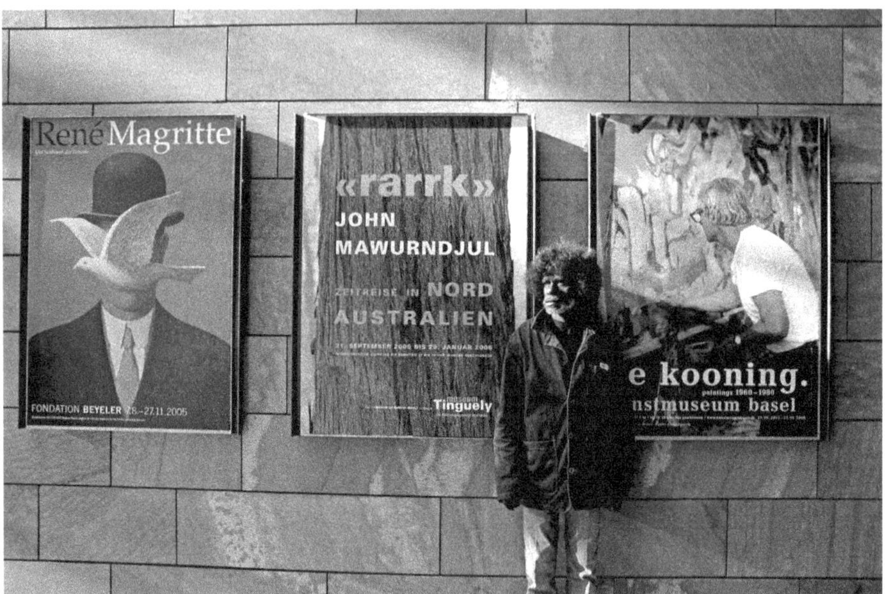

Pl. XXVI: John Mawurndjul in Basel in front of the Museum Tinguely, 2005 (Detail). Photo Erika Koch.

Kitty Zijlmans

Intercultural perspective as context: beyond othering and appropriation? The case of John Mawurndjul

Introduction

Contemporary art from the so-called non-Euro-American world often finds itself in the awkward position of being sandwiched between practices of 'othering' on the one hand and that of appropriation on the other by the various art institutions and media of the international art world. This issue is even more striking in the case of contemporary Aboriginal art, an art practice that draws on a long tradition of representing culture-specific issues and concepts but which, at the same time, reflects upon today's world in present-day contexts and debates. To outsiders, Australia's Aboriginal art is therefore both alien and familiar; in the case of John Mawurndjul, indigenous materials are used and his subject matter reflects his home region of Mumeka but as a form of representation, of communicating a distinct sense of 'world-experience', it opens up to interpretation and evaluation by a wider, international audience including art historians and art critics. Accepting that challenge as an art historian means to discuss and interpret these works as *art* from specific art historical/theoretical frames of reference. Aren't we, by doing so, appropriating these works, discussing them regardless of their cultural background? Or do we need to 'other' this work, not to exoticise it but in order to access it, by taking account of its proper context? Both options and their implications will be discussed in this paper.[1] Is it possible to develop a feasible intercultural perspective that respects the 'own-ness' of the work in question without alienating or assimilating it? The challenge lies in the task of extending the discipline of art history to an intercultural field of art histories.

In this contribution, I will focus predominantly on the exposition of a cross-cultural perspective. I have taken John Mawurndjul's work as my starting point and not as a case study, as the subtitle may suggest. In order to discuss Mawurndjul's work as a case study, I first need a theoretical framework to be able to elaborate fairly on the work, and I hope to present such a framework in this contribution.

---

1 An abridged version of this paper entitled 'An Intercultural Perspective in Art History: Beyond Othering and Appropriation' is published in Elkins, J. (ed.), *Is Art History Global?*, Routledge, London/New York, 2007, pp. 289–298.

Biases

How much one is biased became clear to me when, in 1999, Mieke Bal asked me if I would participate in the PhD reading committee of Gerald McMaster's thesis titled *The New Tribe.*[2] I said yes, being greatly interested to learn more about the subject. I assumed that I was going to read a study on contemporary *Australian* Aboriginal art associating the term 'Aboriginal' immediately and exclusively with Australia. It never even occurred to me that *aboriginal* meant something like 'from the beginning', 'indigenous' 'autochthonous'. The study I was going to read was about Aboriginal contemporary *Canadian* art, from artists we refer to as 'Indian', a denotation McMaster rejects in favour of the emotionally less charged term 'Aboriginal'. I greatly enjoyed reading his thesis, being introduced to Aboriginal contemporary installation art from a country that I have come to know very well over the past 25 years.

Another bias, this time not on my part, surfaced when after the meeting of the committee, another member expressed her surprise at the question I had posed to the candidate. McMaster had discussed the installation works of artists such as Rebecca Belmore (who participated in the 2005 Venice Biennial in the Canadian Pavilion), James Luna (also in Venice in 2005, in the collateral programme, invited by the Smithsonian's National Museum of the American Indian), Edward Poitras, Mary Longman, Shelley Niro and many others. He emphasised how the art works allude to a critical discourse related to issues such as identity, ethnicity, history, mythology, language, stereotyping, marginalisation, but rarely, or hardly at all, to other – perhaps I should say here – Euro-American contemporary art. My question was related to this artistic context and to a critical discourse regarding these art works. My fellow committee member was surprised that I viewed these works primarily as installation art, that is: as one example of this genre, and hence as a work of art in the contemporary context of a global art system. Working from a postcolonial perspective, for her it was an unexpected, even limited, contextualisation; for me as an art historian it was the apparent way of accessing this, or any, art. Not regarding these works as art would have left me bereft of a frame of reference, and me 'jobless'. Was this an act of appropriation?

I would like to discuss here the complex problem of dealing with contemporary art – I use the word 'art' indiscriminately, merely to point out a group of objects that have been attributed a specific valuation (call it art) – contemporary art, then, that stems from cultures that until very recently have not been looked at from the viewpoint of the discipline of art history. My thesis is that art history is indeed equipped and could further provision itself in order to access and understand Aboriginal art. What we need is an intercultural perspective.

2 McMaster, Gerald, *The New Tribe. Critical Perspectives and Practices in Aboriginal Contemporary Art*, PhD thesis, University of Amsterdam, Amsterdam, 1999.

Wrong both ways

Contemporary art from the so-called non-Euro-American world often finds itself in the awkward position of either being neglected completely, or being sandwiched between practices of 'othering' on the one hand, and of 'appropriation' on the other by the various art institutions, media and venues of the international art world. The first option is not an option at all when taking seriously the creative practices of whatever people from whatever place. The other two practices are related to power structures and the institutionalisation of the art world, but at least they make us aware of the fact that the encounter with 'other' art is problematic. Why?

From within the Aboriginal culture that produced the work there is no problem; problems arise when a viewer from outside that particular discourse steps into the debate. I will always remain an outsider where art from a non-Western culture is concerned. I am Caucasian, female, Northern European, academically educated and work at a European university. The subject of my teaching and research is art. Not wanting to sink into the quagmire of the question 'what is art', I plead that art is what is introduced to me as art, by an artist or an art institution. Art is a valuation and is *always* institutionalised; it *always* comes to us mediated through some kind of discourse or institution. This also implies leaving the idea of art relatively open to be defined by the instances, the historical modalities.[3]

Institutionalisation, art as valuation, and globalisation are intrinsically connected to the history of European expansion and domination in the world over the past centuries. Although many of us now look back on these practices very critically,[4] they did shape the world as we know it today. Australia is not an exception to this pattern. The Aboriginal peoples of Australia have lived on the land for over 50,000 years, and only from the 18th century onwards did they come into contact with Europeans; from that moment on Australia started to become Europeanised. In 1606, a Dutch ship spotted the west coast of the continent, but the Dutch were not much interested in such a remote and desolate place. The British however 'discovered' the much more accessible and favourable east coast but initially used it mainly as a place of banishment for its criminals – a fate people, even children, suffered for the slightest offence.[5] At present, the majority of the population is of European, mostly British, descent, and only a mere one percent is Aboriginal. The country is regarded as a Western country; it is a constitutional democracy and a member of the Commonwealth. The Aboriginal peoples are a small minority and their social circumstances contrast sharply with the attention and valuation their art now receives in the international art world.

In a Leiden lecture series on approaches to contemporary art, guest speaker Annette van Ham, curator at the Aboriginal Art Museum in Utrecht, remarked that only since the

---

3 Summers, David, *Real Spaces. World Art History and the Rise of Western Modernism*, Phaidon, London, 2003 and Summers, D., et al., 'The Art Seminar', in Elkins J. (ed.), *Is Art History Global?*, Routledge, London/New York, 2007, pp. 113–175.

4 Mosquera, Gerard, 'The Marco Polo Syndrome. Some Problems around Art and Eurocentrism', in Kocur, Z. and S. Leung (eds.), *Theory in Contemporary Art since 1985*, Blackwell , London, 2005, pp. 218–225.

5 See Hughes, Robert, *The Fatal Shore*, Pan Books, London, 1988.

1970s has Aboriginal art been designated as 'Art' (with a capital A) and hence has become visible, that is, part of an *art system*. Although it is an art practice that belongs to an age-old tradition of bark-, rock- and sand painting, body decoration and rituals – practices which for a long time only in anthropological circles were referred to as art – it only recently became part of the art system and started to be studied from an art historical perspective.

Leaving aside for the moment the economic aspect of a lucrative market, I would like to ask again: is this an act of appropriation? If we consider the international/global art system as being shaped only by the Euro-American art concept, then it is; if we take the art system as a domain that is still fuelled by practices that vary widely in form and content but have as common denominator the way peoples express and give surplus value to their being, it is not. Art is a concept that gives room to a wide scope of practices and interpretations, and it has been co-shaped for centuries by the impetus from various cultures.[6]

This observation, however, does not solve the problem of how to access, in this case, Aboriginal art. The paradox is that either way we approach it, as 'alien' or as 'own', we seem to be biased. Alienating means making Aboriginal art different, and that often means making it less equal or leading it to disregard; not paying attention to its differences, however, ignores the characteristics of this art and de-contextualises it. This would imply: wrong both ways. Nonetheless, we have to proceed. In my opinion as an art historian, which implies being part of the institutionalised art system, we need to both include and 'other' Aboriginal art in order to rate it on its merit.

From Eurocentrism towards art histories

Rating Aboriginal art at its true value, though, is not an easy thing to accomplish – for what does it mean? In his article *The Marco Polo Syndrome*, Gerardo Mosquera, adjunct curator at the New Museum of Contemporary Art in New York, critiques the attempts to overcome the problem of Eurocentrism and Western domination. For him, "Eurocentrism is the only ethnocentrism universalised through actual world-wide domination by a meta-culture, and based on a traumatic transformation of the world through economic, social and political processes centred in one small part of it."[7]

Despite the Western world's growing self-critique, Mosquera still observes the perpetuation of the distortion that is produced by the West's one-sided (unilateral) perspective and the existing circuits of power. If Third World cultures (Mosquera's typification) want to take part in today's dynamics they should not isolate themselves in traditions, but instead – so Mosquera argues – make traditions work within the new epoch by vigorously adapting them, by making contemporary art from their own values, sensitivities and interests. According to him, de-Eurocentrism in art is not about returning to purity, but

---

6 See Araeen, Rasheed, 'A New Beginning: Beyond Postcolonial Cultural Theory and Identity Politics', in Araeen, R., Cubitt, S. and S. Ziauddin (eds.), *The Third Text Reader, on Art, Culture and Theory*, Continuum, London/New York, 2002, pp. 333–345.

7 Mosquera, G., 2005, in Kocur, Z. and S. Leung (eds.), *op. cit.*, p. 219.

about adopting postcolonial 'impurity' in order for cultures outside the West to express themselves. This would result in a syncretistic, contemporary culture that in each case connects to various contexts, be they local, national or international. Art for him, and I agree, is linked to cultural specificity but possesses a polysemic ambiguity open to diverse readings. He proposes that the West should take an equally pluralistic view of its *own* art, and, by doing so, revise Western culture. For Mosquera, intercultural involvement implies a critical evaluation of art practices from both sides. Intercultural communication includes not only seeing but also listening.[8]

What Mosquera is pointing at in his critique is the cultural asymmetry implied. The West set the standard, and the Rest could either adapt, or was traditionalised and exoticised in institutional settings such as ethnographic museums. Mosquera critiques the apparent obviousness of this standard as well as its claim of being entirely of Western descent.

I tend to agree with Mosquera that the idea of a purely 'Western' art setting the standard is a misrepresentation of such a multifarious complex as the prevailing international art scape. For centuries art has been fed by a diversity of cultural sources and impulses, and it can never be tracked down to one single point of origin. We cannot however un-write the art history that has been written, nor deny Western Europe's significance for the emergence of the modern art concept as we know it today. What we can do, and what has already been happening for the past decade, is re-evaluating *how* art history was written and questioning *why* it happened in such a way, and subsequently re-interpret the past from a multicultural perspective and work towards the writing of art histor*ies*, of systematic as well as historical studies on the entire scope of art. As a point of departure, two issues are important: first, to take art as a panhuman property, and second, to take into account art's openness to diverse readings and generation of meanings. I will now elaborate somewhat on these matters.

Art is a specific form of making the world your own, of acquiring, getting hold of the world (in German *Weltaneignung*), and we do that by creating symbols. The use of symbols is a unique characteristic of humans and therefore art can be seen as a panhuman expression.[9] Turning to the second point, a work of art never has just one meaning attached to only one context; that would make it either a historical documentation, or mere decoration. A key characteristic of art is that it opens up to (new) interpretations time and again. Otherwise it would be a self-contained ontological entity, enclosing its one and only meaning and denying both the interpreter's share in the generating of meaning as well as the role of changing contexts in the interpretation of art. To paraphrase Norman Bryson, art works have a potential of meaning that is generated by different frames. Context, or as he proposes a 'frame', is not naturally given but something that we as researchers make.[10] My frame relates to an intercultural perspective.

---

8 Mosquera, G., 2005, in Kocur, Z. and S. Leung (eds.), *op. cit.*, pp. 221–223.

9 Kaiser, Franz-W., *Kunst Wirklichkeit. Untersuchung von Arten der Weltaneignung*, PhD thesis, University of Leiden, Leiden, 2006 [publication forthcoming].

10 Bryson, Norman, 'Art in Context', in Bal, M. and I. E. Boer, *The Point of Theory. Practices of Cultural Analysis*, Amsterdam University Press, Amsterdam, 1994, pp. 66–78.

Intercultural perspective

How do the above-stated arguments help us to formulate an intercultural, or cross-cultural, perspective? I understand the term 'intercultural' as in the Latin meaning of 'inter amicos', among friends: 'inter culturas', among cultures. As a strategy that relates to a diversity of art forms and cultures, an intercultural perspective consequently is based upon a multidisciplinary approach. It addresses art history, philosophy, anthropology, language and culture studies, sociology, even bio-evolutionary and neuroscience. No researcher covers the entire field of academic disciplines alone; rather, we participate in it, each starting from his/her own expertise. Consequently, the research starts with the researcher's clarification from which perspective he or she is operating. Thus, 'showing your colours' makes clear where you come from, academically as well as personally, what position one takes and what the aim of the research is. It makes equally clear that conclusions drawn from the research are expertise-bound, and therefore limited in scope, relative and not absolute, but all the more dynamic.

Thus, for me, key issues for the formulation of an intercultural perspective with a strong art historical, i.e. art theoretical (in German: *kunstwissenschaftlich*) emphasis centre on the following concepts that I will now briefly discuss – there is no hierarchy in this listing, nor is it exhaustive:

1. World art studies. The concept is taken from John Onians, who was the first to use this term to open up the study of art history to a global scale.[11] At Leiden University we have adopted John's phrasing, and World Art Studies is now used to designate a field of study that covers contingent art histor*ies* (of the 'non-Western' world)[12] and, at the same time, aims at developing the concepts and approaches to an integrated, i.e., multidisciplinary study of art, as a panhuman phenomenon.[13] The two strategies do not exclude each other; rather, they keep in balance the 'inclusion/othering' dichotomy.

2. Inclusion and othering. I connect the two by taking seriously what has been presented to me as art – however unfamiliar the works may seem – and thus include it into my research; at the same time I remain aware of the 'own-ness' or 'otherness' respectively of the art works. Thus, including/othering are two sides of one and the same coin. 'Othering' implies connecting art to its cultural background; one of the accesses to a work of art is via its cultural background that can play either a larger or smaller role. Hence, 'other' artistic practices are incorporated and by doing so, art history is revised and extended at the same time.

11 Onians, John, 'World Art Studies and the Need for a New Natural History of Art', *Art Bulletin* 78 (2), 1996, pp. 206–209.

12 Van Damme, Wilfried, *Beauty in Context. Towards an Anthropological Approach to Aesthetics*, E. J. Brill, Leiden, 1996.

13 Zijlmans, K. and W. van Damme (eds.), *World Art Studies. Exploring Concepts and Approaches* [forthcoming, Amsterdam].

3. Cultural diversity and syncretism. We all share culture but the (concept of) culture differs greatly, or rather, the term 'culture' is used in various ways and contexts. It is not just connected to a people, a tribe or a nation, but also to a metropolis, specific areas or provinces, to social stratification, specific groups or scenes, and the like. The one word covers a plethora of meanings and attributions, so we have to handle the notion of culture with care. What, for example, is meant by John Mawurndjul being an Australian Aboriginal artist? His social and cultural background is related to an Indigenous people of Australia, but this matters, I would argue, only when connection to that context is made by the art works themselves. In the case of John Mawurndjul this is obvious, and hence relevant. However, it does not make Mawurndjul or his work a synecdoche; it still matters how his work relates to this, and other contexts. I will come back to this later. The other term I mentioned, syncretism, refers to the assumption that in the course of time all cultures (I almost hesitate to use the word) in one way or another have been influenced and changed by intercultural contacts and exchange, which makes them syncretistic. This is an ongoing and therefore dynamic process. International contemporary art is a powerful example for syncretism, John Mawurndjul's work may prove to be far less so.

4. Centre/periphery. The centre/periphery model is taken as a flexible one. There is no fixed centre, the centre is (or in historical research, was) where the action is (was), seen from the perspective of the art in question. In some (many?) cases, the West may well be only the periphery. The centre/periphery view also applies to the canon. An intercultural perspective rejects the idea of a fixed canon, it is neither static in space nor in time.

5. Frames and contexts. Different framings will produce different readings, different interpretations. To determine what the relevant context is in which to study an art work is one of art history's most demanding problems. Art historical research mostly deals with historical topics. The historical past as such is gone, leaving behind all sorts of material objects, texts and data. To determine what facts, historical events and aspects are significant largely depends on what the researcher is aiming to elucidate. This applies to research into the past as well as to that of the present. Apart from being aware of one's own practices of framing, the research has to critically evaluate the existing discourse (framings) on the subject, to trace norms and values behind it, and take into account possible cultural differences.[14]

6. Role of technique and materials. Art comes as a material and is created by a technique; obvious as they are, these aspects are often overlooked as agents for the production of meaning in both creation and interpretative practices.[15]

---

14 Schipper, Mineke, *Beyond the Boundaries. African Literature and Literary Theory*, W.H. Allen, London, 1989.

15 See Wagner, Monika, *Das Material der Kunst. Eine andere Geschichte der Moderne*, Beck, München, 2001; and Westgeest, Helen, 'Identity and Materiality – Cultural Studies in Artistic Practice', in Coumans, A. and H. Westgeest (eds.), *The Reflexive Zone: Research into Theory in Practice*, School of the Arts, Utrecht, 2004, pp. 188–201.

7. Materiality versus immateriality. In his dissertation entitled *Condensed Reality*, the anthropologist Pieter ter Keurs of the National Museum of Ethnology in Leiden emphasises the importance of the study of material culture, that is to say: the materiality of the objects, in his case from two small island groups in Papua New Guinea and Indonesia. He understands the mere material presence of an object as a cultural fact and introduces the concept of 'material complex'. For ter Keurs, a material complex is a "material object with the meanings condensed in it or evaporated from it";[16] it refers to the object and its socially constructed meanings.[17] The subject's activities towards the creation or construction of meaning condense into the material object but, in the course of time, again evaporate from it due to changing contexts and functions; in the course of the process it will have new meanings attributed to it. In ter Keurs' view, "the subject is changing in the way it deals with objects and (…), although the physical object seems to remain the same, the material complex (the material object and the ideas *condensed* in and *evaporated* from it) is also changing."[18] In my opinion, Pieter ter Keurs' idea of material objects as metaphors, as condensation cores for ideas, concepts and values in culture, addresses both the material object as such and the subjects' part (maker and recipients) in the generation of meaning, as well as the changes that occur over time.[19] He stresses the importance of studying the materiality of the object together with the processes of condensation and evaporation of meaning This is also a very useful approach to works of art. While art works are often seen as 'concepts', the potential of the art work's materiality in the production of meaning is often underestimated.

8. Art History. Last, but certainly not least, there is the body of approved art historical methods and concepts. In my opinion, every art work can be subjected to a formal analysis, placed in relationship to other works, either from the past (diachronic) or from the present (synchronic), from its 'own' culture as well as from others, and, as long as it is relevant to do so, be appraised for its stylistic quality, eloquence and power of expression, for its technical skill, mastery of the materials, even aesthetics. In order to do so, one needs to be fully informed and aware of one's own point of departure (in my case art history) and biases; only then can we contribute to the discourse, by sharing our knowledge, perception and insight.

Concluding remarks

I am not an expert on Aboriginal Australian art; the art works I have seen were in ethnographic and art museums, such as the Aboriginal Art Museum in Utrecht, and in art gal-

16 Keurs, P. ter, *Condensed Reality. A Study of Material Culture, with Case Studies from Siassi (Papua New Guinea) and Enggano (Indonesia)*. PhD thesis, University of Leiden, CNWS Publications, Leiden, 2006, p. 70.

17 Ibid., p. 201.

18 Ibid., p. 195.

19 Ibid., p. 205.

leries; additional information I have acquired from television (e.g. the 1990 documentary *The Quest of Jimmy Pike*, an artist from the Walmajarri), through the internet (723 hits on John Mawurndjul alone!), specialist literature and through books such as Bruce Chatwin's *The Songlines* [1987], that I really enjoyed reading, or the *The Fatal Shore* [1988] by Robert Hughes, who recounts the gruesome fate of a large number of convicted men, women and children that were shipped from Great Britain to Australia between 1787 and 1868. Of course I am influenced by this knowledge, and it plays a role when looking at John Mawurndjul's art, all the more so because it is contemporary traditional Aboriginal art. The two terms 'contemporary' and 'traditional' do not contradict each other, nor are they meant as valuation but merely as position markers: the works are produced now, in the present, and they show to a certain extend some traditional ways, techniques and iconography of a particular Australian Indigenous artist. To acquire insight into his work, his position in the Australian as well as in the international art world, I need to proceed in the way I have outlined above. There are many questions to be asked, leading to many answers that need thorough discussion from changing viewpoints. An intercultural perspective, hence, is a dynamic way of learning, of acquiring access to unfamiliar art works. The final question with regard to the right approach boils down to the basic question that David Summers posed in a recent discussion: does it work?

Further Reading

Bal, Mieke, *Travelling Concepts in the Humanities. A Rough Guide*, University of Toronto Press, Toronto, 2002.

Dissanayake, Ellen, *Homo Aestheticus: Where Art Comes From and Why*, University of Washington Press, Seattle, 1992.

International Journal of Anthropology, Vol. 18 (4), 2003 (Special issue on the conceptualisation of World Art Studies).

Onians, J. (ed.), *Atlas of World Art*, Laurence King, London, 2004.

Tacon, Paul S. C., 'Indigenous Modernism: Betwixt and Between or at the Cutting Edge of Contemporary Art', *Bulletin of the Conference of Museum Anthropologists* 27, 1996, pp. 33–55.

Zijlmans, K., 'Pushing Back Frontiers: Towards a History of Art in a Global Perspective', *International Journal of Anthropology* 18 (4), 2003, pp. 201–210.

Zijlmans, K., 'East West Home's Best. Cultural Identity in the Present Nomadic Age / East West Home's Best. Masalah Identitas Budaya dalam Era Nomad, Kini' in Ang, T., Ekel, F., Jaarsma, M. and R. Jungerman (eds.), *GRID, a Collaborative Project between the Artists Tiong Ang, Fendry Ekel, Mella Jaarsma, Remy Jungerman*, Cemeti Art House, Yogyakarta, 2003, pp. 81–88.

Anne-Marie Bonnet

Dilemmata of otherness

To speak at a cross-cultural symposium on Australian Indigenous art makes me feel somewhat fraudulent since, I must confess, I am in no way a specialist on Aboriginal art.[1] Am I outing myself as one of those Western people in search of exoticism, primitivism, and difference? Why? What for? Speaking as an European art historian have I any chance of not being seen as having a colonial perspective, as being an accomplice in a process of dispossession or 'otherisation' or 'de-otherisation', depending on the point of view? Is there a way out of the hierarchy implicit in the dichotomy between me and the 'other', between a Western and a non-Western contribution to cultural interaction? Is there a possibility of turning the tables; why can't the addressing one be the other? The first time I started reading about Aboriginal culture, it was indeed its difference to my own that attracted me: the other concept of time, of relationships/parentage, the role of myth and so on. In no way did I feel superior or more civilized, on the contrary, I felt poor, small, restricted and realised the one-sidedness and specificity of my own structures.

The vertigo of the unknown, of loosing reference marks attracted me: I was at loss with my usual tools. The more I read, the more it retained its otherness, and that was the attractive and incentive aspect.

I would like to be able to approach foreign/other/ also non-Western cultures without being blamed, or feeling guilty, without feeling like an aggressor, as doing violence to the approached 'other'. Why is my approach bound to be discriminating? In the aftermath of post-structuralism and postcolonial studies we have learnt that each approach constructs its object, that there is no naive belief in some kind of innocence or objectivity: But is there a way out of dualism or subject/object relationships into one of exchange between equals? Must there always be a hierarchy of gender, language, class or nation? Colonialism has meant the transformation of an Indigenous culture into a subordinate culture (Olu

1 The following text is mainly kept in the form of a 'speech'; it is more a report on a work in progress, articulating more doubts and asking questions than rendering firm statements or being a finished theoretical essay. I decided to leave it in its process-oriented form. I want to thank Seán Shanahan for his patience and concern while thinking and writing this essay and Christian Kaufmann for the helpful editorial rearrangement.

Oguibe):[2] Can't postcolonial approaches generate new modes, new forms of encounter or exchange? There have been lots of discourses and reflections about the models of interaction between cultures, we have all heard of contamination, hybridisation, syncretism, critical appropriation, etc. Is there no escape from the model of the so-called 'authoritative observer' that disempowers, victimises or dehumanises the 'observed'?[3] Here and now?

In the context of this interdisciplinary symposium I wish to ask what the specific contribution of art history could be? But first I want to make clear that I distinguish between academic, university-bound art history and its institutional/museological counterpart, the former being less dependent on representational/curatorial concerns, and maybe also freer from the art market's or collectors' interests.

I would like to try the experiment of an approach where the 'other' encounters the art historian, unrestricted by hierarchical positions: how can the 'contact zone'[4] between the two be conceptualised beyond the 'power-mode'?[5] In this contribution I will ask more questions than I can provide answers to, this is still a work in progress, an experiment. I will try to propose parameters for a dialogue (as an art historian, not from a sociological, ethnographic or political perspective) to get closer to Aboriginal art. I'm here to learn ...

It is an approach in three steps:
The first brings me, I hope, as close as possible to the art of John Mawurndjul. In a second step I would like to say a few critical words to current trends in art history, and in a third step I would like to discuss the multiple modes of otherness and the need to reconstruct the views of our discipline accordingly.

2 Oguibe, Olu, *The Culture Game*, University of Minnesota Press, Minneapolis, 2004.

3 Mosquera, Gerardo et al. (eds.), *Over Here: International Perspectives on Art and Culture*, New Museum of Contemporary Art New York, Documentary Sources in Contemporary Art, Vol. 6, The MIT Press, Cambridge (Mass.), 2004, pp. 106–107.

4 Papastergiadis, Nikos, 2004, 'The Limits of Cultural Translation', in Mosquera, G. et al. (eds.), *op. cit.*, p. 336.

5 By 'power mode' I mean the usual art historical approach to art (management of meaning) in which art works are used to show how bright one is, or to illustrate some preconceived theory of imagery or aesthetics, or to argue against a colleague, etc. This kind of art history I once qualified as a 'bachelor's machine', as it is used mainly to retain a safe distance to the work of art, or to tame it, to keep its specific qualities (non-rational bewilderment, etc.) under the control of hermeneutics. Like Duchamp's bachelor who never touched the bride and found a solitary onanistic solace; in the same way most art history is autistic, establishing the rules of approach in advance and only looking for illustration or confirmation of its own intellectual prejudices. Instead of recognising the challenge by, and through, art practices that deal with the world in their own specific terms that demand mediation, not interpretation (in the sense of colonisation by de-otherisation).

What is the specific otherness of Aboriginal art/images/works?

What is my specific otherness[6] in view of Aboriginal art[7]? How do we construct our differences? What for?

Usually one is first fascinated by the idea of the Dreaming and it's obvious otherness, until one realises that it is an invention of early Western anthropologists and archaeologists, a projection[8] of their idea of otherness, 'primeval wilderness' or 'archaic thinking'. This tells more about Western expectations and otherisation mechanisms than it does about the specificity of Australian visual culture/art.

The most fascinating aspect, apart from the visual/aesthetic pleasure that flows from the alterity of Aboriginal art works, is to realise that they cannot be approached and easily decrypted by the usual tools (stylistic or iconographic methods), their language and means of expression having a totally different agency of form/content and conveyance of meaning. Here the modes of dealing with the world are obviously different from the intellectual rationalisations of Western culture. Judith Ryan believes the attraction of Aboriginal art is lodged in its aesthetics and iconographic otherness: its iconographic system is at variance with the Western one, manifesting a different thought mode, belief and view of the world, all signs incorporating multiple levels and ways to be read or interpreted. Meaning is based on a system of symbols and signs, the use of which is restricted to certain persons in certain circumstances. The information is contained on different levels of worldly, sacred and secret knowledge.[9]

Possibly one of the first qualities of otherness in visual productions by Aborigines is the 'steadiness' and continuity. These visual products relate to age and tradition, they seem to be close to an art practice that goes back 40,000 years. In times of accelerated cultural shifts and mixes, of loosening one's territorial affiliation, 'traditional' Aboriginal works seem to incorporate the "discrete, stable, coherent and unique", to convey a "clear self-image and present a distinctive worldview"[10] and to have a contemporaneity the long past

---

6 Ryan, Judith, 'Kunst der Aborigines Australiens: Andersartigkeit oder Ähnlichkeit?', in Lüthi, B. (ed.), *A<u>r</u>atjara – Kunst der ersten Australier: traditionelle und zeitgenössische Werke der Aborigines und Torres Strait Islanders*, Du Mont Verlag, Köln, 1993, pp. 49–64.

7 In the impressive *A<u>r</u>atjara* catalogue, in which the problems of postcolonial approach to Aboriginal art are reflected on, the authors speak mainly about works, and Judith Ryan reminds us that: "Although the art of the Aborigines originally was made out of a specific demand or collateral product of colonisation and growing contacts between whites and blacks, it nevertheless gives the producers a means of expression and recognition and has become a means for social equity." Ryan, 1993, in Lüthi, B. (ed.), *op. cit.*, p. 49.

8 After William Rubin's *Primitivism* exhibition, the debates with McEvilley and also the famous *Magiciens de la terre* exhibition there were many discussions about the primitive, the tribal, etc. in art, and we learned that most concepts are seen as discriminating, as Western projections, as taxonomies within a hegemonic, colonial approach, and that they use exoticisation or folklorisation, etc. But over the last 20 years, globalisation and postcolonial discourses have taught us to look for the marks of differentiation and many non-Western thinkers and artists have entered the discussion forum.

9 Ryan, J., 1993, in Lüthi, B. (ed.), *op. cit.*, pp. 50– 51.

10 Papastergiadis, N., 2004, in Mosquera, G. et al. (eds.), *op. cit.*, p. 330.

of which is still vivid. Are there different forms of contemporaneity in Aboriginal art, for instance in urban practices by Aborigines (see below).

Aborigines' works obviously convey beliefs, values, mythologies, have spiritual, psychic, psychological and physical dimensions, and are embedded in a holistic process of cultural identity and mnemonic functions. They have holistic qualities for communities, which Western works and practices lack: does this view possibly reflect a projection of nostalgia[11] in Western society that is based on individuation and in which culture has become specialised, diversified and atomised into micro- and sub-systems and socio-topes and which is constantly adjusting to the quickly changing demands from the art world?

Western culture and art are familiar with the proliferation of symbols and systems within which micro-groups communicate. But Aboriginal art too is not homogenous and there are several 'Australialities'/Aboriginalities (depending on geographic location and/or the community the art belongs to) but they seem less idiosyncratic. This art seems to have resisted the disempowerment of colonisation, to have saved earlier forms of knowledge and to be able to "to reinscribe the narrative of solidarity and unity" (John Mawurndjul) or it may even "present new cultural symbols and practices through which individuals come to understand their position in the world"[12] (see Pam Johnston below).

A very special renegotiation of tradition and modernity appears to be accomplished in Aboriginal art practices. I do not wish to evaluate this accomplishment by taking Western modernity as the benchmark of human progress and saying that the 'other' lives in its own present (Papastergiadis). We all share the same presence and contemporaneity, even if we express them differently (no scale, no hierarchy): there are multiple modernities. No one is more 'modern' than the other; we may have, or live, different modernities, the specificity of each can only be lived/felt/thought in relation to the other, without hierarchy or prejudice. What strikes me in Aboriginal visual/art practices is the different quality of distilling present and past. Why should Western 'hypermodernity'[13] (consumerist, pluralist, materialist, perverted by the market etc.) be the measure of all things? I do not believe the 'other' – here I mean the Aboriginal person – "can only speak with authority about his or her own past."[14] And I do not approach it out of dissatisfaction with my own culture, modernity or whatever, in search of purer, more authentic, original ways or modes.

No work – including Western ones – can be hermeneutically rationally explained and colonised; one can only translate it, offer approaches to it. With Aboriginal art works this seems to be even more the case; their art reminds us especially of the otherness of art. This may be so because they seem to have been less 'pasteurised' or 'domesticated' by commodification – the fine arts industry – and globalisation.

11 This is not meant as pure regression or as a legitimate strategy for the search of lost origins, or even as a 'noble' expression of nostalgia … to find something in the 'savage ' present of the other (Papastergiadis, N., 2004, in Mosquera, G. et al. (eds.), *op. cit.*, p. 332).

12 Ibid., p. 331.

13 Jimenez, Marc, *La querelle de l'art contemporain*, Editions Gallimard, Paris, 2005.

14 "… while the Western artist is imbued with the melancholy privilege of living in the present. It is this burden of dissatisfaction with modernity that spurs the search for its own innocent origins in the "Other"." Papastergiadis, N., 2004, in Mosquera, G. et al. (eds.), *op. cit.*, p. 332.

In fact, one should distinguish between 'contemporary art' that already has become institutionalised and acknowledged, and which has gone though the filter of the art world, and 'actual art'; in other words, the art, which is actually, really in the making.[15] In the symposium programme we read "in Australian terms" and "contemporary Australian Aboriginal art": what are 'Australian terms" and what does 'contemporary' mean? Who decides about contemporaneity? Who means what with 'art'? Where? When? What for? Do other modes of continuation/transformation of bark paintings or 'abstraction' exist, beyond John Mawurndjul's approach? What does 'abstraction' mean in the Aboriginal system of signs and symbols that has a different and specific way of dealing with mimesis and/or representation?

Let's take a look at a few examples of different forms of 'contemporaneity'/ 'contemporaneities', for example at a performance of *The Darlinghurst Syndrome* by Fletcher Jetspree at Green Park, Darlinghurst, in 1995,[16] or at a graffiti (a visual memory by Woolloomooloo residents of Edison Berrio, murdered by the Sydney Police during the Olympic Games) in Woolloomooloo, which is felt as an important form of expression for the dispossessed, "a method of reclaiming power" (Pam Johnston);[17] or think of the works of Tracey Moffat. The performance artist, inscribing and weaving his own history[18] into a specific urban site, the graffiti artists in Woolloomooloo, and Pam Johnston (who, for instance, gives trees[19] to children, exactly their size, in order for them to grow together) are conscious community artists (others include Jo Darbyshire, Owen Kelly, Marla Guppy). By appropriating international art forms they purposely articulate issues and aspects of current Aboriginal, urban contingencies. As Pam Johnston explains, the graffiti artists in Woolloomooloo get arrested for their graffiti because their works are not perceived as fine art. They are the forms of expression of a certain generation that are not on the gallery circuit, in other words, outside the institutional culture. Are they less art for that? This is certainly true of graffiti all over the world, but maybe inscribing sites has a longer and deeper significance in Aboriginal culture. Just think of the art on the walls of the rock shelters in John Mawurndjul's country under which people lived during the wet season. How can these forms of artistic expression be recognised as art, without becoming fine art and entering a "process of dispossession, a form of colonisation, in which artists are complicit?"[20]

---

15 In that sense see also Jimenez, M., 2005, *op. cit.*, p. 327.

16 Darlinghurst (New South Wales): "He moved around the park accompanied by his own words ... stopped and stalked, yelled, he named and owned every inch of that park and the surroundings with his own words, they told his story, his life ..", after Pam Johnston, in Mosquera, G. et al. (eds.), *op. cit.*, p. 106.

17 Johnston, P., 2004, in Mosquera, G. et al. (eds.), *op. cit.*, p. 108.

18 "That performance in the park was the first time, apart from Aboriginal ceremonies, that I heard a human memory weave itself into the landscape in which we were surrounded. ... In that performance there was an owning of a place, of an identity – a naming of the often invisible that is usually only interpreted by an authoritative observer." Pam Johnston, ibid.

19 Johnston, P., 2004, in Mosquera, G. et al. (eds.), *op. cit.*, p. 114.

20 Ibid.

Tracey Moffat refuses to make reference to Australian or Aboriginal roots, wanting 'only' to be an international artist; maybe because she thinks of fine art as being a better category? Maybe her point is to avoid becoming fine art herself, of retaining the specificity and real significance of her work? The fact that Aboriginal cultures continue to have a special link to time and their own history and that they are still being dispossessed by the drama of 'fine artisation' is quite obvious. But isn't this one of the topoi of every modern art, the fear of having lost its link to real life and authenticity (isn't this a formulation for refusing the de-otherisation in one's own culture?), while, at the same time, striving to be a real, true and authentic expression of life? In the end, isn't fine art in Western culture the commodification of otherness, the taming of a specific disturbing alterity, the essential difference of dealing with the world that all art forms convey?

The problem lies not in the visual products, the art forms or the practices themselves but in the ways and structures by which they are turned into fine art, according to standards established by institutions.[21] We all know the institutions – often we are part of them ourselves – which are driven by their own interests (of control, distribution, profit). It's very easy to forget the cause, and to cause only the effect.

This leads me to the second point that I am interested in as art historian.

What is the subject of art history?

Is it 'art and visual culture' or mere 'imagery', so-called image-science?[22] Replacing an 'art history'[23] approach to non-Western art by the so-called *Bildwissenschaft*-approach does not promise more tolerance or less prejudice towards objects from other cultures. It is just another construction created by Western gatekeepers of art history to retain control over the discourses that now run on a global scale. The concept of *Bild* (image) in German is such an unspecific concept/category that it seems open and liberal: it's only an instrument of discourse.

What other modes of approach are there? Last but not least: if art historians only speak of 'images', who is going to be responsible for art? The 'art world', stronger and more powerful than ever? If we neglect or avoid dealing with the concept of art, how can differences be established in the broad field of visual culture? What art is or can be has been changed profoundly, not only by modernity but also markedly by contemporary art practices, that no longer just represent the continuation of a history of transgressions or herald the arrival of the 'new'. In the last thirty years other aspects have been at stake in the art field: it is no longer about the limits and the mapping of the fields of creation but rather "about the

21 Like the art market, art history, etc.

22 This is a short 'aside' focused on German academic art history, which in certain respects aims at giving up the concern for art, and concentrates on 'images' and visual products only.

23 Even in Western culture, what 'art' is has always to be defined; the concept has a long and multi-layered history which is in danger of being given up. For example, in 'Western culture' things were turned into art, which, in their essence, were not art when they were made – altar paintings, for instance, now in museums – and, since DADA and Duchamp, and later Pop Art, everyday objects can become art (high and low).

inadequacy of traditional concepts of art, work, artist to realities to which they obviously no longer fit/correspond."[24]

I am also rather sceptical about the new trend of so-called anthropological approaches favoured by certain art historians. What does this mean? What anthropological means is very vague and I am diffident of this kind of ahistorical generic humanism. Are we not all just human beings? I fear that the so-called anthropological turn in art history might bring on new essentialisations.[25] The same people who declared the end of history – for whatever reason – now propagate 'anthropology', another facade or camouflage of WASP liberalism.

Why reduce all artistic strategies to mere issues of visual expression and imagery: with the concept of 'image' many visual strategies that are not based on images become reduced,[26] not to mention the multitude of artistic strategies that are not visual, or object bound, but deal for instance with situations, processes or spaces, etc. The concept of 'image' alone cannot convey the very specificity of bark painting in Aboriginal art,[27] the role of the materiality of the support as well as its formal and its iconographic or iconological aspects. As is generally known, the bark support operates as a metaphor for communities such as the Yolngu and Kunwinjku and mediates their way of seeing the world. In addition, its organic qualities, its significance as a piece of the land itself in which the artist is rooted, must be taken into account too; this aspect, the role of the colours and their basic ephemeral character are seminal for Aboriginal paintings. The 'usual' approach would be to compare Aboriginal art with pointillism, minimalism or abstract art: this makes no sense because there is no concept of abstraction in Aboriginal culture; Aboriginal art is a form of communication,[28] a language, the forms and structures of which are bound to specific practices, places, etc. In their making and in their reading they evoke special powers and bring to life beings in modes unknown to Western culture. But this is the same as when scholars in 'classical' art history go looking for the roots of abstraction, for instance in *The Book of Durrow*. There one can observe how figuration is introduced into a culture that so far was only ornamental: is it primitive or abstract? Neither of the two: what looks abstract does so only in retrospect, when we project our own criteria backwards, focusing only on superficial formal aspects without regard for the way these forms deal with the world.

The concentration on 'image' focuses on the surface, on visual phenomena, and does not deal with important aspects like the fact that 'images' are embedded in different cultures of images (identity, memory etc.) in both production and reception (role of art in

---

24 Jimenez, M., 2005, *op. cit.*, p. 21.

25 Already in 1989 Sally Price articulated similar doubts; see Price, S., *Primitive Art in Civilized Places*, Chicago University Press, Chicago, 1989.

26 I prefer to use the notion of image in a restricted sense, as signifying a material product referring to a named or otherwise defined cultural or natural entity, notably excluding all sorts of abstract, mental representations.

27 Nota bene, when I speak of 'Aboriginal art' I don't mean it is a homogenous entity. I know there are many different forms and contents, depending on the community the work comes from; I do not wish to deny its multiplicity and diversity ... allow me the generalisation for the sake of easier expression.

28 Ryan, J., 1993, in Lüthi, B. (ed.), *op. cit.*, p. 51.

reified culture, or its opposite, in oral or non-oral tradition, etc.). Thinking only in the category of 'images' and giving up the art dimension, means waiving the possibility of differentiating cultures of images, different art practices or art cultures; there exist art practices besides fine arts. It is well known that original Aboriginal art is linked to ritual purposes, and that the signs and symbols are only understood by initiated persons in very precise circumstances: since knowledge means power, being able to read and interpret them acquires a very special dimension and signification in Aboriginal culture. Contemporary Aboriginal art[29] is a purposeful transformation of old models into profane works produced for sale to an international audience. Judith Ryan speaks of original Aboriginal art as a "fossil spur out of a world without time," while contemporary Aboriginal art is born from a vivid dynamic process.[30] Contemporary art has deep connections to its origins but it is created under different conditions and for other purposes. Nevertheless, it is a vehicle for very specific Aboriginal needs and demands (see part 3 below).

What art is, or can be, has to be defined and enables differentiations in the broad field of visual culture. To understand the meanings and possible roles of art and visual culture in questions of representation in different cultures requires a reflection on more complex structures than only the definition of what an image is/could be: besides aesthetics, there are anthropological, political, socio-cultural and economical aspects involved in art historical and postcolonial discourses, which the concept of image does not cover. Aspects and issues of context, functions of visual practices are not dealt with when one focuses on questions of defining what an image is. Art and visual culture are tools, modes of reflecting the world in ways that cannot be reduced to problems of image configuration. 'Images' are only one form of visual/cultural production which always depends on a communication circuit, on an institutional or cultural web through which an image circulates, is produced and works or is used or 'consumed'. Art/visual culture is no longer only a question of mere aesthetics, invention of new images or languages, but rather of discursive strategies that are necessarily encompassed within institutional structures, with their own cultural politics being defined from the margins.[31]

In Western (or Euro-American) art historical, or so-called art anthropological, approaches there is still an implicit bias towards the 'universality' of their own practice, while non-Western practices are approached as 'ethnographic otherness'; the anthropological polish masks only badly this unreflected prejudice,[32] which leads to forgetting the limiting blinds that obscure the view from one's own position.

Languages and, even more so, academic/hermeneutic cultures shape cultural systems and the world; although we are globalised and believe to be international there are fundamental differences – be it only the different colonial pasts – in our way of approaching

---

29 Ryan, J., 1993, in Lüthi, B. (ed.), *op. cit.*, pp. 49 – 63.

30 Ibid., p. 49.

31 Peluffo Linari, Gabriele, 2004, 'Autonomy, Nostalgia, and Globalization: The Uncertainties of Critical Art', in Mosquera, G. et al. (eds.), *op. cit.*, pp. 52ff.

32 "... deep seated belief that western artists must always transcend their particular context and be representative of a universal perspective." Papastergiadis, N., 2004, in Mosquera, G. et al. (eds.), *op. cit.*, p. 332.

culture, art, and the 'other'. For instance, in two recent articles in the fine arts section of the *Süddeutsche Zeitung* the increasing value of Aboriginal art was praised; this was interpreted as a sign for the recognition of its status as fine art rather than as a product of ethnographic handicraft.[33] Who decides upon how to approach what? What does it change, or mean, if we approach Aboriginal visual products as fine art? And if we start comparing it for instance with the work of Paul Klee this is not very significative since the similitude is only superficial and does not say much about specific content, form, mode of expression and function of the imagery. Will a possible acknowledgment as fine art change the otherness of Aboriginal art, or our understanding of it? "If the critical discourse of contemporary art engages with artworks from other cultures, will it also embrace other histories of practice, introduce new conceptual schemes for interpretation and appreciation? In short, how will the foreign suddenly be made familiar? Will the different between different cultural practices alert us to the silencing that occurs by the very rules of representation in the discourse of art? Or will that which remains untranslatable summon a critique to the very language of art and culture?"[34]

In order to find out more about the relevance of otherness in the context of appreciating art works, we need, in a third step, to take a closer look at the concept of multiple modes of otherness.

Otherness: traps or chances?

I wish to propose an approach to otherness outside the dialectic opposition me/the 'other' (or Western/non-Western) in order to flesh out an in-between[35] form of encounter/exchange, where the meeting of two othernesses allows each one to experience its own specificity and difference at the same time, while looking for ways to escape the 'culture game' in order to transform understanding from de-otherisation – which results in a taming of the difference to make it my own – into an acceptance of difference. If one chances to live the reciprocity of acceptance and otherness, then difference can become a catalyst of the self for both parties engaged in the dialogue. Should not every approach towards something be a dialogue with an interest for the other?[36] Isn't friction with one's counterpart the basic mode of, or the fuel for, an encounter?

Speaking of difference: here there is a basic double-bind involved. On the one hand, difference is wanted and attractive, on the other it can also become a trap? Why? Who

33 'Kunstmarkt' Report, *Süddeutsche Zeitung*, September 2005.

34 Papastergiadis, N., 2004, in Mosquera, G. et al. (eds.), *op. cit.*, p. 342.

35 In-between: some form of 'hyperculturality' rather than interculturality? Is this possible? See Han, Byung-Chul, *Hyperkulturalität, Kultur und Globalisierung*, Merve, Berlin, 2005.

36 Whatever interests I have, I'll be prejudiced by otherness in gender, race, culture … but doesn't our post-modern, post-structuralist and post-colonial consciousness allow for new ways of dealing with alterity.

defines difference, establishes the criteria?[37] To whose benefit? From a non-Western perspective, for example, the use of difference is felt in another way: while earlier on the West rejected 'difference', it now seems to follow a "demand for difference"[38] as Olu Oguibe has stated. Difference should be a positive quality, not a defect. It is ever-diminishing theoretical heresies that engender the discourse on otherness.

Maybe we need sympathy rather than empathy (pseudo-understanding)? And if we wish to understand, 'understanding' should be conceived in Levinas' sense[39] who remarks that when we understand something we usually have taken away that which was foreign or strange, and have colonised, 'de-othered the other', taken away what was different and unknown. Instead of this type of taming of difference we should stand up for the right to alterity and even "to opacity that is no enclosure within an impenetrable autarchy but subsistence within irreducible singularities."[40] In this sense I would like 'to turn the table' and, instead of stressing the otherness of the 'other', express the feeling of my own difference, accept my own lacunae, deficiencies, doubts, fragility, vulnerability, limits and the chance of claiming new dimensions, of being de-otherised or otherised myself. To achieve this there should be no "preconceived transparency of universal models."[41]

Well then: how to approach the 'other' without entering the 'culture game'? As a Western art historian, am I doomed to be incorporated in the Western imperialistic globalising and globalised discourse? Why must the Western critic always act as an authoritative observer, disempowering or victimising[42] the observed? The Western approach[43] is always linear and logic, as if difference could be dealt with in a linear, accumulative mode. In fact, we should try other ways (see below the notion of 'weave'). Beyond, beneath, as well as before the dichotomy Western/non-Western there exist, by implication, already many other forms: female/male, white/black, theoretician/practitioner (i.e. producer of secondary and primary discourses/facts/evidences), rich/poor, etc. Which are the driving, dominating ones? Instead of applying a dichotomy, an opposition, a dialectical approach to a dialogue in the

---

37 The 'other', understood as a school for differentiation/ for the self/ for acceptance would mean 'equality', if the other is neither more nor less just an other 'equal'/same. The 'one' and the 'other' are different but have the same value, are just deviating experiences of intensity and of experiencing the world. As academic humanities and histories learned from feminisms and gender studies, new capacities of seeing/recognising/acknowledgement, Western culture could learn from dealing with others, with non-Western cultures, more differentiated views, new values, more modesty and self-criticism.

38 Oguibe, O., 2004, *op. cit.*, p. XV.

39 Levinas plays with the etymology of the French verb 'com-prendre', which can be read literally as 'take something away'; he sees this as the 'taking away' of alterity, understanding therefore usually means de-otherisation.

40 Glissant, Eduard, 2004, 'For Opacity', in Mosquera, G. et al. (eds.), *op. cit.*, p. 253.

41 Glissant, E., 2004, in Mosquera, G. et al. (eds.), *op. cit.*, p. 255.

42 "The Millennial intake of humans as opposed to nonhumans, or who wins the lotto and the role of the arts in the process", Johnston, P., 2004, in Mosquera, G. et al. (eds.), *op. cit.*, pp. 106–107.

43 Over the last years not only Western interpreters have approached non-Western artists, works or visual practices ... non-Western artists, curators and critics apply independent practices and interpretations to affirm their own positions. ... are they not equal partners? Intellectual peers? See Oguibe, O., 2004, *op. cit.*, p. XV.

linear mode, maybe one should revert to a 'polylog'[44] to avoid polarisation and schematisations (such as the opposition of two fix points), avoid hierarchy by a rhizomatic, process-oriented and dynamic access. The encounter is not homogeneous and linear, but works on different levels that are intricately related and not easy to schematise (appeal, rejection, double-bind, visual, affective, rational, etc.). To avoid dualism should one use opacity as a solution for intrinsic discrimination? Maybe Glissant's concept of the 'weave' as a structure of communication could be an alternative. Here one could make a link to Glissant's "right to opacity" and his idea that instead of thinking of humanity as an entity one should consider "the divergence of humanities" and take it into account as a mode of communication: "Opacities can coexist and converge, weaving fabrics. To understand this truly, one must focus on the texture of the weave and not on the nature of its components ... Thoughts of Self and of Other here become obsolete in their duality."[45]

This approach demands more modesty than the usual (authoritative), hermeneutical theoretical dogmatisms. It would require an openness and acceptance of one's own limits (unusual in academia); one should keep awake the "questioning essential to any relation"[46] and forget the rigidity of convictions and the kind of conventional academic approach that is merely a kind of search for a self-fulfilling-prophecy, a quest for illustrating pre-established theories.

My proposal is the following: basically art is already the fundamental other dimension that demands translation, communication, mediation, even in its own culture, i.e. the culture it originates from. Art is the 'other way' of approaching the world, of dealing with it; thus the art historian becomes a mediator of plural modes of otherness.[47] This mediation involves inter-subjective dialogue across cultural boundaries or modes of expression, an interpretation and transformation of the original statement, thereby creating something of a new statement.[48] What, among other aspects, makes this approach seminal is the idea of reciprocity and of mutual understanding:[49] while I mediate the other, I change and become altered myself. In this mode there is no omniscient or authoritative interpreter and a victimised, interpreted representative; both parties are involved in an interactive exchange.

But what are the standards, and why are they established? By whom, and what is their aim? What is their function? How can the equality of claims be established? In our case especially: what are the standards of/for 'modernity' when approaching Aboriginal art? Who decides whether bark paintings are handicraft or art? The art market? Do we have to

---

44 Waldenfels, Bernhard, *Topographie des Fremden. Studien zu einer Phänomenologie des Fremden 1*, Suhrkamp, Frankfurt am Main, 1997, p. 228.

45 Glissant, E., 2004, in Mosquera, G. et al. (eds.), *op. cit.*, p. 253.

46 Ibid.

47 Mediation seems a more appropriate concept than translation because mediation comprises all the dynamics of translation, i.e. the disrupting and transforming of sense/context; while translation suggests a mere mirroring, mediation conveys the notion of two entities (or 'two others') interacting in a dynamic mode, not of one approaching and acting on the other.

48 In adaptation of Birgit Meyer's concept of translation, see Papastergiadis, N., 2004, in Mosquera, G. et al. (eds.), *op. cit.*, p. 338 (from Meyer, B., 'Beyond Syncretism', in Stewart, Ch. and R. Shaw (eds.), *Syncretism/Anti- Syncretism*, Routledge, London, 1994).

49 See tribute to Papastergiadis' concept of translation, in Mosquera, G. et al. (eds.), *op. cit.*, p. 339.

acknowledge the criteria of the art market and institutionalised networks "that circulate art objects from all over the world and constantly create hierarchies of significance, what frameworks are available for judging between artworks from different cultures? Can practices that were previously categorised as 'Other' suddenly emerge within the parameters of modernity's self-identity?"[50] Which modernity? One should also stop the talk of centre and periphery: it is an arrogant prejudice that confirms the unreflected, Western-centred (Euro-American centred), art-market-guided mapping of cultural, visual and artistic practices. Do we need universal standards of art? Are not all cultural practices and perspectives legitimate?

First one should say clearly what is meant by art (not only fine art), what it is and what it not is, and then ask ourselves: why is this now an issue? Even in Western culture there is not only one kind of art, but many forms, concepts and strategies, ranging from mere objects of decoration, or works that are merely aesthetically pleasing, to investigations of social and political complexes; there are affirmative and critical (material and spiritual) ways to reflect the complex world, many paths to contribute to the construction of history and memory, of dealing with cultural identity problems, etc. Which art are we speaking of? The one dealt with on the international market, or the bigger, real-existing, broad palette of artistic practices in both Western and non-Western countries? Private art or public art? What do we expect from art? What interests drive research? Is it the control of the high grounds of interpretation, the so-called 'management of meaning'? Falling into this trap can only be avoided by strictly adhering to modesty and reciprocity, and by building on mutual interest. Such good practices would help to undermine positions serving unilateral interests of power.

Conclusion

In its specific otherness the art of Aborigines – traditional, contemporary, current – provides a particularly vivid incentive for rethinking our ways of approaching art practices,[51] of opening our minds to new aesthetic experiences, of creating a new way of looking at the world. I have my doubts about the usefulness of its recognition as fine art. Are Western art museums not mere terminals, mausoleums for formerly vibrant practices, and reservations for things that have become harmless? Maybe the Western art museum first needs redefining[52] as a place of vivid relevant practices – then it would possibly make sense to integrate Aboriginal art. We should cultivate differences and specificities instead of domesticating and 'pasteurising' them by turning them into fine art.

50 Ibid. p. 340.

51 ... what in fact all art practices do!! Isn't their main 'function' a more sensitive, vivid, even exacerbated apprehension of being in the world?

52 I highly recommend Alfred Gell's *Art and Agency: An Anthropological Theory*, Clarendon Press, London, 1998, from which one can learn something about the necessity of defining the characteristics of each culture's inherent aesthetics, Western as well as non-Western.

Part 3
Between Europe and Australia: from local to global

Christian Kaufmann and Richard McMillan (†)[1]

From bark to art: Karel Kupka between Arnhem Land and Basel

Introduction

In the transition of paintings on bark from objects of ethnographic interest to works of artistic value several persons have played an important role; one of them was Karel Kupka (1918–1993, see fig. 26). The aim of this presentation is to coordinate evidence of Karel Kupka's achievements in Australia (as documented by Richard McMillan in the appendix) with the view of the former curator for Oceania at the Basel Museum der Kulturen. The success of the exhibition on the first Kupka collection from Arnhem Land at the Basel museum in 1958 marked an important point in this transition. The museum commissioned Kupka in 1955/56 and again in 1960 to collect and document bark painting, and to portray the artists producing it. I try to shed some light on the specific conditions that prevailed in the 1950s and early 1960s. At the end of this period bark paintings from northern Australia, executed by individuals who were known by name, were being accepted as genuine works of art while the painters were being recognised as contemporary artists by a comparatively small, yet significant museum audience in Europe.

The story of success also tells a tale of misunderstandings. Ironically, not the least point of attraction at the time was the general feeling that artists like Paddy Compass Namatbara, Jimmy Midjawmidjaw or Billy Yirawala and others had inherited, in an uninterrupted line of tradition, an art approach that went back to mesolithic, or even palaeolithic times, in short: back to the dawn of art. As questionable as this approach was, it marked then and there also a difference between Aboriginal art and art from the Pacific Islands, and it left a long trail of continuing fascination. While helping to popularise the art of Indigenous Australians at an early stage, this stereotype prevents still today Western audiences in European museums,

---

1 Richard McMillan died of a cerebral tumour on July 12, 2006. He had read the version of this paper sent to him on April 6, 2006, and had raised no comments. Subsequent alterations concern style, not facts. It was Richard's wish to see the full documentary appendix to his original contribution for the «*Rarrk*» catalogue in print. Sadly, his health did not permit him to attend the «*Rarrk*» Symposium in Basel. We shall remember him as an art historian who was keen on discovering hidden values in his contemporaries' artistic oeuvres, and generous in connecting others to his deep knowledge.

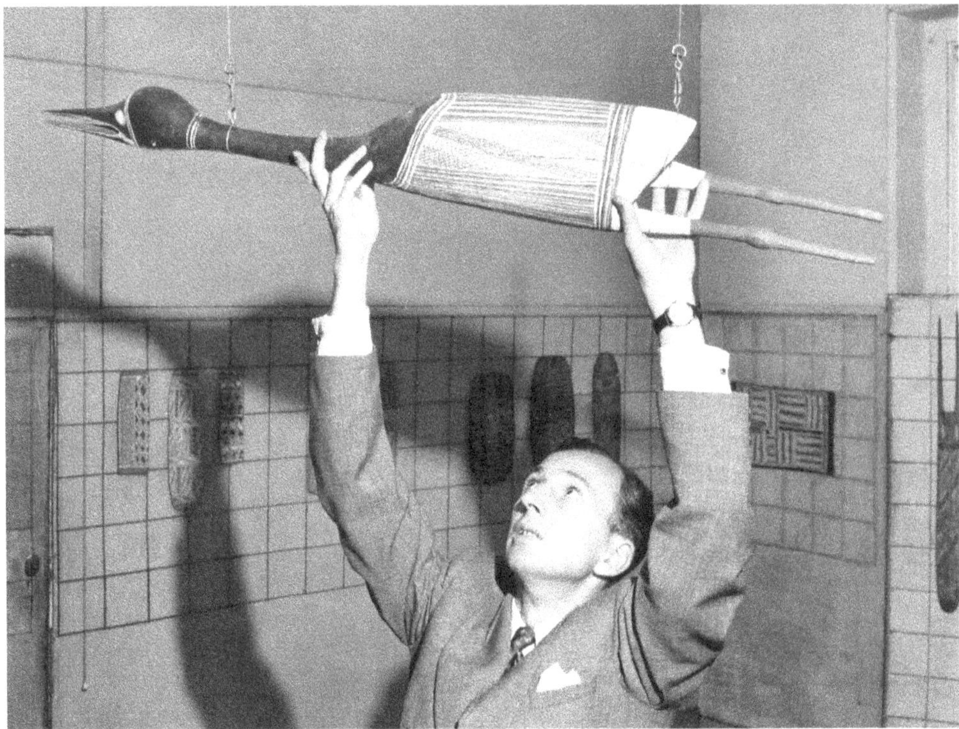

Fig. 26: Karel Kupka displaying in 1956 in Sydney (probably at East Sydney Technical College) a wooden sculpture by Bininjiwui (Djambarbuingu), *Jabiru*, mother stork, the female Black-necked Stork, *Ephippiorhynchus asiaticus* (formerly *Xenorhynchus asiaticus*) (now in the Museum der Kulturen Basel, length 98 cm, Va 1023; see fig. 29) Photo Brindle, L 22085, ANIB; Courtesy Michèle Souëf, Kupka Archives, France.

both in art museums and in ethnographic museums, from truly appreciating the contemporary artist's hard work. A substantial part of the public and even some museum professionals give preference to evaluating a contemporary artist's roots in early history, rather than trying to become familiar with his oeuvre and his message as such.

Early perspectives of art in anthropology

For those readers who are either non-anthropologists or non-German speakers (or perhaps both) it might be wise to start by saying that the discussion on whether non-European cultural products may have properties that qualify them as art in our traditional sense of the term is part of an intellectual dispute that goes back in German anthropological discourse for more than one hundred and ten years to such names as Ernst Grosse, Karl von den Steinen, Felix von Luschan, Konrad Th. Preuss, Emil Stephan, Augustin and Elisabeth Krämer-Bannow, Franz Boas (who was German-born and -educated), Ernst Vatter, Eckard von Sydow, and last but not least, Leonhard Adam, author of *Primitive Art*, who moved to Australia after the Nazis took over in Germany. These are but some of the names of the debate between 1893 and 1939, a debate that specifically touched upon the art forms from the Pacific and the Pacific Rim. While the debate, to begin with and at least partially, paralleled the one launched by Alfred Cort Haddon in the United Kingdom, also in 1893, it diverged considerably in the late 1920s and early 1930s. In fact, at least for anthropologists writing in German in those years, not addressing questions on art, or explicitly dealing with them – when art as a term always has had its universal implications – marked a sort of hidden dividing line. There were those who avoided the issue of art as being too open to subjective interpretation; they preferred to believe in hard facts corroborated by natural science; however, they often carried over the study of phenomena that were of interest to physical anthropology into a method of studying culture that led them on to the path of racist theories. On the other hand there were those who shifted their focus in anthropology from skulls, physical anthropology and material culture to art styles, art works and artists, guiding them to an anthropology of the individual self.[2] This hidden line of orientation partly owes its power to the echoes of the vivid interest that European artists, at first especially Cubists and, only shortly later, Expressionists, then Dadaists, and finally Surrealists of different orientations, took in art forms from Oceania. All these artists' movements were, despite World War I, part of international networks. We can only hypothesise that Karel Kupka was stimulated to go and search in Australia for the roots of art by ideas stemming from one of these sources.

Among anthropologists and art historians, discussions remained limited to those using the same language. Only during and after World War II these separate discussions in the USA and the UK as well as in Germany and in France slowly merged into an international exchange of opinions. Most notable were the initiatives of certain individuals and institutions in New York City (and elsewhere) to encourage the acquisition of knowledge about non-European art through a change in goal setting in museum activities. The focus was on the art works of American Indians, West Africans and Pacific Islanders. It is strange that despite the efforts of Charles Mountford as well as of Ronald and Catherine Berndt during the post-war years, especially in the USA, Aboriginal art did not become part of the canon – it was not integrated into the Rockefeller collection, which in 1957 became New York's Museum for Primitive Art and therefore Australian Indigenous art is still today only marginally represented in the Department of Arts from Africa, Oceania and the Americas at the Metropolitan Museum of Art in New York.[3]

2 For Felix Speiser, an anthropologist with a PhD in chemistry, this transition occurred in the decade from 1924 to 1933, see Kaufmann, C., 'Felix Speiser's Fletched Arrow: A Paradigm Shift from Physical Anthropology to Art Styles', in O'Hanlon, M. and R. L. Welsch, *Hunting the Gatherers. Ethnographic Collectors, Agents and Agency in Melanesia, 1870s-1930s*, Berghahn, New York and Oxford, 2000, pp. 203–226; John Layard, Margaret Mead and especially Gregory Bateson, all of them a generation younger than Speiser, are clear examples for this trend in Pacific anthropology.

3 Despite the fact that art works of Aboriginals were included in a show on the Art of Australia, 1788–1941, held at the Museum of Modern Art, New York in 1942.

Things took a slightly different turn in Europe, at least in France and in Switzerland, partly also in Germany, and Karel Kupka is one of the key figures in this process. Because this past continues to pattern the present, it is worth looking at it in more detail.

Who was Karel Kupka (1918–1993)?

According to Michèle Souëf,[4] whose knowledge is based on Karel Kupka's own archive of field drawings, field photographs and notes, Karel Kupka was born in 1918 in Prague where he studied law and also art. He was a distant nephew of Frantisek Kupka (1871–1957), the Cubist artist, with whom he sometimes gets mixed-up (as in the introduction to the catalogue of the 1969 exhibition in Prague). Karel Kupka was posted to Paris after the liberation by the allied Czechoslovakian forces. He was transferred to his country's embassy but then resigned in order to pursue his studies in law and, at the same time, to enrol at the École des Beaux-Arts in Paris. There he became an active member of Jean Souverbie's studio. Kupka's works were first exhibited in the Salon des Moins de Trente Ans in 1947/8. He survived in France by selling the art he produced in Paris and St Tropez, some of which was principally geared to attracting buyers.

How did Karel become a collector?

We don't know for sure how Karel Kupka became interested in the art of the Aborigines during these years. In any case, he prepared for a first trip to Australia in 1951 and left Europe in a flying boat. However, the plane crash-landed off Malta into the Mediterranean and Karel lost his entire equipment and his passage; but somehow he made it to Australia on a passenger boat. He seems to have been accommodated by artists then resident in Sydney such as Carl Plate, Stanislaus Rapotec (perhaps on a later trip only), the poet and writer Ronald Robinson (who had a keen interest in Aboriginal oral tradition), as well as Paul Haefliger (born in Frankfurt but of Swiss origin). Paul Haefliger had published as early as 1942 in *Art and Australia* (for whom he seems to have worked as an editorial assistant)[5] an illustrated paper on Aboriginal art. Karel Kupka started studying Aboriginal art in as many museum collections as he could visit in Australia. He also managed to establish good contacts with Professor A. P. Elkin, chair of Anthropology at Sydney University.

Back in Europe, Kupka introduced himself to Alfred Bühler, director of the Basel Museum of Ethnography and, at the same time, professor for cultural anthropology

4 See Souef, Michèle in Dussart, F., *La peinture des Aborigènes d'Australie*, Editions Parenthèses, Marseille, 1993, pp. 9–16.

5 I would like to acknowledge Mr. Peter Boehm's (of Bremen and Sydney) information regarding the itinerary of Paul Haefliger (Frankfurt/Main 1914 – Bern 1982): Sydney, Kyoto, London, Paris in 1938/39 (Colarossi and Grande Chaumière), Haefliger left Sydney for Mallorca in 1957.

(or ethnology in the English sense of the term) at Basel University. Bühler had close personal connections to contemporary artists in Basel and beyond, Meret Oppenheim being his sister-in-law; he favoured a reorientation of his museum's activities, with a focus on art from non-European cultures – art in the broad sense of the term – including all kinds of tangible works produced with an aesthetic drive. This approach would eventually lead him to include the art of individual weavers from India, Indonesia and Japan working with reserve-dye methods. Around the time Karel Kupka first met Bühler, the latter had just curated (1954) together with the Swiss anthropologist Paul Wirz a carefully designed exhibition on art works from the Sepik area of Papua New Guinea, showing mainly sculptures and paintings. At that time the director of the Basel Public Art Museum, Georg Schmidt, was a member on the board of the Basel Museum of Ethnography. Earlier, in the 1930s, Georg Schmidt had put on a series of art shows at the Gewerbemuseum (Museum of Arts and Crafts) together with Bühler's predecessor, Felix Speiser, as well as with Bühler, Wirz and Eugen Paravicini. These were temporary exhibitions devoted to art works from specific parts of Melanesia and Eastern Indonesia, displayed in a very sober manner in the style of *Neue Sachlichkeit* or Bauhaus, then still very avant-garde. In the 1950s, Georg Schmidt also encouraged Bühler to hire two young artists and art teachers as exhibition assistants for the Museum of Ethnography.[6]

At any rate, Karel Kupka, probably in 1955, managed to convince Alfred Bühler to the point where the latter promised him CHF 20,000 (which would probably have been the equivalent of his own salary for a full year, if not more) if Karel succeeded in bringing back a collection of works by contemporary Arnhem Land painters. As there are no traces of these early exchanges and the correspondence relating to it, nor of Karel's presentation folder full of drawings made in the Department of Anthropology at the University of Sydney (where R. Berndt's collection was then being kept) or in the National Museum of Victoria in Melbourne and elsewhere in Australia, we do not know the answer to two questions: a) How, that is on the strength of which arguments, did Kupka succeed in convincing Bühler?,[7] and b) did Kupka receive a payment in advance? If not, how did he manage to get underway? We only know from the remaining records that the final payment – increased to CHF 25,000 in the meantime – was settled precisely when his first collection, established in 1956, went on show in Basel in June 1958. For Bühler it was actually far more difficult than he had anticipated in his enthusiasm to raise the required sum from a number of private sources – public funds for acquisitions were, as always, far too limited. The works collected by Kupka came mainly from eastern Arnhem Land, especially from Milingimbi and from Yirrkala (Yolngu people), but also from Groote Island, Bathurst Island (Tiwi) and Port Keats. With the money he received in 1958 Kupka was able to plan his second

6 Lenz Klotz and Rudolf Hanhart, personal communication R. Hanhart, September 2005. As a young, part-time curator at the art museum of St. Gallen, Hanhart succeeded in organising in 1955 a show of local individual painters with a farmers' background from the Appenzell region.

7 Kupka mentions in *Peintres aborigines* "que ses copies dessinées" were "à peu près la seule recommandation qui [lui] permit d'entrer en contact avec le Musée ethnographique de Bâle." See Kupka, K., *Peintres aborigènes d'Australie*, Publications de la Société des Océanistes 24, Musée de l'Homme, Paris, 1972, p. 30.

trip to western as well as to eastern Arnhem Land in 1960, – which was, as we know today, to be decisive both for his collecting activity as well as for his own contribution to anthropology.

Karel's aims and his impact in Sydney

Karel's impact in Sydney was quite substantial, as Richard McMillan documented in detail in the unabridged, original version of his contribution to the *«Rarrk»* catalogue.[8] The collection Kupka put together for the Basel Museum in 1956 was first presented at two venues in Sydney: in November 1956 at the influential art school of the East Sydney Technical College and, in the following month, at the Bissietta Gallery. Both events found mention in the afternoon newspapers and were visited by an audience primarily consisting of artists and their supporters (Cook, 16.11.56: 13 and 04.12.56: 26, Appendix items C.8 and C.9), although the *Sydney Morning Herald*'s headline had warned of *A Parisian in Pursuit of our Aborigines' Art* (Staff Correspondent, 15 November 1956, p 2.) on the eve of the first opening. At the second venue, A. P. Elkin, the respected anthropologist and co-author (with Ronald and Catherine Berndt) as well as editor of *Art from Arnhem Land* (1950) held the opening speech. In his function as editor of the scholarly journal *Oceania*, Elkin invited Kupka to contribute a summary of his fieldwork. When the article *Australian Aboriginal Bark Paintings* appeared the following year, Kupka was introduced by the editor as one who had studied Aboriginal art, not only in museums, but also in Arnhem Land where he had "spent several months amongst the local artists, observing them." Kupka concluded his text with the words: "This most popular and widely known form of Aboriginal artistic expression [bark painting] is nowadays flourishing more than ever... More painters, and competent collectors should be interested in Aboriginal work, and, by good choice, encourage this true art. Public art galleries should follow the example of the Queensland Art Gallery in Brisbane, where three bark paintings, well exposed, add happily to its fresh and youthful collection."[9] Kupka also contributed an account of his first visit to Arnhem Land to *The Missionary Review*, in acknowledgement of the support of his work by the Methodists. Although unmentioned, the supervisor who was also a keen supporter of artists, Rev. Edgar Wells, was at Milingimbi between 1949–59, as were many important artists. "During my trip in and around Arnhem Land I collected bark-paintings from practically every area where they are made. Those from Milingimbi are amongst some of the best."[10]

8 In my role as editor of the *«Rarrk»* catalogue I have, with his consent, integrated here the parts of Richard's texts which we had to leave out in the catalogue due to lack of space; see the appendix to this contribution.

9 Kupka, K., 'Australian Aboriginal Bark Painting', *Oceania* 27 (4), 1957b, pp. 264–267, see also appendix below, item A.2.

10 Kupka, K., 'Artists and Workers in Arnhem Land', *The Missionary Review*, 65 (9), 1957a, pp. 8–9, see also appendix below, item A.1.

Whether by sheer coincidence or not, the first visits by Dr. Scougall and Tony Tuckson, then assistant director of the Art Gallery of New South Wales, to Yolngu artists in Arnhem Land fall into the same two years; both men acquired some of the works they saw on the spot and then donated the paintings to the Art Gallery in Sydney.

By the time of Karel Kupka's second visit to Australia in 1960, the interest of people active in the world of art museums in Aboriginal art was growing, though still at a modest rate. Kupka's supporter and friend Paul Haefliger had retired from the Sydney Morning Herald in 1957. Still, Karel Kupka was given the opportunity to launch a text in the press on how urgent it was to encourage and organise further research into Aboriginal arts and artists; his text appeared in two main daily newspapers in Australia, starting with the Sydney Morning Herald. There Kupka demanded the establishment of a national study centre for Aboriginal arts.

The matter seems to have been given priority by the Federal Government of Australia, which already had started deliberations about coordinating studies on Aboriginal culture and art. Kupka also gave a slide lecture in Sydney in November 1960 on his experiences with Arnhem Land painters, at a time when the first travelling show of Aboriginal art (including the Mountford pieces donated by the Federal Government) was presented in the art museums of the six states, with Tony Tuckson as curator (Tuckson 1960/61).

When Karel returned to Australia in 1963, this time with a commission to collect on behalf of the newly created National Museum of African and Oceanic Arts in Paris (on the initiative of André Malraux, author of *Le musée imaginaire*, and French minister of culture), he also received substantial support in Australia from the fund for urgent research, made available in order to build up the Australian Institute of Aboriginal Studies. With these funds Kupka was to establish a separate collection for the Institute. This additional commission led to some confusion and was followed by rather vicious disputes between the representatives of the Institute and Karel Kupka. In the appendix below, Richard McMillan documents this dispute on the basis of archival material and shows how A. P. Elkin succeeded in arranging a fair deal and how he made sure that Kupka was cleared of accusations, which he, Elkin, considered to be unfounded (see appendix, section B).

As a footnote we should add that the Bishop of Darwin, through the mediation of Father Frank Flynn, had invited Karel Kupka in 1956 to realise a painting of a black or Aboriginal Madonna for the Darwin Cathedral. Kupka used motifs from bark paintings in the background in order to create an appropriate visual context.

Karel's impact in Basel and in Switzerland

From Sydney and Canberra in 1964 we have to go back six years in time. Kupka's first collection of 1956 went on show in Basel in June 1958. Though the venue was the Museum für Völkerkunde and Schweizerische Museum für Volkskunde Basel, where previously one or two shows on European peintres naïfs, or folk art, had been held, the presentation was one that followed the standards of art museums of that period. Neutral artificial light created by filtered fluorescent tubes gave the impression of a well-lit room,[11] without the objects being disturbed by sharply delineated shadows. Karel Kupka came to Basel for the preparation of the exhibition at least once. He also provided field photographs and a text for the little exhibition booklet. The lower parts of the wall and the modular panels that could be erected across the room were covered with a coarse, greyish linen fabric – exactly the same material as was used for the walls of the renowned Basel Museum of Art. The exhibited works were mounted against the wall and on a platform in the middle of the room, protected by glass panels. Of course the space available in the Museum für Völkerkunde was much more limited than in the Museum of Art, and there was a shortage of security staff too. The modular panels displayed enlarged photographic prints with portraits of artists and artists at work, as well as short, concise texts. Sculptural works in wood, all of them painted, and one flexed bark were presented in showcases.

The show that was planned to last for two and a half months until the end of August 1958 had to be extended by four weeks due to the large public interest; this, of course, also meant additional workload for the director and his assistants because there was a continuous demand for guided tours.[12] The press reviews ranged from positive to enthusiastic, much depending on the kind of information provided to journalists by the museum. The wooden sculptures received special attention and were looked upon as a real novelty, demonstrating in the words of one critic, that evolution in art was possible by leaving behind tradition. The human figures in the show were "unlike any other sculpture," and the cranes in flight were the "most beautiful creations to be seen of an art coming from the origins," because as sculptures they were "as simply speedful bodies full of expression, yet painted with natural pigments in a highly developed form devoid of figurative or nature-bound reference." To man, expressing himself as an artist was therefore even more important than proper housing or clothing.[13] According to this view, bark paintings became art because their authors were also capable of creating sculptures; this was taken as testimony of their ability as artists to create forms that belong to traditions, yet express individualised meaning. Unfortunately, no overall report was published on the impact created by the show.[14] One only knows that

---

11 Exactly the same tubes were installed in the galleries of the Basel Art Museum (they were retained in some of the rooms during the latest 2006 renovation!).

12 It is worth noting that Bühler used two different lines of argument, one for fundraising ("to add an important ethnographic collection from an area still poorly represented in the existing museum collection, stemming from a very archaic people etc."), and one for publicly announcing the exhibition ("work of artists, individual artists from the dawn of art etc.") (quoted in museum records V_0292/1957–1958). Despite the potential conflict by inherent contradiction, nobody at that time took offence.

13 Jpb in *National-Zeitung Basel*, Nr. 270, 16 June, 1958.: "... Traditionen verlassen. ... Hier wird nun mit den neuen Holzschneidewerkzeugen eine völlig neue Kunst geschaffen; ... entwickelt sich jetzt eine ganz eigenartige Plastik: So gibt es Menschenfiguren, die sich mit keinem anderen [Werk] vergleichen lassen, und an der Hinterwand prangt ... etwas vom Schönsten, was es an urtümlicher Kunst überhaupt zu sehen gibt – eine Kranichfamilie, Vater und Mutter in der Luft , und das Kleine am Boden, in den ‚naturalistischen' Farben aber in völlig unnaturalistischer großer Form bemalt und plastisch ungemein ausdrucksstark in der Einfachheit des pfeilschnell dahinschießenden Körpers."

14 A different exhibition of Aboriginal bark paintings was held earlier in 1958 at the Kunstgewerbemuseum in Zurich, titled *Rindenmalereien aus Australien*, arranged by Hans Fischli and Willy Rotzler with a set of

Alfred Bühler left the following year for another collecting trip to the Sepik area of Papua New Guinea where he was specially keen on acquiring and documenting objects that would allow for a methodical study of art works, village art styles and individual variation on a comparative, regional level. Bühler was accompanied by a young British anthropologist who in the course of the trip developed his own vivid interest in the anthropology of art and artists. This was Anthony Forge. The results of their collecting and analysis were presented in the 1960 exhibition *Kunststile vom Sepik* (Art Styles of the Sepik), which in a way also echoed Kupka's earlier endeavours.[15] One of Bühler's aims with the 1960 show was to exemplify the potential of an anthropological approach to the study of art in a well defined area as well as presenting it to a wider audience in exhibitions;[16] the emphasis was placed on local histories as reflected in the development of local art styles.

Despite the stunning additions to the collection of works from Arnhem Land brought to Basel by Karel Kupka in 1960 as well as in 1963 – with an important series of works created on Croker Island by Billy Yirawala, Paddy Compass Namatbara and, above all, Jimmy Midjawmidjaw – no follow-up exhibition of the Kupka collection was ever prepared, much to Karel's regret (and recurrent accusations on his part). In 1960 and 1963, Kupka also put together a smaller, yet impressive collection for the Geneva Museum of Ethnography, and, as described in the *«Rarrk»* publication, assembled a collection for the new National Museum of African and Oceanic art in Paris.[17]

---

loans from the Mountford collection of the South Australian Museum in Adelaide (see *Rindenmalereien aus Australien*, Wegleitung 219 des Kunstgewerbemuseums der Stadt Zürich, 11 January – 2 February, 1958); a much smaller exhibition *Australische Urkunst. Rindenmalerei aus dem Museum für Völkerkunde Frankfurt/ Main* was shown at the Göppinger Galerie in January 1959, exhibting barks collected in 1938 and 1954. Agnes S. Schulz, one of the collectors, mentions in the small catalogue that local people in the Kimberley District as well as in Arnhem Land had been encouraged by members of the Frobenius Institute field research team on rock painting to do the paintings "corresponding, however, to old traditions of Australian Aborigines."

15 Bühler, A., *Kunststile vom Sepik*, Museum für Völkerkunde und Schweizerisches Museum für Volkskunde, Basel, 1960; but see also Forge, Anthony, 'Three Kamanggabi Figures from the Arambrak People of the Sepik District", in Newton, D. (ed.), *Three Regions of Melanesian Art: New Guinea and the New Hebrides*, The Museum of Primitive Art, New York, 1960, pp. 6–10; as well as Forge, A., 'Notes on Eastern Abelam Designs Painted on Paper', in Newton, D. (ed.), 1960, *op. cit.*, pp. 12–15.

16 This exhibition was the Ethnographical Museum's contribution to the 500 Year Jubilee of the Basel University; it stood in clear competition to an exhibition on Greek art (which led to the foundation of the Museum of Greek and Roman Antiquities in the following year) and to an important exhibition on the Holbein family of painters, as well as to a double exhibition on recent palaeontological discoveries. The success of the Sepik exhibition led to the planning and preparation of a special show in 1962, devoted to the art of New Guinea in the same rooms that had housed the Greek art show in 1960.

17 Philippe Peltier described the collection as follows:
"The Paris collection of K. Kupka – On his fourth trip to Arnhem Land, in 1963, Karel Kupka put together one last collection. When he got home, it was divided up between several cities: Canberra, Paris and, following an exchange, Basel. This dispersion is explained by the fact that Kupka had several sources of funding: in France, the Centre National de la Recherche Scientifique as well as the young Musée des Arts africain et océanien, whose Oceania department was headed by Professor Jean Guiart; in Australia, he enjoyed support from the AIAS as well as from Professor A. P. Elkin.The Paris collection – formerly held in the Musée des Arts d'Afrique et d'Océanie and recently transferred to the Musée du Quai Branly – numbers 255 paintings and sculptures. To which must be added a donation of 55 paintings, made a short time later from Kupka's "personal collection".

During this period he also wrote his book *Un art à l'état brut* which was published in Lausanne, Switzerland, in 1962 in a very popular series (with a first edition of over 10,000 copies). This book and the intellectual scene surrounding its author, its text and the context of the publication would deserve a study of its own. Kupka played two trump cards: the first addressed the Surrealist movement centring on André Breton (who provided a preface) with his strong disposition towards the "écriture automatique / peinture automatique" according to which a person is able to make super-individual insights into deeper level of human knowledge – an approach that has to be seen against the backdrop of the role of psychoanalysis in both Freudian and Jungian categories, which was very popular at that time, too. The second trump card refers to the interest in prehistoric art, very popular in Europe in the late 1950s due to the renewed interest in palaeolithic rock art through the discoveries in, and publications on, Lascaux and Altamira, as well as on rock art from North Africa (reported by André Lothe), South Africa, Indonesia and north-western Australia. Especially the latter regions became popular in Germany through publications by Helmut Petri and Andreas Lommel. As Aboriginal painters were considered to be closest to the rock art tradition, it followed that their art practice must be seen as a direct heritage of the people of palaeolithic or, at the latest, mesolithic ages. There was no evidence for these theories but they fitted in very well with the Surrealist approach – as did the concept of the Dreaming.

Karel's impact in Paris

Kupka's *Un art à l'état brut* must have been quite a success in Paris too. At least it paved the way for him to a part time job as a chargé de mission at the newly established Musée des Arts Africains et Océaniens (MAAO). In view of his planned thesis on the painters of Arnhem Land at the École des Hautes Études en Sciences Sociales (EHESS) under

---

While the Paris collection, in comparison with that in Basel, is not the most important numerically, it is significant from the standpoint of the history of its constitution. As the starting point of Kupka's thesis, which he defended in 1969, it was composed to substantiate an innovative approach to painters and their place in society. First remark: with the exception of a few works by Yirkalla (9 paintings) and Groote Eylandt (10 works) artists, the main corpus of the collections comes from Croker Island, Milingimbi and Maningrida. Kupka focuses on three production centres. Second remark: while the names of forty-five artists are listed, the figure is deceptive. Some are represented by only one piece, others by large series. Third remark: a single subject (figures or myths) may be treated by several painters. This attention paid to three sites, to a few creators and, finally, to certain subjects, is not without intent. Kupka wanted to show that in those times of sweeping social change and artistic production they were indeed artists in the Western sense of the term, that is to say painters capable of interpreting myths, of expressing their judgment on a subject, whatever the constraints imposed by law or ritual. As he maintained: 'the Aboriginal painter constructs his own pictural architecture which is personal and totally subjective. It is not his intention to describe the way things look but to express his judgment, and that is why he transforms them so freely.' This idea, which was novel at the time, rested on an acute sense of observation and many discussions with the painters. Recent developments in Australian painting show that it was well founded." Philippe Peltier (February 2005); see also Peltier, Ph., 'Karel Kupka, the Key Witness', in Ducreux, A.-C., Kohen, A. and F. Salmon (eds.), *In the Heart of Arnhem Land, Myth and the Making of Contemporary Aboriginal Art*, Musée de l'Hôtel-Dieu, Mantes-la-Jolie, Paris, 2001, pp. 33–36.

Professor Jean Guiart, he became a member of the CNRS, the national centre of researchers. Kupka's museum mission also enabled him to combine his efforts as a collector for at least three institutions as well as for himself – this last collection was to eventually end up in an Australian institution (in 1984 it was acquired by the National Gallery of Australia in Canberra). In 1966 Kupka became a French citizen. In 1969 he defended his thesis before a jury chaired by the distinguished prehistorian and anthropologist André Leroi-Gourhan. The meeting was held in the room of the MAAO where Kupka's collection was on permanent display. Much to Karel's regret the printed version of his thesis did not visually convey the importance he gave to the personality of each individual artist he had met in Arnhem Land (45 of them were documented by him between 1956 and 1963).

Especially on Croker Island where, together with several Kunwinjku artists, he formed a kind of artists' school, a true spirit of cooperation and trust must have developed. When he departed in September 1963 a special ceremony incorporating painted sculptures was prepared and held for, and with, Karel Kupka. The objects he received as a gift reflect the basic types of sacred objects with *rarrk* body painting.[18]

Karel's presented his findings in the exhibitions mentioned above – in Sydney (1956), Basel (1958), Geneva (1962), Paris (1964), later also in Prague (1969) – as well as on a Qantas-sponsored exhibition tour to Rome, thereby establishing these painters as a sort of canon for all subsequent collecting and/or exhibiting projects in Europe. In the eyes of the audience, the texts provided by Kupka for these exhibitions added the necessary touch of seriousness to the documentation. The individual artists' works as well as their names thus became part of any potential history of art in Australia as seen from a European perspective. This important step gained new significance when, in the mid-1970s, museums and institutions in Europe were permitted by their boards to acquire the works of contemporary artists from Papua New Guinea, later also from Vanuatu and New Caledonia, following in the steps of Ulli and Georgina Beier's cutting-edge initiatives.[19]

---

18 See illustrations in Perkins, H. (ed.), *Crossing Country: the Alchemy of Western Arnhem Land Art*, Art Gallery of NSW, Sydney, 2004, p. 193; and in Kaufmann, C. and Museum Tinguely (eds.), *Rarrk – John Mawurndjul: Journey Through Time in Northern Australia*, Verlag und Druckerei Schwabe AG, Basel, 2005, pp. 209 (left) and 221.

19 Beier, Ulli, 'Kauage' in Heinemeyer, Eva (ed.), *Matias Kauage: Malerei aus Papua-Neuguinea*, Ausstellung Künstler der Welt 3, Haus der Kulturen der Welt Berlin, Cantz, Stuttgart, 1990; Boulay, Roger, 'Préface' in Dussart, F., 1993, *op. cit.*, pp. 7–8; Heermann, Ingrid, *Tingting bilong mi. Zeitgenössische Kunst aus Papua-Neuguinea*. Schriftenreihe Dokumentation Bd. 8, Institut für Auslandsbeziehungen, Stuttgart, 1979; as well as Heermann, I. and U. Menter, *Gemaltes Land: Kunst der Aborigines aus Arnhem Land, Australien*, Linden-Museum Stuttgart/Reimer Verlag, Berlin, 1994; Raabe, Eva, *Im Auge des Betrachters: Kunst und Sehen in Papua Neuguinea*, Museum für Völkerkunde [now: Museum der Weltkulturen], Frankfurt a.M., 1998; compare also the history of the collection of contemporary art at the Tjibaou Centre in Nouméa: Cochrane, Susan, *Bérétara: Contemporary Pacific Art*, Halstead, Sydney/Nouméa, 2001.

Australian Indigenous art compared with art from the Pacific

Before that could happen, the works of the Kupka collection were compared to both the existing and the newly arriving collections from Melanesia. More often than not, museum visitors and museum curators – and here I include myself as the curator then responsible in Basel, mea culpa, mea maxima culpa – made a distinction between Aboriginal art and art say from Lake Sentani (where bark cloth was used as a surface for painting) or from the Sepik where painting on sculptures or even on flat sago petioles plays an important role. It took me an overly long time to compare directly works from the different traditions on the same level. To a certain extent, I may say, Karel Kupka stood in my way. Having got to know him at a time when he was already strongly affected by his throat problem, and with Australian colleagues expressing their critical views about him, I was very sceptical about his selection of works, which I thought of too biased. "Should these paintings be art because Kupka himself was an artist of some sort?", I, the son of two art historians, asked myself, being very critical of applying the notion of art to works from traditions where the concept of art was not known. It was only much later, when I came to realise to what extent my own selection of works from specific areas and individuals in Papua New Guinea (as well as the selection made by other fieldworkers at the same time) was equally biased, that the Kupka selection became really significant to me. As the *«Rarrk»* exhibition proves, this change of mind did not come too late. Of course, an important part of paradigmatic change is to learn to understand why and how the weight of established traditional prototypes and patterns had been overemphasised as against the continuous change through contemporary practice.

Further questions – not conclusions

What can we learn from these experiences? Institutions are even more prone than are individuals to 'see' only what they have been taught to know. Though art as a notion is constantly being redefined, therefore being constituted or recreated again and again by the viewer in terms of types, materials and forms, the role and importance of the visual impact of original works is rarely acknowledged. Images expressed (as opposed to digital snapshots), whether in static form or by bodies in movement, always reveal something which is at least partially hidden, whether you are aware of it or not. In the case of Karel Kupka, in my opinion his written texts were less important in getting the creative work of named individual artists from Arnhem Land recognised as art than was his work as a collector and exhibitor of their works, and as a narrator of the iconographic comments and stories the artists had told him.

In fact, different types of motifs and of painting techniques might have provoked quite different reactions in any European audience. The small barks with fine, non-figurative *rarrk* motifs from Yirrkala (see fig. 27), for instance, suggested a link with a constructivistic and reductionistic, thus conceptualising approach, then en vogue in Europe, while *mimih* and *mam* figures (see fig. 28) were seen as having a resemblance to imaginative surrealism.

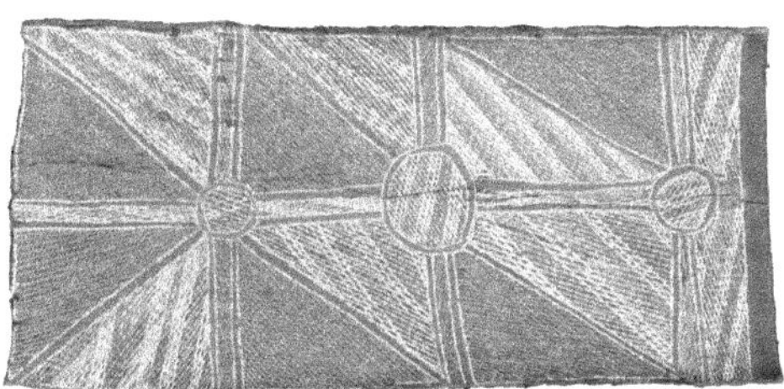

Fig. 27: Bubani (Djambarbuingu), *Water and water hole*, earth pigments on bark, c. 20 x 40 cm, Milingimbi, Crocodile I., Arnhem Land. Museum der Kulturen Basel. Coll. K. Kupka 1956. Va 906. Photo Museum der Kulturen Basel.

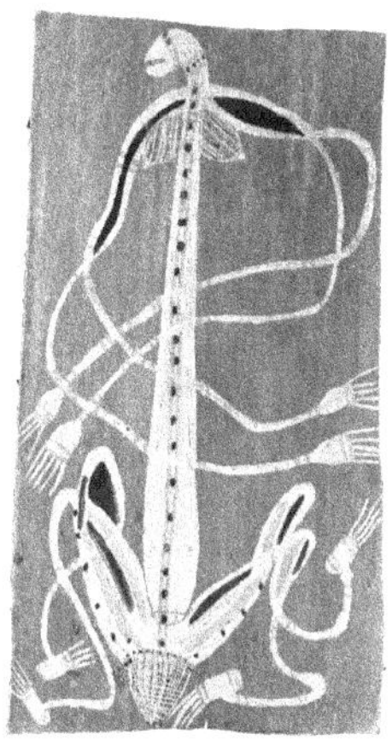

Fig. 28: Jimmy Midjawmidjaw, *Mam, evil spirit,* earth pigments on bark, 103.5 x 55.5 cm, Croker Island, Arnhem Land. Museum der Kulturen Basel. Coll. K. Kupka 1963. Va 1341. Photo Museum der Kulturen Basel.

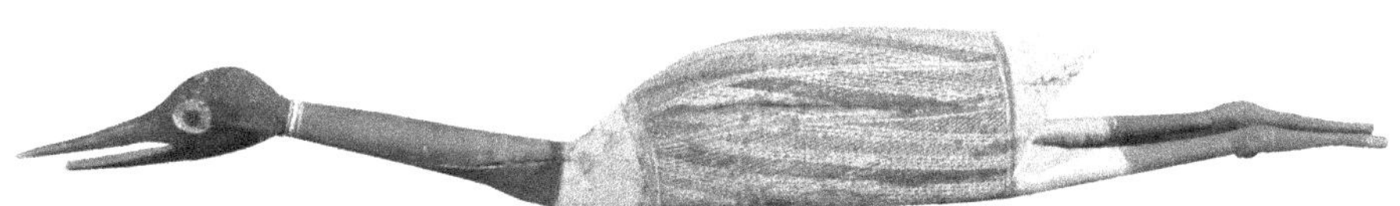

Fig. 29: Bininjiwui (Djambarbuingu), *Jabiru*, father stork , the male *Ephippiorhynchus asiaticus* (see also fig. 26; the two birds form a pair, the eye of the adult female is orange, of the male dark). The *jabiru* bird belongs to the moiety yirritya, opposite to the artist's own, where he replaced the missing knowledgeable members (according to Karel Kupka, 1972:110–111); wood, pigments, length: 121 cm, Milingimbi, Crocodile Island, Western Yolngu, Arnhem Land. Museum der Kulturen Basel. Coll. K. Kupka, 1956. Va 1024. Photo Museum der Kulturen Basel.

What we do not know is the kind of dialogue Karel Kupka had with the Kunwinjku and Milingimbi artists who were painting their works for him. Did he give them guidelines? Did he reject works? And if so, were rejected works destroyed (or were the same barks repainted)? What we do know is that, for him, the relative freedom of the artists to choose a meaning for the forms they painted was an important criterion for their ascribed status as artists. Apart from singing popular French songs with them (as Jessica de Largy Healy told me recently), did Karel show them illustrations, for example from Elkin's book *Art in Arnhem Land*?[20] Or museum pamphlets from the Australian Museum and others? Or images by European cubist painters? And how would his Aboriginal painter friends have reacted to his drawings of works painted by an earlier generation of Oenpelli artists, which he had spotted in a museum down south? What did they think of his *Aborginal Madonna* in the Darwin Cathedral? And finally, does painting on bark – like rock art – create its own brand of afficionados – among artists as well as among collectors? We need at least to try to answer these questions in order to find out in which context the 1963-generation of Bininj artists (see fig.29) were creating their works. To them, in a way, Karel Kupka probably was their first arts adviser.

Appendix: Karel Kupka in Australia
Richard McMillan's Annotated Bibliography and List of Documents with reference to Karel Kupka's activities in Australia:

A. Works by Karel Kupka (texts and photographs)

1. --- 1957a, 'Artists and Workers in Arnhem Land', *The Missionary Review*, 65 (9): pp. 8–9.
"As a painter I have been interested in Aboriginal art for many years. To satisfy my curiosity I studied all available information abroad and made a trip to Australia in 1951. ... During the dry season of 1956 I criss-crossed Arnhem Land and the surrounding areas of the far north. ... I collected bark-paintings from practically every area where they are made." Kupka mentions visits to Yirrkala and Milingimbi, Yilkarri Katani's paintings of the Wagilag sisters, and the "National Art Gallery of Queensland in Brisbane, which is the first to exhibit three fine bark-paintings among other contemporary paintings ... ."
2. --- 1957b, 'Australian Aboriginal Bark Painting', *Oceania* 27 (4): pp. 264–267.
Summary of field-work undertaken in 1956; Kupka describes figurative painting of the interior of Arnhem Land and Groote Eylandt, ceremonial art of the coast, Port Keats 'retranscriptions', and Tiwi painted baskets; he warns against over-production: "Many white artists have been artistically killed by their weakness, in being willing to satisfy the demand for the artistically worthless ..."

20 It contains photographs of two works of magic motifs, a woman with an unborn child and a man, both by Midjamidjaw, see Elkin, A. P. et al, *Art in Arnhem Land*, F. W. Cheshire, Melbourne, 1950, plates 15 and 16; see also appendix below, item C.42 (Taylor, L.).

(p. 267). "More painters and competent collectors should be interested in Aboriginal work, and by good choice encourage this true art. Public galleries should follow the example of the Queensland National Gallery in Brisbane, where three bark paintings, well exposed, add happily to its fresh and youthful collection." (p. 267)

3. --- 1957c, *'Bark Painting from Northern Australia'*, Legend Press, Sydney.
One A3 sheet, folded to 12 x 16 cm., includes six colour illustrations of barks and a photograph by Kupka of Yilkarri Kitani painting a Wagilag Sisters story; also six paragraphs in small type describing bark painting.

4. --- 1958, *Kunst der Uraustralier*, (ed. A. Bühler), Museum für Völkerkunde und Schweizerisches Museum für Volkskunde, Basel.
Preface and introduction by Alfred Bühler, professor of ethnology at the University of Basel and director of the Basel Museum of Ethnology. Short catalogue (16 pages and six b/w photographs) to a special exhibition from 14 June to 31 August 1958 showing the material collected by Karel Kupka. Two articles in German by Kupka (1. Origins and Contents of the Collection, 2. On the Art of the Early Australians).

5. --- 1960a, 'Centre for Aboriginal art', *Sydney Morning Herald*, 11 June.
Includes three photographs by Kupka. Written in 1959, possibly as part of an application to the Bollingen Foundation in New York; the text is also part of a 'Statement of project' found in the Elkin Papers' (see below B.7), "Kupka" folder.

6. --- 1960b, 'Why not a Centre for Aboriginal Art?', *West Australian* (Perth), 2 July. Includes two photographs by Kupka. The text is identical to the one of 1960a.

7. --- 1961a, 'Kunst der australischen Ureinwohner', *Der Landbote* (Winterthur, Switzerland) 10 April. Includes 3 photographs by Kupka. Not seen.

8. --- 1961b, 'Les survivants du mésolithique australien', *Courrier des Messageries Maritimes* 63, (July–August). Original title: A la rencontre des âges. Includes six photographs by Kupka. Not seen.

9. --- 1962a, 'Kunst der ausralischen Ureinwohner', *Thurgauer Zeitung* (Switzerland), 23 June. Includes three photographs by Kupka. Not seen.

10. --- 1962b, *Un art à l'état brut: peintures et sculptures des aborigènes d'Australie*, La Guilde du Livre and Editions Clairefontaine, Lausanne.
With a text by André Breton and a preface by Alfred Bühler, professor of ethnology at the University of Basel and director of the Basel Museum of Ethnology. Nine chapters, short bibliography, two fold-out sheets of captions for 70 illustrations.

11. --- 1963, 'Le Chant des morts', *Courrier des Messageries Maritimes* 74, (May-June).
Includes nine Kupka photographs. Not seen.

12. --- 1964, 'Daingannngan. Artiste de la terre d'Arnhem', *Journal de la Société des Océanistes*, Tome XX, No. 20, pp. 45–55.
Includes two Kupka photographs of artists and two of barks. Interview with Kupka conducted by Father Patrick O'Reilly, Secretary General of the Société des Océanistes, prefaced by a biographical note mentioning Kupka's distant relationship to "Francois" (Frantisek) Kupka (1871–1957), his own vocation as a painter inspiring his research in Arnhem Land, his *Un art à l'état brut* of 1962 and his illustrated lecture for La Société des Océanistes in January 1963, from which the interview derived. O'Reilly says he attempts to retain Kupka's spontaneity and characteristic manner of speaking.

13. --- 1965, *Dawn of Art: Painting and Sculpture of Australian Aborigines*, Angus & Robertson, Sydney / Viking Press, New York.
With a foreword by A. P. Elkin, and a preface by André Breton (in French with a translation by John Ross). English version of A.10, translated by Kupka himself, checked by A. P. Elkin. M. Souef (see below C.37) claims this title has also been translated into German and Czech, but

editions and publishers have not been seen by this writer. An annotated list of some reviews in English appear below.

14. --- 1966, 'Les écorses peintes d'Australie du Musée et Institut d'Ethnographie de Genève', *Bulletin Annuel du Musée et Institut d'Ethnographie de la Ville de Genève* 9, pp. 23–50.
Beginning with 'generalities' about "arts called primitive" Kupka continues with a survey of the literature on bark paintings: he criticises Mountford for not including the names of the artists whose work he collected. He then summarises exhibitions, including Tuckson's in 1960–1961. He describes artists' techniques, materials and procedures of work, then his own research methodology. He then analyses the collection of the Geneva Museum, gathered by Wells, Kupka and others from Milingimbi, Yirrkala, Croker Island, Oenpelli, Port Keats and Groote Eylandt.

15. --- 1967, 'Cazeneuve, Jean', *Encyclopédie Larousse de poche l'ethnologie*, Larousse, Paris.
Includes photos by Kupka. Front cover: the painter Djawa working, Milingimbi; back cover: bark painting by Djulwarak, Milingimbi; p. 43: head-and-shoulders of an anonymous figure captioned 'Australien' in the chapter titled 'Les primitifs actuels'.

16. --- 1969, *Austrálie. Osobnost primitivniho malire*, Napratkovo Museum, Prague.
Catalogue edited by Erich Herold and Zdena Teisingerova. 22 pages, several black and white illustrations of barks and one artist portrait.

17. --- 1972, *Peintres aborigènes d'Australie*, Publications de la Société des Océanistes 24, Musée de l'Homme, Paris. Kupka's thesis, formerly titled *Anonymat de l'artiste primitif*, according to Peltier (2001). Four letters from Kupka of 1965–66, two on Musée des Arts Africains et Océaniens letterhead, relating generally to documentation for this publication, to Hal Missingham, Director, William Boustead, Conservator, and Tony Tuckson, Deputy Director, all of the Art Gallery of New South Wales, with replies. Can be found with the Tuckson Papers at the AGNSW Research Library.

18. --- 1975, 'Le système des sous-sections matrimoniales dans la famille aborigène d'Australie', *Journal de la Société des Océanistes*, Tome XXXI, No. 49, pp. 435–466.
A. P. Elkin's prefatory note in English refers to Dr. Kupka's numerical representation of the north-east Arnhem Land problem of integrating an established norm of matrilateral first-degree cross-cousin marriage within the Aborigines' subsection (eight-section) system.

19. --- 1980, 'The Aborigine Artists of Arnhem Land: Australian Bark Paintings. *UNESCO Courier* 30, pp. 9–14.
Editor's introduction: "Karel Kupka, French ethnologist of Czech origin, is a research officer with France's National Centre of Scientific Research, and is currently studying the basis and purpose of art in the 'primitive' family."

20. --- 1980, _____ and Alain Testart, 'A propos du problème Murngin: le système de sous-sections', *L'Homme* 20 (2), pp. 71–90.
"Les données ont été recueillies sur le terrain par K. Kupka lors de missions effectuées en Terre d'Arnhem entre 1956 et 1975; l'analyse et le dépouillement ont été réalises en commun" (p. 71, footnote). Criticised by Keen 1988 (see below C.16).

B. Archival documents concerning Karel Kupka

1. "Collection K. Kupka constituée au cours de trois voyages en Australie," 1964, PMS 943, Australian Institute for Aboriginal and Torres Straight Islander Studies Library, Canberra. 35 pages typed by Kupka for the Basel Museum of Ethnology.
2. "Répertoire de la collection 1964 du Musée des Arts Africains et Océaniens (Mission K. Kupka, 1963–64)", 1964, MS 263, Australian Institute for Aboriginal and Torres Straight Islander Studies Library, Canberra. Photocopied typescript supplied by Father Patrick O'Reilly, Secretary General of the Société des Océanistes.

3. "Collection of bark paintings and carvings of Arnhem Land (N.T.) made by Karel Kupka in 1963 for the Australian Institute of Aboriginal Studies", 1976, PMS 942, Australian Institute of Aboriginal and Torres Straight Islander Studies Library, Canberra. 105 items; eight pages typescript.
4. Elkin, A. P. Personal archives of Professor A. P. Elkin, P130, Archives and Records Management Services, University of Sydney: Series 29, "Australian Institute of Aboriginal Studies," item 9. Correspondence and papers concerning Karel Kupka; and Series 44 "Personal correspondence general 1956–1979." Guide available at http://www.usyd.edu.au/arms/archives, under Personal Archives E-G.
5. McCarthy, F. D. "Report on Karel Kupka", PMS 1098, 1963, Australian Institute for Aboriginal and Torres Straight Islander Studies, Canberra. Doc 63/68, AIAS Interim Council Meeting 18–19 October 1963. Includes excerpts from previous meetings' minutes (30 April–1 May, 28–29 June) setting forth some basis for McCarthy's conversations with Kupka on 10 and 14 October in Sydney, who, he reports, as maintaining that none of his collection belongs to the Institute, and that he believes he should retain what he has bought with his own money. Details of how he has financed this apart from Institute funding.
6. _____. "Report by executive member on collection made by Mr. K. Kupka in Arnhem Land", PMS 104, 1964, Australian Institute for Aboriginal and Torres Straight Islander Studies, Canberra. A copy of J. A. Barnes' memo of 15 December 1963, and McCarthy's report of 28 January 1964, Doc 64/107, see below. Barnes describes how Kupka "went on to deprecate the scientific value of his annotations."
7. _____. "Report on Kupka Collection", Elkin Papers (see above B.4), P130, Series 29, item 9: "Correspondence and papers concerning Karel Kupka." For AIAS Interim Council meeting of 21–22 February 1964, agenda, item 5(e): Note by acting chairman W. E. H. Stanner recommending the suspension of Kupka's appointment. McCarthy gives details of three Kupka collections: one on order from two missionary sources in Arnhem Land but not yet in Sydney; one in Sydney but not shown to AIAS, and the one from which, on 27 December 1963, W. C. Wentworth, A. P. Elkin and F. D. McCarthy chose 50 barks from Croker Island, five from Milingimbi, six from Groote Eylandt, 30 sculptures and poles from Milingimbi and four sacred boards from Groote Eylandt. McCarthy then records that Kupka departed on 13 January 1964 aboard the SS *Fairstar* without having a customs export permit signed by the Australian Museum.
8. _____. "Report on Visit to Europe", Australian Institute of Aboriginal Studies Document 67/554, March 1967, Australian Institute for Aboriginal and Torres Straight Islander Studies, Canberra. McCarthy visited Basel, where he mentions seeing material collected by Clement, Strehlow, Webb and Handschin. A section headed "Karel Kupka" describes a meeting at the Musée National des Arts Africains et Océaniens in Paris: "The whole of his collection was set out in a large hall. Unfortunately, even though I made an appointment to see him, most of the paintings were facing the walls and could not be seen; others were visible in a portion of the completed exhibition."
9. Tuckson, Tony. Papers, Research Library and Archive of the Art Gallery of New South Wales. Particularly an exchange of letters from 1965–1966 between Kupka and Hal Missingham, AGNSW Director, Tuckson, Art Gallery of NSW Deputy Director and informal curator of Aboriginal art, and William Boustead, Art Gallery NSW Conservator; seeking information of use from the Musée National des Arts Africains et Océaniens, the Centre for Documentation and from Kupka's 1972 thesis publication.

C. Published accounts, references to Kupka

1. Bennett, David H., 1980, 'Malangi: The Man Who Was Forgotten before He Was Remembered', *Aboriginal History* 4 (1), pp. 43–47. Details of Kupka's 1963 involvement with David Malangi at

Milingimbi, and with an officer of the Reserve Bank of Australia in Sydney. (See also Mundine 1997, 1999, 2000, and particularly 2004 below). The Bank selected an image derived from Kupka's photograph of a bark painted by Malangi to be part of Gordon Andrews' design of a "one dollar" note. A claim for compensation, instigated by an Adelaide journalist (see Pullen 1966, below C.33) and the missionary Superintendent at Milingimbi (see Mundine 2004, below C.25), was settled by the Bank in 1967, establishing an important precedent in copyright, and Malangi's fame.

2. Berndt, Catherine H. and Ronald M. Berndt, 1985, *The World of the First Australians*, Rigby, (1st ed. 1964), Sydney, pp. 449, 450. Brief reference to Kupka's "overall" study of Aboriginal art "seriously criticised" by Berndt (1966; see below, D.1) and a mention of Kupka's inclusion of sculpture in his book.

3. Caruana, Wally, 1993, *Aboriginal Art*, Thames & Hudson, London.
"A significant body of bark paintings was produced in response to the interest in the subject [of sorcery] by the Czech artist, ethnologist and collector Karel Kupka." (p. 28)

4. _____. 2001, 'National Gallery of Australia, Canberra', in Cochrane, S. (ed.), *Aboriginal Art Collections: Highlights from Australia's Public Museums and Galleries*, Fine Art Publishing, Sydney, p. 13. Brief account of purchase of 137 bark paintings and sculpture from Kupka in 1984. Works from Kupka's 1963 collection selected for the Australian Institute of Aboriginal Studies now in the National Museum of Australia are noted by David Kaus on p. 25.

5. _____ and N. Lendon, 1997, *The Painters of the Wagilag Sisters Story 1937–1997*, National Gallery of Australia (exhibition catalogue), Canberra, pp. 13, 28, 32. Also catalogue checklist: 3, 10, 13, 49, 52, 79, collected by Kupka for Basel, Canberra and Paris.

6. Catalano, Gary, 1977, 'Changing Responses to Aboriginal Art', *Meanjin* 36 (4), p. 578. "Berndt may well have been reacting [in his speculations beginning 'No Aboriginal art is introvert…'] to the attempts of artists like Karel Kupka [e.g. in 1957b, see above A.2 to impute a 'soverign artistic freedom' to the tribal artist (Kupka considered Arnhem Land bark paintings as examples of expressionism), but his [Berndt's] observation – even if true! – loses all force when we realise that the contrasted tradition of Western art has been caricatured in the process."

7. Clunies Ross, Margaret and Lester R. Hiatt, 1977, 'Sand Sculptures at a Gidjingali Burial Site', in Ucko, P. J. (ed.), *Form in Indigenous Art: Schematisation in the Art of Aboriginal Australia and Prehistoric Europe*, Duckworth, London / Humanities Press, New Jersey, p. 132 (footnote 3): Kupka (1965: 53) acknowledged referring to ground and sand art in Arnhem Land.

8. Cook, J., 1956a, 'Loan Exhibition of Paintings', *Daily Telegraph* (Sydney), 16 November, p. 13. Mention of a short exhibition of bark paintings at the East Sydney Technical College for the benefit of staff and students, initiated by Kupka.

9. _____, 1956b, 'An Exhibition of Aboriginal Arts and Crafts', *Daily Telegraph* (Sydney), 4 December, p. 26. Admonishment of "art enthusiasts (including our Art Galleries)" for neglect of original and powerful Indigenous artists, whose work Kupka collected for Basel and exhibited briefly in Sydney. "Some pastel portraits made by Mr. Kupka during his trip to Arnhem Land and surrounding areas are the only works on sale."

10. Crossman, S., 1990. "Du 'Gilles' de Watteau à l'art brut de Dubuffet: l'obsédante influence française." In: Crossman, S. and J.-P. Barou (eds.), *L'été Australien à Montpellier*, Musée Fabre Galerie Saint Ravy, Montpellier, p. 57. A reminder of the value of Kupka's choice of André Breton to introduce *Un art à l'état brut*. This catalogue, and particularly Barou's essay 'La plus vieille peinture du monde' is cited in Myers [1998, p. 25, see below C.26] to emphasise the debate between art and science.

11. Flynn, Frank, 1963, 'Aboriginal Madonna and Native Art', in Fynn F. and K. Willey, *Northern Gateway*, F. P. Leonard, Sydney, p. 211–221. Account of the commissioning of Kupka's painting *Aboriginal Madonna* for the Darwin (Roman Catholic) Cathedral.

12. Groger-Wurm, Helen, 1973, 'Bark Painting', in Berndt, R. and E. S. Phillips (eds.), *The Australian Aboriginal Heritage: An Introduction through the Arts*, Ure Smith, Sydney, p. 201 and four repro-

ductions. A mention of Kupka's collecting activity: "K. Kupka, a French artist, has collected bark paintings from Arnhem Land for various museums, and also in 1963 a series for the Australian Institute for Aboriginal Studies now (1973) deposited at the Institute of Anatomy, Canberra."

13. Staff Correspondent, 1956, 'A Parisian in Pursuit of our Aborigines' Art', *The Sydney Morning Herald*, 15 November, p. 2, one photograph. Provocative exploitation of Kupka's installation of his first collection of here-called "tanbark paintings" at the esteemed art school East Sydney Technical College for the benefit of teachers and students. " 'What makes this work so interesting to me is that it has real painter's value,' he said, pointing out a design involving what looked like two cubist fish passing through a field of waving corn." This analogy suggests the correspondent is the German-born painter and *Herald* critic from 1941–1957, Paul Haefliger.
14. Jones, Ph., 1988, 'Perceptions of Aboriginal Art: A History', in: Sutton, P. (ed.), *Dreamings: The Art of Aboriginal Australia*, Braziller/ Asia Society Galleries, New York, p. 171. Kupka and Mountford here contrasted with Berndt and Phillips, who maintained "no Aboriginal art is introvert, planned solely as an exercise in individual expression, or a dissertation on the mental or emotional state of a particular artist" in Berndt, R. and E. S. Phillips (eds.), 1973, *The Australian Aboriginal Heritage*, Ure Smith, Sydney. Kupka was "the European artist who considered that Arnhem Land bark painters were 'expressionists' with 'soverign artistic freedom.'" Page-reference to Kupka 1965 inaccurate; perhaps Kupka 1957b was meant (see above A.2. where these words in fact appear).
15. Kaufmann, C., 1980, ‚Ozeanische Kunst – Warum in Basel?', in Kaufmann, C. (ed.), *Ozeanische Kunst: Meisterwerke aus dem Museum fur Völkerkunde*, Museum für Völkerkunde (exhibition catalogue), Basel. Exhibition shown in Kunstmuseum Basel, 23 Feburary to 27 April 1980; included eight bark paintings collected by Kupka. "Erstaunlicherweise darf sich aber auch die nur wenig bekannte Australien-Sammlung des Basler Museums fur Völkerkunde daneben als eine der umfassendsten in Europa sehen lassen. Sie enthält fünf im Felde gesammelte Komplexe, von denen der erste in den Jahren 1900–1927, der letzte (Sammlung K. Kupka) 1957–1966 ins Museum gelangt ist. In der künstlerischen Ausgestaltung bedeutsame Gegenstände sind in allen Teilsammlungen enthalten." (p. 9)
16. Keen, Ian, 1988, 'Twenty-five Years of Aboriginal Kinship Studies,' in Berndt, R. M. and R. Tonkinson (eds.), *Social Anthropology and Australian Aboriginal Studies: A Contemporary Overview*, Aboriginal Studies Press, Canberra, p. 105. Keen quotes John Barnes on the "aesthetic appeal" of many Aboriginal societies' structures of social organisation. Kupka and Tesart (1980 see above A.20) "continue to construct models of marriage exchange between subsections," despite "more adequate repesentations of Murngin (Yolngu) kinship and marriage" by three named anthropologists writing in English between 1967 and 1978.
17. Lendon, Nigel, 2004, 'Innovation and Its Meanings', in *No Ordinary Place: The Art of David Malangi*, National Gallery of Australia, 31 July–7 November, Canberra, pp. 53, 58. General reference to "the work of anthropologists in the late 1950s" who gave the earliest and most detailed contextual accounts of indigenous art.
18. MacIntosh, Neville W. G., 1977, 'Beswick Creek Cave Two Decades Later', in Ucko, P. J. (ed.), *Form in Indigenous Art: Schematisation in the Art of Aboriginal Australia and Prehistoric Europe*, Duckworth, London / Humanities Press, New Jersey. Kupka is referenced: "... the mental code of the artists' schematisation cannot be cracked without keys provided by highly initiated informants. Realisation of this point is clear in the works of Kupka (1965: 88, 90, 120; 1972: 59–62, 71, 80) ..." (p. 197)
19. McCulloch, Susan, 1999, *Contemporary Aboriginal Art: A Guide to the Rebirth of an Ancient Culture*, Allen & Unwin, St. Leonards, pp. 40, 168. Kupka collects for the "National Museum of Arts, Paris"; later called "Hungarian art collector" involved in David Malangi's copyright claim on the Reserve Bank of Australia.

20. Morphy, Howard, 1996, 'Aboriginal Art: Collectors and Dealers', in *Grove Dictionary of Art*, Grove & Macmillan, London, p. 66. Kupka on the list of "major collectors ... outside Australia."
21. Mundine, Djon, n.d., *The Native Born: Objects and Representations from Ramingining, Arnhem Land*, Museum of Contemporary Art, Sydney, pp. 65, 69–73. Importance of Alan Fidock as agent crucial to Kupka, Tuckson, Scougall, Ruhe and Allen's collecting at Milingimbi. Gives a Poignant–Kupka link, possible dates of Kupka visits to Milingimbi, influence of *Dawn of Art*, Kupka's relations with Dawidi and his family, Kupka making portraits of artists; a retelling the 'dollar note' story from the artist Malangi's point of view.
22. _____, 1999a, 'Saltwater', in *Saltwater: Yirrkala Bark Paintings of Sea Country; Recognising Indigenous Sea Rights*. Jennifer Isaacs Publishing in association with Buku-Larrngay Mulka Centre, p. 22. Kupka on a list of ten collectors who visited Yirrkala after WWII.
23. _____, 1999b, 'The Land is Full of Signs', in Morphy, H. and M. Smith Boles (eds.) *Art from the Land: Dialogues with the Kluge-Ruhe Collection of Australian Aboriginal Art*, The University of Virginia, Charlottesville, p. 91. Mention of Kupka's collecting for Paris and Basel, and *Dawn of Art*; Tom Djawa calls him a 'white blackfella', report of David Malangi's memory of him.
24. _____, 2000, 'David Malangi 1927–1999', *Art in Australia*, 38 (1), p. 69. A sentence describing Kupka's involvement with the 'one dollar' misunderstanding.
25. _____, 2004, 'Some people are stories', in *No Ordinary Place: The Art of David Malangi* (exhibition catalogue), National Gallery of Australia, Canberra, 31 July–7 November, pp. 33–34. Paragraphs describing Kupka's involvement with the 'one dollar' misunderstanding.
26. Myers, Fred R., 1998, 'Uncertain regard: An Exhibition of Aboriginal Art in France', *Ethnos* 63 (1), pp. 15, 18, 21, 29, 40, 41. Breton and Kupka linked in search for purity, "deeper structures of the unconscious;" Kupka's "excellent set" of barks at MNAAO constructed there as "an historically significant and distinctive legacy" to valorise the museum and validate its "contemporary artistic value, since Breton, after all had validated it in his celebratory preface to Kupka's book." See also footnote 4: "With a fabulous eye for the workings of Aboriginal abstraction, recognizing that the Aboriginal artists' abstractions are often undecipherable by others, Kupka appreciated that artistry exists in the conscious 'search for the sign that will be most explicit and comprehensible in its brevity' (1962:116, 1965:107)."
27. _____, 2002, *Painting Culture: The Making of an Aboriginal High Art*, Duke University Press, Durham/London, pp. 68, 118. Kupka had undertaken a "brilliant study of Arnhem Land art in the 1950s" published in 1962; Myers uses Kupka's description of crosshatching's 'design effect' in an interesting comparison to dot painting.
28. Neale, Margo, 2001, 'Queensland Art Gallery, Brisbane', in Cochrane, S. (ed.), *Aboriginal Art Collections: Highlights from Australia's Public Museums and Galleries*, Fine Art Publishing, Sydney, p. 60, 2 footnotes. Kupka quoted from his Oceania 1957 article (see above A.2) on the Queensland Art Gallery showing barks with other contemporary paintings, in a manner which other public galleries should follow.
29. Peltier, Philippe, 1999, 'Australie', in *Le Musée des arts d'Afrique et d'Océanie*, Editions de la Réunion des Musées Nationaux, Paris, pp. 120–123. Details of four barks collected by Kupka.
30. _____, 2000, 'Le Temps du rêve: Religion, art et société aborigènes', in *Australie, le temps du rêve*, (exhibition catalogue). Musée de Picardie, Amiens, 17 June –29 October, pp. 31–55. General essay, colour reproductions of 29 barks, eight sculptures and six other objects collected by Kupka, 3 extended citations from Kupka 1972 (see A.17) about particular barks; exhibition checklist.
31. _____, 2001, 'Karel Kupka, le témoin essentiel / Karel Kupka, the essential witness', in Ducreux, A.-C., Kohen, A. and F. Salmond (eds.), *Au centre de la terre d'Arnhem: Entre mythes et réalite, art Aborigène d'Australie / In the Heart of Arnhem Land: Myth and the Making of Contemporary Aboriginal Art* (exhibition catalogue). Musée de l'Hôtel Dieu, Mantes-la-Jolie, France, 24 June–31 October, pp. 33–38. Translation by Apolline Kohen and Murray Garde. Perspective from France of Kupka's

work; begins in Paris with his defense of his thesis in 1969; reflections on the situation of artists in Arnhem Land where increased production caused Kupka to focus on questions of connoisseurship, value and classification. Kupka's preparation for the missions for Basel and Paris; his 'gift' to the Australian Institute for Aboriginal Studies, and the gift of some of his personal collection to MNAAO in 1964; an analysis of the thesis text; a description of the organisation of the collection at MNAAO.

32. _____, and Djon Mundine 1995, 'Interview with David Malangi', in *David Malangi: La galerie des cinq continents*, Musée National des Arts d'Afrique et d'Océanie, Paris, p. 38. Not seen; quoted by Peltier (2001, see C.31) as the source of this information: "C'est au cours de son [Kupka's] troisième voyage en 1960 qu'un des peintres, Dawidi, lui donne son nom."
33. Pullen, R., 1966, 'New Dollar Owes a Lot to Malangi', *South Pacific Post* (Port Moresby) 11 February. Quotes Kupka about his introduction to David Malangi in 1963, whom he called "one of the great Australian Aboriginal artists." Cited in Mundine 2004 (see above C 25).
34. Robinson, Robert, 1976, *The Shift of Sands: An Autobiography 1952–62*, Macmillan, South Melbourne, pp. 168, 173. "My Aboriginal friends at Port Keats were among my many Aboriginal contacts whose names and locations I gave Karel when he dug me out in Sydney to obtain help and directions in his project."
35. Ryan, Judith, 1990, *Spirit in Land: Bark Paintings from Arnhem Land in the National Gallery of Victoria*, National Gallery of Victoria, Melbourne, p. 17. Kupka's own annotations to his brief mention in this text were shown to me by Nigel Lendon, who interviewed him in Paris in 1991. Kupka added references to his collecting for Basel and Canberra.
36. Sayers, Andrew, 2001, *Australian Art*, Oxford University Press, Oxford, p. 195. "Always alert to the aesthetic dimensions of indigenous art, the Czech-born painter Karel Kupka (who was himself responsible for the creation of a major collection of Aboriginal art) described the Aurukun pieces in his 1965 book *Dawn of Art* as 'true sculpture.'"
37. Souef, M., 1993, 'Avant propos: Karel Kupka (1918–1993)', in Dussart, F. (ed.), *La peinture des Aborigènes d'Australie*, Edition Parenthèses, Marseille, pp. 9–16. Very detailed 2,000-word biography, with a portrait taken in 1956 at East Sydney Technical College, and five colour reproductions of Kupka's pastels.
38. Taylor, Luke 1989, 'West Arnhem Land: Figures of Power', in: Caruana, W. (ed.), *Windows on the Dreaming*, Ellsyd Press, Chippendale, pp. 24, 26, 30; see also illustrations on pp. 79, 123. Reference to five barks from Kupka's own collection purchased by the National Gallery of Australia in 1984.
39. _____, 1996a, 'Yirawala (1903–1976)', in *Grove Dictionary of Art*, Grove & Macmillan, London. "In his youth (Yirawala) moved to Croker Island. Here his works, along with those of such artists as Jimmy Midjaw Midjaw, with whom he lived for a while, were collected by the French anthopologist Karel Kupka in 1963." Reference to Kupka 1972 (see above A.17) where the author spells Yirawala thus: Irvala.
40. _____, 1996b, *Seeing the Inside: Bark Painting in Western Arnhem Land*, Clarendon Press, Oxford, pp. 35, 44–45, 138, 224. A short summary of Kupka's collecting between 1960 and 1963, his collecting barks by Yirawala on Croker Island in those years, and generalisations drawn from his description of X-ray painting in *Dawn of Art* (1965:73; see above A.13).
41. _____, 1999, 'Flesh, Bone and Spirit: Western Arnhem Land Painting', in Morphy, H. and M. Smith Boles (eds.), *Art from the Land: Dialogues with the Kluge-Ruhe Collection of Australian Aboriginal Art*, The University of Virginia, Charlottesville, p. 30. Kupka cited as one of five "large scale, systematic" collectors, which "led to rapid growth in the production and sale of bark paintings during the 1960s and 1970s."
42. _____, 2004, 'Fire in the Water: Inspiration from Country', in Perkins, H. (ed.), *Crossing Country: The Alchemy of Western Arnhem Land Art* (exhibition catalogue), The Art Gallery of New South Wales, Sydney, pp. 117–118, 121. Kupka's relations with artists emphasised; an emphasis in his "col-

lection" (the two references to "the Kupka collection" create an imaginary and transcontinental unity) on individual artists' differences when painting the same subject. Also the artists' sharing of ideas of "how to produce paintings for Kupka" to include "wild sexual energy," *mimih* "more elaborate" than those in local rock art, and "themes of sorcery that were not otherwise commonly seen."

43. Viatte, Germain, 2001, 'Malraux et les arts sauvages', in *André Malraux et la modernité* (exhibition catalogue), Musée de la Vie Romantique. Kupka's research contributes to a climate of change in Paris museums. See also (http://www.quaybranly.fr/ under searchword Malraux).
44. Warren, Guy, 2003, 'Sketches from Life: Fragments of an Autobiography', in Hart, D., Lyndon, N., McDonald, J. and G. Warren (eds.) *Searching for Gaia: The Art of Guy Warren*, Macmillan, South Yarra, p. 174. Mention of being introduced to Kupka by artist and designer Douglas Annand in Darwin in 1974.
45. Wise, Tigger, 1985, *The Self-Made Anthropologist: A Life of A. P. Elkin*, Allen & Unwin, Sydney/Boston, pp. 227, 250. Kupka is described as "a Parisian friend," with whom Elkin was working closely "on producing a truly beautiful book on Aboriginal art," as the work-load in Elkin's 70s continued unabated.

D. Reviews of Dawn of Art.

1. Berndt, Ronald M., 1966, 'Review', *Art and Australia* 4 (2), p. 111. Berndt begins by calling the title "unfortunate ... the approach of an artist, not of a trained observer." Various statements linking living Aborigines with "early mankind" are debunked, but "defects are too numerous to note in any detail." He cites Kupka's sponsorship by the Australian Institute of Aboriginal Studies "as an artist and as a collector," and suggests the book be evaluated as a "personal document of an artist.... If the book had fewer 'anthropological' pretentions and had been more openly 'artistic' it would have been much less vulnerable [to an anthropologist's critique]. ... It is in the sphere of design and feeling, and not meaning, that this volume is valuable ...."
2. Bodrogi, Tibor, 1967, 'Review', *Acta Ethnographica Academiae Scientiarum Hungaricae* 16, p. 201–202. Review contains 2,000 words; a summary, chapter by chapter: "The author did not attach too much importance to ... ethnological aspects... (but by describing) the manner in which ideological associations were materialized by colours and lines, Kupka's work has helped in dispelling obscurity ...."
3. Brook, D., 1965, 'Pictures and Theories', *Canberra Times* 18 September, p. 11, illustration. Photo of Jimmy Midjaw-Midjaw painting the Thunder Spirit. "Mr. Kupka cheerfully brings to his task the most vulnerable of presuppositions, which he offers with the air of a man about to build upon rock: 'The true mission of art, the primordial reason for its existence, is communication ...' and 'In painting his body man created a design and at the same time preceived the existance of form ...' One had thought that art had many 'missions' and many (and different) 'reasons for its existence,' and this reviewer, at least, has never fully understood what it is to 'percieve the existence of form.'"
4. Butler, H. D., 1965, 'Review', *Advertiser* (Adelaide) 4 September, p. 20. Not seen.
5. Marshall, J., 1965, 'Review', *The Australian*, 25 September, p. 11. Not seen.
6. Stanner, William E. H., 1967, 'Review', *Mankind* 6 (10), pp. 257–258. W. E. H. Stanner was Acting Chairman of the Interim (first) Council of the Australian Institute for Aboriginal Studies when Kupka chose not to show all of his 1963 Arnhem Land collection to representatives of the Institute before it was shipped to Europe. Stanner's administration of the affair can be followed in the "Karel Kupka" folder kept with the Elkin Papers at the University of Sydney. Stanner had played a role in an earlier dispute between the Australian National University and the anthropologist T. G. H. Strehlow concerning ownership of material collected while Strehlow was funded by the University (see Hill 2002: 418 & note, 611). Stanner's review begins with a mention of Kupka's collecting for Basel "and other bodies, and on his own account." Unmentioned is the substantial collection which the

Institute selected from work shown them by Kupka before he left Sydney for Paris in January 1964. According to a letter of agreement from the Institute (coincidently sent to Paris after Kupka had left for Sydney) the Institute intended to employ Kupka and give him an "allowance for material to be collected for the Institute" with the expectation that "everything collected is to be offered first to the Institute," although Kupka seems never to have agreed to this. Irregular payments were made by the Interim Council, largely on Elkin's authority, but Kupka also had his own resources. His collecting for the Musée des Arts Africains et Océaniens in Paris clearly took priority over Institute claims. Stanner's review notes the dedication of the book to Elkin, examines the Professor's "cautious" support in the Foreword, and claims to detect his "discreet silence" on four of Kupka's questionable assertions. Stanner maintains the first chapters have "little to say … [consisting of] credulous speculations …" "The underlying posture is that an artist, with but an impressionistic grasp of Aboriginal life and mentality, can by fleeting visits and special sensibility grasp better than anyone else the inward motives and conceptual springs of primitive artists." Four other chapters are on a "superior" level, where Kupka has put "his professional experience as an artist to excellent use … and avoids speculative theorizing." The high standard of the book's production is also commended.

Sally Butler

Translating the spectacle: John Mawurndjul's intercultural aesthetic

> Against all modern superstitions of "liberation", it must be said that forms are not free, figures are not free. They are on the contrary bound: the only way to liberate them is to chain them together, in other words to find their links, the ties that create and bind them, that chain them gently together. Moreover, they connect and engender themselves, and art has to enter into the intimacy of this process. *Jean Baudrillard* [1]

> Tell those balanda ('whitefellas') that it's okay, there is not restriction on looking at my paintings. They can enjoy the paintings but buried inside are secret meanings they don't need to know. My paintings are travelling everywhere now, from Sydney right up to Paris or Germany. Everybody can see them, they can think, learn about my cross-hatching. We, the new generation, are taking our culture to far away places where balanda live. *John Mawurndjul* [2]

Introduction

The foregoing quotations from two of our contemporary 'elders' refer to a process of connecting and travelling forms that are symptomatic of our global era. Jean Baudrillard and John Mawurndjul derive from fundamentally different cultural traditions however they share an outlook of inclusiveness that was once an ideal, but today is an imperative. We now understand that visual forms inherently anticipate 'other' meanings and are structures of thought and sense perception that create and reshape social and cultural groups. As Baudrillard describes it, they "engender themselves" to others. The process of engendering inherent to this global exchange does not transfer meaning so much as it initiates it. New forms of knowledge about 'others' initiate new social and cultural relationships, and we remain in a state of renewal.

---

1 Baudrillard, Jean, *The Conspiracy of Art, Manifestos, Interviews*, Essays, Lotringer, S., (ed.), Hodges, A., (trans.), MIT Press, Cambridge, Mass., and London, 2005, p. 127.

2 John Mawurndjul in an interview with Appoline Cohen, see Kohen, A. and J. Mawurndjul '"I never stop thinking about my rarrk"', in Kaufmann C. and Museum Tinguely (eds.) *«Rarrk» – John Mawurndjul. Journey Through Time in Northern Australia,* Schwabe AG, Basel, 2005, p. 27.

Transference of knowledge in traditional Aboriginal cultures is conventionally ritualised by processes of initiation that also mediate social inclusion.[3] In contemporary circumstances these traditional processes of initiation often provide surprisingly useful frameworks for engaging the new outsiders of the global context. John Mawurndjul is an artist who understands how the contingency of his inherited visual traditions equip him with tools to engage in the restriction and liberation of forms in contemporary art. Engagement in this contemporary dialectic of meaning is one of the most significant aspects of intercultural aesthetics, and Mawurndjul's art epitomises its efficacy.

Mawurndjul understands his formal language of crosshatching, or *rarrk,* as restricted (secret) forms that are nonetheless liberated into a contemporary process of connecting, engendering and learning. In this sense Mawurndjul uses *rarrk* to initiate meaning in a global context where; "Everybody can see them, they can think, learn about my crosshatching."[4] He refers also to the "enjoyment" of *rarrk*, and it is this aspect of enjoyment, or appeal, that is of particular interest in this discussion. Enjoyment and appeal are significant as they provide the spark that initiates engagement, and it is insightful to consider how Mawurndjul engenders appeal for 'outsider/others' in his art. This discussion examines how the intercultural appeal of John Mawurndjul's aesthetic is embedded in a ritualised experience of spectacle – an experience common to both Mawurndjul's traditional Kuninjku ceremonial ritual and the exhibition ritual of contemporary international art.

Intercultural perspectives

There have been relatively few opportunities to appreciate intercultural characteristics of contemporary Aboriginal art because it is conventionally exhibited in a hermetic framework of Aboriginal cultural specificity, or else subsumed into group shows governed by generalised ideological themes. The art is rarely presented in ways where its own internal mobility and development can be appreciated, giving some sense of artists' responsiveness to their contemporary contexts. *«Rarrk» – John Mawurndjul. Journey Through Time in Northern Australia* (henceforth referred to as «*Rarrk*»), was a monograph exhibition that achieved this task in profiling the development of one contemporary Aboriginal artist over a period of 25 years. The artistic scope of this exhibition, together with the exhibition catalogue's extensive research regarding the art, revealed how Mawurndjul's increasing awareness of his 'global audience' is concurrent with transformation and amplification in his use of the *rarrk* aesthetic.

Rarrk is a visual design element that engenders the identity of particular social and cultural groups in Arnhem Land. In Mawurndjul's Kuninjku culture, *rarrk* crosshatching conventionally formed an in-fill function for figurative elements, and was created by ap-

---

3 See Keen, Ian, *Knowledge and Secrecy in an Aboriginal Religion*, Clarendon Press, Oxford, U.K., 1994; LaFontaine, Jean S., *Initiation: Ritual Drama and Secret Knowledge Across the World*, Penguin, New York, 1985.

4 Kohen, A. and J. Mawurndjul, 2005, in Kaufmann C. and Museum Tinguely (eds.), *op. cit.* p. 27.

plication of ochre paint with an extremely fine brush made of natural hairs. Designs were formed from diagonal grids of meticulously drawn lines arranged in different ochre colouring. The «*Rarrk*» exhibition created focus on this aspect of Mawurndjul's art and how the artist developed it as a mode of visual appeal for non-initiated audiences.

«*Rarrk*» drew on certain exhibition rituals that shape the way we see the art. Contemporary exhibitions are conventionally developed with project teams who work collaboratively with artists, if possible. This spirit of collaboration is inherent to the entire industry of producing and exhibiting contemporary Aboriginal art. Long-standing relationships between artists, arts advisers, anthropologists, dealers and curators are the mechanics of the contemporary Aboriginal art industry. Exhibitions develop from collaborations based on these long-standing relationships, and «*Rarrk*» is a pertinent example.

The three curators of the exhibition were Bernhard Lüthi, Christian Kaufmann and Tiriki Onus. Lüthi is an artist/curator recognised most notably for his work in exhibiting Australian Indigenous art in Europe. He was chargé de mission for the 1989 *Magiciens de la Terre* exhibition in Paris and curated *Aṯatjara – Art of the First Australians* that opened in Düsseldorf and toured to London and Humlebaek in 1993/4. Kaufmann's involvement with Australian Indigenous art and culture derives from his extensive career as curator of the Oceania Department of the Museum der Kulturen Basel (1970 to 2005) and lecturer in anthropology at the University of Basel (2000–2005). Tiriki Onus is the son of the late Lin Onus, an Australian Indigenous artist from Victoria who worked collaboratively with Aboriginal clans in western Arnhem Land. Tiriki Onus participated in the preparation phase of the exhibition, during and after the first and second research and documentary trips in 2003/4. During these research trips all of the curators worked closely with Mawurndjul in the development of the exhibition.

Collaboration between these individuals and institutions in developing the exhibition inevitably drew together differing cultural traditions and rituals struggling to resolve themselves into some form of coherent rationale about the art. A sense of cultural intersection was strongly evident in the exhibition. Mawurndjul's status as a Kuninjku elder from the Duwa moiety clan country south of Maningrida in Arnhem Land derives from rituals and values of a visual culture immensely different to that sustaining his status as contemporary international artist.[5] Although the origins of bark paintings seemed very distant to the spaces of the Museum Tinguely, the barks did not seem 'out of place' either.

In the «*Rarrk*» exhibition audiences encountered an interaction between rituals of two ostensibly incommensurable visual cultures. The impression of an ancient but ongoing Kuninjku tradition was signalled by inclusion of bark paintings created in the early to mid-twentieth century. Past traditions also featured in the exhibition's didactic panels and film documentation profiling Mawurndjul's ancestral heritage in the rock art in Kuninjku country. At the same time, the monograph presentation of Mawurndjul's art within the contemporary art space of the Museum Tinguely invoked exhibition rituals of Western

5 Altman, Jon, 'From Mumeka to Basel: John Mawurndjul's Artistic Odyssey', in Kaufmann C. and Museum Tinguely (eds.), *op. cit.*, 2005, (pp. 30–39), p. 31.

contemporary art. Art works were hung with elegant spatial articulation, and organised into the kind of chronological narrative of revelation typified by Western teleological traditions of exhibiting art. A paradox of contemporary antiquity arose in this confluence of ritual, however Mawurndjul's art appeared to transcend the paradox, or more accurately perhaps, his art engaged with it.

Monograph exhibitions are a Western cultural construct with a frame of reference based on individualism and aesthetic characteristics of one artist's oeuvre. Monographs implicitly seek out how an artist's 'signature style' develops. This individualistic construct intrinsically diminishes focus on the collective basis of Mawurndjul's Kuninjku traditional identity. However, there are considerable gains with the monograph construct in terms of how it implicitly maps Mawurndjul's engagement with his more 'global' collective audience. As with many exhibitions today, rituals of display derive from both modernist and contemporary principles. They adhere to concerns for the autonomous artist and art object but also pay heed to the contemporary spirit of inclusiveness referenced in Baudrillard's quotation at the beginning of this discussion. The drifts between autonomy and inclusiveness evident in the exhibition attest to Baudrillard's sense of forms that "are not free."

As the title of the exhibition suggests, the curators identified Mawurndjul's use of the *rarrk* aesthetic as a signifying aspect of his art. Audiences were directed toward transitions in the artist's aesthetic logic as he manipulates and reinvigorates the language of fine crosshatching. At the same time, the exhibition drew attention to Mawurndjul's thematic developments and his increasing focus on the subject of Mardayin ceremony, a thematic focus corresponding to the expansion of the *rarrk* aesthetic.

Rarrk crosshatching occurs in all art works by John Mawurndjul in the exhibition, comprising over sixty bark paintings dating from 1979 to the present, several painted hollow logs and a number of etchings produced by the artist in 2004. Early barks from the Kupka collection (see Kaufmann, C. and R. McMillan, this volume, pp. 137–159) demonstrated in an introductory section how traditional use of *rarrk* was limited to the in-fill of figurative imagery. Likewise, early works by John Mawurndjul focusing on themes of Ngalyod (rainbow serpent), *yawkyawk* (young girl water spirits), and *namarrkon* (female lightning spirit) are substantially figurative in nature, with *rarrk* used only as infill.

Limited application of *rarrk* in these early bark paintings contrasts significantly with the dominance of crosshatching in Mawurndjul's mature style. As Luke Taylor observes in his catalogue essay, during the 25-year period of Mawurndjul's art the use of figurative imagery undergoes transformation in terms of its relationship with *rarrk* non-figurative elements.[6] Mawurndjul progressively transforms the in-fill function of *rarrk* into more spatial and thematic significance. In drawing attention to Mawurndjul's aesthetic developments, the exhibition created awareness of the artist's individual creativity and his deliberated re-interpretation of an aesthetic feature of his art. Mawurndjul refers to these aesthetic

6 Taylor, Luke, 'John Mawurndjul – "I've got a different idea"', in Kaufmann C. and Museum Tinguely (eds.), *op. cit.*, 2005, pp. 42–63.

developments in a quite individualistic sense, claiming it as "my own style, my own ideas."[7] The artist's individual re-interpretation of inherited designs transforms in the monograph context into expressions of signature style.

The artist's concern with engaging contemporary audiences also was apparent throughout the exhibition and supporting catalogue, signalling that an intercultural perspective was an imperative in his art. Mawurndjul's awareness of the global perspective of his art is documented in the catalogue repeatedly in terms of the artist's interaction with arts advisers, curators and audiences and his participation in international group exhibitions. Mawurndjul's participation at numerous international art events exposed the artist to cultural rituals of contemporary art exhibitions.

Experiencing exhibitions

These exhibition rituals are structures of visibility that determine a contemporary politics of recognition. The cultural ritual of modernist exhibitions in particular has been the topic of several recent art history studies, such as Carol Duncan's *Civilizing Rituals: Inside Public Art Museums* and Mary Ann Staniszewski's *The Power of Display.* Staniszewski describes the modernist exhibition ritual as powerful creations that manifest impact well beyond aesthetics, into areas of value, ideology and politics. Contemporary exhibitions maintain these modernist principles.

Mawurndjul's exposure to this politics of recognition was broad. In a twenty-year period from 1986 Mawurndjul's art appeared in at least fourteen international exhibitions across Western Europe, Russia, Japan, India, the United States and South America. Whilst Mawurndjul's art was obviously considered to be in dialogue with other art in these group exhibitions, the artist himself also interacted with the professional milieu of these exhibitions. Jon Altman describes this interaction in his catalogue essay:

> In 1993, Mawurndjul travelled to Dusseldorf for A̲ratjara: Art of the First Australian exhibition, a particularly significant event in his career, according to Moon, [Diane Moon was art co-ordinator at Maningrida Arts Centre at the time and accompanied the artist to Europe] because he engaged with international curators, journalists and art world personalities. Equally importantly, Mawurndjul had opportunity to travel to some major European galleries. At the Rijksmuseum in Amsterdam he was impressed by the Dutch still-life paintings and interiors but was especially taken by the Icon room where he a felt a great sense of reverence.[8]

We will return to this last point regarding reverence in ensuing discussion of the concept of spectacle however for the moment it is significant to make note of Mawurndjul's exposure to modernist exhibition ritual – in terms of its spaces of exhibition; its inscription of world

---

7 Kohen, A. and J. Mawurndjul, 2005, in Kaufmann C. and Museum Tinguely (eds.), *op. cit.* p. 27.

8 Altman, J., 2005, in Kaufmann C. and Museum Tinguely (eds.), *op. cit.*, p. 36.

history; and its human infrastructure. At home in Australia Mawurndjul's involvement with exhibition rituals occurred as early as 1983 when the artist visited Canberra's newly opened National Gallery of Australia with its strong collection of international art. Whilst there he also participated in an exhibition at the Canberra School of Art.

Altman also argues that Mawurndjul's global awareness was enhanced further by his "management of important but burgeoning relationships with a number of art advisers, all of whom were white (or Balanda)."[9] During his career Mawurndjul worked with more than twelve art advisers at Maningrida Art Centre, some of whom were artists and notably a linguist who provided an opportunity that Altman considers was "to provide excellent documentation to accompany Mawurndjul's art, but he was also able to give him his own voice through a series of published interviews and in direct translation at major events like the Sydney Biennale in 2000." Altman describes these art co-ordinators as "cross cultural mediators" who significantly enhanced Mawurndjul's ability to "embrace the fiercely competitive fine art world and ... strive and take pride in excelling in the world of Balanda art."[10]

Kuninjku ways of seeing

It is interesting that Mawurndjul's success in engaging with modernist exhibition rituals does not diminish his deep connection with Kuninjku traditions. In fact, his global awareness seems to enrich his traditional connections. Luke Taylor identifies Mawurndjul in this regard as an intercultural mediator. He writes:

> Having travelled the world and visited some of the most important art museums Mawurndjul understands his intercultural role and understands the term 'artist' as someone who mediates the Kuninjku artistic tradition through his own understanding and inspiration.[11]

Whilst Taylor does not refer to it himself, one of his earlier studies regarding iconography in Kuninjku bark painting identifies an inherited Kuninjku visual skill in mediating different realms of meaning; a skill that would appear ideal for an intercultural mediator. He identifies in the so-called x-ray style of bark painting the metaphoric capacity of the 'divided body' of figurative elements; it generates a process of socialisation and realisation of one's place in the world. X-ray style bark painting is characterised by depictions of human and animal bodies featuring internal organs and skeletal elements. These internal elements are distinctly partitioned into what Taylor describes as a visual semantics that encode complex metaphors linking inside (secret or restricted) knowledge and outside (public) knowledge.

---

9 Altman, J., 2005, in Kaufmann C. and Museum Tinguely (eds.), *op. cit.*, p. 37.
10 Ibid.
11 Taylor, L., 2005, in Kaufmann C. and Museum Tinguely (eds.), *op. cit.*, p. 43.

This strategy of the 'divided body' encourages analogies between the familiar daily life of Kuninjku experience and the more esoteric realm of spiritual consciousness through graphic differentiations between natural and geometric figuration. Use of spiritually connoted stylistic features such as dotted lines and intricate crosshatching are also applied. Taylor argues that learning to read these analogies and negotiating connections between inside and outside meanings is a traditional process of socialisation assisting initiation into a Kuninjku world view.

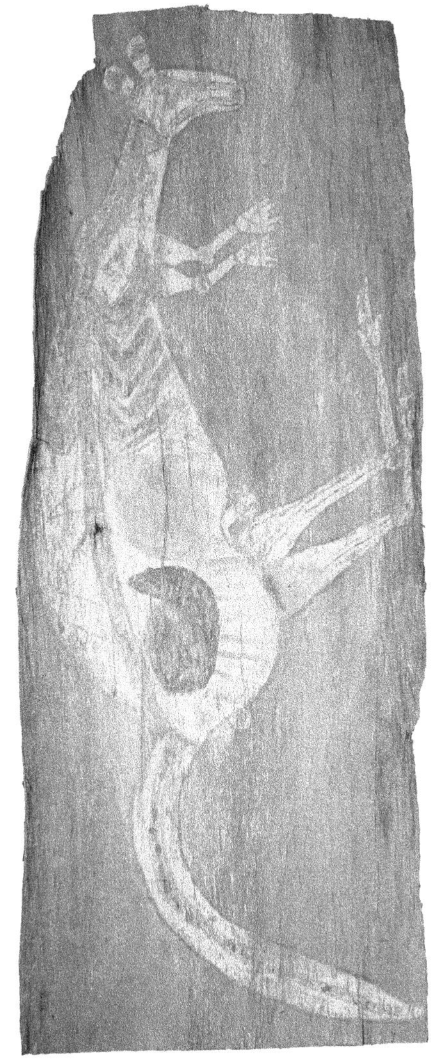

Fig. 30: Painter unkown, *Kangaroo*, before 1931, earth pigments on bark, 120 x 50 cm, Museum der Kulturen Basel. Coll. E. Handschin. Va 356. Photo Museum der Kulturen Basel.

In the context of contemporary art, it is interesting to consider how a visual skill in the art of analogy would be a useful tool for intercultural mediation. Taylor describes how this semantic negotiation of inside and outside meaning extends to an ever-widening stock of personal experience. Mawurndjul's own widening stock of personal experience incorporates his international exposure and intercultural awareness, and arguably extends this process of socialisation into an entirely new dimension of 'outside', rather than 'inside', meaning. In this sense, Mawurndjul's contemporary aesthetic appears as a way of encoding relations between new realms of social experience generated by global cultural engagement. Extension of the 'outside' realm of meaning to an unfamiliar and profoundly uninitiated Balanda audience complicates the dichotomy of inside/esoteric and outside/public meaning because there are now infinitely more different realms of outside meaning. Outside meanings thus range from the familiar realm of everyday Kuninjku experience to the far less familiar realm of global interaction.

Examples of early bark painting in the «*Rarrk*» exhibition illustrate how in the era of early contact symbolic representation in x-ray art consisted largely of figurative motifs of animals and humans recognisable to the familiar 'outside' realm of daily experience.

Kangaroo (see fig. 30) by an unknown artist and dated before 1931 is an example. Taylor describes how these easily recognisable 'outside' motifs are systematically broken down into elements that operate semantically to form analogies with the less familiar inside realm of esoteric knowledge and spiritual significance. This divided body is an aesthetic strategy that conditions familiar visual elements into analogies with less familiar esoteric concepts.

Translating for a Balanda audience

A reverse in this process occurs in the intercultural encounter. The outside Balanda audience is not familiar with even everyday experience. The artist must begin with an unfamiliar 'outside' realm of Balanda visual experience in order to make analogies. The bodies of animals and spirit figures common to mythology are not familiar to them and the artist must find another aesthetic vehicle where analogy, and mediation, can occur.

In this reversal, or complication, of what is inside and outside realms of meaning, Mawurndjul meets the challenge by developing an aesthetic that arguably appropriates an exhibition concept of spectacle, or an abstraction of psychological power analogous to Balanda modernist aesthetics. The defining characteristic of this aesthetic strategy is Mawurndjul's innovative and increasing use of *rarrk* crosshatching. *Rarrk* becomes the principle vehicle for engagement with Balanda audiences. The artist himself refers to the fundamental significance of *rarrk* in his aesthetic on numerous occasions in the exhibition catalogue, and claims it as a vehicle that links past traditions with present circumstances through his own creative innovation: "my own ideas." The following quote from the catalogue is an example:

> When I was a teenager I saw Yirawala and other old people [deceased artists]. I am familiar with their work and learned from them. I have put their knowledge and images into my mind ... We young people [new generation] have changed to using rarrk. White, yellow, red, black, that's what we use in the crosshatching. ... They [early bark painters] took the rarrk from the Mardayin ceremony and put it on bark. They started it and we, the new generation, are doing new things. I make my rarrk different.[12]

Mawurndjul's comments in this quotation remind us that even these early bark paintings were involved in intercultural negotiations. The historical instance of when artists "took the *rarrk* from Mardayin ceremony and put it on bark," underscores how the concept of bark painting as autonomous objects with specifically painted designs actually developed from intercultural exchange. Early anthropologists and ethnographic collectors sought out

12 John Mawurndjul in Kohen, A. and J. Mawurndjul, 2005, in Kaufmann C. and Museum Tinguely (eds.), *op. cit.*, p. 25.

sheets of painted bark that were formerly the decorated walls of bark huts and a new 'tradition' of bark painting emerged.[13]

This demonstrates how Kuninjku traditions employ the versatility of their visual culture as a vehicle of cultural transition over vast differences of time. In film documentation and written catalogue interviews, Mawurndjul draws attention to the connections between his contemporary expression of cultural identity and those of his forebears. The continuity of *rarrk* remains constant in this history of cultural expression.

Mawurndjul's engagement with the international contemporary art market results in an 'elaboration' of the artist's Kuninjku traditions, according to Luke Taylor. The latter's sustained anthropological research into Kuninjku visual traditions cover almost the same period as the 25 years of Mawurndjul's art practice, and provides him with considerable insight into how the art has changed, and in what context. His catalogue essay maps thematic developments in the art, and also draws attention to stylistic changes, particularly the differing approaches to use of *rarrk* crosshatching. Taylor demonstrates how, over the course of several decades, Mawurndjul's use of *rarrk* transformed from a minor role as infill to becoming instead the central element of his art. The following section speculates on how this amplification and elaboration of the *rarrk* aesthetic appeals to an intercultural perspective.

Rarrk as spectacle

There are areas of human experience where an appeal to one's emotional intelligence is more effective than an intellectual, or rationalised, approach. Socialisation often occurs within concepts that are intangible, esoteric, or sense-driven. Indigenous ceremonial traditions, such as Kuninjku, draw heavily on emotive and sensational stimulants to engage and embody audiences into a quite defined expression of cultural identity.[14] The concept of spectacle sits at the heart of much of this emotive and sensational stimulus. Ceremonial body painting and apparel are spectacular, as are the dramatic dance formations performed across the fire-lit stages of grandly designed ground paintings. Ceremonial rituals provide an intense experience of visual spectacle that embeds itself in esoteric paradigms of spiritual belief and social status.

A more detailed discussion of the relationship between ceremony and spectacle is beyond the scope of this essay however focus remains on the visual spectacle's incorporation of intangible or esoteric aspects of experience. Certain concepts are simply too broad, or too imprecise in nature, to be articulated in words. But often a visual image can accommodate this profound generalisation, or provide a concept with an undefined 'presence'. The *rarrk* aesthetic has already been examined in terms of this profound 'presence' by Howard

13 Morphy, Howard, *Aboriginal Art*, Phaidon, London, 1998.

14 Dussart, Françoise, *Walbiri Women's Yawulya Ceremonies. A Forum for Socialization and Innovation,* Unpublished PhD Thesis, Australian National University, Canberra, 1988; LaFontaine, J. S., 1985, *op. cit.*

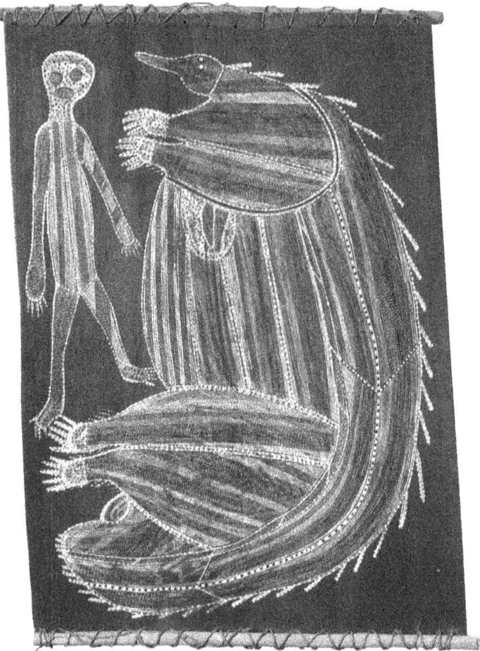

Fig. 31: John Mawurndjul, *Bambil, echidna and mimih*, 1979, earth pigments on bark, 68 x 46 cm, Jon Altman. Photo Archives of the owner. © 2008, ProLitteris, Zürich.

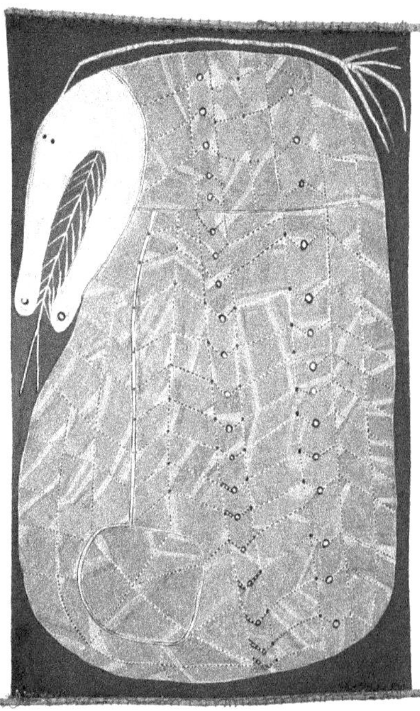

Fig. 32: John Mawurndjul, *Ngalyod, rainbow serpent*, 1999, earth pigments on bark, 153 x 90 cm, L.A. Moran Collection. Photo Carl Warner. © 2008, ProLitteris, Zürich.

Morphy, Judith Ryan and Luke Taylor.[15] The shimmering effect of *rarrk* derives from the visual spectacle of closely aligned lines of varied colours that create an optical energy, or retinal vibration, that is perceived as a form of spiritual, or 'ancestral' power.

It is conceivable that Mawurndjul attempts to harness this spectacular esoteric power of *rarrk* as a 'power tool' for appeal to the global audience. Mawurndjul's reference to his experience of reverence in the Icon room of the Rijksmuseum has arguably as much to do with the exhibition's spectacular 'power of display' as with any perceived understanding of medieval religious practice. However, it does reveal that Mawurndjul perceived a spiritual or metaphysical 'presence' within an art gallery. The relevant context for Mawurndjul's art was not medieval figurative art, but art that was modernist or contemporary in nature. The non-figurative emphasis of much of modernist art instils a sense of intangible subject matter that achieves its power often through imagery that is a cohesive field of visual expression rather than being referential or narrative in nature.

15 Morphy, H., 'From Dull to Brilliant', in Coote, J. and A. Shelton (eds.), *Anthropology, Art and Aesthetics*, Claendon Press, Oxford, 1992, pp. 181–208; Ryan, J. (this volume); Taylor, L. (this volume).

Mawurndjul's art progressively registers a shift toward this field of apparently non-referential imagery. In the development of his art Mawurndjul transforms *rarrk* from the role of infill to that of a complete figure in itself. From his early bark paintings in 1979 to his most recent work in 2005, the most emphatic aesthetic development is a transition from paintings that embody isolated elements of a cultural tradition, to paintings that make a coherent, yet esoteric, statement of his cultural identity. *Rarrk* is the vehicle for this transition.

Mawurndjul's early bark paintings bear the mark of his forebears in the way they depict figures of totemic animals or mythological figures as isolated elements, as in the painting *Bambil, echidna, and mimih*, 1979, (see fig. 31 and pl. XXI). Figures float in space on a plain red ochre background, with coloured bands of *rarrk* forming the infill of the body.

As Mawurndjul's art develops, he brings more compositional cohesion into his art by increasingly filling the pictorial space with either enlarged figures with extensive *rarrk* in-fill, or by using the *rarrk* design to cover the surface. *Ngalyod, rainbow serpent*, 1999, (see fig. 32 and pl. XXII) is an example of where the artist expands the figure of the serpent to almost fill the pictorial surface, and transforms the coiled body of the spirit figure into a complex composition of *rarrk* crosshatching.

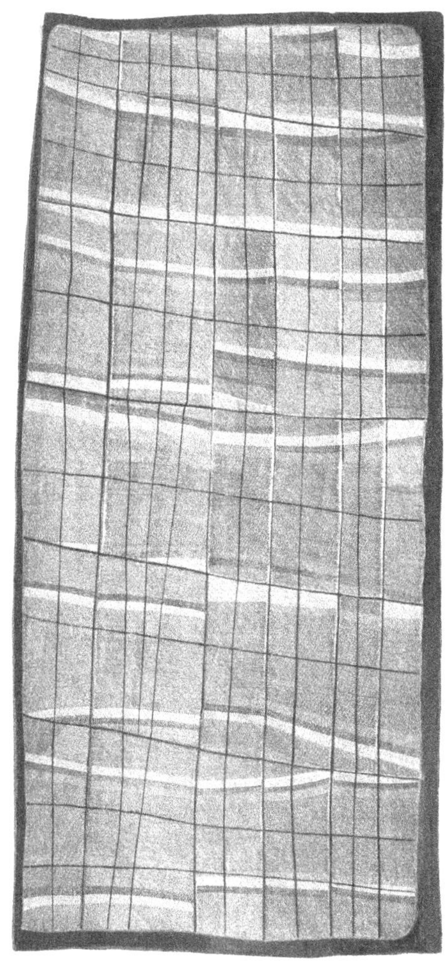

Fig. 33: John Mawurndjul (Kuninjku born 1952), *Mardayin at Dilebang*, 2003, earth pigments on bark, 131.6 x 63 cm, National Gallery of Victoria, Melbourne. Presented through the NGV Foundation by Greg Rosshandler, 2003. 2003.662. Photo National Gallery of Victoria. © 2008, ProLitteris, Zürich.

Figures have disappeared altogether in paintings such as *Mardayin at Dilebang*, 2003, (see fig. 33), leaving the passages of *rarrk* composition as an esoteric, yet cohesive and powerful expression of Kuninjku identity. Reproductions do not convey the spectacle of these intricately worked *rarrk* compositions. They are almost mesmerising in their dynamic organisation and compositional balance, and have an over-riding sense of intangible coherence reminiscent of the all-over field painting of Jules Olitski. Within the modernist exhibition ritual, the optical energy of these paintings translates into a powerful, if intangible, expression of cultural definition.

Jon Altman makes notes of this power when he describes how Mawurndjul creates "ever more powerful artistic statements about this knowledge of the sacred maps of the mythological and sentient landscape."[16] It is a presence of knowledge, or an esoteric statement of self-confidence, that gives this work its power, rather than its capacity to convince on a referential level. Mawurndjul translates a body of knowledge into a ritualistic spectacle capable of appealing to non-initiated 'outsider' audiences.

At the same time as this development in all-over design, the scale of Mawurndjul's art increases and he begins to develop 'big barks'. Mawurndjul's exposure to modernist aesthetics and Balanda art advisers may have inspired his tendencies toward all-over painting. Taylor describes how this aesthetic transformation in the use of *rarrk* is concurrent to Mawurndjul's increasing concentration on the theme of Mardayin ceremony from the 1990s.

As Mawurndjul refines his thematic oeuvre, he shows an increasing propensity to submerge the figurative representation into shimmering fields of *rarrk* patterning, and capture the sensual energy of ceremonial performance.

However, the significant aspect in this aesthetic transformation is in how the artist controls these transformations in ways that sustain a Kuninjku identity of cultural expression. Mawurndjul draws on the essence of Kuninjku visual expression to create a 'signature style' that competes in the global politics of recognition. To use a modernist term, this is the genius of Mawurndjul's art, and where its intercultural efficacy is most apparent.

In the context of Mawurndjul's increasing awareness of the global context of his art it is reasonable to consider that he understands the art object in a different way to his forebears, realising that in its expanded field of reception the image cannot function within traditional narrative formations of cognition and value. The image must exhibit a more autonomous coherence that was not at issue for the early bark painters who did not have the same awareness of the outside context of their art. Mawurndjul is acutely aware that his *rarrk* forms are "travelling everywhere" today, and that they are capable of powerful impact in the politics of recognition.

Conclusion

The «*Rarrk*» exhibition profiles a dimension of intercultural aesthetics in the manner it creates awareness of the contemporary status of the art. This contemporary emphasis serves to incorporate local and global frames of reference, and inclusive and exclusive aspects of meaning. The exhibition engenders a sense of dynamic negotiability between these distinct but overlapping cultural paradigms, and thus avoids the tokenistic mode of recognition often afforded to contemporary indigenous art. This is to say that the exhibition makes a considered and serious attempt to understand specific ways that Mawurndjul's art relates to a contemporary 'global' audience.

16 Altman, J., 2005, in Kaufmann C. and Museum Tinguely (eds.), *op. cit.*, p. 37.

The sheets of bark that originally attracted the attention of anthropologists and ethnographic collectors went into substantial museum collections around the world, however Australian art institutions did not parallel this interest in bark paintings until the later half of the twentieth century. Even less interest was shown by international art institutions. This is why the «*Rarrk*» exhibition is a landmark event. Exhibition of Arnhem Land bark paintings in a contemporary European art museum is a sign of how art has entered into the process of finding the links that connect us. The exhibition, and most importantly the art, anticipates our future.

Further Reading:

Bharucha, Rustom, 'Interculturalism and its Discriminations: Shifting the Agendas of the National, the Multicultural and the Global', *Third Text* 46, 1999, pp. 3–24.

Duncan, Carol, *Civilizing Rituals: Inside Public Art Museums,* Routledge, London and New York, 1995.

Hinkson, Melinda, 'Rarrk – John Mawurndjul: A Journey Through Time in Northern Australia', *Art Monthly Australia* 185, 2005, pp.14–16, 18–19.

Morphy, Howard, 'Aboriginal Art in a Global Context' in Miller, D. (ed.), *Worlds Apart: Modernity through the Prism of the Local,* Routledge, London, 1995, pp. 211–239.

Staniszewski, Mary A., *The Power of Display, A History of Exhibition Installations at the Museum of Modern Art,* MIT Press, Cambridge, Mass. and London, 1998.

Taylor, Luke, 'Seeing the Inside: Kuninjku Paintings and the Symbol of the Divided Body', in Morphy, H., (ed.), *Animals into Art,* Unwin Hyman, London, 1989, pp. 372–389.

Wittgenstein, Ludwig, *Lectures and Conversations on Aesthetics, Psychology and Religious Belief,* Barrett, C., (ed.), Blackwell, Oxford, 1970.

Jean-Hubert Martin

Art of the Aborigines between new-age mysticism and politics

Although not an expert on Aboriginal art I have been occupied with it for many years. In my work as a curator and practitioner of museums and exhibitions I have attempted to apply an integration strategy which involves the inclusion of Aboriginal art works in the field of contemporary art. Most experts who are specialised in Aboriginal arts still make heavy weather of integrating the contemporary art of Aborigines in the common network of values of contemporary Western art. It is a remarkable exception that an Aboriginal artist like John Mawurndjul is not shown in an ethnographic museum, but in a museum of contemporary art like the Museum Tinguely. I appreciate this all the more, considering the fact that one of my main curatorial aims is to expand the rigid Western perspective on art. The scale of values in the arts of today needs re-evaluating in a post-colonial perspective.

Before coming to my specific point let me look back and recount how I first became acquainted with art of the Aborigines at the Sydney Biennale in 1982 where a group of Yuendumu created a ground painting while performing a ceremony. There were long discussions with the artists invited to the Biennale about the validity of religious art in such an event. Many artists maintained that it was impossible to include such a 'traditional' work stemming from a religious ritual. The Paris-based artist Niele Toroni even said if one wanted to include such artists in a contemporary art exhibition one should also consider inviting crucifix makers from Brittany. At that point it became clear to me that there existed a real taboo in the contemporary art world concerning works emanating from cultures without writing. These discussions and thoughts were important for the conception of the exhibition *Magiciens de la Terre* which I put together in Paris in 1989. One hundred contemporary artists from all five continents were invited to exhibit their works. It was the first big exhibition of contemporary art that did not set itself fixed geographic boundaries. Visual creations from all over the world were shown on an equal basis.

We usually operate in the framework of existing Western categories. Up to now, the Western cultural value system has always been the gauge by which the distinction has been made between art and craft, between major and minor genres, between authentic and folkloristic. This taxonomy always seems to win. In order to find a common denominator for the very different practices, I chose the individual artist as a criterion for the exhibition as opposed to the supposed anonymity of so called 'primitive art'. The show did not exclude collective works. But, for example, each participant of the Yuendumu ground painting was individually named in the catalogue and on the labels. It is interesting to note that group-work still exists in the West as a sort of ideal practice. Young artists often start working in groups at the beginning of their career, but the power of the media and the 'star cult' unfortunately urges them to leave the group and to find a way of their own.

It was very difficult for me to select the Australian Aboriginal artists for *Magiciens de la Terre*. I was confronted with a huge production of paintings. The selection was made together with Bernard Lüthi. At the time, three criteria seemed to be important:

– *Support:*
Bark as an image carrier seemed to me very coherent and specific because of the consistency of the material and its link with the environment. I received support for these ideas through my talks with artists, especially with Lawrence Weiner who accompanied me on a trip to the Pacific.

– *Size:*
The form of the painting depends on its support; either it is bark, which obviously cannot exceed a certain size, or it is ground, which gives it a totally different dimension.

– *Technique*:
With artists of the talent of Mawurndjul, the technique of crosshatching (*rarrk*) can attain an extremely refined level. This distinguished him already at that time from other Aboriginal painters. In the same exhibition, paintings of Wunuwun and hollow logs by Wululu were also shown.

Unfortunately one has to say that the interconnection between contemporary art and Aboriginal art has not grown very much since then. The art of Aborigines is developing its own market in Australia and has generated an expanding network of galleries and auctions. The Australian art museums are showing Aboriginal art together with modern works. Regrettably the situation is different in Europe. Many experts still see Australian Aboriginal art as an autonomous bubble. Some critics who specialise in the art of the 20th century, like Werner Spiess, consider Aboriginal art as folkloristic. The Essl Collection in Austria is a remarkable exception for a European public art (not ethnographic) museum that shows Aboriginal art. Another example is (or rather: was), of course, the Musée des arts d'Afrique et d'Océanie in Paris with its aim to be a place of dialogue between the arts of the five continents.

For the integration of Aboriginal art in the field of contemporary art, two issues seem to me very important because they challenge the prejudices held against this strategy: evolution and politics.

Evolution

Many observers still think that Aboriginal art consists of the repetition of given patterns. They are blind for the obvious developments, especially during the last decade. Since the Papunya Tula Movement, new techniques and supports are being used by the artists: canvas and acrylic painting. Dot paintings developed in many new and unexpected directions and led to the discovery of ever-evolving new visual effects. There have been lively discussions within the communities about the secrecy of images and the ownership of images and patterns by clans. In most cases the issues were settled, allowing a great number of paintings to be sold. On the other hand, in some cooperative associations real marketing efforts are being made in conjunction with a control of quality; in this respect the remarkable work of Djon Mundine has received much attention.

The evolution in representing some old narratives can be obvious even to non-initiated viewer. I had the chance of visiting Yirrkala in 1997 and meeting Andrew Blake in order to buy a few paintings for the Musée des arts d'Afrique et d'Océanie in Paris. Among them was the work *Totems Munyuku*, 1996, by Bakulangay Marawili. The story to the painting belongs to the Munyuku clan. It tells of how the ancestors of the Munyuku clan carved up a whale they had just killed and how they threw their tools into the sea after finishing the job. The tools, which were potentially dangerous, formed into two rocks known as Ganapana. In the painting the rocks are symbolised on the one hand by the two black oval forms, and on the other by the two oval forms that are painted on the back of the whales. The two rocks are famous for creating underwater streams. This is shown by the waves that cover the background of the picture. The motive shows that the whales and the tools belong to the Munyuku clan while the stingrays and the other elements belong to the Wasamirri clan. The elders discussed at length whether Bakulangay Marawili was allowed to blend the two stories. In the end the painting was permitted to be shown to the public. Its originality is visible and its complexity distinguishes it from other standard images. The strength of artistic achievement is obvious, even for a non-Aboriginal viewer: the iconography, i.e. the image and its content, are innovative. It shows a procedure comparable to the situation of the Western artist challenging the accepted convention of iconography.

Politics

In museums of modern art religious phenomena are excluded from the discussion, following the Hegelian dogma that underpins modernity.

Since Romanticism, politics have become an indispensable criterion of aesthetic quality. Today more than ever, it constitutes the cornerstone of aesthetic evaluation. The need to combat conservatism and to fight for progressive measures that are beneficial to humanity as a whole has often taken precedence in artistic matters over purely formal questions that have been relegated to secondary status. In the wake of conceptual art, meaning and political discourse have become so prominent that the relevance of the concept is widely assumed to guarantee the pertinence of any form derived from it.

In this context, politics is always envisaged in terms of a balance of power as defined by the West (with Marxist overtones): socialism vs. conservatism, independence vs. colonialism. It is also associated in a most arrogant fashion with the history of Western political struggle. This excludes the peoples from many developing countries whose experience is scorned or pitied because they have not gone through the same historical process.

"Religion is the opium of the people" is one of the most difficult parts of the Marxist heritage to combat or redefine. Enlightened agnosticism remains the progressive highroad for leading the masses from religious and superstitious obscurantism. But other cultures have followed different paths of historical development. Struggles in these cultures have taken a different course and political contest does not invariably imply a negation of things religious.

Europe can be proud of its secular culture. But the fact remains that many rites of passage in Europe are copied from religious life, or have an implicitly religious content.

Oppressed communities in developing countries often unite around traditions with strong religious connotations in order to affirm their identity and oppose domination by a central power. Many campaigning minorities, particularly in countries experiencing internal colonialism, coalesce around religious or thaumaturgic or magical values. One example are the Australian Aborigines.

It is therefore no longer appropriate to apply a simplistic paradigm, condemning visual expression deriving from religious activity as archaising and obscurantist. There are many reasons for this, especially if we accept that a new system of cross-cultural values is needed to replace the ethnocentricity of Western art history, which classified the great civilizations of the past according to a colonialist paradigm, categorising societies without writing as prehistoric.

The principal component of religious art censured by museums today is the one that emanates from funerary rites and magical practices.

Museums of modern art base this practice on the Hegelian doctrine that divorces art from religion. A belief in art in its humanist merits sits ill with the exclusiveness and absolutism of religious art. However, the expressions of religion are unquestioningly identified as art as long as they precede the colonial period. Subsequent works have struggled under a double disadvantage. On the one hand, they do not meet the criteria of agnostic modernity. On the other, they often came into being through contact with Western culture – or Christianity as such – and are therefore rejected by experts as striving too intensively for authenticity.

Throughout the world, many oppressed minorities are resisting assimilation, uniformity and de-culturation by creating and developing their own symbols of identity. In certain regions this amounts to a veritable cultural renaissance.

A belief in the 'liberating' qualities of the philosophy of Enlightenment and in a linear model of its expansion has proved utopian. There are as many wars of religion today as there ever have been.

Threatened peoples unite in seeking their identity in common or shared beliefs. The signs and visual expressions that they thus generate deserve our attention. Almost invariably these works are backed by a history and a tradition. They have in general undergone profound transformations in the wake of globalisation. But often they are firmly anchored in modernity, having integrated modernity's forms and techniques. In many societies this renaissance of rites and their manifestations emerges as a bulwark against globalisation. For some, it is simply a resurgence of the past. But it should be seen in its dialectical relation to modernity; fully aware of modernity, these art forms often attempt to appropriate it.

In our eyes, rites of passage and attachment to the land are among the primary characteristics of Australian Aboriginal societies. Many paintings deal with the very specific Aboriginal attachment to the land, known as the Dreaming. We tend to perceive this spirituality as resulting from the supposedly invariant nature of archaic ancestral societies. But such an account fails to identify a number of vital factors in this artistic phenomenon, which continues to evolve parallel to, but separate from, post-modern tendencies.

When the phenomenon of Aboriginal art began to take off in the 1970s, Aboriginal leaders decided to integrate it into a sort of marketing operation intended to enhance the value of Aboriginal culture in the eyes of white people. At this point rules were drawn up concerning the means by which motifs and images may be diffused and explained.

For the most part these images and motifs belong to clans and are handed down through different lines of descent and cannot be used and reproduced without authorisation. One cannot lay claim to the image of another clan, nor stand in for its owner in explaining it. This traditional iconography is not static but any new interpretation of the myths is submitted to the judgement of the elders. Ultimately these myths are a reinterpretation of history intended to explain the present. Moreover, the present is not simply a matter of spiritual and mystical meditation. On the contrary, the present was brutally imposed by the despoiling of Aboriginal territories, which communities today can only reclaim by way of the courts. This is where politics enters the scene. Societies without writing lack documentary evidence. Thus, Dreaming paintings have on many occasions been brought before the courts to bear witness to such claims. This carries us far away from current paradigms that see traditional art in terms of spirituality and attachment to the ancestral values lodged in the land, and contrast it to our own art, which is perceived as being conscious of political realities and campaigning for the benefit of human progress. When a work of art appears before court in Europe, the issue is either censorship or some conflict over either intellectual property rights or the work's market value.

In the 1960s, when the Aborigines began their resistance against the policy of assimilation that rejected the notion of Aboriginal culture on principle, their primary objective was official recognition of their rights to ancestral territories. Given that in Aboriginal society the rules regulating the ownership of land are closely connected to those governing the ownership of signs, the first concerted communal land claims were argued on the validity of traditional paintings as 'title deeds'.

A remarkable example of the involvement of Indigenous art in politics is the Bark Petition of 1963. In the late 1950s, the Yolngu people of Yirrkala sent a petition to the National Parliament in Canberra, after the government had proposed to lease an area of their land to the French mining company Pechiney. The Yirrkala petition contended an appeal for the recognition of title to their land. Copies of the petition, which was reproduced in English and Yolngu, were fixed to sheets of bark bordered with paintings produced by members of the clans whose lands were affected. The paintings were part of the petition, as Galarrwuy Yunupingu, the son of one of the painters, Munggurrawuy Yunupingu, makes clear: "It was not an ordinary petition; it was presented as a bark painting and showed the clan designs of all of the areas that were threatened by mining ... [It was] not just a series of pictures but represented the title to our country under our law."[1] Even if the Bark Petition did not immediately achieve the desired result, it was the first decisive step in the effort to regain land rights. In 1976, Yolngu land rights were officially recognised when the Aboriginal Land Rights (Northern Territory) Act was passed.

Yolngu have used art to explain their rights to early traders with whom they maintained trade relations for several hundred years. The missionaries in the 1930s learned about the Yolngu way of life with the help of paintings that the Yolngu made for sale. During the following 25 years these activities developed to include major community art works. In 1962, for example, the year before the Bark Petition was submitted, two painted panels were placed on either side of the altar in the Yirrkala church, after Narritjin Maymuru had suggested making them. The paintings were a collaborative work produced by clans of the Dhuwa and Yirritja moieties respectively. They were the result of the syncretistic relationship that developed between Yolngu religious leaders and Methodist missionaries from the 1930s on.

In 1979, the women of Utopia (in the Central Desert) were granted lifelong usufructuary rights to their territory on the basis of their body paintings. The Aboriginal painter Michael Nelson Jagamara, who was invited to the Biennale of Sydney in 1986, stated: "Europeans do not understand about this sacred ground, and the law that governs our interactions with it. We have tried to explain this to them [...] but the Whites do not even recognise our property rights. We do all these paintings, and still they do not understand. They want them for souvenirs to hang on their walls, but they do not realise that these paintings represent the country, all this vast land."[2]

The Bark Petition was followed by the Barunga Statement in 1988. This statement, like the Bark Petition, was a text bordered by paintings. It was presented to Prime Minister Bob Hawke at a ceremony at Barunga (NT) by the two major land councils in the Northern Territory. It shows designs from Arnhem Land and central Australia, representing the provinces of the Northern Land Council and the Central Land Council. The text appealed to the government to negotiate a contract "recognising our prior ownership, continued occupation and sovereignty and affirming our human rights and freedom."[3]

The Aborigines' vigorous and determined struggle for their rights climaxed in the promulgation of the Native Title Act in 1993, which gave them customary rights over lands to which they had ancestral and spiritual bonds. Since then, 15 percent of the Australian continent has been given back to them, but hundreds of cases are still being heard by the courts. The painting *Ngurrara canvas*, on which 39 Aboriginal artists worked, was finished on 3 July 1997 at the National Native Title Tribunal in Pirnini to back up the claims of the population of Fitzroy Crossing in the Great Desert of northern Western Australia.

---

1 Galarrwuy Yunupingu as quoted in Morphy, Howard, 'Art and Politics: The Bark Petition and the Barunga Statement', in Kleinert, S. and M. Neale (eds.), *The Oxford Companion to Aboriginal Art and Culture*, Oxford University Press, Melbourne, 2000, (pp. 100–102), p. 100.

2 Michael Nelson Jagamara in Kleinert, S. and M. Neale (eds.), *op. cit.*, pp. 482–483; see also Johnson, Vivien, *Michael Jagamara Nelson*, Craftsman House, Roseville NSW, 1997.

3 Morphy, H., 2000, in Kleinert, S. and M. Neale (eds.), *op. cit.*, p. 102.

The painting measures ten by eight metres. Each artist painted his own area of the desert country. Some of the artists had never painted before, others were well-known artists, such as Jimmy Pike and Pijaju Skipper. He pointed out: "The big canvas is not an insignificant painting. It is very important. It is *wangarr* (shadow) and *mangi* (spirit or essence which remains when a person has gone). That's what we call it now. We painted all of our country. It is the same as all our smaller paintings. The stories and the bodies of our old people are in their country, our country. We wanted to make *Kartiya* understand our ownership of our country. Bulldozers come into our country and they grade the road right through these places, through those bodies. When the mining company takes the earth away they pull out the *mangi* and take it to another place, they take it away. That's why we are fighting for our country, to keep the *mangi* there in our country."[4]

Far from being the resurgence of a presumably intact, age-old art the authenticity of which is guaranteed by the sacred nature of the painted motifs, the Aborigines' artistic output is largely to be understood in relation to their land rights claims. The paintings show 'areas of territory' with which the Aborigines trace the map of their country, in the heart of which they have lived as exiles for two centuries.

I included the *Ngurrara canvas* in the 2000 Biennale exhibition *Sharing Exoticism* in Lyon in order to compare it with the post-modern political art of the West. More recently I have shown a set of Aboriginal paintings in the exhibition *Art Religion Politics* at the Padiglione d'Arte Contemporanea (PAC) in Milan together with the works of artists from Africa, Asia and Latin America. Aboriginal artists such as Anatjari Tjakamarra, Old Walter Tjampitjimpa, Ronnie Tjampitjimpa and Mick Tjapaltjarri were exhibited next to African and Asian artists as, for example, Frédéric Bruly Bouabré, Cyprien Tokoudagba, Mestre Didi, Jose Bedia, Chara Oquet, Art Orienté Objet and Kazuo Shiraga. An introductory room showed small works by European artists such as Joseph Beuys, Dan Flavin, Lucio Fontana, Yves Klein, Hermann Nitsch and Antonio Tàpies, just as a reminder of the Christian cultural tradition in Western avant-garde. My aim with these exhibitions is to stress the importance of the claim of minority rights being linked to religious visual expressions otherwise ignored by the contemporary art world.

Of course, not all Aboriginal art is political in the sense as I have just defined it, but as a strategy to penetrate the closed circle of contemporary art it might be very useful to insist on the political interpretation of Aboriginal paintings. In this respect Mawurndjul's exhibition in the Museum Tinguely is a very important step. This is why today I regret even more that Jean Tinguely did not take part in the exhibition *Magiciens de la Terre*. I discussed the concept with him at length. He was very interested. Although he sent me some of his beautifully coloured letters on 'magic' we both decided in his studio that the works he had just finished – two years before his death – did not fit in with the exhibition concept. This might be the hidden reason – a sort of 'objective chance' – why today Mawurndjul is presenting his works here. Finally the dialogue of the works is taking place and showing effect.

---

4 Pijaju Peter Skipper as quoted in Dayman, Karen and Pat Lowe, 2000, 'The Ngurrara Canvas', in Kleinert, S. and M. Neale, M. (eds.), *op. cit.*, pp. 493–496.

Till Förster

What is local about local art? Contemporary African artists between international art world and local life-world

Introduction

Since the 1950s, when most African countries entered into a process of decolonisation that deeply transformed the entire cultural sphere, contemporary African art has been a subject of debate. Many Western critics saw contemporary African artists as more or less unsophisticated epigones of modern art or, worse, as somewhat naïve imitators of something they neither understood nor mastered. Contemporary African art had to be profoundly 'African' – and certainly distinct from what was considered to be modern art in general. On the other hand, African artists entering the international art world were expected to subscribe to the assumed universal aesthetic standards of art that, so it seemed, had already proved to be valid for so-called traditional African art. Trapped between modern claims to universality and the demands to remain visibly 'African', many artists in Africa found themselves in a contradictory situation that left little room, if any, for an independent development of their work.

Such contradictions still inform the international art world, in particular with regard to artists that come from regions that were once expected to produce 'primitive', 'traditional', 'ethnic', 'indigenous' or, to take up a more fashionable term, 'local' art. Though the latter term was coined in order to address art that was mainly produced for a local audience, it is increasingly used like the former, drawing a dividing line between 'us' and 'them'. Local versus global may not be much more than a re-coining of the familiar tradition–modernity dichotomy, thus relegating African artists to another realm of artistic creativity.

Hybridity, on the other hand, seems to be an alternative since most artists in Africa work in a setting that does not foster clear-cut distinctions between what is African and what is not. Yet, hybridity and similar terms addressing the interrelatedness of the local and the international art world are still based on the assumption that two (or more) spheres of art production and consumption exist. Furthermore, they often implicitly claim that such a bifurcate merging of the two serves as a reference to the artists and other actors in the art world. Contemporary artists in and outside Africa, however, often try to avoid such binary thinking. They say that they do not care if something is African or not as long as it has some significance for their life. For instance, they would not hesitate to collect plastic garbage in the suburbs of African cities where they live and incorporate it into their assemblages. Outsiders often construe the same act as an appropriation of 'modernity' – of something that initially did not belong to Africa, which was not part of African culture. More often than not, such an interpretation reproduces the dichotomy that it tries to circumvent.

This contribution aims at a clarification of the underlying conceptions that inform the discourse on contemporary art from Africa and elsewhere. It tries to outline the position of the various actors and how this is reflected in their statements about art in and from Africa – regardless of whether it is attributed the status 'traditional' or 'modern'. The article, however, does not intend to provide an alternative or 'more appropriate' description of the situation that most artists from and in Africa have to face. It argues that the social and cultural reality of contemporary African art is made up of actors' points of view and that, therefore, to treat African art as an autonomous fact means reification. To improve the understanding of contemporary art production and consumption in Africa, one has to address specific spheres where the actors' points of view become relevant and shape their practice.

African art

African art has always been constructed by those who looked at it. Still a testimony of 'primitiveness' and early mankind's misconceptions of the body in the 19th century, it turned into avant-garde art when modern artists 'discovered' the very same conceptual qualities during the first decade in the 20th century. As an entity that covered the entire continent and that included most wooden sculptures and their 'cubism' but excluded the 'natural style' of the Ife terracottas, it was again constructed by Western art historians.[1]

Let us first have a look at how so-called traditional African art was supposed to look like – or more precisely, how we anthropologists once liked to look at it. Plate XXIII shows a *korogo* mask of a ropemakers' secret society somewhere in a remote village in northern Côte d'Ivoire. For the spectators, it is easily recognisable by the long ropes of its costume. The mask danced for the elder members of the neighbouring sculptors' secret society on the occasion of a funeral in 1991. The mask was made by the younger initiates of the society, thus demonstrating their skills to the elders, as they do now by performing for them. The visibility of the mask is limited to such occasions: neither the elders nor the young initiates must see it outside its ritual context.

The mask is what anthropologists once would have called an authentic object at an authentic performance – it's not an object produced for an external market, say for tourists or for art collectors. Authenticity is the subtext by which descriptions of such objects and events are informed. It was taken for granted that the mask as an object was exclusively made for this original purpose, that the sculptors knew about their audience and that they made the mask only for this ritual act. As such, as an authentic object, it was appreciated

1 See for example Schmalenbach, Werner, *Afrikanische Kunst aus der Sammlung Barbier-Mueller,* Prestel, München, 1988.

by the general public and by art connoisseurs in particular. Proving that an object had been used in such a ritual setting meant an increase to its value – its artistic value as well as its monetary value on the art market. If one were able to show that the ritual context was a historical one, the better. It was assumed that rites were almost static before the colonial period and, hence, that all objects embedded in such rites were authentic. Most objects were dated 'late 19th' or 'early 20th' century, i.e. in the timeless era when style was still without history and embedded in age old ethnic identities and more or less isolated 'traditional cultures' easily recognisable for those who had the ethnic landscape of pre-colonial Africa in mind.

However, that text has a shadow, as Sidney Kasfir has analysed so brilliantly.[2] The construction of African art as 'traditional' within the wider framework of authenticity meant roughly: art is authentic when produced by local artists for a local audience and not for the market.[3] The notion thus privileges the ethnic group or, if known, the village as the locus of production. They, as cultural entities, take the position of the artist, ignoring individual agency and creativity. At the same time, the idea of authentic African art implies that consumption takes place at the same spot. It neglects the possibility of distribution and in particular the trade of art objects as commodities. In the end, the construction of authentic African art stated that such objects should not be meant and considered as commodities. A traditional art object is produced and consumed in the same place and it is appreciated, for purely aesthetic reasons.

Consequently, this approach is not interested in following the objects beyond the horizon of the local life-world, and from the sites of production to the sites of consumption if the latter lie beyond that horizon, in particular how such objects were passed on from hand to hand, until they became part of museum displays. We are all too familiar with what this meant in economic and political terms: it was the colonial encounter between mainly white, dominant men and black people, who had to hand over their weapons first and then many other items of their daily and religious life. The ethnographic museums founded during the colonial period first received huge collections of 'primitive' weapons – weapons that could not compete with the guns of the coming colonial masters. Later, ethnographic museums collected specimens that were supposed to bear evidence of the otherness of African societies and their arts.[4] When art museums exhibited African art, they mainly did so to evidence the universality of their own aesthetic standards.[5] And when African sculptures

---

2 Kasfir, S., 'African Art and Authenticity: A Text with a Shadow', *African Arts* 25 (2), 1992 pp. 40–53, 96–97.

3 The most prominent proponent of this argument is probably William Rubin, the late director of the Museum of Modern Art's prestigious department of painting and sculpture and curator of the 1984 exhibition *Primitivism in 20th Century Art*; see Rubin, W. (ed.), *Primitivism in 20th Century Art: Affinity of the Tribal and the Modern,* Museum of Modern Art, New York. 1984, particularly his introductory chapter.

4 See Fabian, Johannes, *Time and the Other: How Anthropology Makes its Object,* Columbia Univ. Press, New York, 1983.

5 Errington, Shelly, *The Death of Authentic Primitive Art and Other Tales of Progress*, University of California Press, Berkeley, 1998.

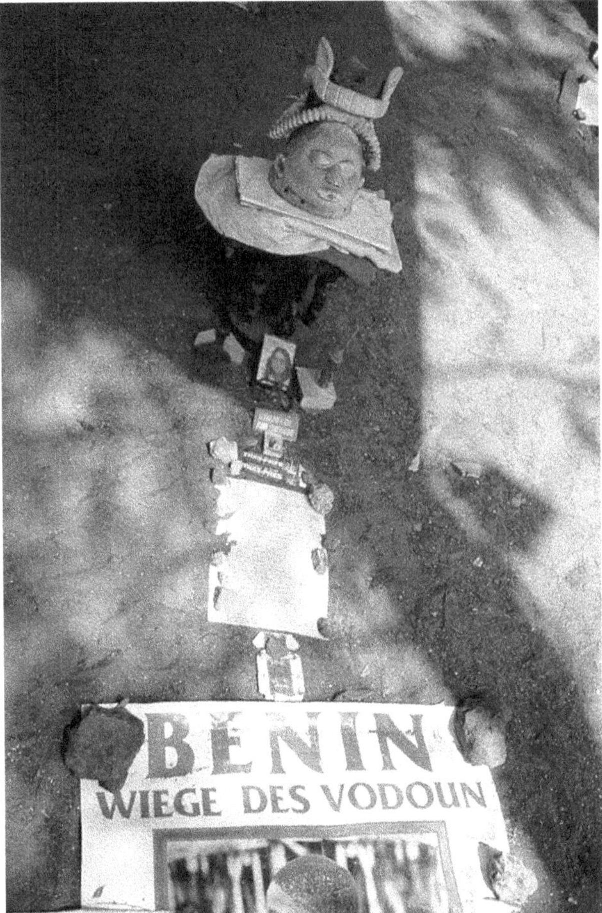

Fig. 34: Georges Adeagbo, *Exhibition*, Dakar Biennale, 1996. Photo after *Anthologie de l'art africain*, edited by N'Goné Fall and Jean Loup Pivin, Paris: Editions Revue Noire, p. 140. Photo © collection Revue Noire.

moved from one museum to the next, they equally changed their status.[6] What was, say, an anthropomorphic pestle from a certain ethnic group became a sculpted figure and maybe a masterpiece from a particular workshop.

However, if authenticity is a matter of the function and audience of an object – as the argument implicitly claims –, then it can change its status according to the context in which an object is embedded. An art object that was destined to be sold to tourists may be incorporated in an existing ritual context. Does this move make it 'authentic'? Also, objects may change their status more than once. A weapon may become an ethnographic specimen and later an art work. But art works may also fall back into other categories, say into that of kitsch or tourist souvenirs, amongst others. They may also be reintegrated into other arte-

6 Price, Sally, *Primitive Art in Civilized Places*, Univ. of Chicago Press, Chicago,1989.

facts and art works as figure 34 demonstrates: it shows a part of Georges Adeagbo's installation at the Biennale de Dakar in 1996. The installation includes a Yoruba *gelede*-mask (top), a tourist poster on Benin advertising in German "The cradle of Vodun", local combs, and industrial tooth-paste, amongst other things. Adeagbo calls his installations 'expositions' and links them explicitly to the multi-facetted history of his home country.

Certainly, deconstructing by re-constructing and playing with objects is not an exclusive privilege of artists – although they are very good at it. Many scholars, among them philosophers, art historians and anthropologists, made inquiries into that field, too. They may prefer to play with notions of art but by doing so they often affect our understanding of what art is, and African art in particular. Their findings are sometimes stated more generally, though at times less vividly. But before analysing what they have to say, we need to remember that the scholarly de-construction of a concept does not necessarily turn it into an obsolete category for others. Authenticity is still a valid interpretative framework for connoisseurs, collectors, many art critics and art galleries that sell 'primitive' or 'traditional' African art.

Art works may have more than one life, as Arjun Appadurai and Igor Kopytoff have shown in their outstanding work on the cultural biography of things.[7] Objects, they say, may have been traded within, between as well as beyond so-called traditional societies. They may adopt the status of commodities more than once and may acquire yet another status again later. Specialists serve as mediators between the spheres, and often as cultural brokers, too. The appropriation of objects as art works is subject to specific societal and historical settings.

It is not too difficult to illustrate their findings. Perhaps the weapon mentioned earlier used to be a commodity when it was sold on a local market, say, somewhere in the Belgian Congo at the end of the 19th century. The customer perhaps used it for defence before handing it, more or less voluntarily, over to the colonial officer. He then perhaps sold it to another African, or the officer may have donated it to the Royal Museum in Tervuren or he may have preferred to sell it on the curio market back home in Brussels. Whatever its itinerary was, it is obvious that the object changed its status from commodity to weapon or art work every time it was integrated into a new context, the museum being just the last one.

One question, however, remains unanswered: is any object suited for this transformation into an art work? Or do they need certain properties in order to be suitable for integration into an art collection or an art museum? Predictably, the answer depends on who is speaking to whom. Representatives of the art world often claim that an object needs certain characteristics that let them recognise it as art.[8] The other position is more radical

---

7 Appadurai, A. and I. Kopytoff (eds.), *The Social Life of Things: Commodities in Cultural Perspective*, Cambridge Univ. Press, Cambridge, 1986.

8 I use the term in the sense of Howard Becker (Becker, H., *Art Worlds*, Univ. of California Press, Berkeley, [9]2003), George Dickie (Dickie, G., *Art and Aesthetic: An Institutional Analysis,* Cornell Univ. Press, Ithaca, 1974) and Arthur Danto (Danto, A., *The Transfiguration of the Commonplace*, Harvard Univ. Press, Cambridge Mass., 1981), i.e. as an institution that reproduces a specific discourse on art and embodies it in its commercial transactions.

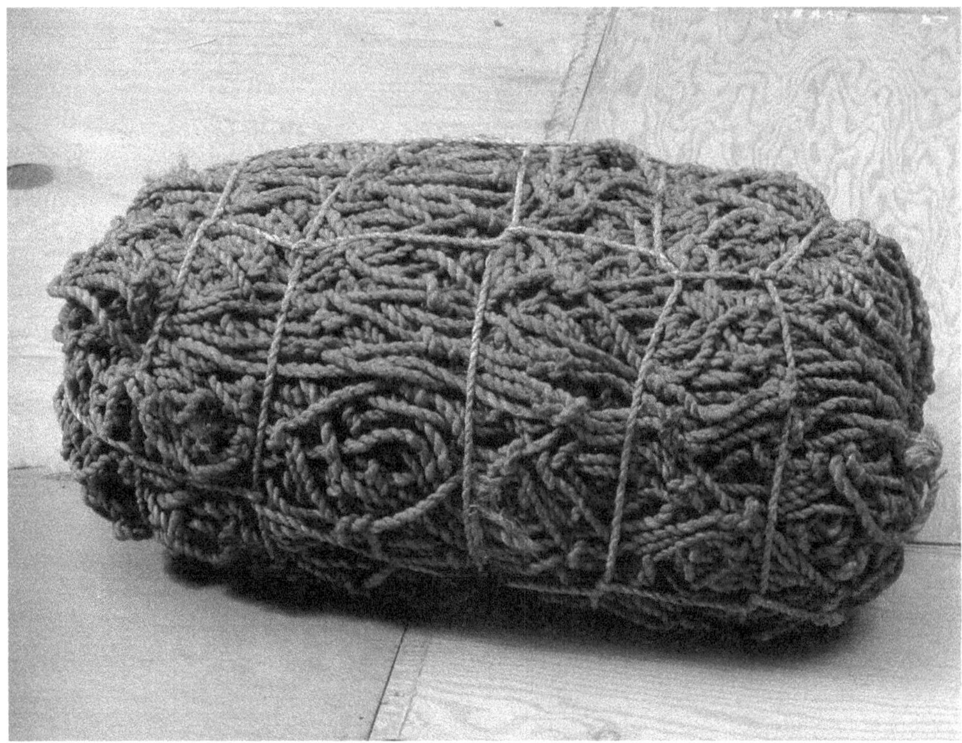

Fig. 35: Hunting-net, Zande, Zaire (Uele River region), fiber, length 59 cm, collected by Herbert Lang in 1910, Museum for African Art, New York. Photo provided by the author.

and states that no essential quality enables the spectator to distinguish art works from other objects – art is based on a practice of looking at objects.

Probably one of the most famous African objects to illustrate this is a hunting-net (see fig. 35 and also this volume Morphy pp. 75–102). It was collected as an ethnographic specimen by Herbert Lang in 1910 among the Zande in what was then the North Eastern Belgian Congo. Much later, in 1988, it was displayed as an art work in the exhibition *ART/artifact* at the Centre for African Art, New York, now the Museum for African Art.[9] It was accompanied by an article by Arthur Danto, who, in his contribution, elaborated on the contexts that allowed modern artists, for instance Picasso, to identify African objects as art works. The 'discovery' of African art, he wrote, "... was only possible because painting and sculpture in [the early 20th century] had undergone changes of a kind that made the values of African art *visible*."[10] Danto illustrated his argument that context makes something art

9 See Vogel, Susan (ed.), *ART/artifact: African Art in Anthropological Collections*, Prestel, München, 1988.
10 Danto, A., 1988, 'Artifact and Art', in Vogel S., (ed.), *op. cit.*, (pp. 18–32), p. 19, my emphasis.

with a story about two fictive peoples, the Pot People and the Basket Folk. Both produce objects of similar appearance, but the Pot People value their pots as art while the Basket Folk do the same with their baskets. The preferred objects are "thick with significations," Danto[11] writes, but they look like the objects of the other 'tribe'. The hunting-net of the Zande also serves as an illustration: spectators only appreciate it as art when it is integrated in a particular context, in this case the art show of the Museum for African Art.

There was widespread criticism from scholars, but a harsher political critique came from African artists and intellectuals. They claimed that African art per se is a construction, and even Africa as a societal or cultural entity is, says Valentin Mudimbe (1988), an invention of the West.[12] And it goes without saying that African art as a framework for the analysis of style and workmanship is as much a construction as the unity of the entire continent.

Hence African art is a construction of the art world, itself an institution of modernity. This has considerable implications. The concepts of authentic, indigenous, local arts still aim at 'othering' artists and excluding them from the one international art world. As a matter of fact, there is neither a necessity for a concept or term called 'African art' nor for any other 'local art' for that matter – apart from applying it for the sake of labelling objects and books that deal with these objects in Western museum displays, exhibitions, book fairs or in data bases facilitating quick access. African artists produce in ways that are not different from those of other artists in the world. To base access to the international art world on regional or ethnic identity rather than on artistic quality should never be accepted. To do so would mean relegating art labelled 'African art' to anthropological museums, instead of answering to its inherent call for access to mainstream art museums.

Over the last twenty years it has become a well-established practice in a number of Western art museums to display works of African art from unknown workshops exactly in the same way as works by known European masters or as any other recognised art, i.e. in a white cube (or a black one, if you prefer). In some cases, African and European art works were displayed side by side, as in the *Primitivism in 20th Century* art show at the Museum of Modern Art in 1984. Let us recall that this was meant to acknowledge the universal aesthetic standards of both Western and African art.

But wait: haven't we heard that art works have no essential quality that allows us to distinguish them from ordinary objects? Who then decides on the quality of a particular object? If one assumes that the art world does, then one has to analyse it as a social institution where specific actors are less, or more, powerful than others and interact according to their chances.

11 Ibid, p. 23

12 Mudimbe, V., *The Invention of Africa: Gnosis, Philosophy, and the Order of Knowledge*, Indiana Univ. Press, Bloomington, 1988.

Africa between the local and art for art's sake

Speaking in general, there does not seem to be a need for difference, and indeed, most artists from Africa today do not accept to be the 'other' of us Europeans, or the West in general. They want to be coequals and contemporaries. But critics are of course quick to reply. They say that this is to deny difference and that Africans and their art should remain different. This leads right into the heart of the dilemma: on the one hand, African artists are expected to subscribe to the standards of international art – standards that pretend to be universal – on the other, they should remain African, recognisably African.

I quote Nzante Spee, a Cameroonian artist: "Whatever you do, whatever you say, you won't escape them."[13] And Soro Coulibaly, an artist from Côte d'Ivoire, adds: "C'est comme une piège: ils t'obligent d'obéir les deux côtés."[14] Indeed, there are but few options to escape this dilemma: you have to play with your identity. And I would argue that African artists today do precisely this. They are invited to do so, to be subversive. Moreover, they are obliged to be subversive. I will come back to this point in a moment.

If art is really art for art's sake, then in any art museum there is no longer the need to label art as 'African' or, for that matter, 'US American', 'Japanese', or 'Swiss'. In addition, many if not most African artists today would strongly reject any notion of localised art, indeed, they would get really upset if you called their works 'indigenous', or African or, worst of all, ethnic – they just happen to be artists from Africa, they say.

Can art be out of time?

On the other hand, until the late 1970s and to some extent even later, the international art world often saw the attractiveness of African artists precisely in the fact that they came from a 'remote' part of the world – one that was not yet touched by the evils of Western civilisation. Artistic creativity of Africans was often constructed as 'pristine' and therefore superior to the disillusioned modern man and his fractured experiences.

This discourse has been deconstructed, too, not least by social anthropologists like Johannes Fabian[15] and James Clifford[16] and later by writers such as Kwame Appiah (1996).[17] But the situation of African artists in regard to their participation in the international art world has not changed much. Their position remains ambivalent to contradictory: on the one hand, they are expected to subscribe to standards of 'aesthetic quality' that claim to be universal, on the other hand, they should be recognisably 'African'. How 'African' is a

13 Personal communication, October 2004.

14 Personal communication, December 1992.

15 Fabian, J., *Time and the Other: How Anthropology Makes its Object*, Columbia Univ. Press, New York, 1983.

16 Clifford, J., *The Predicament of Culture: Twentieth-Century Ethnography, Literature, and Art*, Harvard Univ. Press, Cambridge Mass., 1988.

17 Appiah, K. A., 'Why Africa? Why Art?' in Phillips, T. (ed.), *Africa: The Art of a Continent*, Prestel, München, 1996, pp. 21–26.

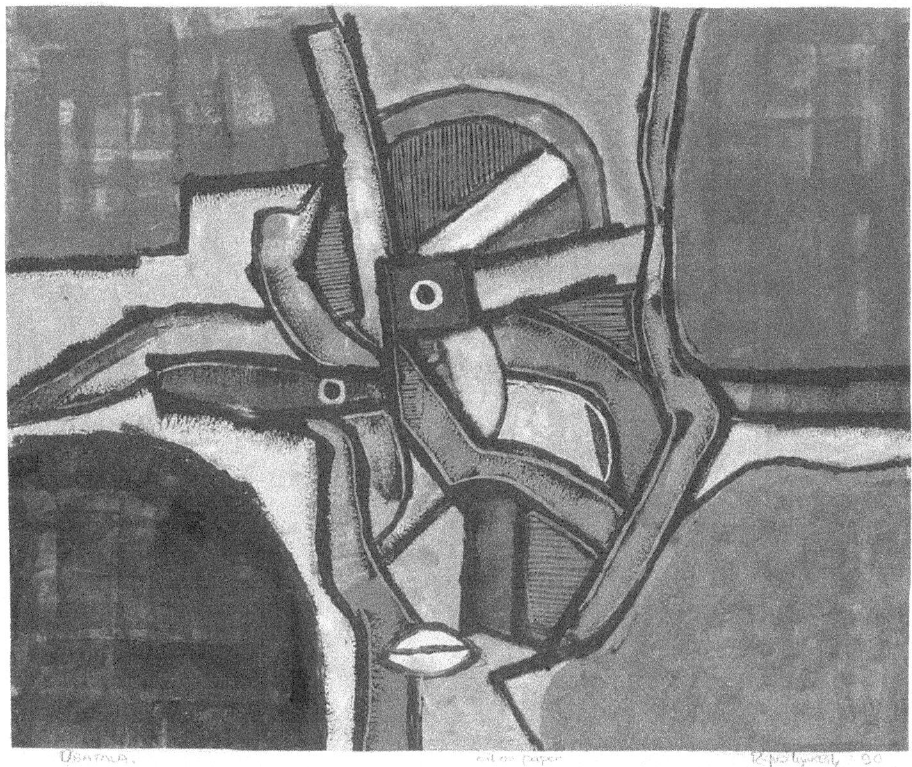

Fig. 36: Rufus Ogundele, *Obatala,* 1990, oil on paper, 39 x 49 cm, Coll. Iwalewa-Haus, Bayreuth. Photo Archives of the author.

painting like the one by Rufus Ogundele reproduced above (see fig. 36)? Rufus Ogundele refuses to answer this question. It's Ogundele, he says. This brings us to the key problem: who judges what Ogundele does?

Standards of quality

Whatever standards of quality one applies, it is obvious that they are set right in the centre of the art world if you understand it to be a societal institution.[18] When seen from the margins, it appears to be an institution of predatory exchange, appropriating the arts of others and submitting it to its own standards. Africa and African art may be inventions of the West, but so is the art museum itself. Art museums and their exhibitions are institu-

18 See footnote 8.

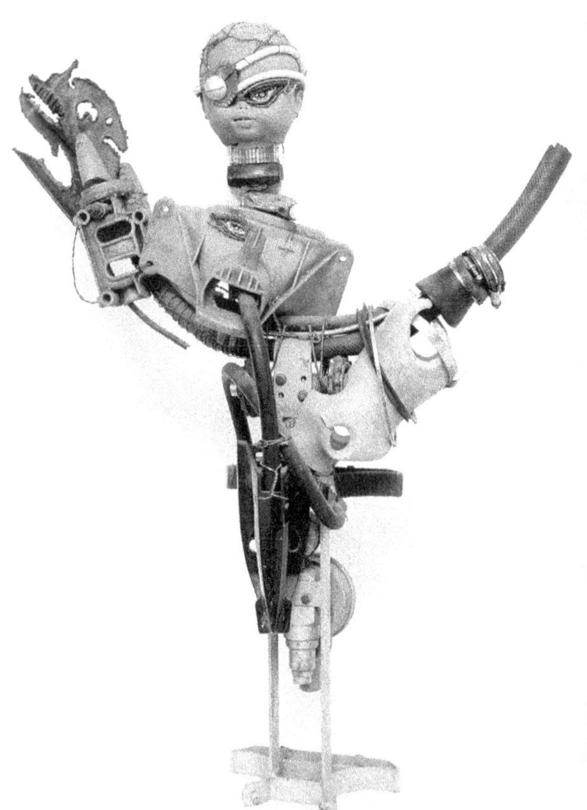

Fig. 37: Joseph Francis Sumégné (Douala, Cameroon), *La poupée*, 1995, assemblage, c. 80 cm, Coll. Doual'Art. Photo Archives of the author.

tions of modernity, highly charged with ideology.[19] Moreover, contrary to one of the basic assumptions of modernity, universal standards of aesthetic judgements failed in the past and it does not seem that they are becoming any more reliable today.

Indeed, the vivid competition of museums for contemporary art around the globe will hopefully grant diversity, more appreciation, with less conformity of opinion. Despite the globalisation of art consumption by way of multilevel exchange (as guided by commercial, artistic, political, tourist or idealistic interests), the social and cultural background of art production, distribution and even consumption remain different in specific contexts, at least partially. The de facto interaction of local and global strands thus will produce different art forms from place to place. By using, among others, terms like hybridity, flows,

19 See, among others, Thomas McEvilley's essays on this issue (e.g. McEvilley, Th., *Art and Otherness: Crisis in Cultural Identity*, Documentext McPherson, New York, 1992).

glocalisation[20] observers and art critics try to cope with this growing interrelatedness. To stay within my own discipline, social anthropology, let us have a look at what this can mean. When walking through an African city, say Dakar, Abidjan, Lagos, or, in this case, Bamenda, Cameroon, one soon notices the incredible diversity of pictures and images. Photos, paintings, prints on paper as well as on cloth merge with other media, among them TV, video and, more recently, the internet. African cities, for instance, seem to be a huge trash bin for the industrialised world where one can only survive by putting the bits and pieces together that were left over from those who are better off. Douala in Cameroon, where Joseph Francis Sumégné lives, is a case to the point (see fig. 37). It's a world of permanent struggle that is reflected in such works.

Flows, hybridity, ambiguity, syncretism or more precisely, syncretisation, glocalisation and other terms are very fashionable today. There is hardly a publication on contemporary African art today that does not make use of them. But they are also very fluid in themselves, and besides celebrating mixture or re-mixture – as we all do in times of globalisation –, they have two major disadvantages: they are not suited for empirical enquiry. Celebrating hybridity, mixture and re-mixture, as a recent exhibition in Düsseldorf and elsewhere was titled,[21] does not help much to understand such processes in regard to agency and creativity, individual and social, nor does it give us an instrument at hand to address questions of domination. If you talk about circulation, meaning the flow of ideas and objects, you do not talk about dependency and exploitation. Many artists in Africa actually criticise this one-sided understanding of globalisation.

Hence, the interaction of the local and the global is a topic for many African artists, and so we as scholars have to address it, too.

Intermediality

Some people may be overwhelmed by the media, but it seems more likely that they more or less actively appropriate them in their own terms. So did Nigerians, for instance, who now have a film industry that even challenges that of India. Scholarly inquiry needs clear concepts, not metaphors, to cope with all these interactions and processes. I will try to present one here – just one, and in a preliminary way: the concept is that of intermediality.

Pictures and images, too, move across medial borders, as you can see in the picture below (see fig. 38): this hair relaxer is sold in the US, the Caribbean and across Africa. Fanta – actually an acronym for Fantastic African Naturally Talented Artist – uses it as a model for his signboards. If the package is from Hong Kong, the faces may have almond

20 A neologism, coined from the Japanese by the sociologist Roland Robertson to cope with the interaction between the local and the global as co-existing interpenetrative principles; see Robertson, R., *Globalisation: Social Theory and Global Culture*, Newbury Park, London, 1992 and 'Glocalization: Time-Space and Homogeneity-Heterogeneity', in Featherstone, M. (ed.), *Global Modernities*, Sage Publications, London, 1995.

21 See Njami, Simon (ed.), *Africa Remix: Zeitgenössische Kunst eines Kontinents*, Hatje Cantz, Ostfildern, 2004.

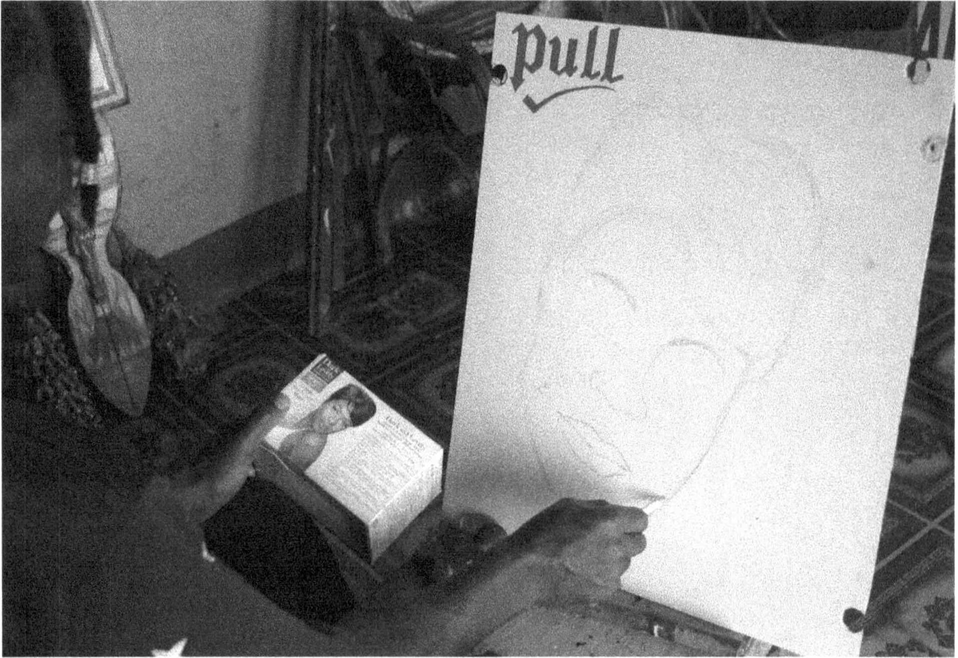

Fig. 38: Fanta Bengy creating a signboard for a hair stylist, after a photograph on an imported hair relaxer product. Photo Till Förster, April 2005.

eyes, but more often than not he paints faces located somewhere in the middle between African, Asian and European physiognomies. What he paints, however, is also subject to interaction with his customers. If, say, a hairdresser wants the picture of a Nigerian hairdo, the painter is likely to reproduce one from the many prints of Nigerian hairdos sold on the market. Competition is high, and he may lose his customer if he refuses.

Another example – one that we are currently addressing in a research project – is the intermediality of photography and painting. Unlike in our own history, photography in Africa arrived first in most societal settings, i.e. before painting. The first studios began offering their services to the urban population in the last two decades of the 19th century. However, pictures and images were also appropriated from the West. Marilyn Monroe's photos are familiar to many painters in Bamenda where we found this one in a workshop of a signboard painter who participated in an anti-AIDS campaign (see fig. 39).[22]

What results from this interaction are, for instance, new genres that do not exist in the Western medial landscape. Malam, another artist from Cameroon, is very consciously subversive, as becomes clear from work that that he showed in a Douala suburb in October

22 This example is drawn from an ongoing project. Hopefully, there shall be more to report about this process within the next two years.

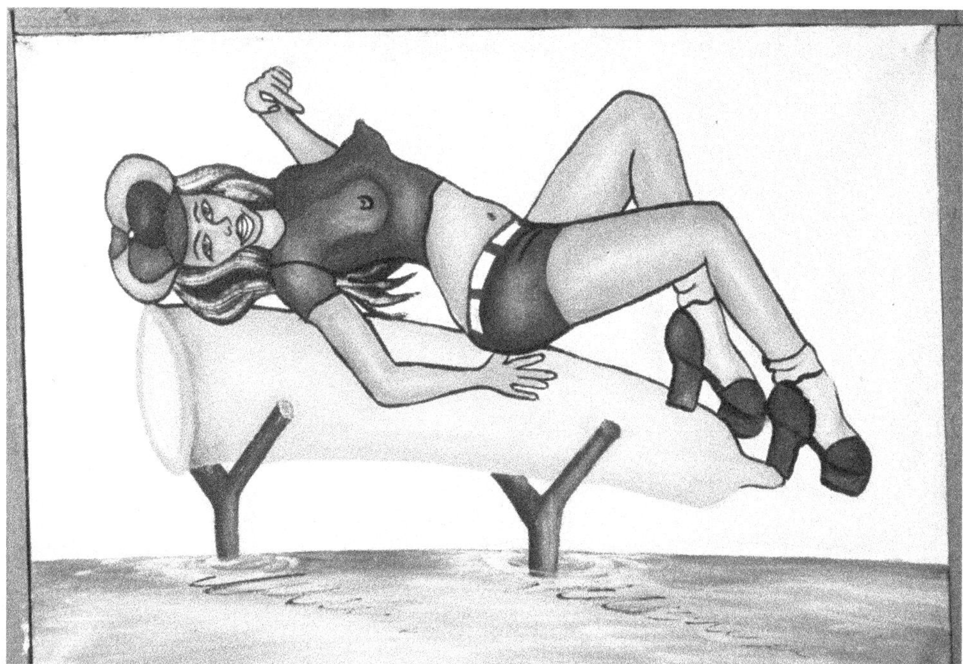

Fig. 39: An anti-AIDS campaign signboard, supposedly inspired by photographs of Marilyn Monroe, Bamenda, Cameroon. Photo Till Förster, Oktober 2003.

2002. Spectators were shocked by the apparently dead bodies in the swamp that separates two popular quarters of the city. They were made of styrofoam and floated on the surface of the murky water. Malam had butchered a ram and put the head of the dead animal on the Styrofoam bodies. It was meant as a metaphor for the state of the city. Malam wanted "... to reveal what lies beneath the surface of everyday life".[23] Photos were later put on the internet in order to gain a wider, non-local audience.[24]

Conclusion

Let me return to my initial question: what is local about local art? The answer is probably disappointing. It depends on how the actors – the artists and others – practise what we call local art (for the lack of a better term). But, and that's a strong but, there also exist constraints and forces that lie beyond their control, and many of the artists are aware of this. Local versus global might be a false dichotomy, and I am convinced it is (if stated as simply

23 See http://www.vmcaa.nl/vm/magazine/hopebox/spotlight002.htm, March 16, 2007.

24 See http://io.pensa.it/node/77?PHPSESSID=7eda5b4a6cfe84e259e55735cd395399, March 16, 2007.

as it often is). As scholars it is our obligation, at the same time, to cope with the heritage of our disciplinary history as well as with our cultural and institutional adherence in general. Concepts such as intermediality, if applied to defined social and historical settings, might help to identify the passageways between the local and the global. Seen under the aspect of the practice of the actors – and, notably, when looking empirically at practice through the actors' lenses – local and global often merge into one horizon.

Part 4
Tomorrow's museums for today's art

John Onians

30,000 years of Australian art – a neuropsychological approach

Usually, when we try to sum up what is known about the art of a particular area of the globe over a very long period, as Andrew Sayers has effectively done in his book on Australian art,[1] we synthesise the knowledge accumulated by different disciplines. As a result, the treatment of the earliest art will reflect the opinions of archaeologists, that of the art of indigenous peoples, will reflect the opinions of anthropologists, and that of the art of more recent immigrants the opinions of art historians. The result is valuable in its own right, but it does have shortcomings. One of the most important of these is its inability to offer a single perspective on all the art produced in an area from the earliest times until the present, and a corollary of this is the lack of opportunity for reflection on the similarities and differences in that art.

The approach adopted here is intended to make up for these shortcomings. It relies on the knowledge of art gathered by archaeologists, anthropologists and art historians but reviews it using a single framework which provides the basis for asking and answering new questions. It starts off from different premises. One is the recognition that the environment of Australia has not changed in its basics throughout the period that humans have lived there, another is the recognition that all those humans were/are basically similar, being members of the species *Homo sapiens*. It thus explores the extent to which the story of Australian art can be understood in terms of the reaction of biologically similar brains and bodies to a physically similar geography. To do so it relies on two recent advances in neuroscience. One is the recognition of the importance of neural plasticity for the formation of the individual's brain. The other is the importance of mirror neurons for the shaping of the individual's behaviour.

Some neuropsychology

Neural plasticity is the key to understanding why, although we are all born with basically similar brains, we all grow up to see and experience the world differently. The basic prin-

1 Sayers, Andrew, *Australian Art,* Oxford University Press, Oxford, 2001.

ciple of neuroplasticity is that throughout our life our brain changes its configuration in response to changes in the individual's experiences and actions. We are all born with 100 billion neurons, each capable of having up to 100,000 connections to other neurons. What makes us different from each other is the way those connections form and fall away in response to our experiences. Thus, in terms of vision, the more often we look at a particular object the more connections will form between the neurons involved, so strengthening our preference for looking at it, or, for that matter, things that share its distinctive visual properties.[2] This means that, to the extent that each of us has looked intently at different things, we will have different visual preferences and to the extent that we have looked at similar things, as people have who live in the same place or period, the more our preferences will be similar. The predictability inherent in this property of our neuropsychology is an extraordinary resource for anyone seeking to understand the history of artistic activity because it predicts that if you know what somebody has been looking at with attention, however remote from you they may be in time and space, you will be able to identify preferences that are liable to affect the character of the art they make or look at – and that without knowing anything of their language or culture. Indeed you will know their preferences as they cannot have done because the neural processes that lead to their formation are buried far below the surface of consciousness, which is why people cannot express them in words.

While the principle of neuroplasticity helps us to appreciate why people who live in the same environment have similar visual preferences, 'mirror neurons' help us to understand why people who live together adopt similar movements. They are the key to our tendency to imitate each other. They were first identified only ten years ago by researchers in Parma, Italy.[3] What Rizzolati and his team noted was that, when one monkey observes another doing something with its hand, particular neurons in the pre-motor cortex of the observing monkey, that is those which would normally fire before he performed the same action, also fire, although in fact no signal is transmitted to the motor cortex and no movement results. The observer monkey thus acquires the neural equipment necessary for him to perform the action simply by seeing it executed by another. Many experiments later it has become clear that this means that the observer monkey understands not only what the other monkey is doing and how, but why he is doing it, as is shown by the way the same mirror neurons fire at the simple sound of a peanut being cracked. Indeed it is now recognised that the existence of many such neurons in the primate brain gives us and our relatives an unconscious understanding of what our fellow primates are doing, an understanding that is fundamental to our sense of empathy. Watching the motor actions of others is enough to give us an understanding of what they are doing and why, and gives us that understanding automatically.

2 Tanaka, K., 'Neuronal mechanisms of object recognition', *Science*, 262, 1993, pp. 685–688.

3 The first important article was Rizzolatti, G., Fadiga, L., Fogassi, L. and V. Gallese 'Premotor Cortex and the Recognition of Motor Actions', *Cognitive Brain Research* 3, 1996, pp.131–141. For a recent survey see Rizzolatti, G. and L. Craighero 'The Mirror Neuron System', *Annual Review of Neuroscience* 27, 2004, pp. 169–192.

We can see how an understanding of two such neural mechanisms can transform our understanding of art. For a start it reminds us that the actions of the artist are not only affected by his or her experience of art, but by his or her experience of all the visual environment, including the movements of those around them. Since everything that someone sees is liable to affect their neural networks and so influence their visual preferences and their bodily movements, if we want to understand their relation to art we need to find out about all their visual experiences, including the emotions that go with them. Above all we need to know what they have been looking at most intently, since it is intense looking that particularly affects neural formation.

Different neuropsychologies, different views

We can get an initial sense of where this may lead us by comparing an Aboriginal painting with the flag adopted by the European colonists. Each tells us something about differences in the visual engagements of the two groups, yet together they reveal shared concerns. While the Australian flag represents the heavens, the painting chosen, *Warlugulong*, inspired by the story of the ravages caused by a bushfire in the Dreaming, and executed by Clifford Possum Tjapaltjarri and Tim Leura Tjapaltjarri, shows the earth (see fig. 40). More precisely, like much Aboriginal art made by the same community it shows the earth's surface. Interestingly too, unlike most paintings of the land in other traditions, for example those of China or Europe, it views the earth from above, recording relationships in two dimensions. There are several reasons for the preference for such a view. One is certainly that since much of Australia is lacking in food-producing plants, and is either very dry or very wet, those looking for things to eat spent much of their time looking down at the ground searching for the footmarks of the animals they were hunting and signs of such edible vegetables as underground tubers. Another reason for the emphasis on the earth's surface is that, since the populations spent much time on the move in the search for resources, they were exceptionally dependent on mental maps, and these not only recorded resources needed for daily life but preserved the memory of the movements of ancestors in the past in what is often called the Dreaming.

Neither of these reasons affected the ancestors of the modern Chinese or Europeans who, by 5,000 BC, were typically sedentary and dependent on agriculture. For them, the typical view was one of a familiar landscape from a fixed point. Only when the Europeans travelled by sea did their typical perspective change, as the need to navigate by the stars required them to frequently look up at the sky above, searching for significant constellations. Since all those Europeans who travelled to Australia in the first one and a half centuries of settlement arrived by sea, that experience would have been a habitual one. Moreover, the sight of the particular constellation shown on the flag was especially reassuring. The Southern Cross had been so named by the first Europeans who crossed the equator in the 16th century. Not only did it mark the South Pole as the Pole Star did the North but by its cross shape it seemed to mark out the new territory as chosen for Christian domination. It is in this sense that the flag and the painting document different views but similar concerns.

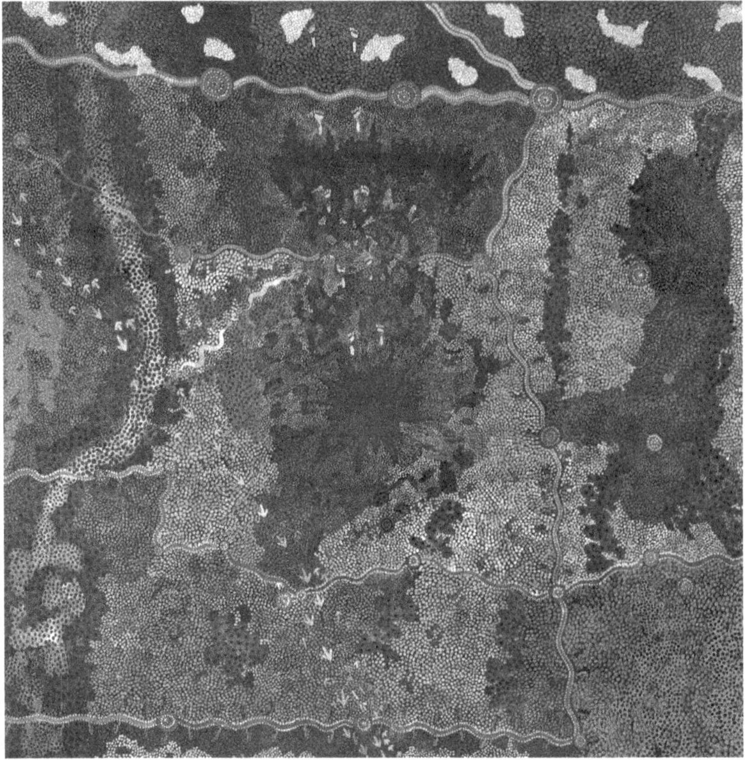

Fig. 40: Clifford Possum Tjapaltjarri and Tim Leura Tjapaltjarri, *Warlugulong*, 1976, synthetic polymer paint on canvas, 168.5 x 170.5 cm. Purchased 1981. Collection: Art Gallery of New South Wales. © Courtesy Aboriginal Artists Agency/2008, ProLitteris, Zürich. Photograph: Christopher Snee.

The flag, like the painting of the Dreaming, gave a reassuring sense of the existence of a higher authority for territorial rights. Nor is it a coincidence that these two images share this function. It was precisely because the two groups made rival and mutually incompatible territorial claims that the assertion of rights was so necessary.

Different responses to the same rocky landscape

There were many other ways in which the contest between the two groups was expressed in the similarities and differences in their experiences of the environment. The descendants of the first arrivals had been particularly influenced by a particular feature of much of Australian geography: the rocks that dotted the landscape. Seen through their neural apparatus they became testimony to the meaning of life in the Dreaming. One group of rocks they saw as kangaroos relieving themselves in a river, while elsewhere two rounded projections they saw as the buttocks of sisters disappearing underground. More angular stones were seen as weapons or chunks of meat. Uluru, also known as Ayers Rock, one of several outcrops in the centre of Australia that are the world's largest free-standing boulders, carried the petrified relics of many events, including the hole made by Tjati when he tried to extricate his *kali* or throwing stick, as well as solidified vestiges of other items of his equipment and of his body itself. These objects, throwing sticks, other equipment and bodies were the things that had had the greatest impact on the formation of their visual neural networks and so it was these that their neural make-up inclined them to see. The neural apparatus of the later European arrivals, being shaped by different experiences and imaginings led them to see very different things in the stones of their new home. It was their frequent visual experience of wool packed for profitable export that helped them to see Woolpack Rocks and it was dreams of the material world they had left behind, dreams such as those that might have filled the head of the Victorian lady in Claxton's 1859 *An emigrant's thoughts of home* that helped them to see in the new landscape such things as the Looking Glass and Dressing Table Rocks. And when they saw Cathedral Rock, Mitre Rock, the Crown of Thorns and the Twelve Apostles, they saw the material paraphernalia and spiritual powers of the Anglican Church whose agency they believed would protect them from the avenging spirits of those they had disinherited. Neuropsychology explains how neural networks shaped by things we have seen, or even only imagined, predispose us to look for those things. It also explains why we see them when they are not there. It is the neurochemistry of our emotions, our desires and fears that exert such pressure on our visual system that we see things even when they are absent.

Different responses to the same illusion

Shared basic properties of the human neural apparatus thus ensure that different communities see different things in the same substance, uncarved rock, depending on their emotional situation. This is a phenomenon we can appreciate through our own self-awareness. There are other differences in vision, however, that also depend on the common properties of our neural apparatus that are more insidious because no amount of reflection can make us aware of them. Take for example the different response some optical illusions can provoke. The anthropologist Haddon a hundred years ago noted such differences in the response to optical illusions between Torres Straights Islanders and Europeans and more recent, more rigorous experiments confirm them. In the 70s Dawson, Choi and others showed that while all Europeans interpret the well-known Muller-Lyer three line illusion (see fig. 41) wrongly, seeing the bottom line as longer than the middle one and the top one as shorter, even though they are really all equal, Indigenous Australians have no problem seeing them as being the same length. They explained the error of Europeans in terms of the distinctive properties of their experience. Modern Europeans spend so much time surrounded by cuboid objects in which angles towards them are acute and those away from them obtuse that they learn to infer that lines with acute angles at the ends should be shortened and those with obtuse angles lengthened. What we now know is that it is not a ques-

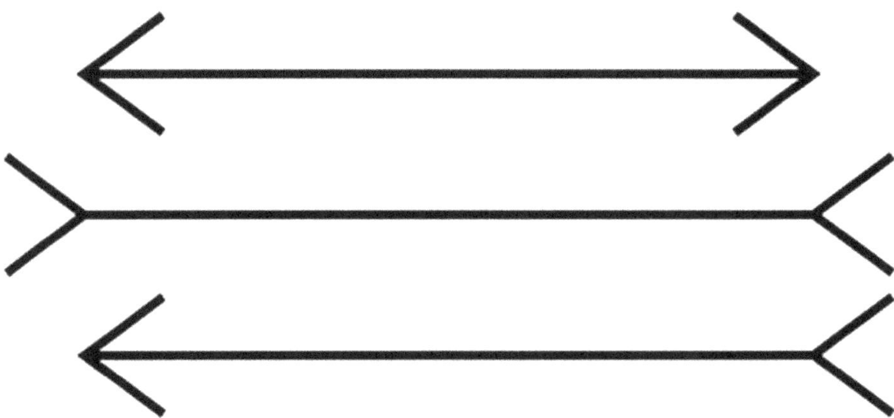

Fig. 41: Müller-Lyer diagram. Archives of the editors.

tion of inference because that would imply that it was something over which they would have control. Rather it was because their neural networks would have been so reconfigured that they produce this response however hard the individual concerned thought about it. It is sobering to realise that the hunter/gatherers, who have been thought of by some as less mentally aware and critical than smart city dwellers, see the lines correctly. Not only have they spent less time surrounded by cuboid objects, but their success as hunters depends on the making of correct mensural judgements of factors such as the length and weight of a boomerang or a spear.

This does not mean that Indigenous Australians are immune to illusions or even all see in the same way. There have, as far as I know, been no tests run on the different Aboriginal populations living in the different areas of Australia but they have been run on Africans occupying a similar range of natural environments. A team led by Segal, Campbell and Herskovits in the 1960s presented a range of illusions to different African populations living in such contrasting environments as open desert, rainforest, savannah and rocky valleys and found that they had very different susceptibilities. For example, when shown two lines of the same length, one horizontal and one vertical at right angles to it, the population living in the desert thought the vertical line was much longer, as do we, while those in the rainforest saw it as the same length. The researchers credited this difference to the impact of the natural environment. The desert dwellers, who frequently saw lines, such as paths and rivers, running into the distance for many miles, 'inferred' that vertical lines were longer than they looked, while those who lived in the rainforest, who never experienced that phenomenon and who were used to measuring trees both growing and felled, saw them as the same length. The consistency of the test results showed that the neural networks of these communities had indeed been modified by passive exposure to the environment and other tests showed similar effects on other communities. Since the environments of Australia have a similar range of variation we can be fairly sure that the different Aboriginal populations manifest a similar variety. Neither in Africa nor anywhere else has anyone yet explored what the consequences of this might be for artistic production but since the consequence of the exposure of people in the European tradition to cuboid objects was the spread of one-point perspective with converging lines it is likely that the impact on the art of Indigenous Australians was also important.

The origins of art in Australia

If such differentiation in perception is due to the neural plasticity mentioned at the beginning, the origin of art in Australia, beyond the making of cupules, may be ultimately the product of the other phenomenon noted at the beginning, mirror neurons. There is much discussion about the dating of the earliest rock art in Australia but most people agree that among the earliest may be that from the Koonalda cave from perhaps 30,000 or 20,000 years ago (see fig. 42). This consists typically of parallel vertical striations and in this has a resemblance to some of the earliest European art found ten years ago in the Chauvet cave and securely dated to 30,000 BC. In both cases the parallel lines are close to earlier scratches made by animals, bears in Chauvet and at Koonalda probably large marsupials. The reason for the parallel emergence is almost certainly the impact of mirror neurons. When the humans saw the scratches on the walls – and they may even have seen the animals making them, – the mirror neurons in their pre-motor cortex were activated and this activation led at least some of them to move their hands in a similar way, so making marks with their stone tools like those that the other animals made with their claws. Although the first markings are likely to have been made quite spontaneously, under the impulse of quite unconscious neural mechanisms, once made they are likely to have provoked a conscious reaction, so encouraging others to imitate them, which is why there is much early art in Australia that consists of such apparently random linear markings.

The date of the earliest figurative engravings and paintings is not clear but by 5,000 BC we have a sense that local traditions were developing, with the so-called 'dynamic figure' tradition appearing in Arnhem Land of the north east and so-called Bradshaw figures and eventually Wandjina figures in the mountains of the north west, while, later, a grand figure style also developed in the area to the south centred on the present Sydney Harbour. Many of these traditions, including those of Arnhem Land, continued down to the present. Such continuity is exceptional in the history of rock art around the world and must largely depend on the relative stability of the populations and the scale and prominence of the art which ensured that generation after generation within the same communities had their neural networks – and so their visual preferences – shaped by their exposure to earlier monuments many of which they continued to repaint or add to. As a result many areas of Australia, like Arnhem Land's Kakadu area or Ubirr Rock, became virtual national galleries open to the public for thousands of years. There can be little doubt that this continuous exposure to major works of painting greatly strengthened the visual preferences of

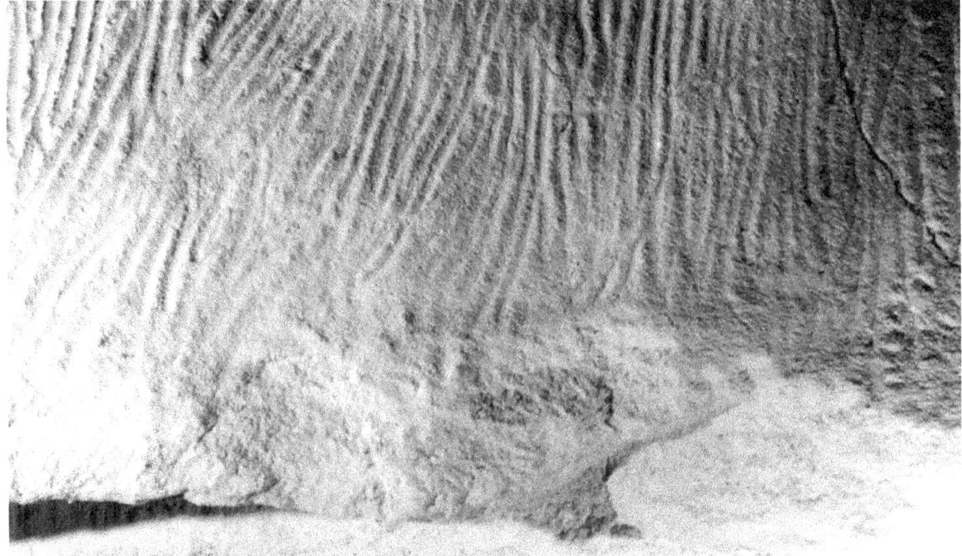

Fig. 42: Rock markings, Koonalda cave, South Australia. Photo Archives of the author.

succeeding generations of painters and ensured that their work was charged with a power rare in rock art, which in many other areas of the world was an activity that was soon abandoned as populations either moved away from where the art was prominent or turned to other forms of art, such as that attached to architecture, which was always more liable to be destroyed and which was often far from the public eye. This is why Aboriginal art, although it lacked the support of academies, museums and written records, has transmitted its authority across the millennia and is in many ways the longest and strongest continuous art tradition anywhere. All this is largely due to neuropsychology. On the one hand, neural plasticity ensured that a particular formal vocabulary was exceptionally deeply embedded in the visual cortex of all members of the community. On the other, mirror neurons also ensured that the manual skills that were regularly manifested in a highly visible way during the painting of bodies on such occasions as rites de passage were transmitted from generation to generation. Elsewhere in the world the act of painting was typically less visible, making the transmission of its techniques over long periods more difficult.

Different responses to the same trees

The principles of neuropsychology had other implications for the two populations. For example, they affected the responses of both Aboriginal inhabitants and Europeans to the gum trees, which, like the rocks, form a dominant feature of the Australian landscape. Gum trees have many defining properties. One is their scent, which, like the smell of the cedar that in the ancient Near East was thought to be the smell of the entombed Osiris, gives it one of the attributes of an animal-life form. Another attribute that suggested life is the tree's deportment, swaying to left and right, while another is its tendency, like some animals, to shed its skin which often has an unusual blue tonality. These properties made the gum trees living beings to the Aboriginals and this affinity between them and the trees is well expressed in the many paintings done by John Glover in the 1830's in which native trees and native peoples are shown together. The contrast between the way Glover represented the trees that provided the setting for the Aboriginal corroboree and those that he shows surrounding his own estate in Tasmania is striking and documents the extent to which he has empathised with the Aboriginals' sensibilities. Other Europeans were not so happy with the blue gums. A painting of another estate by von Guerard shows that such was the aversion of its owners to their swaying forms that they took care to plant the environs of the house with European trees, both deciduous and pines, because these would grow straight, as should the back of a Victorian soldier or school girl. The response that the wandering limbs of the wayward gums triggered in the mirror neurons of uptight Europeans made them so uncomfortable that they tried to exterminate them, rather as the more vicious among them tried to do with the native inhabitants. In both the 19th and the 20th centuries there are many documented examples of such 'arboreal ethnic cleansing'.

Perhaps they were right to sense that the gum trees might affect their own carriage. I have certainly wondered whether the deportment, bordering on the slovenly, of many late 20th century descendants of Europeans, well embodied in the stringy and rangy look of Crocodile Dundee or the slobbering Barry Mackenzie, is not at least partly the result of their keeping company with such disorderly trees whose impact on their mirror neurons is so patent.

Certainly the gum tree has been rehabilitated recently. This is well shown both by the painting of a ghost gum by Albert Namatjira, one of the first Aboriginal artists to adopt European techniques in the 1930s, and by the 1973 photograph *The impossible tree II* by the European David Moore.

Different needs, different searches

An additional disadvantage of the native trees, especially in the 19th century, was that they looked so like girls in coloured dresses that the two could easily be confused, as can be seen in F. E. McCubbin's painting *Lost* from 1886. It was not only the trees that made it much easier to get lost in Australia than in England. It was also the vastness of the untamed wilderness. It was this property, along with the land's isolation, that encouraged the British government to choose to make Australia a penal settlement before they made it a colony, and it is not surprising that some of the transported convicts escaped into the wild where they became members of a new loose community of outlaws. Once in the outback they hunted and were hunted down, as is seen in Tom Roberts' painting *Bushranger* from 1895, where the gunman is as hard to find as the girl in *Lost*. Their spirits haunting the bush, such outlaws soon became heroes of a European/Australian Dreaming and a view of the world from the outlaw's point of view is provided by the series of paintings by Australia's best-known artist of European extraction, Sidney Nolan, whose celebration of the bushranger

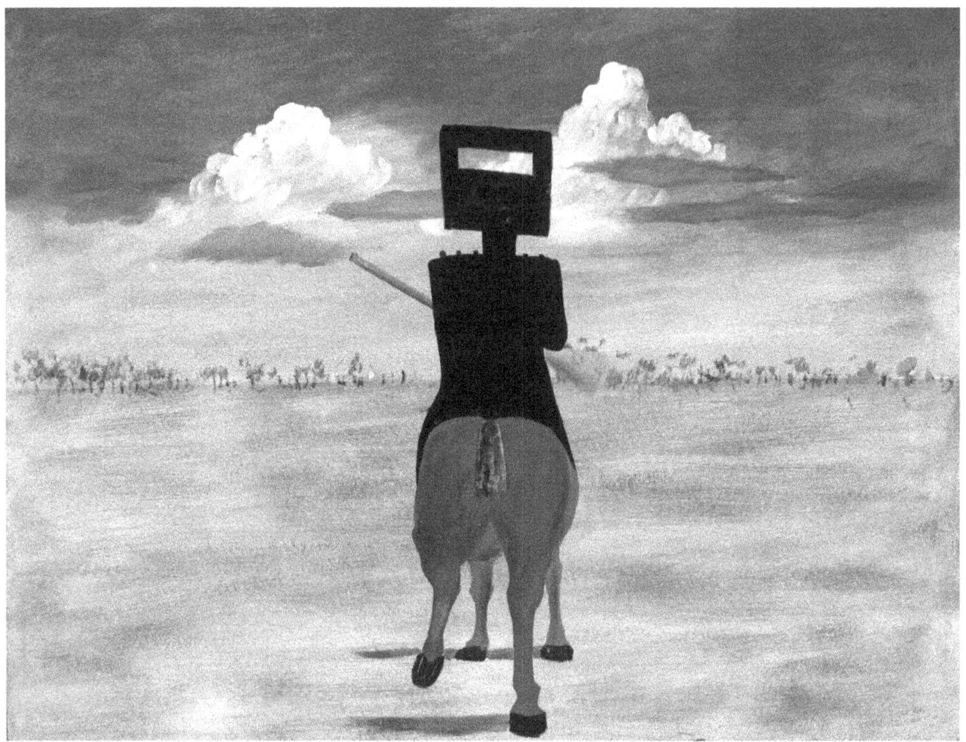

Fig. 43: Sidney Nolan, *Ned Kelly*, 1946, enamel on composition board, 90.8 x 121.5 cm, National Gallery of Australia, Canberra. Gift of Sunday Reed 1977. © NGA 76.277. Photo National Gallery of Australia.

Ned Kelly was inspired by his time spent in remote Western Victoria from 1942. In *Ned Kelly*, 1946, (see fig. 43) the anti-hero is shown as an antipodean Don Quixote as he scans the bush for his victim or his nemesis. But no type of 'looking' so obsessed the immigrants as the search for gold. The gold rush of 1851 was the first of many that drew hopeful diggers into the bush and they too became figures in the European/Australian Dreaming, as we see in Dale Frank's great painting of *The miner's rich vein and a double portrait of the possible miner from the front – triple portait*, 1983. The painting virtually turns the modern gallery-goer into a miner as he or she searches in the swirls of yellow for both gold and a hidden face. Each new type of searching that the unique environment of Australia forced on its European migrants strengthened their capacity to look, creating a Dreaming of searching and embedding the proclivity ever deeper in their neural apparatus.

Perhaps the greatest beneficiary of this European/Australian proclivity to search for the nearly invisible was the art tradition of those who had preceded them. The tradition of Indigenous art was always one of secret knowledge and ambiguous imagery, and this made it particularly appealing to a community neuropsychologically adapted to difficult searches. When Aboriginal art came increasingly into the public eye between the 1930s and the 1990s those who saw it were primed to engage with its mysterious imagery. Indeed a painting like Turkey Tolson Tjuppurrula's *Straightening spears at Ilyingaungau* of 1990, which recalled a combat between ancestral groups in the bush, evoked something of the hide-and-seek associated with the conflict between bushrangers and the law. More explicitly rewarding to the searching eye is Mawundjurl's own *Ngalyod, rainbow serpent, devouring the yawkyawk girls* of 1984, where the viewer searches for the girls just as he or she might in *Lost*.

If an established proclivity for searching prepared viewers for one aspect of Aboriginal art, the advent of flying did this for another. In Australia, due to the absence of roads and railways in many areas, the aeroplane took on the role as a normal mode of transport that it did nowhere else on the planet and European immigrants and their descendants now found themselves experiencing the land where they lived in the same way as the Aboriginals – who had long possessed a flying machine of their own, the boomerang – as viewed from above. Mawalan Marika's *Map of painter's travel by plane from Yirrkala to Sydney* of c. 1960 wittily brings out the similarity between the view of Australia from a modern plane and the way it was traditionally represented in illustrations of the Dreaming.

Different memories: pain and pleasure

The artistic traditions of the Aboriginal inhabitants and the recent arrivals may be coming closer together in the air but on the ground they are further apart than ever, as is demonstrated by a series of monumental expressions of Aboriginal anger. One is *The Aboriginal memorial* created in 1987/8 to express the Aboriginal view of the 1988 Bicentennial celebration of the establishment of British authority in New South Wales. In this extraordinary memorial consisting of 200 traditional hollow logs decorated by a group of Ramingining artists, the dead rise, as if in an army, marshalled along a passage-way representing the Blyth River of their ancient home. And the anger lives on today, as in the work of Fiona Foley who has mocked the exploitation of her community in a series of photographic self-portraits and more recently brought her passion to the University of East Anglia and the shadow of the Sainsbury Centre. In the summer of 2005 she created a compelling work that reminded viewers of the exploitative and violent nature of colonisation not just as an Australian but a global phenomenon, with sacks of salt recalling the issue that brought Gandhi his first political power piled on a mound, its grass clipped and coloured to resemble swelling female genitalia (see fig. 44 and pl. XXIV). The most powerful element of the installation was, however, an upturned rowing boat. This might have been the plaything of a holidaymaker on the adjoining lake, and that is how it came over to most of the polite British visitors, but to Fiona it sent shudders down the spine. A boat being rowed ashore from a larger vessel was usually the first artefact that confronted not just Aboriginal Australians but all the peoples colonised and exploited by Europeans since the 15th century.

As Fiona and I looked at her installation I realised we were looking at it with different neural apparatus. While in my brain the rowing boat was linked to images of freedom

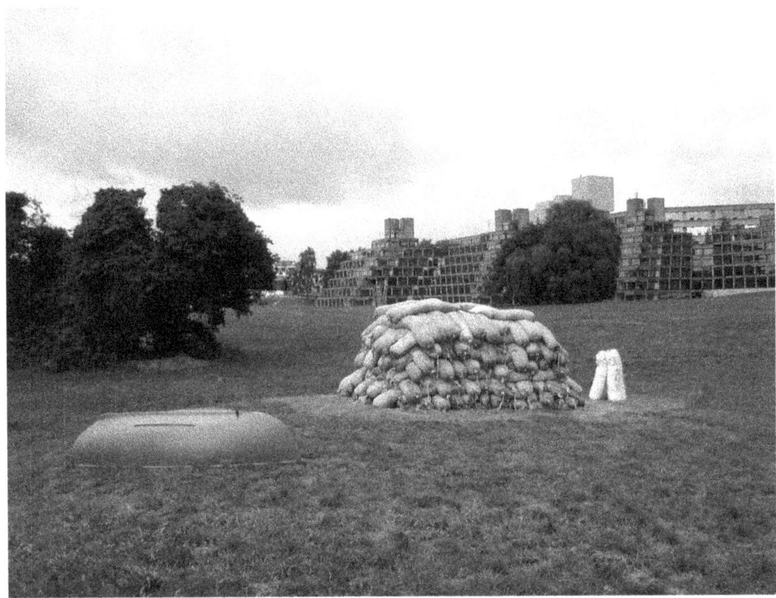

Fig. 44: Fiona Foley, *Dandi March*, 2005, rowing boat, 241 khadi bags, salt. Contribution to *Out There*, installation series, summer 2005, University of East Anglia, Norwich. Image courtesy the artist. Photo Sainsbury Centre for Visual Arts, University of East Anglia, Norwich.

and relaxation by a string of neurons bathed in dopamine, in hers it was linked to scenes of aggression and rape by a burning relay of synapses fired by adrenalin. Watching her put the finishing touches to it on a summer afternoon in Norwich I realised that although her eyes and mine seemed the same the brains which gave meaning to everything they saw and made were profoundly different.

Paul S. C. Taçon

The Creativity Centre: where science meets art

"Arts and sciences are branches of the same tree ... directed towards ennobling man's life, lifting it from the sphere of mere physical existence and leading the individual towards freedom" *Albert Einstein*

"Leonardo da Vinci was as much a scientist as he was an artist; in fact he drew no distinction between the two. In his hands a pencil became as accurate as a scalpel or a microscope in peeling back the secrets of nature and getting to the truth of things" *John Bell, 2005 (Australia's leading Shakespearean actor and director)*

Introduction: art meets science

On 21 September 2005, immediately prior to the Basel Symposium on John Marwurndjul, held at the Museum Tinguely, a special panel discussion took place in front of a large audience. The subject was 'art meets science'. Twelve individuals of diverse art and/or science backgrounds were assembled for the panel.[1]

The main conclusion of the discussion was that artistic creativity is not really very different from scientific creativity but both artists and scientists have a publicity profile problem, especially compared to sports stars. Artists and scientists need to better promote their work and new ways of promotion should be explored, including new art-science-technology 'museums' or 'galleries' like the Tinguely. I elaborated on this in detail a couple of days

1 These included some Symposium speakers, F. Hoffmann-La Roche staff, Museum Tinguely Director Guido Magnaguagno and others from Basel. The discussion was organised by Niggi Iberg (People & Communication – Pharma Research Basel, F. Hoffmann-La Roche) and chaired by myself.
Christian Kaufmann and Claus Volkenandt are thanked for inviting me to write up the Creativity Centre idea and for valuable comments that improved this paper. The organisers and hosts of the John Mawurndjul exhibition and symposium are thanked for inviting me to participate and for a solid week of inspiring events and encounters. Griffith University (Queensland, Australia) is thanked for support and a creative work environment.

later, in one of the concluding discussions of the Mawurndjul Symposium. In this brief paper the idea of a 'creativity centre', a new type of 'art meets science' place, is explored.

The rise of creativity places

For many thousands of years rock art sites, whether deep caves, rock shelters, rock platforms or outcrops of boulders, were the places where humanity displayed the results of human creativity in long-lasting ways. The images at these sites reflect concepts of art and science; anatomy and aesthetics; conceptions and perceptions; principles and belief. These first 'art gallery-museums' became places where future generations learned about history, experience and creation. They were cultural centres where people of varying ages came in contact with place, the past, traditional knowledge and many aspects of creativity and creation in visually exciting ways.

With the advent of writing a new kind of institution devoted to human creativity emerged: libraries to house the tablets, scrolls, papers and books that quickly proliferated. In the 19th century special museums and art galleries were created in buildings but usually were widely separated from each other. The art of Europeans went to galleries[2] while that of Indigenous Australians, Americans and Africans more often went to museums. The art of Asians was divided between the two types of institutions and debates about differences between so-called 'art' and 'craft' emerged. In the 20th century, science centres and technology parks were developed to showcase great achievements in these areas of human creative endeavour. Towards the end of the century, cultural centres became common in many countries as Indigenous peoples worked with other segments of societies and nations to create places highlighting their achievements. Curiously, some are near rock art sites. And in the late 20th Century many rock art sites were also replicated, especially in France, where they became *new* museums that faithfully reproduced some of the world's *oldest*. Rock art theme parks have also been established: places where exploring the past can be fun as well as educational.

Thus, in the world today there are five main types of institutions where the products of creativity are displayed, interpreted, celebrated and researched. These are museums, art galleries, science centres, libraries and cultural centres but the problem is they are invariably separate places with differing agendas. However, the boundaries between them are slowly dissolving, with museums and science centres incorporating certain forms of art and art exhibitions into their programs, art galleries hosting exhibitions inspired by science, cultural centres displaying art and science products alongside each other and libraries increasingly having exhibitions of the sort previously confined to either museums or art galleries. The Museum Tinguely is an excellent example of the emerging new hybrid. And John Mawurndjul's exhibition is one of the latest displays to spark much debate at the Tinguely,

2 Art galleries in Australian terms are what art museums are to a continental European or American audience while museums in this text refer to Natural History museums (and their Ethnographical sections).

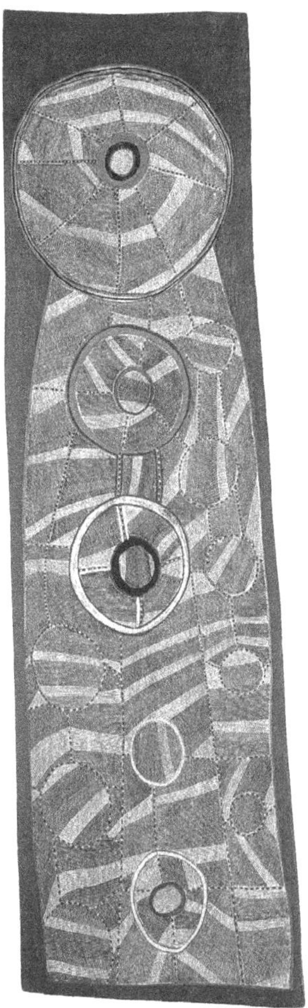

Fig. 45: John Mawurndjul, *Billabong at Milmilngkan*, 1993, earth pigments on bark, 175 x 49 cm, Aimé & Jacqueline Proost Collection. Photo Carl Warner, Brisbane. © 2008, ProLitteris, Zürich.

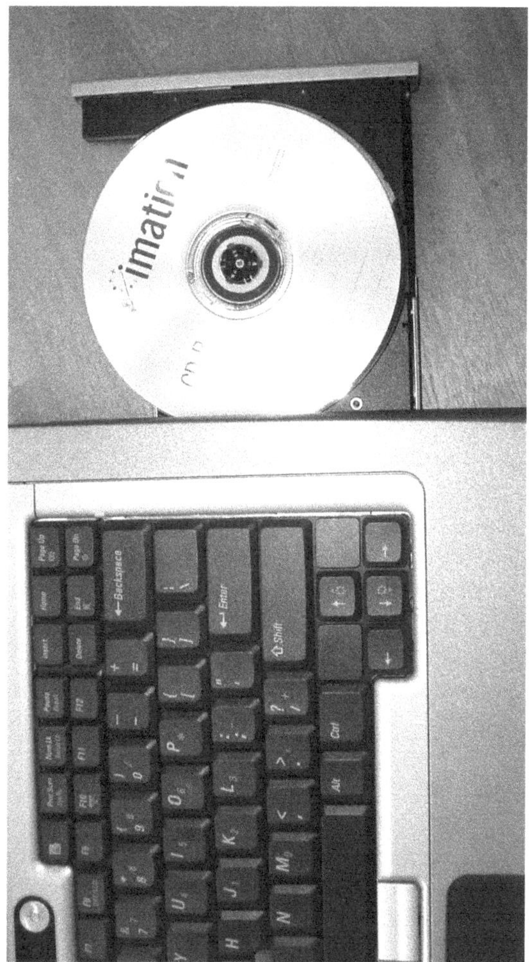

Fig. 46: Computer and CD, 2006. Photo Paul S.C. Taçon.

especially as to where such work is best placed – in a modern art gallery or a traditional (ethnographic) museum?

In response to this, I propose we consider a new type of 'museum-gallery' for the future. This new type of centre would focus on human creativity in a general sense, rather than classifying and splitting categories of objects, intellectual culture and so forth along so-called art-science, ethnographic-Western or other ethno- or discipline-centric lines. These new places would be called 'Creativity Centres' (see figs. 45–46).

The Creativity Centre

At this extraordinary venue visitors will encounter a convergence of art, science and technology. This centre, housed in an architecturally exceptional building, will be a world first where creative science and creative arts combine in unique ways to inspire, educate and communicate the importance and excitement of human creativity. It will be a combination: science centre, art gallery, natural history museum, science museum and creative arts centre are all rolled into one. But these varying aspects will not sit side-by-side as separate entities within the building. Instead, they will be combined in different ways to showcase the best of the world's creative achievements. Science will be made sexy. Creative art will become accessible. Exciting educational and cultural experiences will be provided for all age groups so that the importance of creative art and science in people's daily lives will be communicated.

Communication will be at the heart of the Centre, with science, art and creativity itself demystified. However, the 'magic' and excitement of discovery and creation will not be lost as there will be an emphasis on encounters with real objects. The social impact of science and art on people will feature with the objective of highlighting both relevance and necessity. Art and science will be seen as both serious and fun. Scientists and creative artists will be shown to be heroes as much as sporting stars are. Stereotypes will be dismissed. The beauty of genius and its evolutionary importance will be explored. Creativity, innovation and invention, and their material expression, will be at the core of everything driving the Centre.

Facilities would include:

– The Symbolic Space Gallery devoted to profiling diverse material culture and imagery used in symbolic expression.

– The Contemplation Gallery where the aesthetics of objects are emphasised.

– The Art-Science Creative Collaborations Gallery where unique work by artist-scientists, such as interactive digital or mechanical life-forms, the model-drawings of Leonardo da Vinci or the relationship between mathematical models and ornamental motifs that play with geometrical forms would be featured.

– The Human Evolution Arena that explores how culture has shaped who we are, with facilities to continually update discoveries and debates.

– Experience Space, a unique interactive digital art exhibition place.

– Performance Space, a state of the art 500-seat combination stage and data/digital video projection theatre that can also be used for lectures, major visiting speakers and artists' performances

– Other semi-permanent and temporary exhibition spaces with state of the art display technology. Here the work of particular individuals, such as Leonardo da Vinci or Jean Tinguely (and their machines) or of John Mawurndjul and his contemporaries in non-metropolitan societies (and their paintings, see fig. 47) would feature. Various cultures would be profiled as well as differing approaches to the expression of creativity.

– A Creativity Discovery Space with programs for children and creativity resources for all visitors to access.

– Research, preparation, conservation and collection spaces for processing exhibits and housing a new creativity collection, including a 'Big Brother Room' the public can look into from various vantage points.

– A purposely-designed press or media conference room with video link-up facilities to anywhere in the world.

– An e-Library that would archive digital art and science products, digital art and science publications and various types of electronic applications.

This would be the most amazing venue of its type in the world and a major tourist drawcard. The Centre would provide a new educational and cultural venue where both art and science are promoted and profiled in a comprehensive manner. It will purposely be non-traditional in its approach, designed to actively engage visitors and to provide them with an unusual mix of creative science and art experiences. It would be designed to be environmentally friendly and cost-effective to manage. It would be

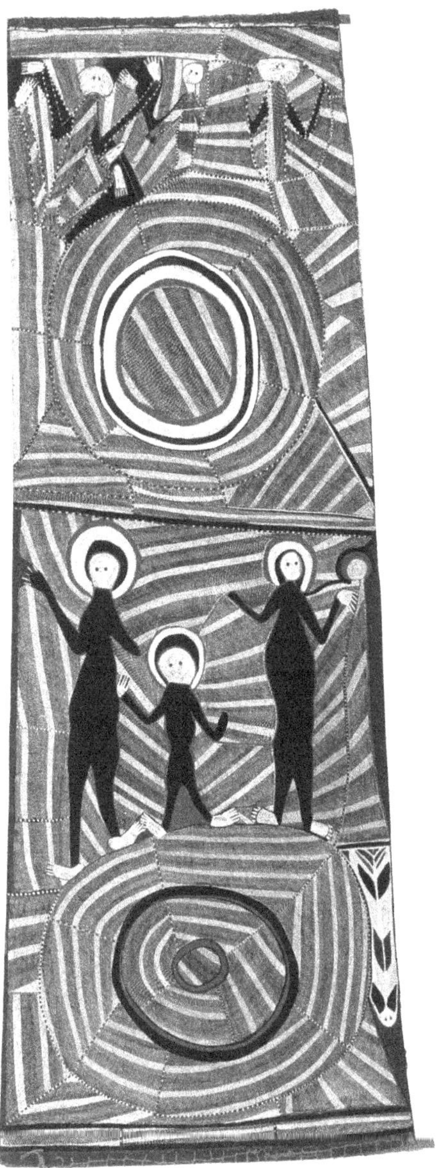

Fig. 47: John Mawurndjul, *Mimih at Milmilngkan*, 1989, natural pigments on eucalyptus bark, 249 x 95 cm. Purchased 2002. Collection: Art Gallery of New South Wales. © John Mawurndjul / 2008, ProLitteris, Zürich. Photograph: Brenton McGeachie.

the sort of place people can come back to time and again, having different educational and entertainment experiences each time. It would be very different from a 'Science Centre' in that the Creativity Centre would achieve balance between the original impact of creativity in science (through tracing ways that lead to discoveries) or in art (through drawing the beholder closer to the original works as well as to the human creativity embodied/materialised in those works), and the un-obtrusive techniques of modern audiovisual communication. Visitors that would get the most out of the Creativity Centre would be those who start to reflect on what they are seeing, get provoked into thinking and ask questions.

New creations and the future

Artists and scientists are especially concerned with creativity but all humans are creative. At some point in the distant past human creativity took us on a different evolutionary path from other creatures. Initially the survival of our ancient ancestors depended on their ingenuity, creation and culture. Soon human creativity pervaded every aspect of existence, with creativity not only expressing human identity but also changing the world and every living creature within it. Resulting material culture has been particularly pervasive. We now live in a human managed, if not constructed, world. But some of our creative acts have been unintentionally or purposively destructive. As a result, the planet is now changing more rapidly and unexpectedly than before. Tomorrow our survival may again be at risk, testing the limits of human creativity in the process. Creativity centres could help educate about the importance of human diversity, ingenuity, lateral thinking, material and symbolic expression, assisting with the development of creative solutions to both new and old unresolved problems in the process. But they should be designed not just to display the incredible range of past and present achievements but also to inspire new creations, debate and reflection. These centres would be the latest and most elaborately engineered places where people could explore the nature of creativity, existence and the human-defined universe, something begun long ago with the first rock art sites.

Marianne Eigenheer[1]

Rendering visible – new practices for old institutions

TO SEE is – as it always has been – difficult. But globalisation has brought into the discussion new instruments, a better understanding not of only distinctions, but also of the need to cross borders, in science, in art and in politics.

On old world maps, mapmakers wrote, "there be dragons!" describing the unknown as often frightening. But as soon as explorers began penetrating the more distant regions of the world, the monster-marked patches disappeared. But there are, however, still many dragon-infested areas on our mental map, of how the different parts of the world work together, and, for example, the question of how the boundless range of cultural expressions may somehow fit together.

The good news is that since recently scientists have been learning to map our interconnectivity in many different fields [see e.g. this volume John Onians pp. 199–210]. Their maps are shedding light on our web-like universe. Many surprises and challenges are emerging that we would not have dreamed of 10 years ago. Naturally these emergent views that scientists and artists are now working with are not at all new, but today we have to deal with the immense complexities of levels and layers of a globalised world, together with the micro-cosmos of one's private destiny. Networks, not only intellectual and cognitive networks, are present everywhere and are thus part of our life experience. There is no way of falling out of touch with the world anymore.

The idea to reconnect different levels and layers of culture or society in an analytical way in order to gain new insights and to obtain better comparative knowledge has been consistently in discussion within institutional structures. It is interesting how these ideas appear and disappear in institutions which we are familiar with through our own work. Take as an example the ideas developed by a great German curator and academic of the 1930s, Alexander Dorner, who was driven out of Germany by the Nazis and found asylum in the United States.[2] He reached a new understanding of the relationship between

1 Unfortunately the author was not able to participate as a discussant at the symposium in Basel, due to illness. The editors regret that her views were therefore missing as a basis to the final discussion.

2 Dorner, Alexander, *Überwindung der «Kunst»* (Original title: *The Way Beyond «Art»*, New York, 1949), Fackelträger-Verl., Hannover, 1959.

exhibited objects and the space in which they are shown. His focus was on the interactions between the public, the artist and the curator. His understanding of the flow and otherwise moving world of cognitive and spiritual energy as being inside objects is, in many ways, contemporary to approaches of today. So, perhaps real glimpses into ways of understanding are always CONTEMPORARY as long as they remain mobile and do not become static, in other words, as long as they are not merely describing something but rather re-creating it.

It is with ideas such as these that we have been working on in our projects at ICE, the Institute for Curatorship and Education in Edinburgh. And, it has been crucial for me to bring into the discussion my position as a practicing artist. At times this has been challenging and controversial with regard to my position as an art historian and as a curator.

I will never forget the discussion I had in 1997 outside Port Vila in Vanuatu with some local colleagues. At the same time Documenta X was being presented in Kassel – far away and in a different context – but perhaps with different and simpler words we were talking about the same issues and why it was so important for us to be artists working together. The moment that animated our discussion was when I had the opportunity to view my colleagues' art works and we were able, through our discussion, not only to look at the work but actually see it.

This was also the visual starting point of my quest into how the creative and artistic process starts for artists from such a different background. By expressing my own experiences as openly as possible, trust between us was able to grow, and with this trust came a genuine exchange of ideas.

A major question that grew from our discussions was the following: how can an exhibition create a quiet space where artists can talk together, trust each other and not be affected by the fear of competition, or 'loosing face'? The question revealed that artists do not a priori have a better understanding and knowledge of art, or of other cultures, than the public in general.

A year later, a stay in Perth in Western Australia, gave me several opportunities to talk to Indigenous Australian women (of whom only some were artists). Without the common ground of some kind of shared spoken language we had to find other ways of expressing ourselves and found these by drawing simple lines which we were able to communicate. Again: by starting to draw lines myself we were able to create an actual space for a real discussion, not only with words, but with gestures, body language and visual language.

We discovered that, as women from Aboriginal and European backgrounds, we shared many experiences and this was a rather incredible moment for us all. As we were really and authentically communicating about our lives and our ideas we soon learned more about each other and our similarities and differences. This only happened because there was no way for us to start an 'art' discussion (where often immediately differing, competitive positions are taken). The essential experience was to look at a creative process and allow a visual world to grow.

This observation led to other questions: how can creative processes of communication start? And how can a situation be created that helps to protect the intimacy of the personal world that will potentially be revealed? How much do we have to know of the culture of the other who is sitting before us?

In 1998 we[3] invited two female Kanak artists from Noumea to work in Basel with two Swiss artists and together create an exhibition,[44] called *Antipode.* We will never know the contents of the discussions between the four women, but the weeks spent together were very successful. And interestingly enough the exhibition revealed that an intensive communication had been established between the four. For the exhibition viewer it became apparent that there existed many more layers to the relationships between the four artists; possibly more than they themselves were aware of.

A well-known backdrop to this situation leads to yet an other question: in a world where, metaphorically speaking, too many women still live on another planet, where clearly they use different visual languages, how can art exhibitions be made to present these relatively unknown visual idioms? This is especially relevant to artists from countries where women have no rights and no personal voice in public anyway. While artists do not have to 'illustrate' a personal situation within their work, they may work from the base of a personal experience in order to develop a personal language. But, how can an exhibition be developed that shows these processes of artistic experience? Perhaps it is through artistic exploration as a sort of research and not just through another documentary form of anthropological questioning that the difference of art, craft and cultural experience can be shown in a non-competitive way.

The experience of working in pairs with different roles – such as an artist with an artist, a curator with an artist, a writer with an artist (or vice versa) – is helping us to bridge our differences. In the process of creating works or putting together an exhibition a space of trust will develop, allowing questions to come more easily. It sounds so simple but perhaps the most difficult thing to remember (in the process of the globalising art world) is how difficult it is to see, and to learn to really see, because it is not enough to simply read or listen to well-prepared definitions. One of the most difficult points for all of us as artists, curators, writers and scholars seems to be the acceptance of change and movement, not only in the 'outside' world but also in our close, personal realm; changes and movements that happen every day, every minute. Going back to the old wisdom that everything is in flow: the younger generation, the networking generation, now accesses global streams of information and technology and uses them without problem; this is another way of thinking and behaving, a mode of communication that does not always lend itself well to rigid institutions (based in firm, brick and mortar buildings).

Looking at the work of an artist such as John Mawurndjul (with Kay Lindjuwanga, his wife, as co-artist) which is so obviously contemporary yet embedded within cultural tradition, we have the incredible opportunity to discover the lines of the network of creativity. The practice of creativity that exists under the surface of theoretical understandings is today as important as it was when the first human beings started to express themselves by

3 The International Exchange and Studio Programme, Basel (Internationale Austausch Ateliers beider Basel, iaab), of which I was then a co-director under the auspices of the Christoph Merian Foundation, Basel.

4 At the private Margrit Gass Gallery, Basel (now closed).

using their hands to do something connected to the outside world and to their personal territory.

It would be interesting to view John Mawurndjul's work and examine the quality of his lines and drawings alongside artists such as Agnes Martin, Emma Kunz or Ruth Vollmer; to examine how John's work resonates within the contemporary art world.

The final question is, how do we show in an exhibition the very difference of expression that lies at the heart of art. And, how do we present different types of art works in a way that helps us understand the differences? These are questions that are being discussed in many parts of the world. The discussion is intense, especially between artists. How can an exhibition really 'show' what an artist is doing or saying? In what respect does showing the differences between cultural expression lead to the creation of new ways of seeing and also lead one to a closer understanding of these cultural differences? Is there a way to attract the gaze of the public, perhaps by developing exhibitions that are not so homogeneous but create a heterogeneous situation in a new way, by setting a stage that identifies the differences? In order to gain an audience that can actively explore the joy of seeing rather than experience the fear of consuming? Or, will this remain a dream?

One should never forget that ideas and theories are useful, but practice is what often brings us down to earth very quickly, not only in the areas that this symposium dealt with. We have in the art world a hierarchical structure that is hard to overcome. Many conferences and events try by creating a forum for communication and by exploring ways to deal with the power games of politics, positions, finances, sponsorship, etc. that lurk behind the art scenes all over the world. Talking about theories and opportunities is interesting and stimulating, but what is the next step?

A revelation for me was an event in Tbilisi in Georgia early in September 2005: we responded to an invitation by some curators, artists and art historians from Tbilisi to come as a group of artists and curators to discuss how communities that feel they are excluded from the international art scene – a bit like outlaws – could be included. It was a positive week of discussions, with teams working together and open discussions taking place but when we started to work up some form of documentation, all the good ideas were soon forgotten and the process became competitive; in the end I had to accept that it was worth discussing and exploring ideas but what was really required from my group was money for a publication. It seems so much easier to follow well-trodden paths than to take the risks of attempting something new (it was like playing with the instrument of guilt that we live in a 'better world'). All the Bienniales in recent years that have shown works by artists from across the globe do not really assist in creating a better visual understanding of cultural and artistic differences; too often they merely present a colourful surface, frequently quite superficial, because an important point is often missing: time for looking at something.

In these events we could explore ways of dealing with different truths and of living happily together. But how can these be expressed in an exhibition? Seeing means to see different realities concurrently, but how?

So many times over the years working in the varied fields of art and cultural research have I struggled with being an artist, an art historian, a curator and a human being living a normal life at the same time. In the process of finding order for myself within all these facets of my life and trying to join all the different threads together it has been incredibly important to spend time as a practising artist because it enables one to move on and take risks. And, it hurts nobody because the battlefield is paper, canvas or some other tangible material. In today's world of new media this creative aspect is increasing for everybody, e.g. digital and mobile photographs, blog-writing or creating homepages can help one to find balance and a personal position (for some seconds) in a world that is moving and changing so incredibly fast. Perhaps the museums have to steer this course in order to survive? Could they become, as universities are starting to do, perpetually mobile with regard to their location in cultural space?

Conclusion

To get cultural diversity to be universally recognised as well as accepted as a global asset is what keeps communication alive on an international level. To keep it working as an effective tool requires investment from many people and institutions that are familiar with different cultural backgrounds and traditions. Why and how should artists in this process be more appreciated as partners for these institutions? The 'why' is clear: because the artists practice, and have done so for a very long the time, and through their practice have created communication channels in many visually effective languages. The 'how' is a matter that deserves a special effort, on the part of the artists as well as the institutions and their representatives. Developing new ways of intelligible visual communication through novel forms of presentation could be a major step in the right direction: ultimately, for the broad audience to SEE!

Bernhard Lüthi

Recognising Indigenous Australians: a new context for art

Having the retrospective on John Mawurndjul in two European museums that otherwise gear their strategies to the presentation of the works of classical European Modernism and contemporary Western art is the realisation of a long-standing idea. It refutes a prejudice often articulated by Western art theory, namely that non-Western, so-called traditional artists are completely in the grasp of their 'cultural traditions' and do not command the potential for innovation. The *«Rarrk»* exhibition clearly showed that this is not the case, and that the works of artists like John Mawurndjul not only incorporate many layers and facets, but speak for themselves and are accessible through viewing and perception. Thus the exhibition can be understood as a response to changing times and as a sign that even in old Europe art history is gradually realising that their exclusively Euro-centred approach is on the way out and becoming a model with neither value nor justification – a step that has been taken already in Australia (see pls. XXV–XXVI).

Ever since the late 1970s and early 1980s, when Western concepts of, and views on, the validity of geographical boundaries, art, culture and cultures, and the historical connections and the geopolitical realities that grew from them began to be questioned it has become increasingly evident that, in the nearer future, contemporary art in all its manifestations will not be able to avoid revising and updating its practices and perception of self.

Where questions of style, of ideas defined by aesthetics and contents, and of movements articulated either by individual artists or by groups of artists are concerned, visual arts and other forms of artistic expression have, at least for a limited period of time, something in common – they carry a date of expiry. Against the background of sweeping geopolitical, religious and cultural change the cross-, trans- or intercultural project is no longer merely a matter of changing fashion or the expression of a craving for novelty, it has become tangible reality. Even though stubborn opposition is foreseeable, this cultural realignment, or whatever you wish to call it, will become a permanent feature in the world of exhibitions and museums.

John Mawurndjul's retrospective was organised by a team of three curators: at the Australian end by the artist Tiriki Onus, son of the late Lin Onus, and at the European end by Christian Kaufmann, curator of the Oceania Department at the Museum der Kulturen for many years, and, in the role of the initiator, by myself (what am I: artist, or mediator in intercultural affairs?). Laurentia Léon braved all the logistical storms while Guido Magnaguagno, director of the Museum Tinguely, stood at the helm and navigated the project safely through the yet unchartered, and thus dangerous, waters of local cultural politics. Of course the project could never have been realised without the patient cooperation of the artist himself, John Mawurndjul, who was assisted by Appoline Kohen, the current arts director of the Maningrida Arts and Culture in Maningrida. In Ivo Kummer we had a brilliant film-maker who, together with his crew, succeeded in creating an impressive portrait of the artist in his home environment; the images projected on the screen provided a guideline for the viewers and inspired them to develop their own way of encountering and reading the works presented in the rooms of the 'white cube'. Not listed here by name are the innumerable assistants, lenders, hauliers, film-technicians and exhibition staff, to name but a few, who worked in the background on putting the show together, on producing the catalogue and readying the visual material or on organising the symposium. They all contributed to making the exhibition the success it was. And last but not least: a big thankyou goes to the generous sponsor of the event – to Roche!

The project's early history

What is striking about many of the people involved in this project – and which, as a matter of fact, and apart from those mentioned above, has not been addressed yet – is their professional background: quite a few of them are artists, others are people who, in the past, have acted as cultural activists behind similar projects in Australia or, in the wider sense of awakening intercultural practical and discursive action, in many other parts the world. For the process of opening up the field of contemporary visual art, the 1970s and 1980s were critical and decisive decades, not only in Australia but also in Africa, Latin America and Asia, and, of course, also in Europe. But the full story of this development is still waiting to be written.

The last point is worth noting because, unknown to many, in Australia it was artists of originally European descent who were among the first to recognise the value of Indigenous art and grant it more attention. Instead of merely taking the works of Aboriginal artists as ethnographic artefacts that belonged to the world of anthropological research, they looked upon these creative products – originally painted on rock and later transferred to bark or canvas, or sculpted in wood – as works of art; the same is true of the more ephemeral ground paintings and sculptures. One man who stands representatively for this group of white Australians is Tony Tuckson who, as an artist, was associated with the Australian avant-garde but who also collected the works of Indigenous artists in his role as a senior staff member at the Art Gallery of New South Wales in Sydney. Also worth mentioning, particularly in the context of the *«Rarrk»* exhibition, is Karel Kupka, the Czech-born lawyer and artist, who visited Australia, particularly the northern parts of the country, several times in the early 1950s. For the artist Kupka it was beyond doubt that – apart from being of anthropological interest – the works he collected from Indigenous painters and sculptors were autonomous and creative accomplishments of high aesthetic value.

Allow me here to go into a little more detail on the above-mentioned, in order to make it clear that intercultural work is never an individual matter; successful projects are always the outcome of collective work and explicitly include the collaboration of Indigenous artists, activists, administrators and, in recent times, also of Indigenous curators, in other words, of people who are part of the culture(s) under discussion.

With the first *Australian Perspecta*, 1980–1981, staged by the Art Gallery of New South Wales and curated by Bernice Murphy, a new leaf was turned over in terms of viewing and valuating Indigenous art in Australia – ten years prior to the trendsetting, hotly disputed exhibition *Magiciens de la Terre* that was staged by Jean Hubert Martin and a team of curators at the Centre Pompidou / Grande Halle de la Villette and which is to be seen as a critical reaction to the *Primitivism in the 20th Century* exhibition that was organised by the New York Museum of Modern Art in 1984. Five years earlier, on the occasion of the Sydney Biennale in 1979, Bernice Murphy had insisted that not only artists of European descent but also representatives of the Australian Indigenous art world should be invited. In the following years this became the accepted standard for all large national and international survey exhibitions of contemporary art in Australia – namely the *Australian Perspecta* and the *Sydney Biennales* – with one notable exception: the 1990 *Biennale*, whose artistic director René Block was, ironically, a European, slid back into the old pattern and invited no Indigenous artists. The only two references to the 'First' Australians are to be found in a contribution to the exhibition catalogue and in the title *The Readymade Boomerang – Certain Relations in 20th Century Art*, as if European artists had never either heard of, or referred to, non-European art, particularly African and Oceanic art. In her contribution to the catalogue titled 'Marcel who? (The Readymade in the Context of the Province)', Bernice Murphy tried at least in words to cushion the embarrassment of not having any Indigenous Australians in the event – an issue she had fought for before the exhibition and has continued to do up to the present day.

Following the period of political activism that had been organised by a broad coalition of solidary black and white Australians in the 1970s, which had strongly focused on the issue of, up to then, denied land-rights – and, most probably, also as a reaction to these events – the 1980s were marked significantly by three developments: first, by the sudden, culturally and politically motivated emergence of creative, contemporary black-Australian art und culture, in conjunction with, secondly, the irrepressible will to create political and administrative instruments of self-rule and to develop cultural self-responsibility, and thirdly, the Australian government's plans and preparations for the Bicentennial of 1988 in which the occupation of Australia in the name of the British crown was to be celebrated. Indigenous Australians refused to participate in the celebrations; the idea of having to celebrate one's own subjugation was looked upon as absurd. In the wake of the protest a new, more rebellious generation began to take shape, focused on a group of culturally sensitised and motivated artists and activists headed by people like Chicka Dixon, Gary Foley, Lin Onus, Jack Davis and Oodgeroo Noonuccal (the writer Kath Walker). Among other things they took over the newly established Aboriginal and Torres Strait Islander Arts Board where the entire staff was of Indigenous Australian descent. This new generation was involved in the launching of a number of groundbreaking cultural-political projects, amongst others the encompassing survey exhibition *Aṟatjara – The Art of the First Australians*, the first of its kind to be shown in Europe. These events and the claims asserted at the time marked the beginning of a political and cultural process that is ongoing to this day, even though it has often been subject to the whims and political agendas of changing governments in Australia. However, over the last decade or so the general climate has deteriorated. This had mainly to do with the conservative – often even reactionary – Howard government that was in power for years and not only showed itself to be uncooperative in a majority of issues but has also repeatedly turned down legitimate claims and even wilfully revoked a number of well-proven achievements. As Gary Foley remarked during the symposium in Basel, seen from the perspective of Indigenous Australians the basic issues still not have been satisfactorily solved. Indigenous people still have to fight for their equal share and status in Australian society (and art).

What conclusions can be drawn from this brief synopsis? It goes to show that in the field of exhibitions and in the process of mediating unfamiliar facts and contexts, as well as in the harsh world of political reality within which contemporary, non-European art has to try to find modes of articulating itself, authentic interculturalism can only grow from a process, in the course of which geographical, mental, cultural as well as individual boundaries are ground down and reduced to a minimum. In other words, interculturalism, the transfer of cultural knowledge and the values and premises associated with it, can only be satisfactorily realised if the culture that is being represented and the voices of its representatives are included in the process, and in collaboration with mediators who themselves do not belong to the culture that is being represented, but who support its cause. In fact, this task could be a chance for European anthropology, provided the discipline is prepared to shed trusted, self-centred and institutionalised, but now obsolete concepts. Or to put it more directly: it could be a chance if European anthropologists are prepared to face up to the fact that the times have finally changed, and if they take into account in their methodology the altered political, cultural and demographic conditions. At least they could then keep pace with the course of ever-changing events. In this respect, their colleagues in Australia are distinctly more open-minded and take their responsibility more seriously.

Art, not anthropology

Given the present geopolitical situation and power relations in the world, we should take into account that when it comes to breaching, or at least crossing, cultural, mental, religious or political boundaries, mediating art and culture is itself a highly politicised venture. Matters become even more complicated when one acknowledges that Western institutions – especially in the world of art and in museum anthropology – follow their own political and strategic agendas, which, at least in their present form, are still geared to demarcation and exclusion, and which need vanquishing.

We have to accept that Indigenous Australian artists – or, for that matter, artists from anywhere in the world – once they have become accustomed to European exhibition practices and the political enmities that the system breeds, will refuse to be banned to, and appropriated by, ethnographic museums any longer. Ethnographic museums are simply not the right place for showing contemporary art, no matter whether we are dealing with European or non-European art. Their task should have a much wider scope. Given a new approach to their discipline, anthropologists could for example for once remain within their own cultural boundaries and study their own, allegedly more familiar environment. They could, just as an example, study contemporary Western art, the modalities of its production and distribution and question its position and role in Western society today, especially since Western artists themselves have started taking these issues into account in their art-producing strategies and have begun challenging them from an anthropological perspective. The opportunity is there, the door is wide open, so is the scope of interpretation. On the other side of the fence, the temples and strongholds of contemporary Western art should be aware that in future not only artists from China – who at present, and in view of the economic potential involved, are very welcome – will come knocking at the door but also artists from cultures that until now have been classed as 'Indigenous', or artists from nations that have up to now usually been labelled and pigeonholed as 'Third World' countries. Not to forget: those parts of the world that used to be the main hunting grounds for anthropologists and ethnographic museums now have their own Biennales.

Seen from this angle, and under the given circumstances, it does not really make sense to build one new museum after the next, as long as these new modes of viewing and forms of organising presentations are not firmly lodged in the heads of curators, museum directors, local politicians and of all the other experts who have, at least until now, argued for the exclusion of 'other' art works on art theoretical and anthropological terms, and, seen from the other side, in future hold the key to their inclusion.

In summary, it appears that in Australia the people responsible for the transfer of contemporary Indigenous art – that is curators, administrators and museum people, and among these particularly the new, younger generation – are seriously thinking about how to best reach the European exhibition scene and position themselves there on a firmer and more sustainable basis. Together with a number of far-sighted individuals, some of whom are no longer around, the generation that is now gradually retiring from the scene has certainly opened the door for them.

At the other end of the line, i.e. at the European end, the situation is in no way easier. On the contrary, in view of the increasingly entrenched geopolitical circumstances, the resurgent xenophobia we are witnessing today, and in conjunction with old and new fears that spell exclusion rather than inclusion, the situation is more complex than ever and is bound to have an impact on the exhibition scene. While in the mid-1990s there was justified hope that the European institutions were in the process of opening their doors to non-European art and culture, these expectations have been dampened in recent years. Today we are witnessing a backlash. This relates not only to Indigenous Australian art, it goes for all forms of contemporary art that have their origin beyond the boundaries of the Western world. But there are exceptions, and these exceptions could lead to a change of mind and of the ruling practice. Although at present it still seems beyond imagination that the John Mawurndjul retrospective would be shown at one of the major temples of art such as the Tate Modern, the National Gallery in Berlin, the Centre Pompidou, the Kunsthaus in Zurich or the Reina Sofia in Madrid, one should not quite give up hope: a change of mind does simply take longer! As we know too well from experience, exhibition practices are subject to constant shifts and changes in strategy; the same is true of the people behind the practices. One has to keep a watchful eye on the scene, preferably directly on site. With this in mind, what about the idea of having in Europe a cultural mission in residence occupied by a Koori, or Aboriginal, representative – which in Australia is normal practice nowadays. It would certainly be worth a try, under the motto: *theory is of no value as long as the art works, and through them the artists, are not visible* – a truth that needs verifying in every new generation.

List of Authors

Jon Altman

Jon Altman is Professor and Director of the Centre for Aboriginal Economic Policy Research at the Australian National University and has an academic background in economics and anthropology. He has a broad economic policy interest in Aboriginal art in Australia, having chaired a national review of the sector in 1989 and assisted the NT government develop an Indigenous Art Strategy in 2003. His anthropological work has focused on central Arnhem Land where he has worked with Kuninjku people since 1979. In 2004 he assisted to curate the Art Gallery of New South Wales major retrospective *Crossing Country: The Alchemy of Western Arnhem Land Art,* and in 2006 he co-curated (with Apolline Kohen) the retrospective exhibition *Mumeka to Milmilngkan: Innovation in Kurulk Art* at the Drill Hall Gallery, the Australian National University, Canberra.

Anne-Marie Bonnet

Anne-Marie Bonnet is Professor of Art History at the University of Bonn (since 1997) where she teaches on the art and culture of the Renaissance, contemporary art history, museology, photography and the new media. Her interests in research focus on the art of the Dürer-period, Auguste Rodin, body and art, photography and painting in the age of the new media. Recent publications include *Kunst der Moderne – Kunst der Gegenwart,* Köln 2004; 'Willkommen in der Jetzt-Zeit ...', in Häusser, H.-J. and K. Imesch (eds.), *Visions of Future. Art and Art History in Changing Contexts,* SIK, Zürich, 2004. 'Am Anfang war das Auge', in *Still Mapping the Moon. Perspektiven zeitgenössischer Malerei* (exhibition catalogue), Kunstmuseum Bonn, 2004; 'Marilyn Monroe: My private Sheroe?', in Hoet, J. (ed.) *'(My private) Heroes',* (exhibition catalogue), MARTa, Herford, 2005.

Sally Butler

Sally Butler, Ph.D., is a Lecturer in Art History at the University of Queensland, Brisbane Australia. She is the author of *Our Way, Contemporary Aboriginal Art from Lockhart River* (University of Queensland Press, St. Lucia, 2007) and curator of a touring survey exhibition of the same name. Her publication and curating experience covers Australian Indigenous epistemology and post-structuralism in Central Desert aesthetics, Indigenous new media art, and cultural politics. Exhibitions curated by Butler also include *The Message Stick, Art from the Lockhart River Art Gang* (1998–2001); and two exhibitions of contemporary non-Indigenous artists: *Sensing the Surface, Photography by Carl Warner* (2006) and *Capricornia, Photography by Shane Fitzgerald* (2006–7).

Marianne Eigenheer

Marianne Eigenheer is an artist and Professor and Director of the Institute for Curatorship and Education at the Edinburgh College of Art. From 1991–1999 she was Artistic Director of IAAB/CMS in Basel and Professor of Fine Arts at the Art Academy Stuttgart, Germany (1997–2007). Her special interests include interdisciplinary projects with scientists, anthropologists, designers, etc. As an artist and a researcher she is especially interested in 'glocal' issues and the new media. Recent publications include contributions in *Patrick Geddes, By Leaves We Live*, Yamaguchi, Edinburgh, 2005; Leutner, P. and H.-P. Niebuhr (eds.) *Bild und Eigensinn*, Bielefeld, 2006; *Kunstforum 186*, Köln, 2006. She is also editor of the ICE Reader 1: *Curating Critique*, Revolver, 2007.

Till Förster

Till Förster is Professor of Anthropology and Director of the Institute of Social Anthropology at the University of Basel (since 2001). His regional focus is on Central and West Africa (Ivory Coast, Cameroon, Nigeria) where he has conducted extensive research since 1979. His special interests lie in art, ritual, modernity and transformation, and political anthropology. Recent publications include: 'Sehen und Beobachten. Ethnographie nach der Postmoderne', in *Sozialer Sinn* 3 (1), 2001; 'Globalisierung aus einer Handlungsperspektive', in Neubert, D. et al. (eds.) *Globalität im lokalen Kontext.* Berlin, 2004; 'Negotiating the Contemporary: Artists in a Globalizing Art World', in Grewe, C. A. (ed.), *Exhibiting the Other: Museums of Mankind and the Politics of Cultural Representation.* Washington, Berlin, 2005; 'Smoothing the Way of the Dead', *Yale Art Gallery Bulletin* 2005.

Christian Kaufmann

Christian Kaufmann, Ph.D., has worked among the Kwoma people of the East Sepik Province of Papua New Guinea, as well as on the islands of Ambrym and Malakula of Vanuatu. He is a founding member of the Pacific Arts Association. From 1970 to 2005 he was Curator of the Oceania Department at the Museum der Kulturen in Basel. Among other projects he initiated and coordinated an international exhibition on the arts of Vanuatu (1996–1997). At the University of Basel he was Lecturer for Museum Anthropology and Art. At present he is an A.B. Mellon Fellow in Art History at the Metropolitan Museum of Art, New York. Together with A. Kaeppler and D. Newton he published *Art Océanien / Oceanic Art*, Citadelles & Mazenod, Paris, 1993 / Abrams, New York, 1997; he recently (2005) co-curated the exhibition *«Rarrk» – John Mawurndjul. Journey Through Time in Northern Australia* at the Museum Tinguely in Basel, Switzerland, and edited the exhibition catalogue.

Apolline Kohen

Apolline Kohen is the current Arts Director at Maningrida Arts & Culture. She puts together an average of 25 commercial exhibitions per year for Maningrida Arts & Culture. She has also initiated two major international projects for Maningrida Arts & Culture: the exhibition *In the Heart of Arnhem Land: Myth and the Making of Aboriginal Art*, Musée de l'Hotel-Dieu, Mantes-La–Jolie, (June-October 2001) and the cultural exchange *Crossings* between Indigenous artists from Maningrida and French artists (2001 and 2003), which resulted in the presentation of a mixed media performance at the 2003 Darwin Festival. She has worked on the exhibition *Crossing Country: the Alchemy of Western Arnhem Land Art* presented at the AGNSW from September to December 2004. In 2006, she co-curated with Jon Altman the exhibition *Mumeka to Milmilngkan: Innovation in Kurulk Art* at the Drill Hall Gallery, Canberra.

Bernhard Lüthi

Bernhard Lüthi is a free-lance artist and curator with a special focus on intercultural projects. In 1988/89 he was project manager of the exhibition *Magiciens de la Terre*, Centre Pompidou / Grande Halle de la Villette. At the same time he developed together with the Aboriginal and Torres Strait Islander Arts Board of the Australia Council and the former Power Gallery of the University of Sydney (now Museum of Contemporary Art) the concept for the exhibition *Aratjara – The Art of the First Australians* which opened in Düsseldorf in 1993, before travelling on to the Hayward Gallery in London and the Louisiana Museum in Humlebaeck. From 1999 to 2001 he worked together with Jean Hubert Martin and others on the realisation of the exhibition *Altäre – Kunst zum Niederknien* which opened the new Museum Kunst Palast in Düsseldorf. In 2005 he co-curated the exhibition *«Rarrk» – John Mawurndjul. Journey Through Time in Northern Australia* at the Museum Tinguely in Basel, Switzerland.

Guido Magnaguagno

Guido Magnaguagno is Director of the Museum Tinguely, Basel, Switzerland. After receiving his degree in Art History at the University of Zurich, he joined the Kunsthaus Zürich (1980–2001), first as a Curator and later as a Vice-Director, where he curated many notable exhibitions and published extensively on issues of modern art. Since 2001 he has been the Director of the Museum Tinguely, ranked as one of the most innovative art museums in Switzerland. In 2005 the Museum Tinguely showed the retrospective exhibition *«Rarrk» – John Mawurndjul. Journey Through Time in Northern Australia* and hosted the symposium out of which the present volume developed.

Jean-Hubert Martin

Jean-Hubert Martin is a Museum Curator of international renown. He was Senior Curator at the Musée national d'art moderne in Paris (1971–1982) and later its Director (1987–1990). From 1994–1999 he was Director of the Musée national des arts d'Afrique et d'Océanie and Director General of the Museum Kunst Palast in Düsseldorf (2000–2006). Next to many other important projects he curated the ground-breaking *Magiciens de la Terre* exhibition (1989) and the *Biennale d'art contemporain* in Lyon (2002). The Museum Kunst Palast in Düsseldorf opened in 2001 with the acclaimed exhibition *Altäre – Kunst zum Niederknien* where Jean Hubert Martin displayed 68 contemporary altars from 34 different countries, thus once more evidencing the significance he grants interculturalism in art and art history. He has published extensively on issues of modern art and curating.

Richard McMillan (1944–2006)

Richard McMillan was a sculptor and scholar, deeply involved in the world of art as a freelance art historian. He established the *catalogue raisonné* of the artworks of Tony Tuckson (1921–1973). On the basis of this work, McMillan attained a Masters Degree from the College of Fine Arts at the University of New South Wales. While working on Tony Tuckson's biography, McMillan also discovered Karel Kupka's involvement with Australian Indigenous artists. His publications include *The Drawings of Tony Tuckson. The Establishment of a Comprehensive Inventory. Problems of Dating Considered in Regard to This and New Biographical Material* (MA thesis, University of New South Wales, 1997) and 'Karel Kupka in Australia: Artist, Collector, Writer, Anthropologist' in Kaufmann, C. and Museum Tinguely (eds.) *«Rarrk» – John Mawurndjul. Journey Through Time in Northern Australia* (exhibition catalogue), Museum Tinguely, Basel, 2005.

Howard Morphy

Professor Howard Morphy is Director of the Centre for Cross-Cultural Research at the ANU, Canberra. He has conducted fieldwork in Arnhem Land, Northern Australia, and in the Roper Valley. He is at present researching the life and art of Narritjin Maymuru. He has collaborated on many films of Arnhem Land ceremonial performance with Ian Dunlop of Film Australia. He has published widely in the anthropology of art, aesthetics, performance, museum anthropology, visual anthropology and religion. He was editorial advisor for the Aboriginal section of *The Dictionary of Art*. His books include *Ancestral Connections: Art and an Aboriginal System of Knowledge*, University of Chicago Press, Chicago, 1991; *Rethinking Visual Anthropology*, (with Marcus Banks), Yale University Press, New Haven, 1997; *Aboriginal Art*, Phaidon, London, 1998. Recent publication are a CD-ROM *The Art of Narritjin Maymuru*, ANU E-Press (with Pip Deveson and Katie Hayne) and *Becoming Art. Exploring Cross-cultural Categories*, Berg, Oxford and New York, 2007.

John Onians

John Onians is Director of the World Art Research Programme in the School of World Art Studies at the University of East Anglia. Among many other issues his research interests include perception, cognition and the biological basis of art. He was founding editor of the journal *Art History* and has recently edited the first *Atlas of World Art* (2004). His books include *Bearers of Meaning. The Classical Orders in Antiquity, the Middle Ages and the Renaissance*, Princeton University Press, Princeton, 1988; *Classical Art and the Cultures of Greece and Rome*, Yale University Press, New Haven, 1999; and *Neuroarthistory. From Aristotle and Pliny to Baxandall and Zeki*, 2007.

Judith Ryan

Judith Ryan is Senior Curator of Indigenous Art at the National Gallery of Victoria, Melbourne. Her special interest is Indigenous Australian art of the 20th century – its diversity, dynamism and transformation in the face of social change. She has curated over thirty exhibitions of Aboriginal art and has published widely in the field. Her publications include *Mythscapes: Aboriginal Art of the Desert*, NGV, Melbourne, 1989; *Paint up Big: Warlpiri Women's Art from Lajamanu*, NGV, Melbourne, 1990; *Spirit in Land: Bark Paintings from Arnhem Land*, NGV, Melbourne, 1990; *Images of Power: Aboriginal Art of the Kimberley*, NGV, Melbourne, 1990; *Ginger Riley*, NGV, Melbourne, 1993; *Raiki Wara: Long Cloth from Aboriginal Australia and the Torres Strait* NGV, Melbourne, 1998; *Remembering Barak*, NGV, Melbourne, 2003; and *Colour Power: Aboriginal art post 1984*, NGV, Melbourne, 2004.

Paul Taçon

Paul S.C. Taçon is Professor of Anthropology in the School of Arts, Griffith University, Queensland, Australia. Joining Griffith in 2005, he leads *The Human Question* research program. He was based at the Australian Museum, Sydney since early 1991 and was Principal Research Scientist in Anthropology from mid-1998 to early 2005. He has conducted archaeological and ethnographic fieldwork since 1980, with over 65 months field experience in remote parts of Australia, Canada, Myanmar, southern Africa and elsewhere. Paul Taçon has co-edited three books and published over 130 academic and popular papers on prehistoric art, body art, material culture, colour, cultural evolution, identity and contemporary Indigenous issues.

Luke Taylor

Luke Taylor is Deputy Principal – Research at the Australian Institute of Aboriginal and Torres Strait Islander Studies and Adjunct Professor at the Centre for Cross-cultural Research at the Australian National University, Canberra. He is an anthropologist who specialises in research with Aboriginal and Torres Strait Islander artists. He has written a number of books on Aboriginal art including *Seeing the Inside: Bark Painting in Western Arnhem Land*, Clarendon Press, Oxford, 1996; *Painting the Land Story*, National Museum of Australia, Canberra, 1999; and is co-editor with Jon Altman of *Marketing Aboriginal Art in the 1990s*, Aboriginal Studies Press, 1990. He was Curator and then Senior Curator in the Gallery of Aboriginal Australia at the National Museum of Australia for ten years from 1990 to 2000.

Claus Volkenandt

Claus Volkenandt is an art historian and lecturer at various universities in Germany and Switzerland. He has recently concluded a 'Habilitation' research project on the concept of abstraction in the work of Piet Mondrian and has worked extensively in the field of intercultural art history. Recent publications include 'Hermeneutik', in Pfisterer, U. (ed.) *Metzlers Lexikon Kunstwissenschaft*, J.B. Metzler, Stuttgart/Weimar, 2003; *Rembrandt: Anatomie eines Bildes*, Wilhelm Fink Verlag, München, 2004; Volkenandt, C. (ed.) *Kunstgeschichte und Weltgegenwartskunst. Konzepte – Methoden – Perspektiven*, Reimer, Berlin, 2004; 'Indirektes Zeigen von Wirklichkeit. Zur Abstraktion bei Piet Mondrian', in Hoppe-Sailer, R., C. Volkenandt and G. Winter (eds.) *Logik der Bilder. Präsenz – Repräsentation – Erkenntnis*, Reimer, Berlin, 2005, 75–88.

Kitty Zijlmans

Kitty Zijlmans studied art history at the University of Leiden, the Netherlands, and was appointed Professor of Contemporary Art History and Theory at the University of Leiden in 2000. Her main interest is in the fields of contemporary art, art theory, and methodology. She is also especially interested in the ongoing intercultural processes and globalisation of the (art) world. Recent publications include 'Documentary Evidence and/in Artistic Practices', in Rakier, M. and M. Schravemaker (eds.) *Right About Now. Art and Theory since the 1990s*, Amsterdam University Press, Amsterdam, 2007; Zijlmans, K. (ed.), *Site-Seeing. Places in Culture, Time and Space*, CNWS Publications, Leiden, 2006), and 'Pushing Back Frontiers: Towards a History of Art in a Global Perspective', *International Journal of Anthropology* 18 (4), 2003: pp. 201–210.

Index

Aboriginal and Torres Strait Islander Arts Board, 225
Aboriginal art, 45, 52, 113, 116, 121, 125ff, 129, 133, 162, 175, 176, 179, 181,
  acceptance of, 75–76, 224
  discourse on, 83, 100
  interpretation of, 79
  history, 78–79, 84, 101, 206
  ontology of, 80
  politics, 19, 27–28, 127–128, 179–181, 225–226
  writing on, 79
  vulnerability of, 53
  see also non-Western art
Aboriginal Arts Board (AAB), 23, 56
Aboriginal memorial , 1987/88, 209
Adam, Leonhard, 139
Adeagbo, Georges, 186–187
  Exhibition, 1996, 186 (fig.)
African art, 81,
  contemporary, 183
  traditional, 183
  construction of, 184ff, 18
  in comparison, 189
  invention of, 192
Altamira rock art, 146
Antipode, exhibition, Basel, 219
Aṟatjara – Art of the First Australians, 1993/94, exhibition, 163, 226
Arnhem Land
  central, 47, 51
  eastern, 24, 35n, 84, 94, 98, 141
  north-east, 66, 67, 84, 96, 152
  western, 20n, 35n, 61, 63, 66, 142, 163
art and anthropology, 14, 76, 81–82, 104, 107, 111, 138–139, 226ff
ART/artifact, exhibition, 188
art galleries and museums, exhibiting in 14–16, 139, 143ff, 162–164, 175–176, 177, 211ff, 225, 227
Art Gallery of New South Wales, 13, 142, 224, 225
Art Orienté Objet, 181
Art Religion Politics, Milan, exhibition, 181
Asia Pacific Triennale, Brisbane, 100
Asian art, 212
Australian Institute of Aboriginal Studies, 143
Australian Perspecta, 1980–1981, exhibition, 225

Bamabama story (Yolngu), 89, 92
bark painting,
  development of, 61, 63, 71
  specificity of, 68, 129
  structure of, 33–35, 69
  tradition of, 14, 31
Bark Petition 1963, 179
Barunga Statement 1988, 180
Bathurst Island (Tiwi), 141
Baudrillard, Jean, 161
Bauhaus, 141
Bawinanga Aboriginal Corporation (BAC), 24, 53, 55ff
Bedia, Jose, 181
Belmore, Rebecca, 114
Berndt, Catherine, 139
Berndt, Ronald, 139

Beuys, Joseph, 181
Bicentennial celebration, 1988, 209, 225
Biennale, Dakar 1996, 187
Biennale, Lyon 2000, 181
Biennale, Sydney 1979, 225
Biennale, Sydney 1982, 175
Biennale, Sydney 1986, 180
Biennale, Sydney 1990, 225
Biennale, Sydney 2000, 42, 166
Biennale, Venice 2005, 114
Bininjiwui, artist, 149
  Jabiru, coll. 1956, 149
Bininj Kun-wok, language, 20
Birriya Birriya, artist, 96
bir'yun, brilliance 67
Bissietta Gallery, Sydney, 142
Block, René, curator, 225
Boas, Franz, 138
Book of Durrow, 129
Bouabré, Frédéric Bruly, artist, 181
Bradshaw figures, 205
Breton, André, 146
Bubani, artist, 149
  Water and water hole, coll. 1956, 149
Bühler, Alfred, 140, 145
Buku-Larrnggay Mulka Art Centre, 89n
Burada, language community, 23
buwuyak, technique (Yolngu), 93

Canadian Aboriginal art, 114
Cathedral Rock, landmark, 203
Centre Pompidou, Paris, 225
Chauvet cave, 205
Claxton, Marshall, 203
Clemenger Contemporary Art Award, 43, 69
Cobourg Peninsula, 63
Cooke, Peter, 24
Coulibaly, Soro, artist, 190
Croker Island, 64, 69, 96, 145, 147
Crown of Thorns, landmark, 203
Crossing Country: the Alchemy of Western Arnhem Land Art, exhibition, 13, 20, 50, 55
Cubism, 139

Dadaism, 139
Dangbon country, 95
Darbyshire, Jo, 127
Darlinghurst Nation, 127
Davis, Jack, 225
Dekurridji, dialect, 21
delek, 33, 43, 68
Didi, Mestre, artist, 181
Dilebang, sacred site, 55
Dixon, Chicka, 225
djang, ancestral place 32, 36, 62, 71
Djet story (Yolngu), 89, 92
Djinang, language community, 23
Djómi Museum, 12
Documenta X, Kassel, 1997, 218
Douala, Cameroon, 194–195
Dorner, Alexander, curator, 217
Dressing Table Rock, landmark, 203

East Sydney Technical College, 142
Eastwood, Danny, 127
École des Beaux-Arts, Paris, 140
École des Hautes Études en Sciences Sociales, Paris, 147
Elkin, A. P., 140
Essl Collection, Vienna, 176
European art, see Western art
Expressionism, 139

Fanta, artist, 193, 194 (fig.)
Fitzroy Crossing (Great Desert), 180
Flavin, Dan, 181
Flynn, Father Frank, 143
Foelsche, Paul, 61, 63
Foley, Fiona, 209–210
  Dandi March, 2005, 209, 210 (fig.), **pl. XXIV**
Foley, Gary, 225
Fontana, Lucio, 181
Forge, Anthony, 145
Frank, Dale, 208–209
  The miner's rich vein, 1983, 208

Gagadju artists, 66
Ganalbingu, Luluna, 68
  Bumuri/Wayarre – Lunggurrma figures, 68 (fig.), **pl. X**
Ganalpingu, language community, 23
Gandhi, Mahatma, 209
Garig artists, 63
Gillespie, Dan, 24
Glover, John, 207
Groote Island, 141
Grosse, Ernst, 138
Gumana, Gawirrin, 67, 70
Gunwinggu (Kunwinjku), 26
Gupapuyngu, Lipundja, 68
  Wild honey figure, 68 (fig.), **pl. IX**
Guppy, Marla, 127

Haddon, Alfred Cort, 139, 203

Ife terracottas, 183
Ilgar artists, 63
Indonesia, 120
Iwaidja artists, 62, 63

Jagamara, Michael Nelson, 180
Jetspree, Fletcher, 127
  The Darlinghurst Syndrome, 1995, 127
Johnston, Pam, 127

Kakadu area, 206
Kakodbebuldi, sacred site, 42
Kalarriya [Kalareya], artist, 95
Kanak artists (New Caledonia), 219
Kangaroo, before 1913, unknown artist, 167 (fig.)
Kelly, Owen, 127
Klee, Paul, 131
Klein, Yves, 181
Koonalda cave, 205, 206 (fig.)
korogo mask (Ivory Coast), 184, **pl. XXIII**
Krämer, Augustin, 138
Krämer-Bannow, Elisabeth, 138
Kubarkku, Mick, 22, 54
Kudjarnngal, sacred site, 55
Kulunba, Anchor, 21
Kuningbal, Crusoe, 22, 54
Kuninjku,
  bark painting, 69, 166–167
  cultural tradition, 163, 166, 169
  dialect, 66n
  identity, 164
  language, 13, 20n
  community, 20
  return to country, 22, 54
  social history, 20–23
Kuninjku art
  body painting, 35, 41, 66, 169
  arts movement, 26, 58, 59
  history of, 19ff, 25, 31, 54
  as fine art, 24
  compared to Yolngu art, 94ff
  forms of representation, 33
  marketing of, 53ff
  motifs in,
    bambirl, 32
    birlmu, 32
    Buluwana, 25
    lorrkkon, 25
    Lumaluma, 97
    Mardayin, 32, 39–44, 66, 96
    mam, 148
    mimih, 25, 32, 33, 96, 148
    namarrkon, 32, 164
    namorrorddo, 25
    ngaldadmurrng, 32
    Ngalyod, Rainbow Serpent, 32, 36–38, 97, 110, 164
    yawkyawk, 25, 32, 108–111, 164
  transformation of, 25
Kuninjku artists, apprenticeship, 32, 34, 36
Kunststile vom Sepik, exhibition Basel, 145
Kunwinjku,
  culture, 20
  dialect 20n, 66n
  artists, 62, 66, 97–98, 147, 148
  language area, 66n
Kunwinjku/Dangbon School, 95

Kunz, Emma, artist, 220
Kupka, Frantisek, 140
Kupka, Karel, 20, 64, 138 (fig.), 224
  artist, as an, 143
    Aborginal Madonna, 1956, 143, 150
  background of, 140
  collector, as a, 140ff, 143, 148
  exhibition in Sydney 1956, 142, 147
  exhibition in Basel 1958, 143–144
  exhibition in Geneva 1962, 145, 147
  exhibition in Paris 1964, 147
  exhibition in Prague 1969, 147
  impact in Sydney, 142
  in Paris, 146ff
  second visit to Australia, 142
  Kupka collection Basel, 17, 137, 164
  Kupka collection Geneva, 145
  Kupka collection Paris, 145–146
  publications by, 150–152
  archival documents on, 152–153
  published references to, 153–158
  reviews of thesis *Dawn of art*, 158–159

Lake Sentani, West Papua, 148
Lang, Herbert, collector, 188
Lascaux, rock art, 146
Leroi-Gourhan, André, 147
likanpuy painting (Yolngu), 90
Lindjuwanga, Kay, 18, 219
Longman, Mary, 114
Looking Glass Rock, landmark, 203
Luna, James, 114
Luschan, Felix von, 138

Macassans, 90
Magiciens de la Terre, exhibition, 39, 163, 175, 181, 225
Malam, artist, 194–195
Malangi, David, 98
Malraux, André, 104, 143
Mandarrk, Wally, 22
Mandaynjku, artist, 96
Manggalili, clan (Yolngu), 86
Manggalili paintings (Yolngu), 87
Maningrida Arts and Culture (MAC), 12, 23–27, 47–52, 53, 56, 166
Maningrida area, language groups, 48 (map, fig. 8)
Maningrida region, 21 (map, fig. 2)
Maningrida, township, 12, 20–21, 54
Marawili, Bakulangay, 177
  Totems Munyuku, 1996, 177
Marawili, Djambawa, 93, 100
Mardayin, ceremony, 39, 66, 72, 164, 168
Mardayin, motif, 32, 39–44, 66, 96
Marika, Mathaman, 67
  Wawilak ceremony, 67 (fig.), **pl. VIII**
Marika, Mawalan, 209
  Map of painter's travel by plane from Yirrkala to Sydney, c. 1960, 209
Marralwanga, Peter, 21, 54, 66, 95, 96, 97, **pl. I**
  Two rock wallabies, 1979, 95 (fig.), **pl. XVII**
Marrkolidjban, 20
Marrkolidjban II School, 96
Martin, Agnes, artist, 219
Mawurndjul, John,
  aesthetics, 167–168
  art of, 9, 113, 119, 161, 176, 219
  artistic development, 32–33, 36, 39, 54–55, 164, 169
  awards, 43, 69–70
  early works, 31, 33–35, 164, 171
  exhibitions, 70, 165–166, 223, **pl. XXVI**
  iconic translation in works, 110,
  image of self, 12, 14
  in Paris, 17, 51, **pl. IV**
  member of Mumeka/Marrkolidjban School, 96
  middle work period, 36–39
  presentation of works in museum, 15, 164
  productivity, 55
  recent works, 31, 39ff, 172
  secret/sacred in art, 39–41, 66, 71–72, 166–168
  style in painting, 99
  works

Bambil, echidna and mimih, 1979, 170 (fig.), 171, **pl. XXI**
Ngalyod, rainbow serpent, devouring the yawkyawk girls, 1984, 36, 37 (fig.), 209, **pl. II**
Ngalyod, 1988, 39
Mimih at Milmilngkan, 1989, 39, 40 (fig.)
Rainbow serpent's antilopine kangaroo, 1991, 38 (fig.), 39
Billabong at Milmilngkan, 1993, 213 (fig.)
Mardayin ceremony, 1999, 42
Mardayin ceremony, 1999, 99 (fig.), **pl. XIX**
Ngalyod, rainbow serpent, 1999, 170 (fig.), 171, **pl. XXII**
Mardayin ceremony, 2000, 42
Mardayin at Kudjarnngal, 2003, 43, 68, 70 (fig.), **pl. III**
Mardayin design at Dilebang, 2003, 71 (fig.), **pl. XI**
Mardayin at Dilebang, 2003, 71 (fig.), 171 (fig.)
Yawkyawk, young girl – water spirit, 2005, 108–111, 109 (fig.), **pl. XX**
work steps, 11, 69, **pl. XXV**
Maymirrirr, artist, 88
Maymuru, Banapana, 86–87, **pl. XV**
Maymuru, Bokarra, 86–87, **pl. XIV**
Maymuru, Galuma, 93
Maymuru, Mändjilnga, 86, 88
Maymuru, Narritjin, 67, 84, 86–88, 98, 180
Djet story, 1967, 87 (fig.), **pl. XII**
The Marawili tree at Djarrakpi, 1976, **pl. XIII**
McCubbin, F. E., 207
Lost, 1886, 207
mediaeval art, 16
Melanesian art, 148
Metropolitan Museum of Art, New York, 139
Midjawmidjaw, Jimmy, 64, 96, 137, 145
Sorcery figure, 1975, 64 (fig.)
Mam, evil spirit, coll. 1963. 149
Milaybuma, David, 96
Yingarna, 1983, **pl. XVIII**
Milingimbi, 66, 141, 142, 150
Milmilngkan, outstation, 11, 14, 55
Mithinari, artist, 86, 98
Mitre Rock, landmark, 203
Modernism, European, 11
Moffat, Tracey, 127
mokuy sculptures (Yolngu), 67
Moon, Diane, 55, 165
Moore, David, 207
The impossible tree II, 1973, 207
Morning Star story (Yolngu), 92
Mountford, Charles, 100, 139
Muller-Lyer three line illusion, 203, 204 (fig.)
Mumeka, 23, 54, 113
Mumeka/Marrkolidjban School, 95–96
Mundine, Djon, 177
Murphy, Bernice, curator, 225
Musée des Arts Africains et Océaniens, Paris, 143, 145, 146, 176
Musée du quai Branly, Paris, 17, 50–51
Museum for African Art, New York, 188
Museum of Art, Basel, 144
Museum of Ethnography Basel, 137, 140, 143
Museum of Ethnography, Geneva, 145
Museum of Modern Art, New York, 189, 225
Museum for Primitive Art, New York, 139
Museum Tinguely Basel, 108, 175, 181, 211, 212

Nabarlambarl, artist, 95
Nabarrayal, artist, 95
Nadjamerrek, Lofty Bardayal, 65–66
Bark shelter, 1987, 65 (fig.)
Ngalyonddoh djang, 2005, 65 (fig.), **pl. VII**
The female rainbow serpent beneath waterlilies in her sacred billabong, 1991, 94 (fig.), **pl. XVI**
Namatbara, Paddy Compass, 63, 96, 137, 145
Namarnday spirits, early 1960s, 63 (fig.), **pl. VI**
Namatjira, Albert, 207
Namirrkki, artist, 96
Namirrki, Ivan, **pl. I**
Namunjdja, Clark Bubbuwanga, **pl. I**

Nangunyari-Namiridali, artist, 96
National Gallery of Australia, Canberra, 76n, 147, 166
National Museum of Victoria, Melbourne, 141
Nest of emu eggs, unknown artist, 1948, **pl. V**
Neue Sachlichkeit, 141
New Caledonia, 147, 219
Ngalyod, Rainbow Serpent, 32, 36–38, 97, 110, 164
Nganjmira, Robin, 96,
Nganjmira School, 96
Ngurrara canvas, 1997
Nguleingulei, Dick, 95
Niro, Shelley, 114
Nitsch, Hermann, 181
Njiminjuma, Jimmy, 33, 54, 96
Nolan, Sidney, 208
    Ned Kelly, 1946, 208 (fig.)
non-Western art, 13, 115, 128, 139, 212
    concept of, 76–77, 104
    as artefact, 82
Noonuccal, Oodgeroo (Kath Walker), 225
Nouvel, Jean, 17

Oceanic art, 137
Oenpelli, 66n, 95
Oenpelli artists, 150
Ogundele, Rufus, artist, 191
    Obatala, 1990, 191 (fig.)
Olitski, Jules, 171
Onus, Lin, 163, 223, 225
Oppenheim, Meret, 141
Oquet, Chara, 181

Panofsky, Erwin, 106
Pacific art, 148
Papua New Guinea, 120, 147
Papunya Tula Movement, 24, 177
peintres naïfs, European, 143
Picasso, Pablo, 188
Pike, Jimmy, 181
Pintupi artists, 79n, 85n
Plate, Carl, 140
Poitras, Edward, 114
Port Essington, 63
Port Keats, 141
Port Vila, Vanuatu, 218
Preston, Margaret, 76n
Preuss, Konrad, 138
primitive art, 175
Primitivsm in 20th Century, exhibition, 189, 225

Queensland Art Gallery, Brisbane, 142
Quest of Jimmy Pike, documentary, 121

Ramingining artists, 209
Rapotec, Stanislaus, 140
rarrk, crosshatching, 12, 32–33, 34–35, 35n, 36, 41, 66, 71, 147, 148, 162–163, 164, 168, 171, 176
«*Rarrk*», exhibition: 9, 14, 17–18, 20, 31, 70, 148, 162, 172, 212–213, 223, 224–226
Rijksmuseum, Amsterdam, 165, 170
Roberts, Tom, 208
    Bushranger, 1895, 208
Robinson, Ronald, 140
rock art, 11, 146, 163, 205–206, 212
rungkalno, silhouette, 34, 69

Sainsbury Centre for Visual Arts, 209
sand sculpture *yingapungapu* (Yolngu), 90
Schleiermacher, Friedrich, 106
Sepik River, Papua New Guinea, 141, 144, 148
Shiraga, Kazuo, 181
Skipper, Pijaju, 181
Souverbie, Jean, 140
Spee, Nzante, 190
Speiser, Felix, 141
Spencer, Baldwin, 66
Spiess, Werner, 176
Stephan, Emil, 138
Sumégné, Joseph Francis, artist, 193
    La Poupée, 1995, 192 (fig.)
Surrealism, 139, 146, 148
Sydow, Eckhard von, 139

Telstra Aboriginal and Torres Strait Islander Art Award, 70
Thomson, Donald, 84
Tbilisi, Georgia, 220
Tinguely, Jean, 181
Tjakamarra, Anatjari, 181
Tjampitjimpa, Old Walter, 181
Tjapaltjarri, Clifford Possum and Tim Leura, 201
  Warlugulong. 1976, 201, 202 (fig.)
Tjapaltjarri, Mick, 181
Tjuppurrula, Turkey Tolson, 209
  Straightening spears at Ilyingaungau, 1990, 209
Tokoudagba, Cyprien, artist, 181
Toroni, Niele, 175
Torres Straight Islanders, 203
Tuckson, Tony, 142, 224
Twelve Apostles, landmark, 203

Ubirr Rock, 206
Uluru, 203
Utopia (Central Desert), 180

Vanuatu, 147
Vatter, Ernst, 139
Vollmer, Ruth, artist, 220
von den Steinen, Karl, 138
von Guerard, Eugene, 207

wangarr marr (Yolngu, ancestral power), 67, 85, 91, 93
wakinngu painting (Yolngu), 90
Walmajarri people, 121
Wandjina figures, 205
Wanyubi, artist, 98
Western art, 9, 15, 126, 162–163, 175, 212, 223, 224
  art history, 78–79, 100, 104–108, 130
  concept of, 76, 116–117
  fine art category, 78, 82
  ontology of, 80
Wirz, Paul, 141
Woolloomooloo, Sydney, 127
world art, 10
Worringer, Wilhelm, 104
Wululu, artist, 176
Wunuwun, artist, 176

yawkyawk, 25, 32, 108–111, 164
Yilpara settlement, 93, 98
Yirawala, Billy, 40, 42, 66, 96, 97, 137, 145, 168
Yirrkala, 66, 87, 89, 141, 148, 179
Yolngu, 31, 66–67, 84, 179–180
Yolngu art, 75ff, 85–86, 97ff, 180
  bark painting, 84, 88
  foreign influences, 90–91
  history, 89, 93, 98, 100–101
  production, 93
  secret/sacred, 66–68, 90, 93
  theory, 84
Yuendumu artists, 175
Yunupingu, Munggurrawuy, 179

Zande, 78, 188

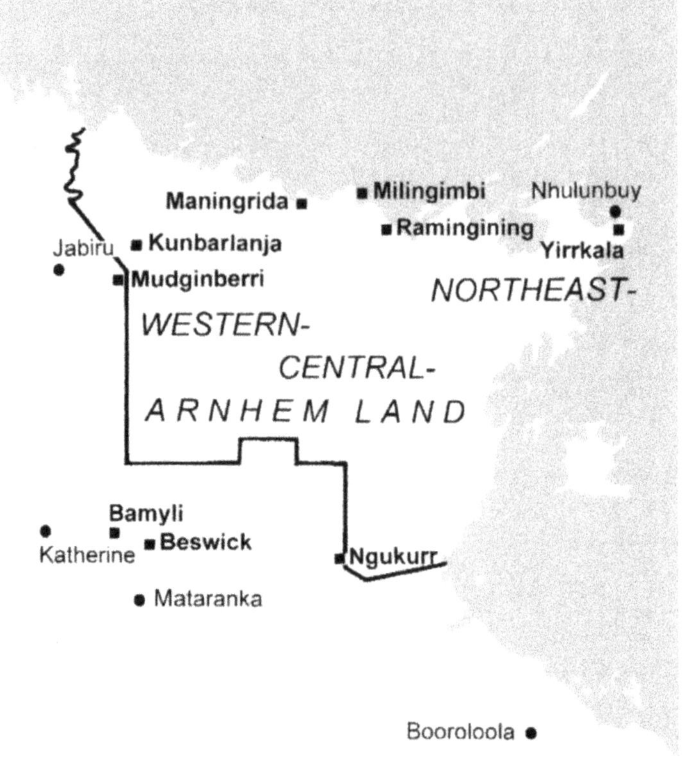

Fig. 48: Map of Arnhem Land, Northern Territory, Australia. Archives of the editors.

www.ingramcontent.com/pod-product-compliance
Lightning Source LLC
La Vergne TN
LVHW060933110826
845155LV00042B/721

* 9 7 8 0 8 5 5 7 5 6 6 6 6 *